# The California Probate Paralegal

# The California Probate Paralegal
## SECOND EDITION

Dianna L. Noyes

CAROLINA ACADEMIC PRESS
Durham, North Carolina

Copyright © 2014
Dianna L. Noyes
All Rights Reserved

Library of Congress Cataloging-in-Publication Data

Noyes, Dianna L.
  The California probate paralegal / Dianna L. Noyes. -- Second Edition.
      pages cm
  Includes bibliographical references and index.
  ISBN 978-1-61163-452-5 (alk. paper)
  1. Probate law and practice--California--Popular works. 2. Executors and administrators--California--Popular works. 3. Legal assistants--California--Handbooks, manuals, etc. I. Title.

  KFC205.N69 2013
  346.79405'2--dc23

2013020639

Carolina Academic Press
700 Kent Street
Durham, North Carolina 27701
Telephone (919) 489-7486
Fax (919) 493-5668
www.cap-press.com

Printed in the United States of America
2019 Printing

# Contents

| | |
|---|---|
| Introduction | xiii |
| **Chapter One · Introduction to Probate, Estate Planning and Administration** | 3 |
| Probate, Estate Planning and Estate Administration in California | 3 |
| The Paralegal's Role in Probate and Estate Planning | 4 |
| Ethics and the Paralegal | 5 |
| Other Malpractice Concerns | 7 |
|     Confidentiality | 9 |
|     Ethical Wall | 10 |
|     The Paralegal's Role | 10 |
| Probate Code and Other Relevant California Codes | 11 |
| The Paralegal's Role | 13 |
| What is Probate? | 15 |
|     History | 15 |
| United States Probate Laws | 16 |
| Testate and Intestate Succession Defined | 16 |
|     Testate Succession | 16 |
|     Intestate Succession | 16 |
|     Probate Code § 240 | 18 |
|     Probate Code § 6240 | 19 |
|     Community Property | 22 |
|     Surviving Spouse | 22 |
| Effect of Dissolutions on Probate | 24 |
|     Divorced But No New Will | 24 |
|     Failure to Provide for Wife and/or Children | 25 |
|     Posthumously Conceived Child | 26 |
|     Spousal Property Petition | 26 |
|     Distribution of Intestate Estate | 26 |
|     Escheat | 27 |
|     Ancillary Probate | 27 |
|     Fiduciary | 27 |
|     Key Terms | 27 |
| **Chapter Two · Estate Planning** | 29 |
| Succession Planning | 29 |
|     Military Testamentary Instrument | 30 |
| Probate Avoidance | 30 |
| Wills | 32 |

|  |  |
|---|---|
| Requirements of a Valid Will | 32 |
| Holographic Will | 32 |
| Statutory Will | 33 |
| Pour-Over Will | 34 |
| Attestation and Witnesses | 34 |
| Codicil | 35 |
| Preparation of Wills | 36 |
| Execution of the Will | 39 |
| Typical Will Preparation | 41 |
| Key Terms | 43 |

## Chapter Three · Wills — 45

|  |  |
|---|---|
| Specific Will Provisions | 45 |
| Identification of Testator | 45 |
| Pour-Over Wills Related to Trusts | 47 |
| Obligation to Pay Debt and/or Taxes | 47 |
| Reference to Contract in Testator's Will | 47 |
| Distribution of Property | 47 |
| Naming of Executor | 49 |
| Defining the Executor's Powers | 51 |
| Period of Time for Executor to Act | 52 |
| Children—Definition and Guardianship Provisions | 52 |
| Trust for Children | 53 |
| No-Contest Clauses | 54 |
| Boilerplate Language | 54 |
| Simultaneous Death | 55 |
| Rule Against Perpetuities | 55 |
| Self-Proving Affidavit, Attestation, Signature of Witnesses | 56 |
| Research and Interesting Wills in History | 56 |
| Key Terms | 56 |

## Chapter Four · Probating an Estate — 59

|  |  |
|---|---|
| Probating an Estate | 59 |
| Probating the Will | 59 |
| Probating an Intestate Estate | 61 |
| Testate Distribution | 66 |
| Retaining an Attorney | 67 |
| Formal Probate Proceedings | 69 |
| Administrator or Personal Representative | 70 |
| Preparing the Petition and Lodging the Will | 70 |
| Other Documents Submitted with Petition for Probate | 73 |
| Citation | 74 |
| Waiver of Bond/Purchase of Bond | 74 |
| The Hearing and Notice Requirements | 75 |
| Preparation of Judicial Council Forms | 78 |
| Key Terms | 78 |

## Chapter Five · Probate Process Continued — 101

|  |  |
|---|---|
| Probate—Part II | 101 |

| | |
|---|---|
| Request for Special Notice | 102 |
| Appointment of Probate Referee | 102 |
| Inventory and Appraisal | 104 |
| Creditor's Claims | 106 |
|     Payment of Creditor's Claims | 109 |
|     Payment of Medi-Cal Liens | 110 |
| Sale of Property | 111 |
| Overseeing the Estate During Administration | 112 |
| Petition for Final Distribution | 113 |
| Preparing the Petition for Final Distribution | 115 |
| Statutory Attorney and Executor Fees | 117 |
|     Statutory Attorney and Executor Fees | 117 |
|     Extraordinary Fees | 119 |
| Special Considerations When Preparing the Petition for Final Distribution | 120 |
| Hearing on Petition for Final Distribution | 120 |
| Order for Final Distribution | 121 |
| Distribution to Heirs/Beneficiaries | 121 |
|     Preparation of Judicial Council Forms | 122 |
|     Key Terms | 122 |

**Chapter Six · Transfer of Property Without Estate Administration** — 143

| | |
|---|---|
| Community Property, Surviving Spouse, Domestic Partner, Joint Tenancy | 144 |
| Community Property | 145 |
| Separate Property | 146 |
| Types of Ownership | 146 |
| Joint Tenancy | 147 |
|     Basis | 148 |
| Petition to Determine Succession to Real Property | 148 |
| Small Estates Set-Aside | 149 |
| Transfer of Small Estates Without Administration | 150 |
| Spousal Property Petition | 151 |
| Information Regarding Property Transfers | 154 |
|     Real Property | 154 |
|     Motor Vehicles | 154 |
|     Mobile Homes | 155 |
|     Bank, Savings & CD Accounts | 155 |
|     Stocks and Bonds | 155 |
|     Mutual Funds and Money Market Accounts | 156 |
|     Savings and Treasury Bonds | 157 |
|     Other Personal Property | 157 |
|     Preparation of Judicial Council Forms | 157 |
|     Key Terms | 157 |

**Chapter Seven · Trusts** — 165

| | |
|---|---|
| Inter Vivos or Living Trusts | 165 |
|     Trust Administration Overview | 166 |
|     Attorney and Executor Fees | 166 |
|     Confidentiality | 167 |
|     Reduce Taxes | 167 |

| | |
|---|---:|
| Flexibility | 168 |
| Protection from Creditors | 168 |
| Distribution to Beneficiaries Is Expedited | 168 |
| Grantor, Settlor, Trustor, Trustee | 169 |
| Irrevocable Trust | 169 |
| Revocable Trust | 171 |
| Advantages of a Revocable Trust | 171 |
| Protection from Federal Estate Taxes | 173 |
| Custodial Accounts | 173 |
| Ability to Amend Trust | 174 |
| Types of Trusts | 174 |
| Revocable Life Insurance Trust | 175 |
| Other Estate Planning | 176 |
| Pour-Over Wills | 176 |
| Creating a Trust | 177 |
| The Nuts and Bolts of the Trust (Mandatory and/or Boilerplate Language) | 179 |
| Trustee Powers | 185 |
| Discretionary Provisions | 185 |
| Revocation and Amendment | 185 |
| Taxes | 186 |
| Provisions for Distribution of the Trust Estate | 186 |
| Outright Distribution to Beneficiaries | 188 |
| Distribution of Specific Items of Property | 189 |
| Distribution with Tax Planning | 189 |
| Disclaimer Trust | 191 |
| Separate Share Trust | 191 |
| Special Needs Trust | 191 |
| Spendthrift Trust Provisions | 192 |
| The Conclusion | 192 |
| Transfers of Property and Other Documents | 192 |
| Key Terms | 193 |
| **Chapter Eight · Collateral Documents** | 195 |
| Certified Abstract | 195 |
| Assignment of Property | 196 |
| Transmutation Agreement | 196 |
| Revocation of Trust | 197 |
| Other Collateral Documents | 198 |
| Funding Trusts | 198 |
| Real Property | 199 |
| Financial Institutions | 201 |
| Motor Vehicles, Etc. | 202 |
| Stocks and Bonds | 202 |
| Mutual Funds | 203 |
| Insurance & Annuities | 203 |
| Retirement Accounts | 203 |
| Mobile Homes | 203 |
| Promissory Notes | 204 |
| Trust Amendments and Restatements | 204 |

| | |
|---|---:|
| Conclusion | 205 |
| Key Terms | 205 |

## Chapter Nine · Powers of Attorney — 207

| | |
|---|---:|
| Powers of Attorney | 207 |
| Limited or Specific Power of Attorney | 207 |
| Durable Powers of Attorney | 209 |
| Naming of Agent/Attorney-in-Fact | 209 |
| Springing Powers | 210 |
| Durable Powers of Attorney and Advance Health Care Directives | 212 |
| Durable Power of Attorney for Health Care | 212 |
| Advance Health Care Directive | 213 |
| Importance of Advance Health Care Directives | 214 |
| Key Terms | 215 |

## Chapter Ten · Trust Administration — 217

| | |
|---|---:|
| Acceptance to Appointment of Trustee | 218 |
| Beginning the Administration Process | 219 |
| Trustee Powers | 220 |
| Making Distributions | 221 |
| Trust Accountings | 223 |
| Compensation | 223 |
| Winding up the Simple Estate Administration | 224 |
| Complex Estate Administration | 226 |
| Property Not Transferred into the Trust | 226 |
| Federal Tax Consequences and Wealth Transfers | 226 |
| Federal Estate Tax Consequences | 227 |
| Applicable Exclusion Amount | 227 |
| Federal Gift Tax | 228 |
| Distributions and Creation of Sub-Trusts | 229 |
| Marital Deduction Trust | 229 |
| Bypass Trusts | 229 |
| Charitable Deductions and Charitable Remainder Trusts | 230 |
| Creating and Funding Sub-Trusts | 230 |
| Funding the Sub-Trusts | 230 |
| Generation Skipping Transfer Tax (GST) | 231 |
| Federal Estate Tax Returns | 232 |
| Trusts with Specific and/or Unequal Distributions and/or Distributions to Charitable Organizations or Others | 233 |
| Creation of Children's, Grandchildren's or Special Needs Trusts | 234 |
| Final Distributions and Termination of the Complex Trust | 235 |
| Final Accounting | 235 |
| Petition for Instructions | 235 |
| Property Located in Another State | 237 |
| Key Terms | 238 |

## Chapter Eleven · Guardianships and Conservatorships — 239

| | |
|---|---:|
| Guardianship | 240 |
| Guardian Ad Litem | 241 |

| | | |
|---|---|---:|
| | Judicial Council Forms (Guardian Ad Litem) | 242 |
| | Guardian of the Person and the Estate | 242 |
| | Petition for Guardianship (Person and/or Estate) | 243 |
| | Judicial Council Forms | 243 |
| | Other Applicable Forms | 244 |
| | Conservatorship | 244 |
| | Judicial Council Forms | 250 |
| | Conservatorship Process | 250 |
| | Limited Conservatorship | 251 |
| | Preparing the Petition for Appointment of Probate Conservator | 255 |
| | Other Considerations | 258 |
| | Key Terms | 258 |

**Chapter Twelve · Other Issues Affecting Probate and Estate Planning** — 259

| | | |
|---|---|---:|
| | Effects of Homicide or Elder Abuse | 259 |
| | Health Care Surrogacy (PC § 4711) | 261 |
| | Public Administrator (PC§§ 7600–7666) | 264 |
| | Priority for Appointment of Administrator (PC§§ 8460–8469) | 267 |
| | Federal "Uniform" Statutes | 269 |
| | Uniform Testamentary Additions to Trust Act (PC§§ 6300–6303) | 269 |
| | Uniform International Wills Act (PC §§ 6380–6390) | 270 |
| | Uniform Principal and Income Act (PC§§ 16320–16347) | 272 |
| | Uniform Prudent Management of Institutional Funds Act (PC§§ 18500–18509) | 273 |
| | Effects of a Registered Domestic Partnership | 278 |
| | Termination of Domestic Partnership/Revocation of Bequests | 278 |
| | Hospital and Health Care Facility Visitation Rights (H&S Code § 1261) | 278 |
| | Taxes and Definitions | 278 |
| | Marital Deduction | 283 |
| | Charitable Gifts | 285 |
| | California Inheritance Tax | 285 |
| | Key Terms | 286 |

**Appendices**

| | | |
|---|---|---:|
| 1A | Table of Consanguinity | 289 |
| 1B | Distribution Charts | 290 |
| 2A | Probate Intake Form | 292 |
| 3A | Sample Will | 295 |
| 3B | Shores Will (Signed) | 301 |
| 4A | Client Fact Sheet (Completed) | 307 |
| 4B | Verification | 310 |
| 4C | Proof of Subscribing Witness (DE-131) | 311 |
| 4D | Waiver of Bond | 312 |
| 5A | Probate Accounting Spreadsheets | 313 |
| 5B | Petition for Final Distribution | 317 |
| 5C | Waiver of Notice | 324 |
| 5D | Receipt | 325 |

| | | | |
|---|---|---|---|
| 5E | Order for Final Distribution | 326 | |
| 5F | Ex Parte Petition for Discharge | 329 | |
| 6A | Affidavit — Death of Spouse | 330 | |
| 6B | Death of Property Owner Assessor | 331 | |
| 6C | Preliminary Change of Ownership Form | 333 | |
| 6D | Declaration for Collection of Compensation Owed to Spouse | 335 | |
| 6E | Affidavit — Death of Joint Tenant | 336 | |
| 6F | Declaration under Probate Code §13100, et seq | 337 | |
| 6G | Spousal Property Petition Attachments | 339 | |
| 7A | Federal Estate Tax Exemption Chart | 343 | |
| 7B | Annual Exclusion Chart | 344 | |
| 7C | Disclaimer Requirements | 345 | |
| 8A | Assignment to Trust | 346 | |
| 8B | Trust Transfer Deed | 349 | |
| 8B | Trust Transfer Deed continued | 350 | |
| 9A | Durable Power of Attorney—Powers | 351 | |
| 9B | Durable Power of Attorney—Care & Control of Person | 359 | |
| 9C | Durable Power of Attorney—Incidental Provisions | 361 | |
| 9D | Durable Power of Attorney—Health Care Powers | 366 | |
| 10A | Trustee Accounting Spreadsheet | 370 | |
| 10B | Petition for Instructions | 372 | |

**Glossary**   377

**Index**   393

# Introduction

Probate and estate planning is an area of the law that affects almost every individual. You cannot say that about most other areas of law. Most of us will go through life without being sued or having to sue anyone. Some, but not all, of us will come into contact with the family court either through divorce or a child custody matter. The vast majority of us, however, will have a family member who has died or will die. Moreover, we will all eventually die and need to have our property passed on to our heirs.

From a personal perspective, each of you should learn something of value from this text that will be useful in your own life. One of the most important personal insights you should gain is that each of us needs to plan for our own death or possible incapacity. From a professional perspective, as a paralegal, I hope you will find this area of law interesting and challenging.

This book will cover the various types of documents a paralegal might be involved in drafting in a typical probate and estate planning practice. Such documents include, but are not limited to, Wills, Trusts, Powers of Attorney, and Advance Health Care Directives. As a paralegal student or entry level paralegal, you will become familiar with the various forms of complex estate planning such as revocable and irrevocable trusts and the many documents that accompany such estate planning techniques. The paralegal student will also learn the various mechanisms for transferring property upon death with and without probate administration.

The text provides practical applications to the basic probate process by providing samples of completed Judicial Council forms required by the California courts. Practical skills, terminology, and discussions of various "real world" applications are provided to assist the paralegal in developing knowledge and skills. Concepts will be discussed. Examples and assignments will be provided so that the student will have a better understanding of how the concept is applied in the legal environment. The student will also learn how to properly manage files and documents, as well as keep accurate timelines and calendar deadlines that are critical to the probate process.

Probate also covers the areas of guardianship and conservatorship. These topics will also be addressed in this text as they are governed, for the most part, by the California Probate Code. In most California Counties, these cases are heard within the probate court system.

There is much terminology utilized in this area of practice, which will be a primary focus of the text. The book is written in a logical manner and therefore terminology will be included as it applies to a particular section. The Glossary at the end of the book will also contain the definitions found in the various chapters, as well as many other definitions and will be in alphabetical order.

This book is written for the paralegal student and entry level paralegal. There are many complex estate planning and probate issues that will not be addressed in this text. Such issues are best learned through advanced seminars and hands-on experience in the law office environment. However, with the basic knowledge and understanding of the topics presented in this book, a paralegal will be ready to take on more complex matters as they become more experienced and knowledgeable.

Probate and estate planning are constantly changing. Changes in California law include Registered Domestic Partners within most of the probate code sections particularly as they relate to the transfer of property held by two persons who have registered with the State of California as Domestic Partners. Most recently the California Supreme Court ruled that individuals of the same sex could marry. It will be likely that some modifications will need to be made to the Probate Code and other related statutes to include language that reflects this ruling. Additionally, both state and federal tax laws may also affect the transfer of property as well as whether the decedent's estate will incur any taxes. These topics will be addressed so that the paralegal has a basic knowledge of how these issues relate to the estate administration process.

Depending upon the complexity of the estate, it may take several years to bring the matter to a conclusion and make a final distribution. Clients and attorneys find that paralegals will be able to keep track of the various statutes, local rules, time-lines, and details throughout this often-lengthy period. The paralegal will be able to continue to work on the administrative tasks, while the attorney can continue to secure new clients, attend hearings, as well as work on complex matters requiring his or her expertise.

A probate and estate planning paralegal will find this work very interesting and rewarding. Some students will take quickly to this area of practice, while others will want to get as far away from it as possible. The probate paralegal must be able to be empathetic while remaining detail-oriented. An organized paralegal with excellent communication and writing skills will excel in this area of practice. Probate and estate administration are well suited to paralegal skills and will reduce the costs to the client.

A probate paralegal should be able to work well with clients as well as be able to work well with the legal team. He or she should also be able to work well with appraisers, actuaries, accountants, court personnel, and others who will be providing services related to the client's finances.

A paralegal working in this area of practice should have a good basic knowledge of finances. Many of the tasks and information acquired will relate to the client's assets. A working knowledge of valuations, appraisals, taxes and other financial areas are a plus. It is not imperative to be an accountant, but it certainly is a benefit to know how to prepare a balance sheet, what is profit or gain, and what is a loss.

This area of practice is "people-oriented." Often a client will come to the office as a result of a traumatic experience, such as the death of a family member. The client will want someone who shows empathy, understanding, and sincerity. Planning for one's own death or incapacity is also difficult for most people. The paralegal will often be the client's link to the firm as the case progresses. The client often comes to ask to speak with the paralegal each time he or she calls. Clients will rely greatly on the paralegal, not only for his or her procedural knowledge and for expertise, but because they feel, they have built a relationship with the paralegal. A wise paralegal will take care that the client does not become too attached to him or her. The paralegal must also make sure not to give advice to the client and commit the Unauthorized Practice of Law (UPL). This is often a very fine line. The paralegal will also need to take care that the client does not monopolize his or her time. As the paralegal comes to know the client and the client finds the paralegal to be kind and empathetic, he or she may call the office constantly. There will be times that the paralegal will have to diplomatically let the client know that he or she cannot spend time conversing with the client. Probate and estate planning clients often are not paying an hourly rate and therefore do not see the cost of the time being spent on the matter. In the event it becomes a problem, the attorney needs to be advised of the situation.

Probate and estate planning are interesting and challenging. There are many other types of laws that interact with this area of practice. A paralegal working in this area of law will come into contact with various business entities, contracts, family law issues, finances, and taxes. There may even be some civil issues that relate, if for example, a decedent died in an automobile accident caused by another person, or died at work as the result of an industrial accident. Rarely are two estates exactly the same. This area of law is multi-faceted and can be very rewarding for a paralegal choosing to work in this field of the profession.

Dianna L. Noyes, M.S., RP®

# The California Probate Paralegal

# Chapter One

# Introduction to Probate, Estate Planning and Administration

## Probate, Estate Planning and Estate Administration in California

This chapter is meant to be an overview of the estate planning and probate process. It contains some historical background regarding how property was transferred upon death by our ancestors. It is meant to familiarize you with the current probate structure, including why we have Wills and the other ways by which assets can be transferred upon death and/or how to avoid probate entirely. This chapter will provide you with an overview of estate planning and the various ways to administer a decedent's estate. The subsequent chapters will contain substantive applications to the California Probate Code and will utilize a hands-on approach as you learn how estates are typically administered and the paralegal's role in this endeavor.

The three primary areas comprising the probate and estate law practice are Probate, Wills, and Trusts. Each of these areas includes other means of transferring property among individuals either prior to or after death. There are also many other types of documents that can be drafted and executed as part of an individual person's or a couple's estate planning needs such as Advance Health Care Directives, Durable Powers of Attorneys, Assignments and/or Transmutations (of property), and Certified Abstracts of Trust.

A law firm specializing in these areas will also likely be involved in Administering Trusts upon a death, where the person has previously created and executed a revocable trust in order to avoid the probate process. This process will be somewhat similar to the probate administration process, but will have some differences because in most cases there is no court oversight.

All of these various mechanisms and the processes for preparing or completing the various types of documents will be discussed in greater detail as you progress through this book. You will also become familiar with the many documents and methods for drafting and preparing documents that compliment the probate, estate planning, and trust administration processes. There are other methods of transferring property upon death, referred to as non-probate transfers. These can include holding property in joint tenancy, naming a beneficiary for an annuity, bank and savings account, insurance policy or other type of "pay-on-death" accounts; mutual funds; pension plans and other "contractual" documents; or by affidavit.

We will also review, research and discuss many other areas of law that impact probate and estate planning such as dissolutions of marriage, tax considerations, pre- and post-marital agreements, and real estate transactions.

Changes in California law with respect to Domestic Partnerships are a more recent development. This issue will also be discussed as it has affected the manner in which documents are drafted, the manner in which the statutes recommend title be held, as well as the implications of transfer of property if one of the Domestic Partners dies with or without a valid Will. As this book is being written the California Supreme Court has ruled that same-sex couples may be legally married. Any references to a valid marriage should include these couples, at this time. However, because it is difficult to know what statutory changes may occur in the future the content of this text has not been modified to reflect this recent decision.

Many estate planning attorneys are also faced with working with elderly clients who lack capacity or competency, face diseases such as dementia and Alzheimer's, Medicare and Medi-Cal issues, social security and disability challenges, and many other issues related to an aging, baby-boomer population. As the average age of the U.S. population is extended and this group's numbers increase, there are new challenges and issues to be resolved. Elder law attorneys may be the first to witness elder abuse, coercion by family members and care-givers and a host of other problems never before encountered within the estate planning profession. One issue in particular involves the ethics of working with elderly clients and concerned family members. The inherent risks will be discussed in more detail under "Ethics and the Paralegal."

You will begin by learning and discussing some of the ethical concerns for paralegals in this type of practice.

# The Paralegal's Role in Probate and Estate Planning

It is important for a paralegal who is involved in drafting estate planning documents including Wills and Trusts, to understand the administration of probate and trust estates, as well as the laws that affect estate taxes and transfers of real and personal property.

Estate planning can be very complex and many firms are specializing in this area of practice. Federal and state inheritance and estate tax laws have changed dramatically in the past twenty years and continue to evolve and change. A paralegal with estate planning knowledge is a valuable asset to the law firm. It is also very important that the estate planning paralegal take continuing education courses to stay current with the many changes and developments in this area of law and to further hone skills and expertise.

The following is a typical job description for a probate and estate planning paralegal:

Assist the attorneys by performing various tasks as follows:

- Prepare and file pleadings and documents in the course of administering a probate or trust estate, conservatorship, or guardianship
- Preparation of federal and estate tax returns—a knowledge of selection of tax year, tax elections as well as the documents and procedures for such elections is preferred

# 1 · INTRODUCTION TO PROBATE, ESTATE PLANNING & ADMINISTRATION

- Coordinate with accountants regarding estate and death taxes; real estate agents regarding the sale of real property; stockbrokers regarding the sales and/or transfer of stocks, bonds and funds and other financial property experts
- Research title of assets and work with actuaries, probate referees, appraisers, and others to value estate assets
- Prepare court accountings for estates, trust, guardianships and conservatorships
- Maintain a working relationship with clients, assist clients in preparing and obtaining financial information for accountings, court filings, and tax documents
- Draft correspondence, research memoranda, petitions, pleadings, and orders regarding probate and estate planning matters
- Draft trusts, wills, trust abstracts, powers of attorney, property agreements, and related estate planning documents
- Coordinate and confer with Superior Court personnel regarding the filing, processing and hearing dates related to probate and estate administration
- Perform legal research and prepare memoranda, shepardize cases related to tax law, probate code, rules, procedures and judicial council

Many of these will be discussed in greater detail as you cover the applicable law and various procedures throughout this textbook.

Review the National Federation of Paralegal Associations, Inc. (NFPA) Roles and Responsibilities publication; it is available on their website at www.paralegals.org.

# Ethics and the Paralegal

The paralegal should be diligent throughout the entire case and be aware of potential conflicts of interest, as well as other ethical considerations. Before meeting the client and/or being retained, a conflict check should be undertaken. The California Rules of Professional Conduct (CRPC) address potential conflicts of interest that are unique to probate and estate planning law. The paralegal should be well versed and understand these Rules. One of the most common potential conflicts would be the attorney representing **both** sides of a probate, will, or trust matter which is called a *person with adverse interest*. The Rules governing this type of representation can be found within CRPC 3-300. The actual *rules* are very simply stated. However, it is more important to read the footnotes which provide guidance, examples, and the reasoning behind the rule along with related case law.

There are many examples of conflict of interest; the following are just a few:

1) If the attorney has a "social" relationship with either or both of the parties;
2) If the attorney has a "confidential" relationship with opposing counsel;
3) If the attorney represented one of the parties and/or immediate family members; or
4) A family member who accompanies an elderly client in order to "help" because there is a question of competency there may be a question as to who is the client.

A potential client may ask the attorney, whom they trust, to act in the capacity of an agent, executor and/or trustee. While the Rules do not prohibit the attorney from acting in this fiduciary capacity, a full disclosure should be made regarding the fees that the attorney could charge the estate. California has set statutory fees for both the attorney for the estate and the executor. If the attorney is acting in both capacities, it may be construed as "double-dipping" on the part of the attorney to receive compensation for serving in both capacities. The client should have the opportunity to include the amount of compensation that the attorney would receive should he or she act as both executor/trustee and attorney for the estate.

There is also an inherent conflict when representing married couples. Some of the most common reasons are as follows:

1) Family Structure—Remarriage, blended and non-traditional families may lead to one partner feeling that a child or other heir is not entitled to their portion of the estate. For example, a stepparent may not wish for their portion of the estate to go to their stepchild. They may feel that their natural children are entitled to the entire (one-half of community property) estate.

2) Differing Testamentary Goals—Spouses may not agree on the type of estate planning, the executor/trustees/agents to be named and how the property is to be distributed.

3) Dominating Spouse—Spouse who obviously controls the other and makes all the decisions without input or consulting the marriage partner.

4) Stability of Marriage—Attorney may question the stability of the marriage, and whether the parties should even be creating estate planning documents if the marriage is not on solid ground as they enter into a trust "agreement."

5) Size of the Estate—The relative size of the estate may be different between spouses. The spouses may marry (second marriage) and one may have significantly more property than the other. The parties may question whether all of the property should be divided equally among all of their children, rather than pro rata shares to each spouse's natural children.

Joint representation of spouses forces spouses to forego the normal expectation of confidentiality and evidentiary privileges. Should one spouse reveal something to the attorney, the attorney may be obligated to tell the other spouse.

Notwithstanding being advised of any conflict or adverse interest and the signing of an *informed written consent*, at such time as the attorney and/or client feels that the confidential information has been or may be disclosed or that the parties realize they cannot agree, the attorney representing them must completely withdraw from the case. Therefore, although it is not strictly prohibited for an attorney to provide dual representation, in many situations it is not advisable. There are many attorneys and/or firms who will require a husband and wife to execute a document acknowledging that estate planning (preparation of wills and/or trust documents) is inherently a conflict of interest as each party may have different interests, especially in situations where they have children from other marriages, or separate property.

Another ethical concern is where registered domestic partners wish to create and execute reciprocal Wills. Since the probate statutes that now incorporate the transfer of property upon the death of a registered domestic partner are so new, this area has yet to be tested. It would appear on the surface that there is clearly an inherent conflict of interest due to the confidential nature of the relationship with each client. One partner's interest may be adversarial to the others'. It is likely that many attorneys will choose not to create reciprocal Wills in these cases and may advise each partner to seek their own attorney.

Due to the growing elderly population and the fact that many people are finding themselves caring for elderly parents, the incidence of elder abuse—both physical and emotional has increased. Adult children are often faced with becoming caregivers, which can take the form of helping occasionally or as a full-time caregiver and having to take over all aspects of the parent's care. This could mean everything from providing food, shelter and the necessities of life as well as taking care of the bills, medical treatment, and such—in other words, become the custodian for the aging parent. Should the parent have failed to prepare the legal documents needed for the child, or some other individual, to provide for this care, some sort of formal and legal path will need to be created. That path could be creating an estate plan or having to petition the court to be appointed as custodian. This process will be discussed later in the text. At this juncture, however, it is important that the paralegal understand the potential conflicts that could arise should there be a question of the elderly person's competency and capacity. An adult child who brings their parent to the estate planning appointment, does all the talking and directing, and pays the fee, is in reality **not** the client. That child may be insulted when the attorney informs him/her that he/she is not the client and that the parent must understand the plans and documents to be executed. If the attorney questions that competency, he/she may not actually be able to ethically provide the proper representation, creation, and execution of the necessary documents.

It should be noted that once the probate or estate administration begins, the person petitioning the Court to be appointed as Personal Representative is the client. This person may or may not be the named Executor or Trustee, if there was a Will. The attorney does not represent the estate or any individual family member, heir, or beneficiary, only the court-appointed representative.

The attorney's position in representing the estate's interests may be adversarial to the heirs and beneficiaries. This is another reason why an attorney should take caution in probating an estate for which he or she drafted the estate planning documents. He or she may have given the testator or settlor specific advice that may be adversarial to the interests of specific heirs as well as the executor and/or trustee's personal interests. Conversely, the same attorney is also the most familiar with the testator's wishes and may feel they are best qualified to represent those interests.

## Other Malpractice Concerns

Errors in calendaring are one of the most common areas of malpractice. It is, therefore, essential that the paralegal understand calendaring if he or she is responsible for that function in the office. If there is another individual assigned to calendaring, the paralegal should always double-check any calendared dates to make sure any and all dates are complete and accurate as it is likely to be the paralegal's responsibility to assure the work is complete and ready for the attorney's review prior to the deadline.

Calendars may be topical, a central firm calendar (which may or may not be computerized), an attorney's personal calendar, and any other calendaring system the firm maintains. The paralegal will often maintain his/her own calendar as a back-up for any of the aforementioned calendaring systems. Calendaring information should at minimum include the client or case name; the document received or filed, from or to whom and on what date; the hearing or appearance date; the date any responses are due (if applicable). Subsequent entries should include any other relevant dates based on the type of document received. Once the documents are calendared, the paralegal should bring them to the attorney's attention. You will need to be diligent in providing copies of the documents received to the client, letting the client know what information the attorney needs in order to respond, giving the client a timeline for providing the information, preparing the responses in proper legal format, and finally providing drafts for the attorney to review and sign prior to sending the final documents and any exhibits (attachments) to the Court as well as to any adverse party or their counsel.

Probate and Estate Administration also include timelines for the filing of various tax returns. The paralegal is often responsible for getting the information needed so that the returns will be completed in a timely fashion. The estate can be liable for penalties and interest for nonpayment of taxes that are due. Dates of all state and federal, personal and estate taxes should be calendared. Additionally, documents required to request extensions should also be calendared, including enough time to insure that the extension is granted. In many law firms, the preparation of tax returns is coordinated with a Certified Public Accountant (CPA) who is knowledgeable in estate administration and the preparation of taxes for same. The CPA will also calendar the appropriate dates, however, they should still be included in any calendaring for the estate. It is always wise to confirm that the CPA has met those deadlines as they occur. Most firms will request that a letter be written and that the letter be copied to the client.

There are a number of charts, workbooks and probate-specific software programs that contain the probate specific timelines and deadlines for filing specific documents and forms. For example, the filing requirements for Notices to Creditors, Inventory and Appraisal and the various Federal tax forms (706, Final Federal Tax Return, etc.) are included in these resources. It would be extremely helpful to have at least one of these tools available for use, to avoid missing any significant dates.

Clerical errors also frequently impact probate and estate planning practices. The failure of an attorney to understand provisions that relate to the disposition of the testator's property and which lead to beneficiaries not receiving the share the testator intended can be a problem in this area of practice. An attorney who is not familiar with drafting Wills and Trusts should refer clients to an attorney who does this kind of work. The paralegal and attorney should also make sure that all estate accountings are accurate, as this is an area where it is easy to make errors. The errors most frequently become known **after** the testator's death.

Clients have been known to sue for malpractice because they do not know what is going on with the case or why the attorney is taking so long to bring the matter to a conclusion. As you learn about the probate and estate administration processes, it will become apparent that these matters often take more time that one would anticipate. However, clients often do not understand the volume of work that must be generated, not only in their matter, but also for the many others that are handled by the firm. It is a good idea for the paralegal to keep the client informed frequently of the progress in the case. This will keep the client informed and happy. A happy client is less likely to bring a malpractice suit and will refer other clients to the firm.

The paralegal should always be careful about *giving advice* to the client (otherwise known as the Unauthorized Practice of Law or UPL). Although it may not be the client's intent, it is very easy to fall into a trap of answering clients' questions. You cannot give that client advice on any legal remedy—even if you know the answer. You must wait to relay the information to the attorney. The attorney will either call the client to advise him or her, or the attorney may (in his or her discretion) ask you to call the client and relay specific information. The client may be extremely emotional and distraught and will want to have an answer right away. However, you **cannot** tell the client what to do. That is considered giving legal advice and is a violation of UPL Statutes.

Your firm may have developed strategies for dealing with certain types of information that may be relayed to the client without the attorney's direct supervision. You should ask if there are any such circumstances, as each firm will be different.

## Confidentiality

The paralegal must never share information about clients and their cases with family or friends and should not discuss a client's case, even with the attorney, in an elevator or other public place where details about the client might be overheard by others. Additionally, one needs to be mindful that in some offices, telephone conversations can also be overheard by others, and legal documents should never be left in areas where other clients or persons coming into the office might be able to see them. In many cases, the smaller law firm may seem more casual than a big firm that practices in the area of litigation. Regardless of the size of the firm—a solo practitioner or several attorneys—the confidentiality of each client must be maintained and be of primary concern to every person affiliated with the law firm.

A common area of growing concern with respect to confidentiality has occurred with the baby-boomer generation and especially among those who are suffering with dementia, Alzheimer's, or some other disease that affects their mental capacity. Many elders are relying more on family, friends, and even caregivers to help them with daily living activities because they can no longer drive or may be unable to understand what was once normal conversation and/or daily business activities. Many elders have difficulty making decisions, paying bills, understanding and executing documents, and such. Thus many times an elderly person will schedule an appointment with the attorney and have his/her child or a caregiver bring them to the meeting. The child or caregiver then wants (or the client wants) to be part of the discussion to make sure that the attorney understands the wants and needs of the individual when creating the estate plan in order to best meet their needs. Letting a child or caregiver sit in the consultation, unless he/she has a valid Power of Attorney is a breach of confidentiality and may waive any attorney-client privilege.

There are courses and other resources offered to attorney and their staff through the Bar Associations that cover this growing area of concern. It is imperative that all legal staff understand whom the attorney represents so that confidentiality and privilege can always be maintained by everyone who comes in contact with the case.

It may be necessary to relay information to an expert such as the CPA, an appraiser or other professional who requires the information in order to perform the work for which they have been contracted. In the event you provide this information to such a person outside of the firm, that individual or company should be reminded of the confidentiality of the information. This is especially true of emails and facsimiles. All emails and facsimiles containing information about clients that are sent via the internet or telephone lines should contain a confidentiality statement.

A paralegal must insure and protect his/her own interests with respect to being protected in the law firm. It is undecided whether Errors and Omissions Insurance extends to the paralegal. Business & Professions Code § 6450 states that a paralegal's work **must** be supervised by an attorney. However, the paralegal's liability may be at question and unprotected. Under the concept of *respondeat superior*, employers are considered liable for any negligence of their employees as long as the employees are working within the course and scope of their employment at the time the negligent act occurred. This concept does not protect the employee. It does, however, extend the negligence to other persons and/or the law firm.

You should discuss this matter with the firm to be clear on whether or not you are listed on their malpractice coverage. You should also have a clear understanding of what information, if any, can be given to a client within the scope of your work and without direct supervision of the attorney.

## Ethical Wall

Probate and Estate Planning paralegals do not seem to change jobs as frequently as litigation and other types of paralegals. However, because the probate "community" may be very small in some jurisdictions, it should be noted that a potential employer needs to be made aware of any cases on which the paralegal is working, particularly where the new employer might represent an adverse party. This would include any type of case on which the paralegal worked when parties are involved in the probate process.

In the event there may be a conflict of interest, an ethical wall may have to be established. The National Federation of Paralegal Associations, Inc. (NFPA) has an outstanding publication titled, "The Ethical Wall," which details the requirements of the ethical wall. I would encourage you to obtain and read that publication.

## The Paralegal's Role

Probate can be a very lengthy process. Over a period of time, the client will come to rely on the paralegal for certain types of information. It is always a good idea for the attorney to inform the client at the beginning of the process of the paralegal's role. Once the firm has been retained, it is also a good idea that the attorney send the client a letter outlining what to expect. The introductory letter can cover the process and procedure, the various time-lines, and who is to be responsible for the various aspects of the matter. In most cases, the client will be the person named as executor or it will be a close family member who wishes to be appointed as the Personal Representative and thus will be considered the Petitioner. This person will need to be familiar with the duties and responsibilities of the Personal Representative or executor. This letter is also a great way of enumerating some of those requirements and fiduciary responsibilities of the client. The Judicial Council has created the Duties and Liabilities of Personal Representative (form DE-147) that the client must sign and which is then filed with the court. The form confirms that the Petitioner(s) has read the list of the duties and responsibilities. It is, however, my experience, that once clients have signed this form they may forget exactly what the roles are in the administration of the estate. The letter serves as an additional reminder and may also contain additional detail not included in the Judicial Council form; the form should be included with the letter so that the client cannot say they never saw and/or read it. Trust Administration is not typically overseen by the Courts, however, the fiduciary duties and responsibilities of the successor Trustee are just as important. Regardless of whether the client is administering the estate through the probate process or trust administration it is important that the client have a clear understanding of the duties and responsibilities.

There have been several cases resulting in Court rulings with respect to malpractice in the area of estate planning. Two such cases are: *Biakanja v Irving* (1958) 49 Cal.2d 647, 320 P2d 16 and *Lucas v Hamm* (1961) 56 Cal2d. 583, 15 Cal.Rptr. 821, 364 P.2d 685.

In both of the above cases, the Court rejected the opinion that attorneys are insulated from accepting responsibility for the acts of careless conduct. Specifically, the Court stated that "negligent attorneys" should not be insulated as an entire group from liability for preparing documents, which they should not be preparing. In *Biakanja,* a "non-lawyer" prepared the Will in question. The Court determined that if it did not hold the non-lawyer liable, then the Court would not be able to hold attorneys liable.

Additionally, the Court determined that the beneficiary was not a client and could recover from the attorney, as the attorney is "liable" when he or she knows the client intends the representation of the non-client. Most significant is that the statute of limitations begins to run when the non-client **learns** of the negligence rather than on the date the act was **committed** (the date the Will was created and/or executed).

Two other cases, although heard in jurisdictions other than California, are significant because they each involve a paralegal.

*In re Conduct of Morin* (1994) 319 Or. 547, 878 P.2d 393. Involved "living trust" seminars presented by an attorney and two paralegals. It was determined that the clients who attended the seminars never actually met with the attorney once they agreed to the service. The attorney "created the situation" where the attorney had the opportunity to commit the Unauthorized Practice of Law (UPL) by failing to supervise and sending the paralegal to meet with the client to gather information, and execute documents.

*In re Estate of Devine* (1994) 263 ILL APP.3d 799, 635 N.E. 2d 581. A paralegal became friends with the client. Bank accounts were established naming the paralegal as beneficiary. A trust was established naming paralegal as beneficiary. The client also had family; however, the paralegal was named as the beneficiary for all of the client's property. The family stated that the paralegal befriended the client for the purpose of inheriting his estate and that she used undue influence over the client so that she would be named as the beneficiary, rather than the natural heirs.

A paralegal should also read and be familiar with the National Federation of Paralegal Associations, Inc. (NFPA) Paralegal Model Code of Ethics. Specifically, the following sections are relevant to the area of estate planning and probate:

EC 1.2(e), EC 1.5(a)–(f), and EC 1.8(a)

# Probate Code and Other Relevant California Codes

There are thousands of code sections that have been enacted by the California legislature that relate to Probate and Estate Administration. Of primary interest in this class will be Probate Code §§ 240–249, which provide for definition of right of representation in relation to the distribution of the decedent's property. Probate Code §§ 6100–6325 set forth the various rules and requirements for Wills. Probate Code §§ 6400–6455 deal with Intestate Succession. Probate Code §§ 7000–12252 provide the guidelines for the administration (probate process) of the decedent's estate. These code sections should be your guidebook and you should familiarize yourself with them.

You will find that there are many other California Codes to which you will need to refer in certain situations. The following is not meant to be an exclusive list, but will give you an idea of the complexity of probate law matters and the other laws with which a paralegal should be familiar.

Service of Documents — Code of Civil Procedure § 413.10

Venue — Code of Civil Procedure § 395(a)

Conservatorship — Probate Code §§ 1400 et seq.

Guardianship — Probate Code §§ 1400 et eq.

Discovery — Code of Civil Procedure §§ 2002 to 2076

There are several California Family Code Sections with which you will become familiar. The following are only two examples of how these two areas of practice often overlap.

Probate Code § 26 defines "child" as "any individual entitled to take as a child ... from a parent whose relationship is involved." You will be well served to look also at the Family Code definition of a child, which indicates that there does not need to be a marriage of two people for there to be a child of the relationship. The probate laws look to the "blood" relationship between parents and children and the Family Code is an excellent resource for defining who is a child. Always read the footnotes/comments regarding any amendments for clarification of when and why the statute was amended.

Probate Code §28 provides for the definition of "community property." The Family Code also provides a similar definition, although it is more concise, it essentially mirrors the Probate Code definition.

Probate Code §37 provides information for Registered Domestic Partnerships as they relate the revisions in the Probate Code.

There are also code sections in the Civil and Family Codes that relate to debts and debtors. There are also several Federal statutes that may come into play in probate matters as they relate to Bankruptcy, the Full Faith and Credit Act, Retirement, Taxation, Medi-care and Medi-Cal.

The paralegal will find many secondary sources, which will be helpful in order to understand more fully the legislature's intentions in enacting laws and the Court's rulings. There are numerous secondary resources that provide history, theory and sample documents to be utilized by the probate law paralegal. Some of these are as follows:*

- The Rutter Group — *Probate*, by Bruce S. Ross, Esq.
- The California Continuing Education of the Bar (CEB) has numerous publications regarding will drafting, probate, estate planning, trust administration, elder law, conservatorship and guardianship
- *Transfer of Property Without Estate Administration* (Continuing Education of the Bar)
- Witkin, *Summary of California Law*
- Witkin, *California Procedure*
- National Academy of Elder Law Attorneys — www.naela.org
- *California Rules of Court*

---

*Author's Note: I find the Rutter Group and the CEB books offer some of the best examples of documents, motions, pleadings and forms for practical use and application in this type of practice. Some Courts may mandate the use of a particular resource as a guideline or checklist for properly prepared documents.

There are numerous other publications and on-line services available and to which your firm may subscribe. It is also helpful to join your local bar association's probate practice section (if they allow paralegal or associate membership) as they may be able to provide you with recent updates, continuing education, and timely information about local court rules, as well as proposed changes to the law, judicial council forms, and other probate-related issues. If you are unable to become a member of the local bar, you should attend their luncheons and other Continuing Legal Education (CLE) offerings as frequently as possible. There are also a number of private continuing education providers who offer courses which are taught by attorneys and experts in estate planning. You might also want to join your local paralegal association, or consider joining the sections of the California State Bar that allow paralegals to join, such as the Solo and Small Firm Practice section. Membership in other associations such as the National Federation of Paralegal Associations, Inc. (NFPA) and the National Association of Legal Assistants (NALA) will also give you an opportunity to network with other paralegals, as well as locate affordable CLE offerings.

# The Paralegal's Role

It is this author's opinion that the practice of probate and estate planning is especially suited for paralegal involvement. Paralegal utilization is vital in keeping the costs down for the client. California has established a statutory fee schedule for Personal Representative's and attorney's compensation. (See Probate Code §§ 10810–10814.) Thus, the fees payable to the attorney can be limited. While the Probate Code does allow for "extraordinary fees," these fees must be detailed and approved by the Court. As such, the Court has the discretion to "cap" the hourly rate for extraordinary fees at the paralegal rate rather than the attorney's normal hourly rate.

The organized and detail-oriented paralegal is an asset to the probate and estate planning practice as much of the work involves working with the client, collecting information, preparing accountings and forms, and drafting pleadings. For the most part, unless the matter is contested, the court appearances, particularly if the decedent died with a Will, are minimal.

A paralegal that has a background in transactional law such as real estate, banking, or in accounting may find the probate and estate planning arenas a perfect fit. The processes involved in probate and estate and/or transferring (funding) revocable trusts will be transactions with which they are already familiar.

The probate and estate planning paralegal should have good people skills. There will be a great deal of client contact and information gathering. It is often done while the client is under emotional stress because the client has recently lost a loved one. The person may be elderly and they may not have any idea where to find the decedent's personal information such as a safe deposit box, bank accounts, deeds, vehicle registrations, insurance policies, and retirement, survivor benefit information or most importantly the decedent's Will or Trust. You may also be working with many individuals such as appraisers, insurance companies, Certified Public Accountants (CPA), probate referees, appraisers, and court personnel. The paralegal needs to be patient and kind while gently steering the client toward the goal of obtaining the needed information.

Your firm may have been retained to represent a person who is contesting a Will or Trust or who has some adverse interest in the decedent's estate. That person could be a previously unknown child or a child who has been disinherited or omitted; the person could be a former spouse who was promised that an insurance policy would be maintained for a minor child. Conversely, your firm may be asked to represent the person who was named as Executor, for example. Any of the above situations may arise that will complicate what is initially considered a simple probate proceeding.

The areas of probate and estate planning are very personal in nature. There are rarely any two cases exactly alike. These matters involve the person's family and financial issues that may be adverse to each other. Most parents want to provide for their children when they are gone. Others are estranged from their children and want to make sure that someone else gets their property and belongings. It is often a very personal struggle when making those decisions. Additionally, the administration and subsequent transfers of property to children of "blended" families may add complexity to the distribution of an estate.

Once the decisions are made and are in writing, such as preparing a Trust and/or Will, and once the person(s) dies, there are those who will be unhappy with the parents' decisions about who will receive their estate. If the parent(s) dies testate, the children may feel that one person is getting more than another or they may feel slighted if one person is named as Executor over the others. The dynamics of a family are ingrained and are very personal. The manner in which siblings have interacted over the years will become even more exaggerated during the probate process. Families who at first glance may seem close have issues with each another: years of "Mom always liked you best," perceived special treatment of one child over another. A child who feels that because he/she was the only child to take care of the parent(s) during their last illness should receive more than the others can bubble to the surface and complicate matters.

Imagine a family who is obviously dysfunctional or blended family members who feel that they are entitled to more of a parent's estate, for whatever reason, or the feeling that upon the passing of a parent, the natural child's share may be transferred to the surviving spouse, who is not the natural parent. A parent may have verbally told a child he/she could have a particular item of personal property, but did not memorialize it in a Will. The natural child(ren) may feel as though they have been robbed of their parent's estate and, particularly, personal belongings, especially items which often hold more sentimental than monetary value. By their very natures, these situations often breed animosity and contempt. Thus, what appears to be a straightforward estate administration becomes a volatile and potentially hostile situation, regardless of whether or not there was a Will.

The paralegal is instrumental in collecting information and maintaining contacts with experts or other professionals who may be needed during the probate process. Once preliminary information such as real property deeds, vehicle titles, business documents, stocks and mutual funds, antiques, collectibles, and other assets the decedent may have owned is gathered, it will be necessary to determine the value of each of those items.

The paralegal will also need to work with the Personal Representative to determine debts, expenses of last illness or burial, as well as the needs of any of the decedent's family members. At the discretion of the client and/or attorney, some or all of the following tasks can be performed by the paralegal:

- Notification of Department of Health Services of any Medi-Cal benefits received by the decedent
- Notify the Post Office; place hold on mail
- Secure residence and/or arrange for moving and storage of property, as necessary
- Location of missing heirs

- Research old stocks and bonds, retirement, pensions, and annuities
- Request Estate Tax Identification Number (TIN) from the IRS, if needed

The above list is not meant to be inclusive. It is just an example of a few of the many tasks for which the paralegal can be responsible during the estate administration. Many more will be discussed as the probate and trust administration processes are discussed in their respective chapters.

# What is Probate?

Probate is the process by which a deceased person's property is transferred to other individual(s) through judicial oversight. A decedent's property was generally presumed to be transferred to any children in some manner. Historically the transfer of property, upon a person's death, varied widely depending upon the culture. Even English Common Law, upon which the United States originally based its laws, evolved greatly over time.

## History

Some cultures would not allow the transfer of property from a man to his wife when he died. In some cases, the property would be transferred to only the male children in the family or to the husband's "side" of the family. Other cultures transferred property to the wife's "side." This area allows for some lively classroom discussion about the various manners in which property was passed between families and especially heirs when there were no Wills to follow. For example, in the Middle Ages in England, only males could inherit real property unless there were no male heirs. In the event there were several male children, only the oldest would inherit the entire real property estate to the exclusion of the other male heirs. This is called the Rule of Primogeniture.

The Egyptians, as early as 2900 B.C. developed methods for a person to provide instructions, while still alive, for determining who would be the owners of property upon death. This power was called testation. The Roman and Greek civilizations also developed rules regarding Wills and the transfer of a person's worldly possessions upon death. You may also recall that many of these civilizations also buried personal belongings with people so that they would be able to carry those things into the "after life."

During the Anglo-Saxon era, Wills were developed and incorporated into common law that became the English Statute of Wills, codified in 1540. Many students will be familiar with the terms "Last Will and Testament." Initially, the Will was for the transfer of real property belonging to the decedent and the Testament provided for the transfer of personal property. Today those terms are considered synonymous and "Will" is the most often used and preferred term. In those early years, real property was the only property with significant value. Thus, the term "real estate" became common.

At that time, people did not have investments, insurance and retirement accounts. Their personal property consisted of clothing, furniture, jewelry and, possibly, livestock. The English "Crown" often allowed the church to oversee the distribution of personal property that was usually distributed equally among any related heirs.

Eventually, primogeniture was abolished, common law was modified, and a unified system was created. The English Parliament eventually passed the Administration of Estates Act in 1925 wherein the age of heirs was irrelevant and there was no preference made for male heirs.

# United States Probate Laws

U.S. Federal law governs federal and estate gift issues that can affect the manner in which some estates are administered. (These issues will be discussed further in Chapter Seven, "Trusts.") Some states have adopted the Uniform Probate Code (UPC) or portions of it that spring from English common law. Probate and the laws of succession of property are usually governed by each individual state. The state of Louisiana is the exception as its probate laws are based on Roman civil law. These individual state laws govern what makes a valid Will and, absent a valid Will, the laws of intestate succession.

See Chapter Twelve for federal and state statutes that further impact California estate planning and probate.

# Testate and Intestate Succession Defined

## Testate Succession

The property passing under a decedent's valid Will.

The concept of Testate Succession is fairly simple. If the person died leaving a valid Will, the property passes as set forth in the Will. (The discussion of what happens when there is a determination that the decedent had an invalid Will appears later in the chapter.) Upon locating the Will, which will also be addressed in more detail later in the chapter, the original Will is lodged with the Court in the County where the person was domiciled. The probate process is then commenced.

## Intestate Succession

The manner in which property passes when a decedent dies **without** a Will. (Probate Code §§ 240–241.)

The laws of Intestate Succession can be very complex. First, let us consider why a person would die without a Will.

The reality is, a good number of people die without a Will. As a young adult (you must be at least 18 years of age or be emancipated to execute a Will in California), you probably have very little in the way of personal belongings that anyone would want. You might own a car, a stereo, sporting equipment, the furniture in your rented apartment, and the clothes in your closet. You may be a student and under the care of your parents. In most cases, there is not much property of value to leave to anyone. The exception might be that you received some type of cash settlement or inheritance which is being held in trust until you are eighteen.

However, as we grow older, get a job, own a home, open a bank and savings account, buy a couple of automobiles, and have a family, we accumulate more "wealth" or things of value. With our job, we might have a small insurance plan (enough to cover burial expenses), retirement plan, 401(k) or similar employee benefits. These benefits are "contractual" in nature and provide us the opportunity to name a beneficiary who will receive any accumulated funds upon death. They are considered non-probate transfers because you do not need to go through the probate process in order for the beneficiary to receive a "gift." These transfers will be discussed in greater detail in Chapter Six under "Transfers upon Death."

If you are married, you probably purchased your home as a joint tenant with your spouse and thus the home also transfers outside of probate. The same is true of bank and savings accounts. Most accounts have the names of both people on the account. The same is true with automobiles if the title on the vehicle is John Smith or Mary Smith. Then it can be transferred by either party without the signature of the other being affixed to the title upon transfer. This is a very common way to hold property and is advantageous because transfers can be made simply and expeditiously if either person dies. Based on this scenario, many people do not feel they need a Will.

However, what if you have children and both you and your spouse (or the child's other parent) dies unexpectedly and without Wills? Who will care and provide for the emotional needs of the children? Who will be responsible for liquidating the estate and providing for the financial needs of the children, including food, shelter and clothing? In the event there is not a Will, a person whom you might not have ordinarily chosen as a guardian of your children can petition the court to be appointed as Guardian for the "person" and/or the "estate" of your minor children.

Probate Code § 3900 defines an adult as anyone over the age of eighteen. Therefore, the implied definition of a child is any person who is under the age of eighteen.

What if your only brother Tommy is a fabulous person. He loves your kids and they love him, but he is fiscally irresponsible? You might want to name him as guardian of the person of your children but name your cousin Samantha as guardian of the estate because she has her act together financially, but is not able to take on the responsibility of the day-to-day care of the children as she is physically disabled. The same may be true for divorced spouses. Obviously, in most cases a person would want the biological parent to care for the children if they passed away. But, what if spouses divorced because there were financial problems that they were not able to overcome? The person might not want the other spouse to have access to the money in the estate that is meant to provide for the children's needs. This will be discussed in greater detail Chapter Two.

You should get the picture of why it is a good idea to have a Will, particularly if you have minor children and want to make sure there is someone of your liking to care for them or to provide for the necessities of life from your estate in the event that you are unable to do so.

A Will also allows you the opportunity to determine who will be the Executor of your estate and the powers that the Executor will have. (Note: Executrix is the feminine version of Executor; the same is true for Testator and Testatrix.) As in the case of naming a guardian for the estate left to your children, do you want a person who has difficulty handling their own finances or who just cannot seem to get things done, to be the person who decides that they are going to petition to probate your estate. This is problematic when he/she learns that an administrator (the person appointed in the absence of a named executor) is entitled to a statutory fee for being appointed as your administrator or Personal Representative? This may not be the best person for the job. The best person may be your most responsible sibling, a parent, an adult child or even a trusted friend. A Will allows you the ability to name any person you feel is responsible enough to carry out your wishes and to find their way through the probate process, usually with the assistance of a good attorney and his/her paralegal.

A person might state they cannot afford to have a Will since attorneys are so expensive or that they just do not have the time. Often, if people can be shown the cost to their estate if they die without a Will, it will convince them that it is money well spent. At the very least, most attorneys will recommend that the person execute a holographic Will (handwritten). Holographic Wills are discussed in Chapter Two. It is the opinion of most legal practitioners, that a holographic Will is better than not having a Will at all.

18   1 · INTRODUCTION TO PROBATE, ESTATE PLANNING & ADMINISTRATION

What happens to a person's estate (real and personal property) if they die without a Will?

## Probate Code § 240

The California statutes provide for property to be distributed in a certain manner in the event a person dies without a Will—intestate. As previously indicated, the courts must look at the manner in which property is held or if there is a named beneficiary. The court will also look at whether the decedent is married and if there are minor children.

Probate Code § 240, states as follows:

If a statute calls for property to be distributed or taken in the manner provided in this section, the property shall be divided into as many equal shares as there are living members of the nearest generation of issue then living and deceased members of that generation who leave issue then living, each living member of the nearest generation of issue then living receiving one share and the share of each deceased member of that generation who leaves issue then living being divided in the same manner among his or her then living issue.

The above paragraph uses the term "issue" when referring to children. In the situation where a person dies intestate, the issue or children may also be referred to as heirs. If a person dies testate (with a Will) the issue will most likely, although not in all cases, be referred to as beneficiaries. (This will be discussed further in Chapter Two.)

The California Probate Courts look to the biological relationship to determine who are the issue or heirs of a decedent who dies intestate. This biological or blood relationship is set forth in what is referred to as the Table of Consanguinity ("the Table") which is used to determine the descendants of the decedent. Your direct descendants would be your children and then your grandchildren. You and any siblings are the direct descendants of your parents and so on. As referenced in the paragraph above, you are also the issue of your parents and your children and grandchildren are your issue. The Table allows the attorney (and his or her able paralegal) to chart the first line of issue or descendants to determine if the decedent had any heirs and who they are. In the event that the decedent does not have any issue (first line descendants), then you must look to the second line of descendants to establish the decedent's heirs. The Table is included as Appendix 1A. Use the following example and the Table to determine who are the heirs in the scenarios provided.

Example #1: Decedent dies intestate and is not currently married. He was previously married and has one stepchild, whom he did not adopt. He did not have any children with his wife. His Father and Mother have passed away and he has two sisters and one brother. Who inherits the estate?

Example #2: Decedent dies intestate and has never been married. However, he has two children, a boy and a girl, with Suzanne. Who inherits the estate?

Your instructor will provide you with more scenarios as part of your class assignments in order to learn how to properly use the Table. There will be other examples provided in the Appendix 1B regarding distribution of property based on a Will and whether the property will be distributed by right of representation, per stirpes or pro capita. (See the Glossary for definitions of these terms.)

In Example #1, you needed to look for the Collateral Relatives. These persons are those who are related to the decedent, but are not his/her issue. They are those listed in the second and third lines of the Table. The Courts always looks to the first line of descendants, when the decedent is not married and has no children, and then to the second line, if there are no descendants in the first line who would be heirs to the estate.

The Courts require that all issue be recognized, even if those children are estranged.

For example: If one of your parents was previously married or had a previous relationship and had a child of that relationship then that child must be notified of the death of the parent even if the decedent did not have a good relationship with the child.

The above section indicates what will happen if the decedent dies without a Will, no spouse, and has issue (children). It does not, however, indicate that the person who died was married and had children. Therefore, the issue of property acquired while the person was married, or community property, must be also considered.

The following is an excerpt from the California Probate Code §6240, which is set forth in question and answer format regarding Statutory Wills. It is relevant at this point as it sets forth why the legislature and courts feel that California citizen's should have a Will and why the Statutory Will was created so that people would be encouraged to, at very least, fill in the blanks of the Statutory Will so that their heirs and the Courts would understand their wishes as to the distribution of the decedent's property. The Q&A, included in the statutory will are a good foundation for a paralegal in order to understand the mechanics, mandatory clauses, and what types of questions a testator needs to ask him/herself and what questions the attorney needs to ask, such as who should be executor and/or guardian, does the executor need to be bonded, and so forth. There is also terminology defined, such as custodian, trustee, and domestic partner, which will be helpful for the entry-level paralegal who wishes to work in the estate planning firm.

## Probate Code §6240

The following is the California Statutory Will form: QUESTIONS AND ANSWERS ABOUT THIS CALIFORNIA STATUTORY WILL.

The following information, in question and answer form, is not a part of the California Statutory Will. It is designed to help you understand about Wills and to decide if this Will meets your needs. This Will is in a simple form. The complete text of each paragraph of this Will is printed at the end of the Will.

1. What happens if I die without a Will? If you die without a Will, what you own (your "assets") in your name alone will be divided among your spouse, domestic partner, children, or other relatives according to state law. The court will appoint a relative to collect and distribute your assets.

2. What can a Will do for me? In a Will, you may designate who will receive your assets at your death. You may designate someone (called an "executor") to appear before the court, collect your assets, pay your debts and taxes, and distribute your assets as you specify. You may nominate someone (called a "guardian") to raise your children who are under age 18. You may designate someone (called a "custodian") to manage assets for your children until they reach any age from 18 to 25.

3. Does a Will avoid probate? No. With or without a Will, assets in your name alone usually go through the court probate process. The court's first job is to determine if your Will is valid.

4. What is community property? Can I give away my share in my Will? If you are married and you or your spouse earned money during your marriage from work and wages, that money (and the assets bought with it) is community property. Your Will can only give away your one-half of community property. Your Will cannot give away your spouse's one-half of community property.

5. Does my Will give away all of my assets? Do all assets go through probate? No. Money in a joint tenancy bank account automatically belongs to the other named owner without probate. If your spouse, domestic partner, or child is on the deed to your house as a joint tenant, the house automatically passes to him or her. Life insurance and retirement plan benefits may pass directly to the named beneficiary. A Will does not necessarily control how these types of "nonprobate" assets pass at your death.

6. Are there different kinds of Wills? Yes. There are handwritten Wills, typewritten Wills, attorney-prepared Wills, and statutory Wills. All are valid if done precisely as the law requires. You should see a lawyer if you do not want to use this Statutory Will or if you do not understand this form.

7. Who may use this Will? This Will is based on California law. It is designed only for California residents. You may use this form if you are single, married, a member of a domestic partnership, or divorced. You must be age 18 or older and of sound mind.

8. Are there any reasons why I should NOT use this Statutory Will? Yes. This is a simple Will. It is not designed to reduce death taxes or other taxes. Talk to a lawyer to do tax planning, especially if (i) your assets will be worth more than $600,000 or the current amount excluded from estate tax under federal law at your death, (ii) you own business-related assets, (iii) you want to create a trust fund for your children's education or other purposes, (iv) you own assets in some other state, (v) you want to disinherit your spouse, domestic partner, or descendants, or (vi) you have valuable interests in pension or profit-sharing plans. You should talk to a lawyer who knows about estate planning if this Will does not meet your needs. This Will treats most adopted children like natural children. You should talk to a lawyer if you have stepchildren or foster children whom you have not adopted.

9. May I add or cross out any words on this Will? No. If you do, the Will may be invalid or the court may ignore the crossed out or added words. You may only fill in the blanks. You may amend this Will by a separate document (called a codicil). Talk to a lawyer if you want to do something with your assets that is not allowed in this form.

10. May I change my Will? Yes. A Will is not effective until you die. You may make and sign a new Will. You may change your Will at any time, but only by an amendment (called a codicil). You can give away or sell your assets before your death. Your Will only acts on what you own at death.

11. Where should I keep my Will? After you and the witnesses sign the Will, keep your Will in your safe deposit box or other safe place. You should tell trusted family members where your Will is kept.

12. When should I change my Will? You should make and sign a new Will if you marry, divorce, or terminate your domestic partnership after you sign this Will. Divorce, annulment, or termination of a domestic partnership automatically

cancels all property stated to pass to a former husband, wife, or domestic partner under this Will, and revokes the designation of a former spouse or domestic partner as executor, custodian, or guardian. You should sign a new Will when you have more children, or if your spouse or a child dies, or a domestic partner dies or marries. You may want to change your Will if there is a large change in the value of your assets. You may also want to change your Will if you enter a domestic partnership or your domestic partnership has been terminated after you sign this Will.

13. What can I do if I do not understand something in this Will? If there is anything in this Will you do not understand, ask a lawyer to explain it to you.

14. What is an executor? An "executor" is the person you name to collect your assets, pay your debts and taxes, and distribute your assets as the court directs. It may be a person or it may be a qualified bank or trust company.

15. Should I require a bond? You may require that an executor post a "bond." A bond is a form of insurance to replace assets that may be mismanaged or stolen by the executor. The cost of the bond is paid from the estate's assets.

16. What is a guardian? Do I need to designate one? If you have children under age 18, you should designate a guardian of their "persons" to raise them.

17. What is a custodian? Do I need to designate one? A "custodian" is a person you may designate to manage assets for someone (including a child) who is under the age of 25 and who receives assets under your Will. The custodian manages the assets and pays as much as the custodian determines is proper for health, support, maintenance, and education. The custodian delivers what is left to the person when the person reaches the age you choose (from 18 to 25). No bond is required of a custodian.

18. Should I ask people if they are willing to serve before I designate them as executor, guardian, or custodian? Probably yes. Some people and banks and trust companies may not consent to serve or may not be qualified to act.

19. What happens if I make a gift in this Will to someone and that person dies before I do? A person must survive you by 120 hours to take a gift under this Will. If that person does not, then the gift fails and goes with the rest of your assets. If the person who does not survive you is a relative of yours or your spouse, then certain assets may go to the relative's descendants.

20. What is a trust? There are many kinds of trusts, including trusts created by Wills (called "testamentary trusts") and trusts created during your lifetime (called "revocable living trusts"). Both kinds of trusts are long-term arrangements in which a manager (called a "trustee") invests and manages assets for someone (called a "beneficiary") on the terms you specify. Trusts are too complicated to be used in this Statutory Will. You should see a lawyer if you want to create a trust.

21. What is a domestic partner? You have a domestic partner if you have met certain legal requirements and filed a form entitled "Declaration of Domestic Partnership" with the Secretary of State. Notwithstanding Section 299.6 of the Family Code, if you have not filed a Declaration of Domestic Partnership with the Secretary of State, you do not meet the required definition and should not use the section of the Statutory Will form that refers to domestic partners even if you have registered your domestic partnership with another governmental entity. If you are unsure if you have a domestic partner or if your domestic

partnership meets the required definition, please contact the Secretary of State's office.

# Community Property

California is a community property state. Therefore, any property acquired during the marriage is presumed to be community property, unless there is a pre or post marital agreement stating that the property is separate property or the property was received by gift or inheritance and the acquisition by those means can be verified. California Probate Code § 28 defines Community Property as follows:

Probate Code § 28 "Community property" means

(a) Community property heretofore or hereafter acquired during marriage by a married person while domiciled in this state.

(b) All personal property wherever situated, and all real property situated in this state, heretofore or hereafter acquired during the marriage by a married person while domiciled elsewhere, that is community property, or a substantially equivalent type of marital property, under the laws of the place where the acquiring spouse was domiciled at the time of its acquisition.

(c) All personal property wherever situated, and all real property situated in this state, heretofore or hereafter acquired during the marriage by a married person in exchange for real or personal property, wherever situated, that is community property, or a substantially equivalent type of marital property, under the laws of the place where the acquiring spouse was domiciled at the time the property so exchanged was acquired.

# Surviving Spouse

Probate Code §§ 100–105 provides for the disposition of property of a married person, as follows:

Probate Code § 100

(a) Upon the death of a married person, one-half of the community property belongs to the surviving spouse and the other half belongs to the decedent.

(b) Notwithstanding subdivision (a), a husband and wife may agree in writing to divide their community property based on a non pro rata division of the aggregate value of the community property or on the basis of a division of each individual item or asset of community property, or partly on each basis. Nothing in this subdivision shall be construed to require this written agreement in order to permit or recognize a non pro rata division of community property.

Probate Code § 101

(a) Upon the death of a married person domiciled in this state, one-half of the decedent's quasi-community property belongs to the surviving spouse and the other half belongs to the decedent.

(b) Notwithstanding subdivision (a), a husband and wife may agree in writing to divide their quasi-community property on the basis of a non pro rata division of the aggregate value of the quasi-community property or on the basis of a division of each individual item or asset of quasi-community property, or partly on each basis. Nothing in this subdivision shall be construed to require this written agreement in order to permit or recognize a non pro rata division of quasi-community property.

The above statutes specifically state that the agreement is to be "in writing." Prior to January 1, 1985, a verbal agreement could be made between the parties as to the manner in which community or quasi-community property could be transferred upon death. Property subject to a pre- or post- marital agreement or property transferred to a revocable trust (see Probate Code § 104.5) for the benefit of both the parties are subject to these provisions as both types of documents are written instruments or agreements. A Transmutation Agreement is also a form of transferring property from one spouse to another and will be discussed in Chapter Seven. (See glossary also.) It is also recommended that you read the comments from this probate code section for clarification and reasoning for the changes, as well as available cross-references. The cases below are part of the reason the judicial council recommended the legislative changes to the statutes.

There is a presumption as to the manner in which title is held. There has been recent case law which clarifies these statutes for the purposes of both probate and family law.

*In re Marriage of Matthews* (2003) 133 CA4th 624, 35 CR3d 1 addressed the issue of how title is held with respect to community property. It is likely that this case will also be used in probate matters to determine if property was community or separate. In this case, the Court did not apply the rebuttable presumption of undue influence. They found that when Wife signed a quitclaim deed transferring the property to her husband in order to refinance the property (he had good credit and she did not) that she signed the deed voluntarily and with full knowledge. They therefore determined that the property was Husband's separate property and not community property.

*In re Marriage of Starkman* (2003) 129 CA4th 659, 28 CR3d 639 involved a revocable Trust agreement that was executed by a husband and wife. The Trust provided that property in the trust be considered community property. The Court held that a reference in the trust is not sufficient to be considered a transmutation of property from separate to community property.

The transmutation must be in a separate **written** agreement as set forth in the Probate Code sections referenced above and below.

These laws now also apply, in most cases, to registered Domestic Partnerships that will be discussed further in Chapter Twelve.

Absent a written agreement to contrary community or quasi-community property, if property is in the possession of any person who is not the surviving spouse, the property is subject to the following provisions of the Probate Code.

Probate Code § 102

(a) The decedent's surviving spouse may require the transferee of property in which the surviving spouse had an expectancy under Section 101 at the time of the transfer to restore to the decedent's estate one-half of the property if the transferee retains the property or, if not, one-half of its proceeds or, if none, one-half of its value at the time of transfer, if all of the following requirements are satisfied:

(1) The decedent died domiciled in this state.

(2) The decedent made a transfer of the property to a person other than the surviving spouse without receiving in exchange a consideration of substantial value and without the written consent or joinder of the surviving spouse.

(3) The transfer is any of the following types:

(A) A transfer under which the decedent retained at the time of death the possession or enjoyment of, or the right to income from, the property.

(B) A transfer to the extent that the decedent retained at the time of death a power, either alone or in conjunction with any other person to revoke or to consume, invade, or dispose of the principal for the decedent's own benefit.

(C) A transfer whereby property is held at the time of the decedent's death by the decedent and another with the right of survivorship.

(b) Nothing in this section requires a transferee to restore to the decedent's estate any life insurance, accident insurance, joint annuity, or pension payable to a person other than the surviving spouse.

(c) All property restored to the decedent's estate under this section belongs to the surviving spouse pursuant to Section 101 as though the transfer had not been made.

Probate Code § 103.

Except as provided in Section 224, if a husband and wife die leaving community or quasi-community property and it cannot be established by clear and convincing evidence that one spouse survived the other:

(a) One-half of the community property and one-half of the quasi-community property shall be administered or distributed, or otherwise dealt with, as if one spouse had survived and as if that half belonged to that spouse.

(b) The other half of the community property and the other half of the quasi-community property shall be administered or distributed or otherwise dealt with, as if the other spouse had survived and as if that half belonged to that spouse.

# Effect of Dissolutions on Probate

## Divorced But No New Will

Most dissolution attorneys will include a provision within the property settlement agreement that states any Will executed during the marriage is now void. Additionally, the Family Law Judgment form (FL-180) states: *Dissolution or legal separation may automatically cancel the rights of a spouse or domestic partner under the other spouse's or domestic partner's will, trust, retirement plan, power of attorney, pay on death bank account, transfer-on-death vehicle registration, survivorship rights to any property owned in joint tenancy, and any other similar interest. It does not automatically cancel the rights of a spouse or domestic partner as the beneficiary of the other spouse's or domestic partner's life insurance policy. You should review these matters, as well as any credit cards, other credit accounts, insurance policies, retirement plans, and credit reports, to determine whether they should be changed or whether you should take any other actions.* This serves as a notice to the parties that they should execute a new will once the divorce is final. What happens if they fail to execute a new will?

Probate Code §6122 states that any gift of property made to a former spouse or domestic partner in a Will previously executed, the former spouse will be treated as though they predeceased the testator. There are exceptions for dissolutions prior to January 1, 1985, however. If that should be the case, the attorney should review the applicable laws carefully to determine what action must be taken.

Another consideration may be the marital status of the parties. As stated in the paragraph above, a dissolution of marriage may have occurred. If the parties have separated, the attorney may need to make sure that the family is provided for during the pendency of any probate matter. However, if the parties have an action for dissolution of marriage filed with the Court, it may affect certain aspects of the probate. Of utmost importance to the Court, will be the care, or the continued care and needs of any children of the decedent, if the children are minors.

The manner in which property is held prior to the dissolution action as well as during the pendency of the matter will be considered by the Court. Many family law attorneys will recommend that the client execute a deed, particularly for the family home, making the parties Tenants In Common rather than Joint Tenants. This is particularly useful if it appears that the Dissolution process will be lengthy or the parties have reached a settlement agreement, but have agreed to jointly own the house for a specified period of time. This will allow each person to determine who will inherit their share of the property rather than have the survivor automatically inherit.

One significant (family law) case relates to a pension plan distribution during the pendency of a dissolution. Regents of University of California v Benford (2005) 128 CA4th 867, 27 CR3d 441. The Court determined in this matter that "an antialienation provision in husband's pension plan precluded distribution of a wife's community interest to her heirs, when she died after filing a dissolution petition but before entry of a judgment dissolving the marriage." A Court order had not been prepared, executed, filed and served on the pension plan that set forth the division of wife's community share in the pension plan prior to her death. Such an order would normally be prepared once the parties had reached an agreement and in conjunction with their property settlement agreement.

## Failure to Provide for Wife and/or Children

The Probate Code also takes into consideration that a person may have married or had a child after the time they executed their Will. Probate Code §§21610—21623 provide instructions for the court should a decedent fail to provide "in a testamentary instrument" for their children and/or surviving spouse.

A testator must knowingly, specifically omit their spouse and/or children in their Will (testamentary instrument) and have stated such. For example, if the spouses made a valid agreement waiving his or her right to receive a share of the decedent's estate and the Will specifies that the spouse and/or child(ren) received some other property (insurance, retirement proceeds, real estate) in lieu of a portion of the decedent's estate passing under the Will, it should be stated in the Will to clarify the testator's intention. However, if no such statement is included in the Will by the testator, the property will be distributed as set forth in those code sections referenced above. These code sections mirror the distribution under intestate succession.

## Posthumously Conceived Child

Effective January 1, 2005, the Probate Code was modified to include provisions for a child who was conceived using genetic material of the decedent after that person's death. Probate Code §§ 249.5 and 249.6 clarify the requirements for distribution of decedent's estate for a posthumously conceived child. Specifically, the use of genetic material of the decedent requires that the Executor of the decedent's estate be notified within three years of the decedent's death in order for that child to be considered a "potential" heir of the decedent. If the Executor is not notified within the three-year limit, the potential heir may be divested of the right to inherit. Section 249.5 provides specific guidelines for the use of such genetic material, including but not limited to stating who has control and use, which must be determined by the donee, in writing.

I recommend that you read these sections. They are interesting, cutting-edge, and evolving law, which incorporate the changes in our society's mores and lifestyles. The legislature recognized that these issues might come to light in the future with respect to the inheritance rights of potential heirs.

## Spousal Property Petition

There is a mechanism for transferring real property to a surviving spouse without having to proceed through the complete probate process when the decedent dies intestate. This procedure is called a Spousal Property Petition. This mechanism comes into play when the decedent died intestate and the property was not held in joint tenancy with the surviving spouse. The actual process of completing the Spousal Property Petition will be discussed in Chapter Six, "Non-Probate Transfers."

The above infers that the property was held as community property with the spouse. If the property was held in joint tenancy, then there is a right of survivorship and the property will be transferred to the surviving joint tenant.

Property held between individuals, as tenants in common will have to be probated based on the decedent's share of the property.

## Distribution of Intestate Estate

While some of the above statutes may seem fairly straightforward it is not the statutes that cause the difficulty in distributing the estate of an individual when they die intestate. It is most often the family dynamics and relationships that cause the many issues that can arise.

In today's society, we have more "blended" families. These are families where adults have married, divorced, remarried and had children with different spouses, and/or adopted step-children, or with individuals to whom they were not married. Which of these "family" are entitled to the decedent's estate? And, at what ratio?

According to California statutes, unless a person has a valid Will, **all** of their children will receive a portion of the estate, along with any surviving spouse. Thus, even if a child is estranged from the parent, or unless they have been adopted by another person, that child will still receive a portion of the natural parent's estate as long as there is no Will. A Will allows a person to "disinherit" a child from receiving any of portion of the estate upon their passing. Disinheritance provisions will be discussed further in Chapter Three.

Another concern to be considered is whether a non-U.S. citizen can inherit property. While this is beyond the scope of this text, it is worth reviewing the Uniform Probate Code §§ 2-111 for an explanation on whether property can be inherited, if the heir-at-law or beneficiary is not a U.S. citizen.

For additional history and information about intestacy consult the Uniform Probate Code which is available at www.uniformlaws.org/probatecode.

## Escheat

Escheat means "that which falls to one." It is the forfeit of all property to the State. Thus, if the intestate decedent dies without any heirs (spouse, children, parents, siblings, or relatives of any degree) the property reverts to the State of California (where the decedent lived). Refer to Probate Code §§ 6404 and 6800, et. seq. for additional information on how the California probate courts and the State deal with escheat estates.

## Ancillary Probate

If the decedent owned property in several states, the issue needs to be determined by the attorney and/or court as to what type of proceeding must occur. Some states may assert claim on property—particularly real property located in their respective states. Other states will require that an Ancillary probate be filed in the non-residence state.

The attorney will need to know what kind of property was owned and will need to research that particular state's laws as to how property is distributed and/or if a probate is required in that state. In the event an Ancillary probate must be filed in the non-resident state, the attorney and/or paralegal will need to research the laws of that state, the local rules, and any other state specific information that will be needed to conduct the appropriate procedure. A law firm may need to be retained in that jurisdiction as well.

## Fiduciary

A person's fiduciary responsibility will be discussed in greater detail in successive chapters, particularly as they relate to a person's capacity as a Personal Representative, Trustee, a Guardian or as an Agent under a Durable Power of Attorney.

Fiduciary is defined as a person who is entrusted with the handling of money or property for another person.

A person whom your firm is assisting in probating a Will or administering a Trust will have a fiduciary responsibility to that person and/or their estate. Care should be taken when working with any client to assure that they are fulfilling their fiduciary capacity in good faith.

## Key Terms

- Confidentiality
- Privileged Communication
- Adverse Interest

- Administrator
- Beneficiary
- Descendant
- Consanguineous Relationship
- Affinity Relationship
- Collateral Relative
- Heir(s)
- Issue
- Intestate
- Statutory Will
- Holographic Will
- Personal Representative
- Testate
- Testator
- Executor
- Fiduciary
- Joint Tenant
- Tenants in Common
- Will
- Non-Probate Transfers
- Guardian
- Rule of Primogeniture
- Community Property
- Surviving Spouse
- Spousal Property Petition
- Escheat
- Ancillary Probate

# Chapter Two

# Estate Planning

Estate planning is the mechanism by which a person makes certain decisions and executes specific documents that will affect how his/her estate will be disbursed upon death.

Estate planning can be as simple as making Will. There are essentially four types of Wills: holographic, statutory, standard Will and pour-over Will.

A "holographic" Will is made simply by writing on a piece of paper who should be named as Executor and who will get your belongings, money and property upon your death. A holographic Will is signed and dated by the person in his/her own handwriting and is **not** witnessed. It is the most difficult type of Will to "prove" since it is not witnessed. See Probate Code § 6111 for the specific requirements of a holographic Will.

A "statutory" Will is one that is a pre-printed form. The person making the Will fills in the blanks and has the Will witnessed.

A standard Will is the document created when the person chooses to seek the services of an attorney who will prepare a customized Will for the individual. There are also various Will software programs available for purchase. These programs may cause problems as the person creating the Will may have no legal knowledge and may omit certain essential requirements. He or she may also fail to include certain provisions that are required in the state in which they live, since these programs are meant to cover all 50 states, U.S. territories, and commonwealths. Additionally, some states require that the witnesses signatures on the Will be notarized, while in others it may be optional, and in still others a notary is not required. The validity of the Will could be called into question in the event the notary requirements for that individual state are not followed.

A pour-over Will is one that is associated with the preparation of a revocable "living" trust and is meant to capture any property that is not placed in the trust.

Estate planning can also include additional documents for the purpose of avoiding the need for conservatorships, guardianships, as well as advance health care directives ("living Wills") and durable powers of attorney. All of these will be discussed in more detail in later chapters.

## Succession Planning

Succession planning is the mechanism whereby a person decides how he/she wishes to have his/her estate distributed after death. This is also referred to as Estate Planning. Such planning may include planning for the distribution of property as well as for the care of oneself, their children, grandchildren, and other family members. A person may want to establish trust funds for the needs and/or education of children or grandchildren. This can be accomplished by creating a Will, Trust or other documents that provide for the transfer of property during a person's lifetime or after their death. The estate plan may also provide for distributions of property to charitable organizations, as well as make specific bequests of items of tangible property and/or cash. Primarily, succession planning is the manner in which a person customizes the distribution of his/her estate according to his/her individual wishes. Contrary to popular belief, estate planning is not just for the wealthy. It is necessary for anyone who has children and/or owns any type of property which requires transfer through probate. Estate planning also typically includes planning for one's inability to make decisions should they become incapacitated.

## Military Testamentary Instrument

Of special note are Wills that are prepared for active military personnel. As you can imagine, it would be difficult for the Judge Advocate General (JAG) attorneys to know the laws regarding Wills in all fifty states.

Soldiers' and Seamen's Wills are covered by Section 551 of the *Floyd D. Spence National Defense Authorization Act for Fiscal Year 2001* codified at 10 U.S.C. § 1044d. The Code provides that a "military testamentary instrument" is exempt from all state laws and formalities. It also provides that the Will should have the same force and effect as a Will prepared in the state where it would be probated and as though it was executed according to, the jurisdiction's governing codes. The Code also sets forth the requirements for the Will, including how to make them self-proving. To date, the Act has not been challenged.

This information is provided so that in the event your office is faced with probating a Will which has been prepared by the Judge Advocate General's office (JAG) and executed by a soldier or sailor, you will be familiar with its basis. It should be treated, in all respects, as though it were a Will created within the state where the soldier or seaman is domiciled.

# Probate Avoidance

The execution of a Will, in most cases, will not avoid probate. A valid Will simply makes the steps of the probate process easier for the named Executor as it may eliminate certain steps that will be required by the Court, if the person dies intestate. This will become clearer as you read and explore the various requirements of Wills later in this Chapter.

In most cases, probate avoidance is the manner by which property is held so that transfer upon death can be made without going through the formal probate process. Examples of probate avoidance are most commonly property held in joint tenancy or an asset that names a beneficiary. A piece of real property held in joint tenancy, such as between spouses and with a child will mean that upon one tenant's death, the property may be transferred to the surviving tenant(s). The same is true if a parent puts a child's name on his/her bank account so that the child can write checks if the parent is unable to do so. Any funds in that account, upon the death of either the parent or the child whose name is on the account, will belong to the surviving "tenant" unless otherwise specified. There are pros and cons to holding title in this manner and attempts to avoid probate which will be covered later in the text. The client should discuss this avoidance tool carefully with the attorney.

Revocable and Irrevocable Trusts, which will be discussed in Chapter Seven, are also, in most cases, used to avoid probate.

Insurance policies, mutual funds, annuities, retirement plans and accounts, IRAs, bank accounts, and other financial accounts usually have a named beneficiary. They are referred to as Pay on Death (POD) accounts or "Totten Trusts." Upon the death of the person who "owns" the account, the beneficiary(ies) will receive the portion of the account that has been designated to them. For example, a married couple may name each other as the first beneficiary of an account and may also name their child(ren) as the secondary beneficiary(ies) and the portion or percentage that each is to receive. When one of them dies, the account manager will pay to the spouse the value of the account, provided that certain contractual obligations have not voided the account. If both spouses die at the same time, the account will be distributed to the children who are named beneficiaries.

The accounts referenced above are considered "contractual" accounts between the owner of the account and the manager of the account or fund. Each type of account has different qualifications. For instance, a life insurance policy is administered differently than a retirement account through one's employer. Insurance policies can have certain qualifications that may affect the distribution of the property to the owner's beneficiaries. For example, some policies will state that if the owner takes his/her own life (suicide) the policy is null and void. Others may state that if the owner dies of lung cancer that was caused directly by smoking and the person stated on the application that he/she did not smoke, the insurance company may hesitate to pay the beneficiary, as it may be a violation of the contract. IRAs, bank accounts, annuities and retirement accounts do not usually have the kinds of conditions placed on them, as do life insurance policies.

Additionally, you need to know that if a beneficiary is a minor, the child will not be able to directly receive an amount more than $20,000 (as of the date of publication). In the event the amount is more than $20,000 or the amount allowed by the IRS under the annual gift tax exclusion (IRC§ 2503(b)), a custodian or guardian will have to be appointed for the "estate" of the child until he/she reaches the age of eighteen. This will be an extra step that will have to be considered, even if there is no formal probate proceeding. Guardianship will be discussed in Chapter Eleven. The amount of exclusion for 2012 was $13,000; however, this amount will likely change in subsequent years. It is also subject to adjustment for inflation. Always check for the current annual allowable exclusion when determining the need for a Uniform Trust for Minor's Act (UTMA) account and/or the amount that is allowed for estate planning purposes. California Probate Code Section 3412 sets the (current) amount at $20,000 as noted above.

Probate Code § 3413(a) currently states that if the amount [to be received by the child] is greater than $20,000, the court, in its discretion, may determine what is in the best interest of the child, depending upon factors such as whether a guardianship exists, the type of property or assets and such.

There are other mechanisms for the transfer of property without completing the probate process. In most cases, however, very specific criteria must be met.

For example, if the surviving parent dies, there is only one adult child and the only property in the estate are a vehicle and a bank account and the total value of those items is less than $150,000, the property may be transferred by Affidavit, whether or not the person had a Will.

The Affidavit procedure will be discussed in greater detail in Chapter Six.

In the event, Husband and Wife, or Registered Domestic Partners have valid reciprocal Wills and own property as Joint Tenants and/or named each other as beneficiaries on all applicable joint assets, it is likely probate can be avoided.

# Wills

A Will is a written document that directs to whom the decedent's property will be given upon the decedent's death. The Will also names the person or persons who will administer the estate of the decedent according to the Will makers' wishes. The Will may also specify other wishes of the decedent, such as who should be appointed as a guardian for any minor child he/she may have, specific gifts or bequests of certain items of property or sums of money, and burial instructions.

## Requirements of a Valid Will

In order to execute a valid Will in California a person must have "testamentary capacity" to create the Will. Therefore, the testator must be over the age of 18 and must be of sound mind. (Probate Code § 6220).

The Will must be witnessed by at least two persons who saw the testator sign the Will. (Probate Code § 8220.) Those persons must date the document, sign their name and affix their address. These witnesses will also be called subscribing witnesses when the Will is submitted for probate. See Probate Code § 6110 for additional information about the proper execution of the Will.

## Holographic Will

A holographic Will, in simple terms, is one that is completely handwritten, signed, and dated, in the testator's own handwriting and it **not** witnessed.

For example, if I sit down, write out whom I want to receive my property when I pass away and who I want to take care of my affairs (the Executor), sign it, and date it, I have created a holographic Will.

If I have three adult children, I can simply name each one of them as executor, commencing with the oldest, or I can name them co executors and state that they get all of my property in three equal shares.

Attorneys and the Courts tend to agree that a holographic Will is better than no Will at all. At the very least, the person has stated whom he/she wants to name as Executor and who should get their belongings. In the case of minor children, it can also state who will take care of the children. **Note that the Court does not consider a computer-generated Will a holographic will — it must be *handwritten*.** See Probate Code § 6111 for further detail on the holographic Will.

Using the above scenario, it would simplify filing the Probate with the Court. The oldest child could seek the services of an attorney and commence the probate process. (See Chapters Four and Five.) Once the process is complete, the estate would be divided into three equal shares as directed in the holographic will.

# Statutory Will

Probate Code §§ 6220, et seq. set forth the requirements of a statutory will in California, as follows:

Probate Code § 6220. Any individual of sound mind and over the age of 18 may execute a California statutory will under the provisions of this chapter.

Probate Code § 6221. A California statutory will shall be executed only as follows:

(a) The testator shall complete the appropriate blanks and shall sign the will.

(b) Each witness shall observe the testator's signing and each witness shall sign his or her name in the presence of the testator.

Probate Code § 6222. The execution of the attestation clause provided in the California statutory will by two or more witnesses satisfies Section 8220.

Probate Code § 6223.

(a) There is only one California statutory will.

(b) The California statutory will includes all of the following:

(1) The contents of the California statutory will form set out in Section 6240, excluding the questions and answers at the beginning of the California statutory will.

(2) By reference, the full texts of each of the following:

(A) The definitions and rules of construction set forth in Article 1 (commencing with Section 6200).

(B) The property disposition clauses adopted by the testator. If no property disposition clause is adopted, Section 6224 shall apply.

(C) The mandatory clauses set forth in Section 6241.

(c) Notwithstanding this section, any California statutory will or California statutory will with trust executed on a form allowed under prior law shall be governed by the law that applied prior to January 1, 1992.

Probate Code § 6224. If more than one property disposition clause appearing in paragraphs 2 or 3 of a California statutory will is selected, no gift is made. If more than one property disposition clause in paragraph 5 of a California statutory will form is selected, or if none is selected, the residuary estate of a testator who signs a California statutory will shall be distributed to the testator's heirs as if the testator did not make a will.

Probate Code § 6225. Only the texts of property disposition clauses and the mandatory clauses shall be considered in determining their meaning. Their titles shall be disregarded.

Probate Code § 6226. (a) A California statutory will may be revoked and may be amended by codicil in the same manner as other wills. (b) Any additions to or deletions from the California statutory will on the face of the California statutory will form, other than in accordance with the instructions, shall be given effect only where clear and convincing evidence shows that they would effectuate the clear intent of the testator. In the absence of such a showing, the court either may determine that the addition or deletion is ineffective and shall be disregarded, or may determine that all or a portion of the California statutory will is invalid, whichever is more likely to be consistent with the intent of the testator. (c) Notwithstanding Section 6110, a document executed on a California statutory will form is valid as a will if all of the following requirements are shown to be satisfied by clear and convincing evidence:

(1) The form is signed by the testator.
(2) The court is satisfied that the testator knew and approved of the contents of the will and intended it to have testamentary effect.
(3) The testamentary intent of the maker as reflected in the document is clear.

A Statutory Will, much like a holographic Will, is better than not having a Will at all. However, as you can see from the Probate Code Sections referenced above, if the testator completes the form incorrectly, the Will is not valid and the estate will need to be probated as though the person died intestate. A person who has little education, some form of dementia, or is elderly might be easily confused by the form and have difficulty completing it.

Very often people who do not have a Will, write out a Will prior to leaving on vacation "in case something happens" while they are gone. Elderly people who have not previously executed a Will may decide that they need to write down their wishes because they have been diagnosed with a terminal illness; however, they do not own much and feel they can't afford to pay an attorney to draft a Will for them.

## Pour-Over Will

A "pour-over" Will is typically the Will that is prepared and executed along with a Trust. This Will's purpose is to define the Testator, identify the executor and most important, names a guardian or guardians of the Testator's minor children. The Will also provides that any property that has not been transferred into the Testator's Trust or which is held pursuant to the General Assignment of property should be transferred as set forth in the Testator's Trust upon their death.

In the event that property has not been transferred into the Trust, the Court will be able to make orders for the transfer of the property based on the provisions in the Trust. It is then essentially a summary type of probate procedure rather than having to complete the entire probate process. This will be discussed further in Chapter Eight.

In most cases, the Testator will name the same person to be the Trustee and Executor. If married, it will usually be their spouse. However, the Testator is not required to do so and may decide to name another individual. It does make it simpler from a trust administration perspective to have the same person named in all capacities.

## Attestation and Witnesses

In California, a Will must be witnessed by at least two witnesses. Some firms will prefer that there are three witnesses. The witnesses do not need to read the Will; however, they must state that they saw the Testator sign the Will.

Self-Proving Will—A self-proving Will is defined as one where the witnesses declare under penalty of perjury that they saw the Testator and each other sign the Will in their presence. The witnesses, referred to as Subscribing Witnesses, must sign and date the Will. The Will should also provide a place for the witnesses to insert their address so that they can be located in the future. In most cases, however, if the Will is self-proving, the witnesses will not have to sign an Affidavit stating they witnessed the signing of the Will (Form DE-131).

In the event the Will is not self-proving, then the Affidavit will have to be completed by each witness declaring that each of them saw the person sign the Will. They are essentially becoming Subscribing Witnesses after the fact.

Make sure that the proper language is included in the Will so that the witnesses are considered Subscribing Witnesses. You will not have to locate them in the future when the Testator has passed away, and you must now probate their Will. It is often difficult to locate the witnesses ten or twenty years from the time the Will was signed. People relocate, they pass away, marry, change their names, etc., all of which may make them difficult to locate.

Attorneys have different philosophies about the execution and witnessing of documents. Some attorneys feel that it is an inherent conflict to prepare a Will and then be a witness to the same document. Others do not see a conflict in witnessing a Will that he or she has prepared. There is no law that precludes this. The attorney may prefer that their paralegal or other member of the legal staff be the witness(es). In that case, a firm may also pay for and encourage a paralegal to become a notary public so that the paralegal can also notarize other necessary and/or related documents for the client.

In California, Wills will be witnessed. They should not be notarized, unless an attorney has advised the notary public to do so. This can be very confusing for the client if they have lived in another state where Wills are required to be notarized. Additionally, some Will drafting software programs provide for both notary and witnesses at the end of the document. Keep in mind that these types of programs are meant to be generic so that they will comply with the law in most states. However, the witness requirements for the various states can be confusing to persons using an "all purpose" will preparation software.

The California State Bar advises that when a notary public is asked to notarize a document that purports to be a will, the notary public should decline and advise the person requesting the notarization to consult a member of the California State Bar. If an attorney recommends that the document be notarized, a notary may do so.

## Codicil

A codicil is a document that modifies or amends a Will. Typically, a person or married couple may want to have their children be their Executors once they have reached adulthood. In the event this is the only change they wish to make in their Will(s) then a Codicil will easily do the trick. If the changes are more complex or the laws have changed which effect the manner of distribution, then it is likely the attorney will recommend that a new Will be prepared to properly protect the person's assets, assure that expenses are properly paid, that an Executor has the appropriate powers to complete the probate process and/or that there is no question as to the manner in which the Testator wished that the property be distributed. Once children have become adults, the guardianship provisions are no longer valid or necessary.

# Preparation of Wills

Each law office will have their own process for preparing Wills for a client. The process may also depend upon the size of the firm. As a paralegal in the law firm you will need to ask the attorney(s) with whom you will be working how a Will and any collateral documents are created and who creates and prepares them.

The most common ways to prepare Wills are:

1) Templates
2) Document Preparation Software

The firm also may utilize a combination of those methods.

The first step in creating any estate planning documents is the gathering of information. In most cases, the attorney will meet with clients who wish to discuss their estate planning needs. Potential clients may not know exactly what types of estate planning they would like to have in place. They may have heard about Trusts. They may feel that they do not own anything other than a house so they only need a Will. On the other hand, perhaps they do not even own a house, but they have minor children. Clients often have preconceived notions about estate planning documents, what they do, and what they will cost. Thus, it is important for an attorney to explain to the potential client the various forms of estate planning, discuss with them the costs, and what documents will best meet their needs.

Once the clients decide what method of estate planning they wish to employ and have retained the firm to prepare those documents, it will be necessary to gather information from the clients in order to properly prepare the documents.

Many firms have a questionnaire form that can be given to either the client to complete or the attorney or paralegal can use to gather the information from the client. If the firm does not have such a questionnaire, it would be a good idea to ask the attorney if you should assist them in creating one so that the information that will be gathered from clients will be consistent. I have provided a sample questionnaire as Appendix 2A. There are also a number of resources that you can use to customize questionnaires, such as the Continuing Education of The Bar estate planning guides and estate planning software. The firm may also have different questionnaires for Wills and Trusts.

The attorney will advise you once he or she has met with the client how the information should be gathered. You may be introduced to the client and asked to sit down with the client and assist him/her in filling out the questionnaire. The attorney may simply ask you to provide the client with the appropriate questionnaire and a stamped, self-addressed envelope so that the client can return the information once it has been completed. Alternatively, the attorney may have already completed the questionnaire and advised you that he or she will begin creating the documents once you (or the appropriate office staff person) have opened the file and performed the conflicts check.

It has been my experience that you will want to review the completed questionnaire whether it has been completed by the attorney or the client as there may still be critical information needed. For example, if the client(s) provided the information to the attorney at the initial meeting, they may not have had full names, birth dates, addresses, telephone numbers, or other information with them at that meeting. Clients often get overwhelmed when completing lengthy forms and will not complete all of the information before it is returned to your office. Perhaps, the client was to provide the office with copies of deeds, insurance policies, bank or mutual fund account numbers, and the names of current beneficiaries on any policies they might own. It is usually the paralegal's function to make sure that all of this information is complete so that the documents are completed accurately and that any collateral documents that must be created (particularly for a Trust) will be included with the estate planning package.

The client may also want to talk with the attorney again regarding the person(s) who will be named as Guardian, Agent, Executor and/or Trustee of the various documents. The client may have changed his/her mind since the initial meeting, may still have questions or needed to ask these person(s) if they would be willing to serve in the various capacity(ies). Additionally, clients may need to discuss their wishes with a potential guardian and/or trustee, especially when it involves young children. The person whom the testator wants to name as guardian of his/her children may not feel they can perform the duties required of them and therefore decline. The testator may have to explore other options at that point. It is wise for the testator to make sure the person they choose is willing rather than wait until the time of appointment to find out this person must decline. There may be follow-up necessary on the part of the attorney and/or the paralegal depending upon the type of missing information before the documents can be drafted.

The paralegal should also ask the attorney if there is a specific deadline associated with the creation and completion of the Will and any other estate planning documents. For example, does the client need to execute the documents before he/she leaves on vacation, has surgery or some other important event? Has a date already been set for the execution of the documents or do you need to schedule this event? You certainly do not want to delay opening the file and getting it to the attorney if the client is going to need the documents completed the following week. In most cases, your office will have several weeks to prepare the documents and to schedule the signing, but you will want to make sure that you are aware of any important timelines and whether this is a high priority project.

Once the information is complete, the attorney and paralegal will work together to create the documents.

The attorney will advise you on how the documents should be created. The firm may have estate planning software and/or the attorney may choose to draft the initial documents. He or she will then provide you with the drafted documents via the firm's network or by providing you with a disk containing the documents.

There are many estate planning software packages available for attorneys to use in drafting wills, trusts, durable powers of attorney and other related documents. However, these documents do not typically provide the ability to customize the documents for each specific client. That is not to say that a software package is without the ability to provide some customization, but that it may not provide the level of detail and explicit directions needed to meet the particular client's needs. Rarely are two clients exactly the same. As you learn more about the estate planning process and the various types of software available, you will find this is true.

The following are some examples of how some nuances will make each Will different:

Husband and Wife have two minor children. They want all of their estate to go to the two children. They want Wife's sister to be guardian of the two minor children. (Very simple, right?)

Husband and Wife have two minor children. Husband has an adult child from a previous relationship with whom he is estranged. They want all of their estate to go to the two minor children and do not want the adult child of Husband to receive any part of the estate. They want Wife's sister to be guardian of the two minor children.

Husband and Wife have two minor children. Husband was previously married and has a minor child from that marriage. They want all of their estate to go to their two minor children, but want to make a provision for an insurance policy proceeds to be provided for Husband's other child. They want Wife's sister to be the guardian of the two minor children. Husband's previous spouse will be guardian of his minor child with her.

Husband and Wife have two minor children. They want all of their estate to go to the two children. However, one of the children has mental disabilities. They are concerned that if the child receives one-half of their estate it will affect any type of government benefit to which the child will be eligible. They want Wife's sister to be guardian of the person and estate of the child without disabilities. However, the Wife's sister will be guardian of only the estate of the child with disabilities as that child resides in a care facility and the facility (or state) will oversee the "person" of that child.

As you can see, it appears on the surface, at the first meeting, to be a Husband and Wife who just need to provide for the distribution of their estate to their two minor children, at least that's what they told you on the phone.

The Testator, if married or a who has a Registered Domestic Partner, may have separate property he/she wishes to leave to someone who is not considered a direct heir; a spouse or children.

For example:

Testator's family has a cabin in the woods and he/she wants it to be distributed directly to the children and not his or her spouse; or

Testator owns a business (such as a medical practice, law, or public accountant firm) with a partner. A spouse or child is ineligible to receive, operate or own a professional business unless they are licensed to do so. Therefore, the Testator must make provisions for his share of that property (even though technically there may be a community interest in the business) to be distributed according to the applicable laws governing that profession. The spouse or children can receive profit and income as distributed through the business partner(s). This will have to be considered when drafting a Will; or,

The person may simply own property in Joint Tenancy with someone other than his or her spouse. Even though the property would transfer outside of probate, most attorneys will recommend that the Testator state the proposed disposition within the Will to avoid confusion once the Testator has passed away and can no longer speak to ownership and personal wishes. There will be no question about the Testator's intentions or desire to omit a spouse or children as to this property.

Once you gather **all** of the information and get beyond the first scenario, there are a number of slight differences in each situation. An estate planning software package will only let the attorney draft the document with certain types of situations. If the situation is different, the attorney or paralegal is going to have to modify the document(s) to customize them to meet the particular situations.

The firm also may set up templates in a variety of ways. There may be templates to fit certain basic situations for each different type of information. Alternatively, there may be a database of template language to fit certain situations. Looking at the scenarios presented above, there may be templates for the following situations:

- Language about a previous relationship.
- Disinheritance clause stating that Husband's child is acknowledged, but will not receive any portion of the estate.
- Language about a previous marriage.
- Language about specific insurance policy for child.
- Language about dividing the remainder of the estate between the two children.
- Language specifying who will be guardian of the various children.
- Language about a "special needs" Trust to be created for the child with disabilities (this will be discussed in more detail in Chapter Seven); language specifying that a guardian of the estate and person is needed for one child; language specifying that a guardian of the estate only is needed for the child with disabilities.

There are as many different variations of template language that is not considered to be "boilerplate" as there are people and situations. A paralegal can be a great asset in creating and/or saving language to be used in other instances for different clients. Whenever possible do not spend unnecessary time "recreating the wheel" or searching through volumes of documents looking for language used for one client that is needed for another. A database or template file is a great place to save provisions that might be needed at a later date. Try to stay a step ahead of the attorney so that when he or she says, "*I need that language about \*\*\*\*\** (separate property distributions, disinheritance, special needs, guardianship by different individuals and/or person and estate) *that I used for that client about six months ago, it is a similar situation.*" You will be able to quickly find that language so that it can be inserted in the current client's document and then modified as needed.

The downside of using templates is you need to be very careful to eliminate all references to the previous client. Word and WordPerfect allow you to do a global search for a particular name or phrase. Remember, however, that these are not foolproof. I have had situations where I have done the global search and something was missed. I then printed out the entire document in final form and thought it was ready to be signed by the client, only to turn to the signature page and find that the previous client's name is still under one signature line or that the footer was not changed and had to quickly revise and reprint. You will need to read and re-read the drafts. Of course, the attorney will also need to proof each draft and particularly the final draft before the client signs it. (Remember that the attorney may not be the best proofreader either.) In many large firms, it is required that a senior attorney review all of the documents before the client signs them. It saves everyone time and potential embarrassment (not to mention malpractice) if the drafts are accurate. It is always a good idea to have as many people as possible review the documents within reason.

# Execution of the Will

The firm will likely dictate the manner in which the Will is executed. You should ask the attorney his or her preferences so that the document will be in the proper format. Some firms prefer that there be three witnesses to the Will, although California law only requires two. As previously indicated, the witnesses must be over the age of eighteen and should not be related to the Testator or have any personal interest in the Testator's estate. Any person with a contractual agreement with the testator should not be a witness to the Will.

The attorney may have a preference as to how the Will is executed. Some attorneys want lines on each page where the testator and/or the witnesses can initial the pages. This reduces the risk of having alternate pages inserted in the Will at a later date. Some attorneys do not feel it is appropriate for them to be a witness to the Will, while others will witness the Will as well as notarize other estate planning documents. This eliminates the need to find an additional witness and/or a notary public when the documents are executed. The attorney may also prefer that the paralegal be a witness as well as perform notarial services as needed for collateral documents. In instances where the attorney and paralegal are witnesses, if necessary, the attorney will more easily be able to locate the witnesses at such time as the Will is probated.

Attorneys also like to have their staff witness Wills because there is usually less question as to whether the Testator signed under coercion or duress should the Will be contested. If the office staff is not available, for instance if the Will is executed at the Testator's home, the attorney may prefer that people who are younger than the Testator serve as witnesses as they are less likely to predecease the testator. The attorney may ask the witnesses to provide their dates of birth, drivers' license number, or social security numbers so that they can be identified later if needed. Only the address, printed name and signature are **required** on the Will. The other confidential identification information will be kept in the attorney's client file to be used when/if needed to locate the witnesses in the event they move, marry, change their names or pre-decease the Testator.

Even though the attorney has met with the client before, the attorney will want to make sure that the client knows what he or she is signing and that the Will is being signed without coercion or duress. The attorney will confirm that the person is of sound mind, usually by engaging them in informal conversation. At this point, the attorney will also confirm the client has reviewed the Will and that he/she knows the contents and it was prepared pursuant to his/her wishes. This is particularly important when your firm has elderly clients.

It can be very tricky for the attorney if there is any question about the Testator's mental capacity. The attorney will have to broach this subject carefully and with the utmost sensitivity and respect for the client. Frequently you will be contacted by a family member of a person who has been diagnosed with Alzheimer's Disease or some other form of Dementia. The person is worried that his/her loved one has not "gotten his/her affairs in order." The attorney will have to determine if the person is still able to make the decisions about the estate or if the disease has affected any ability to make those decisions. If the attorney determines that the person does not have the mental capacity to do so, it may be too late and the person's estate will have to be probated as Intestate. This is also true of executing other documents such as Advance Health Care Directives and Powers of Attorney (which will be discussed in more detail in Chapter Nine). If the attorney determines that the person is unable to understand and execute these documents, the attorney will be unable to assist them.

A notary who is notarizing other documents, as well as witnessing the Will, has the right to question the person's mental capacity to sign the documents that will be notarized.

The witnesses do not review the Will, nor will they, in most instances know the contents of the Will. The exception would be if the attorney and paralegal served as witness, then they would have been involved with the creation of the document and know its contents. Otherwise, the witnesses will hear the Testator state that it is his or her Will and that he/she is signing it voluntarily. The witnesses will observe the Testator signing the Will. The witnesses will then read the attestation clause, date and sign the Will (and initial the pages if the attorney has requested that they do so); they will enter their addresses on the Will also. As previously indicated, the attestation clause (subscribing witness) states that each person is declaring "under penalty of perjury" that he or she has witnessed the signing of the Will by the testator.

The next step is to make sure that the client has the original copy of the Will. The attorney will also keep a copy for the firm's file. The client may also want additional copies. Oftentimes, the client will keep the original in a safe deposit or fire-safe box and will keep a copy in a desk, filing cabinet, or wherever other important documents are stored. Some Testators will also want to have a copy to give to their Executor(s) and/or their children. No matter how many copies the client wishes to have, he or she should be advised by the attorney that the client makes a clear record and/or informs the Executor where the original Will can be located at such time as it is needed.

The attorney may also want to provide a checklist or reminder information to the client before leaving the office with a new Will. This information can serve as a reminder of things they must do with the Will and also when it's advisable to make changes to documents such as if a beneficiary or executor dies or upon marriage or the birth of a child. If the firm does not have such an information sheet/checklist, the paralegal could prepare a draft for the attorney's consideration upon resources such as CEB or the software packages which may have sample documents and letters for this purpose.

The attorney will also want to let the client know that the client should contact the law firm if he/she needs to make any changes to the Will. Wills that have been altered, even with additions or deletions that are initialed, may be the subject of Will contests. It is important that the client knows that he or she needs to have a Codicil if changes need to be made and that it is important that the Will **not** be altered in any manner.

Upon the death of the testator, a paralegal in an estate planning firm, will receive numerous telephone calls from family members wanting to know if you know if the decedent/testator had a Will. It will likely to be your job to search for, locate the client's file, and determine if there is a Will. Although you should not tell the person calling whether or not a Will exists, you should let the attorney know about the call(s) and provide the attorney with the file so that he/she can contact the person(s) requesting information.

If your firm did prepare the Will for the Testator/decedent, it is likely that the person calling is the Executor or another family member who has been unable to locate the Will. It is also likely that such people/individual(s) will retain the firm to handle the Probate. Recall the ethical considerations of this situation discussed in Chapter One.

## Typical Will Preparation

The following is a typical sequence of estate planning document preparation. Please keep in mind that the firm and/or attorney will dictate exactly how the process is to be completed.

- Attorney meets with client(s), determines estate planning needs and gathers preliminary information.
- Attorney introduces paralegal to client(s) so that he or she can gather more information from the client.

- Paralegal gathers information from client and gives the client a list of other information that will need to be provided, e.g. dates of birth, full names and addresses of siblings, current addresses of children, addresses of people serving as executors, trustees, and/or guardians, copies of insurance policies, mutual funds, bank accounts, deeds and other property.
- Paralegal opens file, performs conflict check and gives the attorney the completed client questionnaire and other documentation gathered.
- Attorney uses estate planning software package to prepare Will and any other agreed upon documents and saves documents to firm data base; or the Attorney advises the paralegal to use a particular template(s) in the firm's data base; alternatively, to customize the Will.
- Attorney gives paralegal the file and informs him or her that the documents are drafted, but that additional provisions need to be included as indicated in the file (unless the attorney has already given the paralegal the file and directed him or her to use a template).
- Paralegal accesses documents, locates templates of various provisions that require insertion in client's documents and saves documents according to the firm's requirements for saving documents.
- Paralegal prints rough drafts for attorney to review.
- Attorney reviews documents and makes changes as necessary and/or advises paralegal of changes to be made.
- Paralegal makes changes as necessary, add or changes footers, page numbers, document names and any other formatting changes as requested by the attorney or required by the firm.
- Paralegal prints second draft of documents, saves second draft and returns file to attorney for review.
- Attorney advises paralegal that the documents are ready for printing of final draft and to schedule appointment for client to come to the office to execute the documents.
- (Optional) Attorney may request that drafts be sent to the client prior to the meeting.
- Paralegal gives documents to attorney for final review. (At this point, the attorney may have a partner or their supervising attorney review the documents.)
- Attorney meets with client(s) and reviews documents.
- Attorney and paralegal witness, or assist with proper witness of, the execution of the Will(s) and perform notary acknowledgments as required on other estate planning related documents.
- Attorney advises client of need to formally change documents, to keep the documents in a fire safe location, and to provide executor with a copy and/or advise him or her where to find copies and originals.
- Paralegal prepares copies for client(s).
- Provide clients with a checklist or informational letter about storing the Will and other documents; when to modify documents; and, formalities in making changes when necessary.

As you can see, a paralegal is very involved in preparation of Wills and other related estate planning documents. Once you become more familiar with this area of law and the drafting of the documents, you will become an integral part of the preparation of Wills and other documents. Your expertise will be valued by the law firm, and you will be given more responsibility in drafting, as well as working with clients. Although it is important, as previously noted, that the attorney meet with the client(s) for the initial appointment as the client(s) will need advice and direction as to the estate planning documents that will best meet their needs. You will likely be the point person to take initial telephone calls, screening the clients and setting up the initial appointments. As you become more experienced, it is also likely that you will spend more time interviewing and gathering information once the attorney has been retained by the client to prepare the agreed-upon estate planning documents.

You are also a second set of eyes and ears for pertinent information that the client may neglect to relay to the attorney. You will also become familiar with many of the boilerplate provisions that are required to be included in Wills or which may affect the manner in which the property is distributed. For example, you will become familiar with the distribution of the estate under Probate Code §246. Thus, if this provision is not included in the Will, you may ask the attorney to verify that he or she wants the property to pass in that manner. If the attorney specifically deleted those provisions, you will then know that it was done purposely rather than by a computer program malfunction or the attorney inadvertently not checking that box as he or she completed the questionnaire in the software.

I am also aware of one software program that does not automatically insert the reference to Independent Administration of Estates Act language (which we will discuss in Chapter Three) under the Executor powers. I noticed this and brought it to the attorney's attention. He thanked me and asked me to begin including it in all the Wills the program created. Eventually, we found that we could "customize" the software. We were then able to add the specific language into the program and all subsequent Wills created by the program contained the specific language that the attorney preferred.

You will also learn as you complete the process of probating a Will that there are other nuances that will help the firm as well as the administrator by assuring that the Will does not have any flaws at the outset. As you gain experience, you may feel more comfortable pointing out language that may seem ambiguous.

These are just a few examples of how you can be an asset to the estate planning firm as you learn the various nuances, increase your skills, and become more knowledgeable about the documents you are helping to create, as well as those that may also be administered by the firm.

A Will template is provided at Appendix 3A. This is a standard format. Your instructor will provide you with instructions and any personal preferences so that you can prepare a draft Will for **yourself**, as part of your assignment for this class.

NOTE: This example should not be considered legal advice or be used as an actual Will for your personal use. It is simply meant for the student to become familiar with the basic requirements, information, and provisions that will be included in most valid California Wills. It is similar to the types of documents you will see in the various secondary sources referenced in Chapter One.

# Key Terms

- Testamentary Capacity
- Military Testamentary Instrument

- Holographic Will
- Statutory Will
- Codicil
- Totten Trust
- Pay On Death Account
- Attestation Clause
- Subscribing Witness

# Chapter Three

# Wills

## Specific Will Provisions

This chapter will focus on some of the specific Will provisions you will encounter when drafting and probating Wills. It is important to have a clear understanding of why the legislature and the courts have determined that certain passages should always be included in Wills and Trusts. Attorneys will also have certain preferences for language to be included in these documents to make the intent of the provision clearer to the client and also so that it will be clearer to the probate court as to the Testator's intentions at the time the Will was drafted.

That being said, there is still a great deal of "boilerplate" language in Wills that would not be included if the client were to write the Will on his/her own. Clients often comment that they do not really know what some of the wording means, but they understand that it needs to be in the document for their protection and because it is the law.

Probate Code Sections 6100 to 6105 set forth the "General Provisions" for the making of a Will, including who can make a Will, the mental capacity needed to make a Will, and that the Will may dispose of property.

Probate Code Sections 21110 through 21356 set forth the "Construction of Wills, Trusts, and other documents." These code sections do not provide exact language as to how the Will should be prepared, but they are a summary of the various terminologies contained in the Probate Code as well as the Will. They also provide a guideline for the transfer of property upon the Testator's death, for the manner of holding title, and who are issue (heirs) and children of issue. They should be reviewed carefully.

As you review the Will template, provided as Appendix 3A, you will note that the Will follows a type of pattern.

## Identification of Testator

First, the Testator is identified; who he or she is and where he/she lives. The Testator must be domiciled in California. In the event the person has been known by different names either currently or in the past, such as maiden name or previous married names, the attorney may also want to include that information. Some firms will also include whether the Testator is a U.S. Citizen to avoid any confusion about the rights to inherit under Uniform Probate Code §§ 2–111.

Immediately after the identification of the Testator, a provision usually follows that states that the Testator revokes all other wills and codicils that he or she may have previously made. As mentioned in Chapter Two, it is always best if the attorney asks the client if he or she has executed a previous Will. If there is a current Will, the attorney will likely offer to destroy the Will upon the execution of the new Will or remind the client that the Will, and any copies, need to be destroyed by any of the methods discussed in Chapter Two.

The introduction also states whether the person is currently married, or in some cases the attorney will add to whom they were previously married. In the event the person is still married, but is separated or in the process of obtaining a dissolution of marriage, that information may also be noted. Likewise, a person who is engaged and who is leaving property to their fiancé(e), he/she may also be mentioned.

Next, the children are listed. Each office will have a preferred method for listing the children (or it may be dictated by the software program, although that can certainly be modified if the attorney prefers it be listed in a certain manner). Below are some of the different ways that children may be listed, particularly if there are children from different marriages or stepchildren.

Single person with two children:

| Child | Date of Birth | Name of Parent |
|---|---|---|
| Sally B. Smith | 01/01/01 | Samuel B. Smith |
| Samuel B. Smith, Jr. | 03/03/03 | Samuel B. Smith |

Married persons with two children (same language applies to both husband and wife):

I have two living children: Sally B. Smith, whose date of birth is January 1, 2001 and Samuel B. Smith, Jr. whose date of birth is March 3, 2003.

Married persons who have blended families (Example is for Wife):

I have three children as follows:

| Child | Date of Birth | Name of Parent |
|---|---|---|
| Sally B. Smith | 01/01/01 | Samuel B. Smith |
| Samuel B. Smith, Jr. | 03/03/03 | Samuel B. Smith |
| Jaime J. Jones | 05/05/05 | John J. Jones, II |

I have the following stepchildren, who are the children of my husband:

| Child | Date of Birth | Name of Parent |
|---|---|---|
| Jeffrey J. Jones | 08/08/98 | Jennifer M. Jones |
| John Jones, III | 09/09/99 | Jennifer M. Jones |

A reference should also be included as to **any** children who have previously died. The Will may simply state that "I have no predeceased children." (See template.) If the testator did have a child that predeceased him or her, whether the child was a minor or an adult, the child's name and date of birth should be noted. The attorney may also want to include the date of death.

For example:

I have one child who predeceased me as follows: Theodore Z. Nugent, whose date of birth was February 14, 1970, and who passed away on December 5, 1975.

These introductory provisions tell the court, the Executor, and any other interested parties the obvious people who will be involved in and who will be required to receive notice of any probate of the testator's estate upon the Testator's death.

## Pour-Over Wills Related to Trusts

In the event the Will is a "pour-over" Will, prepared in conjunction to the Testator's Trust, there will usually be a section that states that the Trust was also created on the same date as Will and that it was executed just prior to the Will. The provisions will also provide for instructions if the Trust (or any portion of it) is found invalid or is revoked by the Testator/Trustee. The Will would then be distributed under the same terms as the Trust.

## Obligation to Pay Debt and/or Taxes

The next paragraph, article, or section (usually the attorney or firm will have a preference as to the headings that are used) generally deals with the obligation to pay taxes, bills, last illness and funeral expenses of the decedent.

This section may appear elsewhere in the document, depending upon the attorney's preference, but it is almost always included somewhere within the document.

## Reference to Contract in Testator's Will

Probate Code § 21700 provides that a person should not be required, by contract, to make a Will unless certain conditions are met. This section also relates to Probate Code §§ 140–147 with respect to a spouse's right to execute an agreement wherein he/she waives property rights and/or transmutes property, within that written document. As you review Wills that were created prior to 1990, you will note that there is not usually a reference in the Will to such contracts. You should review these code sections carefully. In most cases, this reference is to married couples who are making "reciprocal" Wills. The attorney will need to be aware of any pre-marital, post-marital or transmutation agreements, which are contracts under the definition in the code sections, referenced in this paragraph.

In most cases, the attorney will likely include a simple statement in the testator's Will stating that the Will was not created any contractual obligation.

## Distribution of Property

The manner of distribution will also be set forth in the Will. As you can see in the template, the language is very simple. The spouse receives all property if he or she survives the Testator and the children share equally all property if the spouse does not survive the Testator/decedent.

There are many more complex ways of distributing property. The Will could contain a provision for specific bequests of personal property or of money with the residue going to the spouse, children, and/or other named beneficiaries. In the event that the Testator makes a provision for specific bequests, this provision should come first and then the residual language would follow.

For example, Husband's Will may state:

I make the following gifts of personal property:

1) I give my grandfather watch to my brother, Jasper Jones
2) I give my antique model car collection to my best friend, Art C. Fellow

3) I give my restored 1960 Jaguar to my son, John Jones, III

I give the residue of my estate to my wife. If my wife predeceases me, I give the residue of my estate to my children in equal shares. If either of my children predecease me that child's share shall be distributed to his or her issue by right of representation.

Oftentimes, a Will may simply state that the heirs will receive the decedent's property as "set forth in Probate Code Section 240." Most law firms have gotten away from drafting this kind of language, except to use it as a "catch-all" at the conclusion of the distribution provisions so that there is no ambiguity as to the Testator's intent. However, if there was no Will, the decedent's property is automatically distributed pursuant to Probate Code § 240. That code section is stated below:

Probate Code § 240 — If a statute calls for property to be distributed or taken in the manner provided in this section, the property shall be divided into as many equal shares as there are living members of the nearest generation of issue then living and deceased members of that generation who leave issue then living, each living member of the nearest generation of issue then living receiving one share and the share of each deceased member of that generation who leaves issue then living being divided in the same manner among his or her then living issue.

Additionally, Probate Code § 246 provides for the distribution of the decedent's property where there is a Will and/or Trust which provides for the distribution to take place *per stirpes* or "by right of representation." Simple Wills commonly state that the beneficiaries take the property by right of representation or pursuant to Probate Code § 246, which states as follows:

Probate Code § 246

(a) Where a will, trust, or other instrument calls for property to be distributed or taken "in the manner provided in Section 246 of the Probate Code," the property to be distributed shall be divided into as many equal shares as there are living children of the designated ancestor, if any, and deceased children who leave issue then living. Each living child of the designated ancestor is allotted one share, and the share of each deceased child who leaves issue then living is divided in the same manner.

(b) Unless the will, trust, or other instrument expressly provides otherwise, if an instrument executed on or after January 1, 1986, calls for property to be distributed or taken "per stirpes," "by representation," or "by right of representation," the property shall be distributed in the manner provided in subdivision (a), absent a contrary intent of the transferor.

The Will may state that the property is to be distributed "per capita" as set forth in Probate Code § 247. That section states as follows:

Probate Code § 247

(a) Where a will, trust, or other instrument calls for property to be distributed or taken "in the manner provided in Section 247 of the Probate Code," the property to be distributed shall be divided into as may equal shares as there are living members of the nearest generation of issue then living and deceased members of that generation who leave issue then living. Each living member of the nearest generation of issue then living is allocated one share, and the remaining shares, if any are combined and then divided and allocated in the same manner among the remaining issue as the issue already allocated a share and their descendants were they deceased.

(b) Unless the will, trust, or other instrument expressly provides otherwise, if an instrument executed on or after January 1, 1986, calls for property to be distributed or taken "per capita at each generation," the property shall be distributed in the manner provided in subdivision (a).

(c) If a will, trust, or other instrument executed before January 1, 1986, calls for property to be distributed or taken "per capita at each generation," the property shall be distributed in the manner provided in subdivision (a), absent a contrary intent of the transferor.

Care should be taken with respect to the use of ambiguous language. Read the following Will provision, discuss, and think about the interpretation:

"I give $20,000 to my four children: Sam, Sally, Sarah and Seth."

Does the above sentence mean that each child receives $20,000 or that the four children will receive $20,000 to be divided among them, or $5,000 each?

I have included several charts as Appendix 1B, as I personally find it easier to understand the differences between these various distributions when I can visualize them. I hope that you also find them helpful. These charts also include the various manners in which spouses and children receive property depending upon whether the distribution is *per stirpes*, *by right of representation*, or *per capita*, as set forth in the applicable Probate Code sections. Examples are also provided within the relevant Probate Codes for each type of distribution.

## Naming of Executor

The next paragraph typically sets forth who will be the Executor of the estate. In most cases, married people will choose their spouse. The exception may be if you have elderly clients and one of the spouses is unable to "act" on behalf of the other. The Testator will likely want to name someone such as a child, a close friend or other person whom he/she trusts. As previously indicated, it is a good idea to choose a person as Executor who can be trusted, but who will also, hopefully, outlive the Testator so that down the road an alternate does not have to be sought.

Most attorneys will recommend to a client that the client name at least one alternate to serve as Executor, should the first choice be unable to serve for any reason.

The other consideration that the Testator must make when appointing an Executor is whether that person may serve without bond. A person who is appointed to serve as administrator of an intestate estate is, in most cases, required to file a bond. The Testator is allowed to waive the bond requirement for the person who is named as Executor of the estate. However, if the named Executor lives out of the state there will be a bond required. Some Courts will require a bond for an Executor who lives in another County.

The purpose of the bond is to assure that the Personal Representative performs his or her fiduciary duties with regard to the decedent's estate. It protects the estate and beneficiaries from Executors who might be tempted to mismanage the estate. The Executor has a fiduciary responsibility to the Testator's estate and is held to a high standard of care. It will be Executor's duty to manage and sell property and to ultimately distribute the estate assets as set forth in the Testator's Will, or if the decedent died intestate, as set forth in the laws of California. The bond, issued by a surety company, provides "insurance" should the Executor not perform his/her duties as required, and in particular, cost the estate money, the bond may be collected upon by the heirs or beneficiaries to cover the lost portion of the estate.

Normally, if the Testator is appointing a spouse, a child or other trusted person the Testator will state that the bond requirement is waived. However, if the Testator has no family members and is appointing an unfamiliar individual or entity, the attorney may recommend that the requirement to post of a bond be included in the Will.

The naming of an Executor can be particularly troublesome for some individuals. The job of an Executor is considered an honor by many. It means the Testator trusted you to fulfill their wishes. It means that you were considered trustworthy, responsible and reliable.

The attorney will explain the legal requirements and responsibilities of the Executor along with some of the desired characteristics that make a good Executor. This may further confuse the client's desire to do what is "right" within his or her family. As previously indicated, most spouses name each other as Executor. However, what if the person is not married, but has children, or who should spouses name as an alternate after they have named each other?

Clients will often tend to name the oldest child as first alternate and so on down the list by date of birth. However, what if the oldest child is unable to hold a job, has financial difficulties, or another child has personal issues that indicate the child does not have the right characteristics or the ability to fulfill the duties and responsibilities? Or, perhaps, that child is estranged from his/her parents or siblings and there would be intrinsic rivalry if that child were appointed. Perhaps the youngest child is the most levelheaded, trustworthy and honest and would be the best candidate, but the client feels that this will cause animosity between the siblings. This will be an issue that the client will have to resolve based on what the client feels is best overall for the estate at the time of death.

Clients may also want to choose co-Executors, particularly if they have two children and do not want the children to think that the parent preferred one child to the other or where they are not sure that one child can perform the duties by him(her)self, but they do not want to disfavor the child by not making the appointment. Alternatively, Testators with blended families may want to choose a child of each of them to serve together so that the interests of "both families" will be represented. The downside to having joint Executors is that they will **both** have to sign all documents and perform all duties **together**. This can be rather cumbersome, particularly if the children do not live in close proximity. Every pleading, every form, document, deed, policy, account, etc. will require the signatures of both Executors.

The client may choose to name a bank or other corporate fiduciary as Executor. This also has its downside. Unless the person has a large estate, the estate will quickly be depleted not only by the normal Executor fees, but also by additional administrative costs that an individual executor might not charge the estate. If you or I were appointed as Executor of our parent's estate, we probably are not going to charge the estate for mailing letters, telephone calls, photocopies, meetings with the attorney, etc. A corporate fiduciary is going to charge for everything, thus reducing the net value of the estate at distribution.

Another thing to consider is what kind of assets the Testator has accumulated. If the Testator have a business that one of the children is involved with on a regular basis, it might be best if that child were appointed Executor because the child is going to have the knowledge necessary to keep the business running during the course of the probate.

Another family member might not have that knowledge. A corporate fiduciary while understanding business and the structure in general, will likely not have the "inside" knowledge that the family member has. A corporate fiduciary is also not emotionally involved as would be a family member. As previously mentioned, if the business is a professional organization such as a law or CPA firm, medical practice, the Executor will not be able to continue to "run" the business if he or she is not a licensed professional. The attorney will need to guide the client on how to make appointments if that should be the case.

## Defining the Executor's Powers

After naming the Executor in the Will there will be a list of the types of duties the Executor may perform. If the Executor is a trusted individual and is serving without bond, the attorney will usually recommend that the Testator give the Executor broad powers. These may include, but are not limited to, collecting all the decedent's assets, paying his or her debts, liquidating property and distributing the property as set forth in the Will or, as allowed, at his or her discretion. You should read the "powers" in the template (Article IV) to become familiar with some of the types of responsibilities that the Executor will be expected to perform as a fiduciary for the decedent.

Additionally, when naming an Executor, it is helpful to give him/her the broad powers as set forth in the Independent Administration of Estate Act. (See Probate Code § 10400 et seq. and §§ 10502–10586.) Specifically, the powers granted under the "Act" and as set forth in the template Will allow the Executor to perform most of his or her responsibilities without constant, direct Court oversight and more informally. The Executor who will be working with the attorney, will be allowed, for example, to sell the decedent's property in order to pay his or her debts, pay administration costs, and then distribute the "net" estate to the beneficiaries named in the Will. An Independent Administration does not mean that the Executor is not required to fulfill his or her duties and responsibilities, it simply means that the process is less formal and will, in most cases, advance more quickly without having to get permission from the court when taking most actions.

The Executor will be required to file a Notice of Proposed Action with the Court, which requires serving all interested parties with all details and information about the intended sale of the decedent's property. If the Will contains Independent "Act" powers, the Executor will **not** be required to have a hearing regarding the matter. Anyone objecting to the sale must do so within the stated period. If the sale is not opposed, the property can be listed for sale. Once an offer has been made on the property, the Executor would again be required to notify the court and serve notice of the pending sale, including the amount offered on the property. Without Independent "Act" powers, the Executor must request a hearing to confirm the sale. If no objections are raised to the sale price, the property can then be sold. As you can see, just this one responsibility can be quite cumbersome if the Executor is required to give notice and have a hearing for each and every activity that he or she needs to perform. An Executor and the attorney, who are performing their responsibilities under the "Act," will be able to function more expeditiously and effectively if they do not have to have a court hearing for each and every action taken during the course of the probate. Rather the attorney will simply provide *Notice* proposed action to all interested parties and then be able to submit the *Order* for the Judge's signature upon proof of service of the Notice. It is usually the paralegal's responsibility to work with the Executor and others such as real estate agents and/or appraisers, to gather information regarding these transactions. The paralegal will prepare the Notices, attaching copies of required documents, serve them to interested parties, calendar all dates and file documents with the Court.

The "Act" does not mean that the Executor does not have to report his or her activities to the beneficiaries, those requesting *Special Notice,* and the Court. The reporting process under the "Act" includes providing interested parties with information if requested. It also provides that, in most cases, the Executor, with the assistance of the law firm, will provide notice of all activities within the scope of the Petition for Final Distribution. This will provide a synopsis of all activities performed by the Executor during the course of the probate.

## Period of Time for Executor to Act

Also included in most Wills drafted by law firms will be a section relating to the period of time which the Executor may have to act as Trustee, if he or she is appointed as Trustee for any minor children who will receive the decedent's property. Typically, the period of time is 21 years, which, is the length of time it would take for an infant to reach the age of 21 if the Testator died shortly after that child was born. These are referred to as the "Laws of Perpetuity."

As previously indicated, a minor child cannot receive a sum larger than $20,000 from a decedent. Any minor children must have "trust" accounts created for them, and a trustee of the account would need to be appointed. The account is maintained under the Uniform Transfers to Minors Act (UTMA). (The federal statute can be found in Chapter Twelve of this text.) These statutes provide that a donor may make a gift to a minor (donee) and may retain the management as the custodian of the property or may name another person to serve as custodian. The custodian will manage the property, for the benefit of the minor, until the minor reaches majority at which time the property is distributed to the donee. The donor may state whether the donee is to receive the property on the 18th, 21st, or another birth date, such as the 25th, that is determined by the Testator. These types of transfers are relatively simple, and are less complex than creating a Trust. They are also more cost-effective, especially if the value of the property is relatively small. The custodian's duties, powers and responsibilities can be found in the statute.

Thus, the twenty-one year period will provide for this trust account to be held and administered according to any terms set forth in the Will (or Trust) or according to the UTMA if not specified in the Testator's Will. (California Probate Code §§ 3900–3925.) Refer to PC§ 21200 et seq. with respect to the Uniform Statutory Rule Against Perpetuities.

# Children—Definition and Guardianship Provisions

When the Testator has children, whether they are adults or minors, the attorney will provide a definition of children within the Will. Unless otherwise specified, the natural children of the Testator are considered children, this includes children who are "non-marital" children, if the Testator's parentage has been, or can be, established. Children adopted by the Testator are also considered children and have waived any right to inherit from their natural parent through the adoption. Stepchildren (if not adopted) are **not** considered natural children of the Testator. However, a number of firms are including language that includes stepchildren when the Will provides that **all** children shall share equally in the Testator's estate. This means that the children of the Testator and his/her spouse will all be treated as equals in the distribution of the Testator's respective estates.

It is extremely important that the attorney draft these provisions to clearly and accurate reflect the wishes of the client(s) with respect to any and all children to avoid any confusion. Additionally, the attorney work-product—as to the discussion he or she had with the client(s), in the event he or she must testify as to the person's intent after the testator's death may be extremely important to provide verification of the testator's intent.

If the Testator has minor children, a guardian will need to be appointed who will provide for the care of the children if the Testator dies before the children become adults. In most cases, the surviving natural parent of the child would be appointed to serve as guardian. The parents (husband and wife if preparing joint Wills) will also discuss and determine whom they wish to be the guardian of their children if they both should die. This may be a very difficult choice for some people; for others, it is fairly easy.

Another consideration is who will be guardian of the children when there is a blended family. Would different guardians be appointed for the "person" and for the "estate" rather than one guardian appointed for both? Can you appoint a person other than a natural parent to be a guardian where the parents are divorced? The attorney may have to look to the dissolution papers to determine custody and other considerations. What happens when a married couple is appointed as co-guardians and they divorce? Whom does the client appoint as guardian in that circumstance?

As indicated in the previous section, it may be necessary to create a UTMA (custodian) account for any property that would ultimately be distributed to the minor. In most cases, personal property may be given directly to the child, depending upon the age of the child and the type of property. The Executor is probably not going to distribute a motor vehicle to a child of 10. However, the executor may, depending upon the Testator's specific instructions, sell the vehicle and place the funds in a UTMA account or may hold, or have the parent hold, the vehicle for the child if the child is closer to driving age. However, if the Testator left a 13-year-old child a stamp collection because the child had an interest in it, the Executor is likely to distribute that gift to the child.

Thus, you can see that there are differences in guardianship of the person (the actual child) as opposed to guardianship or custodianship of the estate of the child. In most cases, the Wills you will be involved in drafting will be simple and straightforward naming one person in both capacities. However, there are as many differences as there are individual families and relationships, so it is helpful to be aware of the nuances that may come into play in the law office environment.

Your instructor will discuss a few of the many variations regarding naming guardians, particularly in blended families where there may be custody and support issues to be taken into consideration. It should make for a lively discussion.

## Trust for Children

The Testator may provide for a Trust or Trusts to be created within the framework of the Will for any minor children, should the Testator choose not to create a "stand-alone" Trust. These trusts are often referred to as Testamentary Trusts—they do not become effective until the death of the testator. This mechanism allows for the Executor, if he or she is also appointed as the Trustee for such Trust, to hold, administer and distribute the Trust for the child according to the terms provided within the instrument. It eliminates the need for the creation of a custodial account, for which the Testator may not have the funds at the time of executing the Will. Additionally, a custodial account requires judicial oversight. The "Child or Children's" Trust does not usually require judicial oversight. The Trustee has a fiduciary responsibility to maintain the trust property and such standards are usually included within the Will provisions. The Testator may name the guardian of the minor child as the Trustee, rather than the Executor, if they are different individuals. These types of trusts will be discussed in greater detail in Chapter Seven.

A parent should also consider the ability of the Trustee and/or Guardian to be able to provide this service over the long term—this may not be a short-term commitment. If the testator should die, leaving small children, the Guardian/Trustee will need to provide care and support for the child(ren) until the child reaches majority or the specific age set forth in the Will, if past majority in the case of a Testamentary Trust.

## No-Contest Clauses

The simple template Will is included in the Appendix does not include a No-Contest Clause. The No-Contest and/or Disinheritance Clause is usually included immediately after the provisions regarding children, as they are the individuals who Testators would be most likely to disinherit. This may also be referred to as an Omission of Heirs Clause. No-Contest provisions can be found within Probate Code § 21310 et seq.

These clauses usually contain language that states that a specific child or children have been purposely omitted (or not provided for) in the testator's Will. It will also likely state that if any person contests the validity of the Will they will be treated as though they "predeceased" the Testator. In other words, they will not receive anything from the Testator's estate. A Testator may also specifically exclude a parent, sibling or other person who potentially could inherit.

In years past, Testators have often included a clause that stated that the person who contested the Will would receive "one dollar." This was customary as it provided acknowledgment of the person as well as giving the person something from the decedent's estate so the person could not say he/she did not get anything and were erroneously omitted from the Will. It is difficult to contest a Will in which you were named and given $1 or some other small tangible item. It was a means of showing the Testator's specific intent as to that individual. This practice continues today in some firms, but it is not as common as it once was.

## Boilerplate Language

The "meat" of the Will is usually followed by boilerplate provisions. You will see in the template that there is a provision about the Tax Codes and the IRS. There is also a reference to definitions in general. These provisions, although seemingly boilerplate, are necessary as they will provide direction for the Executor as well as the court in determining the manner by which certain activities should be performed or how language should be interpreted. Without those provisions, the intent of the Testator could be questioned, particularly by outside entities such as the Internal Revenue Service. Omitting certain language could trigger tax consequences the Testator would not have wanted or anticipated. It could also cost the Testator's estate additional sums to be paid in taxes, penalties or other fees.

For example, the language with regard to requiring a bond of the Executor may be boilerplate. However, without that language a bond would be required. The cost of the bond is based on the estimated (gross) value of the estate. The bond is issued for one year. Thus, the bond could be substantial. In the event it takes more than a year to settle the estate, the Executor would have to renew the bond on each anniversary date, costing the estate additional monies. Most Testators do not want their estate being depleted by the payment of bonds that could have easily been waived.

## Simultaneous Death

This language provides that if any beneficiary should die at approximately the same time as the Testator and it is inconclusive as to who died first, that the beneficiary should be considered the first to die. This provision is interpreted to mean that if the beneficiary died first, the Testator's estate does not have to be probated first. Without this provision, the law would require the transfer of any property to the beneficiary's estate. That estate could be in the process of probate. The provision allows any distribution that the beneficiary would have received to be distributed directly to the beneficiary's heirs. Essentially, the beneficiary and probate proceedings would be skipped.

For example, a single (divorced) person who has three adult children dies in an auto accident along with one of the children. The 1/3 that the deceased child would have received would go directly to his or her children (the Testator's grandchildren), if any, or as otherwise provided in the Testator's Will.

## Rule Against Perpetuities

In the event, a potential beneficiary will receive a "nonvested" property interest or a power of appointment within the framework of the Will (or Trust), the attorney will make sure that there is language included which cites the Uniform Statutory Rule Against Perpetuities. Probate Code Sections 21300–21115 address the California Statutory Rule Against Perpetuities. (See Glossary for "Rule Against Perpetuities.")

Specifically, Probate Code §21209 sets forth the time period and requirements for the property under this Rule, as follows:

Probate Code §21209(a) If, in measuring a period from the creation of a trust or other property arrangement, language in a governing instrument (1) seeks to disallow the vesting or termination of any interest or trust beyond, (2) seeks to postpone the vesting or termination of any interest or trust until, or (3) seeks to operate in effect in any similar fashion upon the later of (A) the expiration of a period of time not exceeding 21 years after the death of the survivor of specified lives in being at the creation of the trust or other property arrangement or (B) the expiration of a period of time t hat exceeds or might exceed 21 years after the death of a the survivor of the lives in being at the creation of the trust or other property arrangement, that language is inoperative to the extent it produces a period that exceeds 21 years after the death of the survivor of the specified lives.

## Self-Proving Affidavit, Attestation, Signature of Witnesses

The requirements for a valid Will state that the document should contain language that makes the Will self-proving. There should be a declaration that the Testator is of sound mind and has the mental capacity to create the Will. (PC §6100.) The self-proving declaration is not required, however, it makes probating the Will more simple, as it saves several steps.

The Testator and the witnesses should attest to the validity of the Will, that they signed in each other's presence, having seen the Testator sign the Will and that they are making the declaration under penalty of perjury.

Without this specific language, the Court will require that the Witnesses be located and a Proof of Subscribing Witness (form) be completed and filed with the Court. It is much more expedient to avoid this step and make sure that the required language, dates, signatures and attestations are included in the original Will from the beginning. See Probate Code §76 for additional information regarding subscribing witnesses.

Care must be taken in drafting Wills for Registered Domestic Partners. There will be a variety of nuances and phrases that will differ from the typical spouse/husband and wife language which may be taken for granted in reciprocal Wills.

It is important, however, that Registered Domestic Partners execute Wills to specify their intentions with regard to property and any children they may have in order to avoid confusion as to the passing of their estate, potential guardians and any other special requests that they wish to make upon their death. Many of the Probate statutes were changed to include Registered Domestic Partners where previously the law only recognized "marriage." Wills are needed to avoid ambiguity as to the Testator's intent. It will also be important for the Registered Domestic Partners to execute Durable Powers of Attorney and Advance Health Care Directives should they want their partner to be appointed as their Agent should it become necessary. This will be discussed further in Chapter Twelve.

## Research and Interesting Wills in History

Your instructor will provide you with a list of "famous" persons whose estates went through the probate process.

The filing of a Petition for Probate makes the decedent's property, heirs and other personal information public information. This is one of the many reasons why people take steps to avoid probate by creating trusts and other non-probate transfers upon death.

You will find some very interesting reading in this assignment.

## Key Terms

- Right of Representation
- Per Stirpes
- Per Capita Distribution
- Totten Trust
- Uniform Trust for Minors Act (UTMA)

- Custodial Account
- Sound Mind
- Mental Capacity
- Pecuniary
- Bond
- Disinheritance Clause
- No Contest Clause
- Testamentary Trust
- Uniform Transfer to Minor's Act
- Bond
- Corporate Fiduciary
- Guardian
- Custodian
- Reciprocal Will
- Pour-over Will
- Executor
- Simultaneous Death
- Attestation
- Self-Proving
- Witnesses
- Rule Against Perpetuities

# Chapter Four

# Probating an Estate

## Probating an Estate

Probate Code Section 8000 sets forth the conditions for a Probate, as follows:
Probate Code § 8000

(a) At any time after a decedent's death, any interested person may commence proceedings for administration of the estate of the decedent by a petition to the court for an order determining the date and place of the decedent's death and for either or both of the following:

  (1) Appointment of a Personal Representative.
  (2) Probate the decedent's will.

(b) A petition for probate of the decedent's will may be made regardless of whether the will is in the petitioner's possession or is lost, destroyed, or beyond the jurisdiction of the state.

Probate Code §§ 8001–8007 provide guidelines for commencing the probate process. A paralegal working in the area of probate and estate planning should be familiar with these sections. They will provide not only an understanding of the probate process, but also make you aware of why Wills may be created in a certain manner and why more and more people are creating Trusts in order to avoid the probate process.

## Probating the Will

In most cases, a Will must go through essentially the same probate process as an intestate estate. The procedures will follow the same legal process through the Courts with slight variations. The exception may be a Pour-Over Will, which will only need to be submitted or "lodged" with the Court, providing that all the decedent's assets have been funded into the Trust. (This will be discussed further in Chapter Six.)

The first step will be to determine if the decedent had a Will. This will usually involve looking through the decedent's personal papers and other effects at their home. If the decedent is married, then it is likely that their spouse will know if there is a Will, as he or she probably will have executed one also. If both spouses are deceased, the children may know if there was a Will, although this is not always the case. If there were no children, then it will require that someone close to the decedent go through his or her papers and try to locate a Will. It is also possible that the person named as Executor was provided with a copy of the Will. The attorney/firm should also have a copy or may even have the original Will.

While looking for the Will, it is also a good idea to begin setting aside documents, including but not limited to, asset and debt information, insurance policies, title documents, pension and retirement information, etc. that will be needed by the Executor or Administrator and the attorney.

If it is determined that there was a Will, because a copy has been located, but no original can be found after a diligent search, the Court may probate a copy, provided it can be determined by the Court, that no other Will or subsequent Codicil is believed to have been executed since the time the Will was signed. (See Probate Code § 8000(b).)

A Petition for Probate is then filed with the Court so that the Administrator (usually the Executor) can be appointed. Once the Administrator is appointed, the process of locating property, liquidating property as necessary, the payment of debts and distribution to the beneficiaries can begin.

You will note that Probate Code § 8000 states that **any interested** person may commence a Probate, whether or not they possess the Will and/or were named the Executor in the Will. In most cases, in which you will be involved, the named Executor will request that he/she be named as the Administrator of the estate. There are always exceptions to every situation, and you may be involved in a case where a person other than the named Executor wishes to be appointed as the Administrator. This could occur for several reasons: 1) the person is not aware that there was a Will; 2) the person who was named as Executor is deceased or unable to perform their duties as Executor. Therefore, the firm might be representing a Petitioner whose appointment will be contested by the person who was named the Executor. Alternatively, if the person who was named as Executor does not wish or is unable to serve, the firm will need to obtain that person's waiver (or their agent's waiver on their behalf) so that another person may be appointed to act as Executor in the matter.

The following is a sample scenario of a person being named as Administrator when they were not named the Executor.

Testator had a terminal illness and died. She was not married, but had a child with a person with whom she had lived for over 15 years. Prior to her death, she executed a Will naming her child and her significant other, the father of her child (who is over the age of 18), as her sole heirs. The Testator named the significant other as Executor and the child as the alternate Executor. The Testator gave the original Will to the significant other for safekeeping.

Upon the Testator's death, the Testator's sister, who was her only sibling, consulted an attorney and filed a Petition for Probate. The Petition requested that the sister of the decedent be appointed as Personal Representative. The sister alleged that there was no Will and that she was entitled to one-half of the decedent's estate as the decedent was not married. The sister did acknowledge that the decedent had one child.

Upon receipt of the Notice of Hearing and Petition for Probate, the child advises the parent that the Mother's sister had filed an action with the Court requesting that she be named as Administrator.

Of additional note: All property owned by the decedent was owned in joint tenancy with the significant other (house, bank accounts, etc.). The decedent also listed the significant other and the child as beneficiary of all retirement accounts and insurance policies.

The named Executor (significant other) consulted an attorney about the Probate matter. At the meeting, he provided the original Will, copies of all property owned by the decedent evidencing that the property was held in joint tenancy and/or had named him and the child as beneficiaries. The Will stated that the significant other would receive the Testator's portion of the real property along with any other property that was held in joint tenancy; that any other property would be shared equally between the significant other and the child.

As you can probably tell in the above situation, what initially appeared as a fairly simple probate matter to the attorney representing the sibling, has become a more complicated situation, requiring a determination by the court.

## Probating an Intestate Estate

In the event a person dies without a Will, his/her estate must also proceed through the formal probate process. A Petition for Probate will have to be filed and a Personal Representative will need to be appointed. Before we discuss the entire process, let us compare the distribution of the decedent's estate when he/she is intestate as opposed to a person who died testate, with a valid Will, as discussed in Chapter Two. You will begin to see why it is very important to have a valid Will, if the Testator wants the estate to pass in a certain manner.

California Probate Code § 6400 et seq. sets for the requirements for distribution for intestate succession:

6400. Any part of the estate of a decedent not effectively disposed of by will passes to the decedent's heirs as prescribed in this part.

6401.

(a) As to community property, the intestate share of the surviving spouse is the one-half of the community property that belongs to the decedent under Section 100.

(b) As to quasi-community property, the intestate share of the surviving spouse is the one-half of the quasi-community property that belongs to the decedent under Section 101.

(c) As to separate property, the intestate share of the surviving spouse or surviving domestic partner, as defined in subdivision (b) of Section 37, is as follows:

(1) The entire intestate estate if the decedent did not leave any surviving issue, parent, brother, sister, or issue of a deceased brother or sister.
(2) One-half of the intestate estate in the following cases:

(A) Where the decedent leaves only one child or the issue of one deceased child.
(B) Where the decedent leaves no issue but leaves a parent or parents or their issue or the issue of either of them.
(3) One-third of the intestate estate in the following cases:

(A) Where the decedent leaves more than one child.
(B) Where the decedent leaves one child and the issue of one or more deceased children.

(C) Where the decedent leaves issue of two or more deceased children.

6402. Except as provided in Section 6402.5, the part of the intestate estate not passing to the surviving spouse or surviving domestic partner, as defined in subdivision (b) of Section 37, under Section 6401, or the entire intestate estate if there is no surviving spouse or domestic partner, passes as follows:

(a) To the issue of the decedent, the issue taking equally if they are all of the same degree of kinship to the decedent, but if of unequal degree those of more remote degree take in the manner provided in Section 240.

(b) If there is no surviving issue, to the decedent's parent or parents equally.

(c) If there is no surviving issue or parent, to the issue of the parents or either of them, the issue taking equally if they are all of the same degree of kinship to the decedent, but if of unequal degree those of more remote degree take in the manner provided in Section 240.

(d) If there is no surviving issue, parent or issue of a parent, but the decedent is survived by one or more grandparents or issue of grandparents, to the grandparent or grandparents equally, or to the issue of those grandparents if there is no surviving grandparent, the issue taking equally if they are all of the same degree of kinship to the decedent, but if of unequal degree those of more remote degree take in the manner provided in Section 240.

(e) If there is no surviving issue, parent or issue of a parent, grandparent or issue of a grandparent, but the decedent is survived by the issue of a predeceased spouse, to that issue, the issue taking equally if they are all of the same degree of kinship to the predeceased spouse, but if of unequal degree those of more remote degree take in the manner provided in Section 240.

(f) If there is no surviving issue, parent or issue of a parent, grandparent or issue of a grandparent, or issue of a predeceased spouse, but the decedent is survived by next of kin, to the next of kin in equal degree, but where there are two or more collateral kindred in equal degree who claim through different ancestors, those who claim through the nearest ancestor are preferred to those claiming through an ancestor more remote.

(g) If there is no surviving next of kin of the decedent and no surviving issue of a predeceased spouse of the decedent, but the decedent is survived by the parents of a predeceased spouse or the issue of those parents, to the parent or parents equally, or to the issue of those parents if both are deceased, the issue taking equally if they are all of the same degree of kinship to the predeceased spouse, but if of unequal degree those of more remote degree take in the manner provided in Section 240.

6402.5.

(a) For purposes of distributing real property under this section if the decedent had a predeceased spouse who died not more than 15 years before the decedent and there is no surviving spouse or issue of the decedent, the portion of the decedent's estate attributable to the decedent's predeceased spouse passes as follows:

(1) If the decedent is survived by issue of the predeceased spouse, to the surviving issue of the predeceased spouse; if they are all of the same degree of kinship to

the predeceased spouse they take equally, but if of unequal degree those of more remote degree take in the manner provided in Section 240.

(2) If there is no surviving issue of the predeceased spouse but the decedent is survived by a parent or parents of the predeceased spouse, to the predeceased spouse's surviving parent or parents equally.

(3) If there is no surviving issue or parent of the predeceased spouse but the decedent is survived by issue of a parent of the predeceased spouse, to the surviving issue of the parents of the predeceased spouse or either of them, the issue taking equally if they are all of the same degree of kinship to the predeceased spouse, but if of unequal degree those of more remote degree take in the manner provided in Section 240.

(4) If the decedent is not survived by issue, parent, or issue of a parent of the predeceased spouse, to the next of kin of the decedent in the manner provided in Section 6402.

(5) If the portion of the decedent's estate attributable to the decedent's predeceased spouse would otherwise escheat to the state because there is no kin of the decedent to take under Section 6402, the portion of the decedent's estate attributable to the predeceased spouse passes to the next of kin of the predeceased spouse who shall take in the same manner as the next of kin of the decedent take under Section 6402.

(b) For purposes of distributing personal property under this section if the decedent had a predeceased spouse who died not more than five years before the decedent, and there is no surviving spouse or issue of the decedent, the portion of the decedent's estate attributable to the decedent's predeceased spouse passes as follows:

(1) If the decedent is survived by issue of the predeceased spouse, to the surviving issue of the predeceased spouse; if they are all of the same degree of kinship to the predeceased spouse they take equally, but if of unequal degree those of more remote degree take in the manner provided in Section 240.

(2) If there is no surviving issue of the predeceased spouse but the decedent is survived by a parent or parents of the predeceased spouse, to the predeceased spouse's surviving parent or parents equally.

(3) If there is no surviving issue or parent of the predeceased spouse but the decedent is survived by issue of a parent of the predeceased spouse, to the surviving issue of the parents of the predeceased spouse or either of them, the issue taking equally if they are all of the same degree of kinship to the predeceased spouse, but if of unequal degree those of more remote degree take in the manner provided in Section 240.

(4) If the decedent is not survived by issue, parent, or issue of a parent of the predeceased spouse, to the next of kin of the decedent in the manner provided in Section 6402.

(5) If the portion of the decedent's estate attributable to the decedent's predeceased spouse would otherwise escheat to the state because there is no kin of the decedent to take under Section 6402, the portion of the decedent's estate attributable to the predeceased spouse passes to the next of kin of the predeceased spouse who shall take in the same manner as the next of kin of the decedent take under Section 6402.

(c) For purposes of disposing of personal property under subdivision (b), the claimant heir bears the burden of proof to show the exact personal property to be disposed of to the heir.

(d) For purposes of providing notice under any provision of this code with respect to an estate that may include personal property subject to distribution under subdivision (b), if the aggregate fair market value of tangible and intangible personal property with a written record of title or ownership in the estate is believed in good faith by the petitioning party to be less than ten thousand dollars ($10,000), the petitioning party need not give notice to the issue or next of kin of the predeceased spouse. If the personal property is subsequently determined to have an aggregate fair market value in excess of ten thousand dollars ($10,000), notice shall be given to the issue or next of kin of the predeceased spouse as provided by law.

(e) For the purposes of disposing of property pursuant to subdivision (b), "personal property" means that personal property in which there is a written record of title or ownership and the value of which in the aggregate is ten thousand dollars ($10,000) or more.

(f) For the purposes of this section, the "portion of the decedent's estate attributable to the decedent's predeceased spouse" means all of the following property in the decedent's estate:

(1) One-half of the community property in existence at the time of the death of the predeceased spouse.
(2) One-half of any community property, in existence at the time of death of the predeceased spouse, which was given to the decedent by the predeceased spouse by way of gift, descent, or devise.
(3) That portion of any community property in which the predeceased spouse had any incident of ownership and which vested in the decedent upon the death of the predeceased spouse by right of survivorship.
(4) Any separate property of the predeceased spouse which came to the decedent by gift, descent, or devise of the predeceased spouse or which vested in the decedent upon the death of the predeceased spouse by right of survivorship.

(g) For the purposes of this section, quasi-community property shall be treated the same as community property.

(h) For the purposes of this section:

(1) Relatives of the predeceased spouse conceived before the decedent's death but born thereafter inherit as if they had been born in the lifetime of the decedent.
(2) A person who is related to the predeceased spouse through two lines of relationship is entitled to only a single share based on the relationship which would entitle the person to the larger share.

6403.

(a) A person who fails to survive the decedent by 120 hours is deemed to have predeceased the decedent for the purpose of intestate succession, and the heirs are determined accordingly. If it cannot be established by clear and convincing evidence that a person who would otherwise be an heir has survived the decedent by 120 hours, it is deemed that the person failed to survive for the required period. The requirement of this section that a person who survives the decedent must survive the decedent by 120 hours does not apply if the application of the 120-hour survival requirement would result in the escheat of property to the state.

(b) This section does not apply to the case where any of the persons upon whose time of death the disposition of property depends died before January 1, 1990, and such case continues to be governed by the law applicable before January 1, 1990.

There are some additional probate provisions which have not been included, as they are not relevant at this point. Should you be involved in a probate where the decedent died intestate, you will want to review the entire code section. Additionally, Chapter Twelve of this text contains the Probate Code section with regard to the priority of appointing an Administrator for the estate.

The Probate Code also sets forth the determination of children, including adopted children, as heirs of the decedent. It is very important to understand these provisions and concepts as you begin the probate process and ultimate distribution of the estate.

Probate Code § 6450. Subject to the provisions of this chapter, a relationship of parent and child exists for the purpose of determining intestate succession by, through, or from a person in the following circumstances:

(a) The relationship of parent and child exists between a person and the person's natural parents, regardless of the marital status of the natural parents.

(b) The relationship of parent and child exists between an adopted person and the person's adopting parent or parents.

Probate Code § 6451.

(a) An adoption severs the relationship of parent and child between an adopted person and a natural parent of the adopted person unless both of the following requirements are satisfied:

  (1) The natural parent and the adopted person lived together at any time as parent and child, or the natural parent was married to or cohabiting with the other natural parent at the time the person was conceived and died before the person's birth.
  (2) The adoption was by the spouse of either of the natural parents or after the death of either of the natural parents.

(b) Neither a natural parent nor a relative of a natural parent, except for a whole-blood brother or sister of the adopted person or the issue of that brother or sister, inherits from or through the adopted person on the basis of a parent and child relationship between the adopted person and the natural parent that satisfies the requirements of paragraphs (1) and (2) of subdivision (a), unless the adoption is by the spouse or surviving spouse of that parent.

(c) For the purpose of this section, a prior adoptive parent and child relationship is treated as a natural parent and child relationship.

6452. If a child is born out of wedlock, neither a natural parent nor a relative of that parent inherits from or through the child on the basis of the parent and child relationship between that parent and the child unless both of the following requirements are satisfied:

(a) The parent or a relative of the parent acknowledged the child.

(b) The parent or a relative of the parent contributed to the support or the care of the child.

Probate Code § 6453. For the purpose of determining whether a person is a "natural parent" as that term is used in this chapter:

(a) A natural parent and child relationship is established where that relationship is presumed and not rebutted pursuant to the Uniform Parentage Act (Part 3 (commencing with Section 7600) of Division 12 of the Family Code).

(b) A natural parent and child relationship may be established pursuant to any other provisions of the Uniform Parentage Act, except that the relationship may not be established by an action under subdivision (c) of Section 7630 of the Family Code unless any of the following conditions exist:

(1) A court order was entered during the father's lifetime declaring paternity.
(2) Paternity is established by clear and convincing evidence that the father has openly held out the child as his own.
(3) It was impossible for the father to hold out the child as his own and paternity is established by clear and convincing evidence. (c) A natural parent and child relationship may be established pursuant to Section 249.5.

Probate Code § 6454. For the purpose of determining intestate succession by a person or the person's issue from or through a foster parent or stepparent, the relationship of parent and child exists between that person and the person's foster parent or stepparent if both of the following requirements are satisfied:

(a) The relationship began during the person's minority and continued throughout the joint lifetimes of the person and the person's foster parent or stepparent.

(b) It is established by clear and convincing evidence that the foster parent or stepparent would have adopted the person but for a legal barrier.

Probate Code § 6455. Nothing in this chapter affects or limits application of the judicial doctrine of equitable adoption for the benefit of the child or the child's issue.

The above sections set forth the manner in which the estate of the decedent will be distributed according to the law. Your instructor will provide you with some scenarios that should lead to some interesting discussions about what happens to the property and the estate if a person dies intestate.

# Testate Distribution

If a person dies having a valid Will, that person's estate will be distributed according to his/her wishes rather than as set forth in the statutory requirements in the sections above. There are some exceptions, such as the person did not make certain provisions or provide direction to the court regarding certain matters. The example provided in Supreme Court Justice Rehnquist's Will is a good example of the failure to include pertinent language for one's Executor and/or the Court. In such an event, the Court will have to interpret the decedent's Will according to the law when other instructions are absent.

The decedent will have named an Executor (or Executrix) to handle his or her affairs and to be appointed and authorized by the Court to complete the probate process and make the distributions as set forth in the Will. Most people, when appointed as Executor, will retain the services of an attorney, although it is not mandatory, as the entire process can be tricky and cumbersome due to the local Court rules and the time line that is required for such items as Creditor's Claims and other statutory requirements.

# Retaining an Attorney

Regardless of whether the decedent died with or without a Will it is important for the decedent's family, or if they did not have family, someone close to them to contact an attorney for legal advice and to determine what steps need to be taken.

The paralegal is often the first person to talk with the potential client who calls for an appointment. You will be the goodwill ambassador for the firm and your attitude may affect whether the person makes an appointment and/or ultimately retains the firm. Your initial empathy for the person and their loss will come through even on the telephone. The person may find it difficult to talk, so you will need to be patient. Some people may want to tell you everything about the person who was very special to them and who was "taken" from them. You will need to listen and be attentive. For some of you, this will be an acquired skill and for others, it will come naturally. You will need to learn how to communicate with these individuals in order to obtain as much information as possible without spending hours on the telephone with them and, **most importantly**, without giving them advice.

It is helpful if you take notes during the conversation, writing down information whether or not it seems relevant at the time. You can always transcribe your notes into memo form after the conversation, especially if the potential client has scheduled and appointment. It may also be helpful for you to have an intake form handy so that if the person asks what they need to bring, you can provide them with a list of what is on the intake form. The firm may have other specific tasks that it wants you to do. Alternatively, the attorneys may prefer that you simply take the person's name and contact information so the attorney can contact them. You will also want to check for and locate the decedent's file if the firm prepared the Will.

One of the most important things you should initially ask is the person's name and what the relationship is to the decedent. The attorney will probably also want to know the date of death and where the person died. If the person died the day before in another state or even another county, it may not be a matter that requires an immediate appointment. Also, your firm may not be able to handle the matter because of the domicile of the decedent. It is helpful for the attorney (provided the attorney wants you to obtain this information) to have this information prior to the meeting with the client. It may save time, or the attorney may simply want to contact the person by telephone to obtain more information and evaluate whether it is a case that he or she will be able to take. The attorney can also use the information as a starting point during his or her initial meeting by confirming the information that has already been provided and springboard from there. This will also be an opportunity for a conflicts check to be completed.

Once the attorney has met with the client, reviewed the decedent's Will (or determined that there is no Will) and gathered certain basic information, he or she will be in position to advise the client about the next steps. The attorney may determine that a formal probate is not necessary and that the property owned by the decedent may be transferred by some type of summary or non-probate procedure. These procedures will be discussed in more detail in Chapter Six.

For the purposes of information, at this point, it is helpful to know what would constitute a disposition of the decedent's estate without probate administration.

Examples would be:

- All of decedent's property was held in joint tenancy with his or her spouse, children or other persons.
- The total value of the decedent's property (except real estate) is less than $150,000.
- The decedent died testate, is married and has no children. All property is held jointly with his or her spouse.
- Decedent's assets are only those where there is a named beneficiary, such as life, insurance, an annuity, or retirement.

There are many more examples, but these are among the most common where the attorney will usually advise the client that a formal probate proceeding will **not** have to be filed with the Court.

Sometimes the firm will be consulted and asked for advice regarding the probate process as the Executor and/or heirs may feel they can handle the probate process without the help of an attorney. They may not want to pay the statutory fees and costs associated with retaining an attorney. The attorney may concur that it is a simple matter and that an attorney's services are not absolutely necessary. The attorney may also feel that the decedent had so very little in their estate, it does not warrant the hiring of an attorney. This is the exception rather than the rule. There are also paralegals who are very experienced in the probate process and who may be employed by the decedent's heirs, Executor or by the law firm as an independent contractor to fill out the probate documents and forms in their capacity as a Legal Document Assistant (LDA).

Additionally, if the attorney advises the client that a full formal probate is not needed, the client may hire the attorney to prepare certain documents, such as an Affidavit of Death of Joint Tenant and pay the attorney only for that work that was performed.

The attorney may determine that the decedent died in another state and that the probate proceeding will have to be carried out there. This may be confusing to the heirs especially if the decedent executed a valid Will in California and owned property here. However, after the Testator executed the Will he/she retired to Hawaii and became a resident there. The decedent did not execute a new Will in Hawaii. In that event, an ancillary probate may need to occur in California to transfer the real property here, whereas the formal probate will need to occur where the decedent actually resided, in this case, Hawaii.

As with most other legal actions, an initial document must be filed with the Court to commence the case. In Probate, this document is known as the Petition for Probate (Form DE-111). In most instances, the person named as the Executor will be the Petitioner. There is no "statute of limitations" for a Petition for Probate, as there is in other matters. It is conceivable that the named Executor has no knowledge that he/she was appointed or perhaps the Executor has died or does not wish to act in this capacity. Therefore, it may be another individual who is asking the firm to initiate the probate on his/her behalf. While there is not a formal time element, there are, of course, matters that must be dealt with in a timely manner. The disposition of the decedent's person and property are very real and important issues. The payment of the decedent's bills is also of utmost importance.

The client may be asking for authority to dispose of the decedent's remains if there are no other family members or persons appointed to take care of this matter. Once that matter is resolved, the issue of how to pay for that disposition is also critical. The person attending to these matters may not have access to the decedent's money in order to pay for the arrangements out of the decedent's own funds. That person may have to pay out of his/her own pocket, in which case he/she will want to be reimbursed. The decedent may have an insurance policy, which would pay, but without proper notice and authority, the insurance company may not release the funds.

At this point, if the attorney has determined that a formal probate must be commenced and the client has agreed to retain the services of the firm, the paralegal's work will begin in earnest. The Probate Code provides specific instructions for the opening and commencement of administrative probate proceedings. See Probate Code §§ 8000, et. seq.

## Formal Probate Proceedings

There are advantages and disadvantages to formal probate proceedings.
The advantages are:

- Claims against the estate must be identified and satisfied. Once they are, there is no liability against the survivor's share for the decedent's debts.
- Taxes must be paid.
- Testator's wishes are carried out.
- Title to property is cleared and distributed according to the Will or Laws of Intestate Succession.
- Savings on income tax (the estate often pays rather than the Personal Representative of the decedent and/or the beneficiary, which could be taxed at a higher rate).
- Special Administrator or a Professional Fiduciary may be appointed and may be given the authority to operate an on-going business.
- Administrator has a responsibility to make sure that the assets of the decedent are properly maintained, including but not limited to earning interest and increasing the value of the estate whenever possible.

The disadvantages are:

- Probate fees (Administrator and Attorney).
- Time-consuming procedure.
- Delay in selling property and ultimate disposition of estate.

The filing of the Petition should also include the original Will, if any, being "lodged" with the Court. Thus, the first action is to obtain the original Will and have the attorney determine who was appointed as Executor.

Assuming the attorney has been presented with a Will by the potential client, he or she will need to determine if it is the original Will. If it is not the original Will, the original Will should be located. The attorney may ask the client to go to the decedent's residence and determine if the Will is there or if there is any indication that the Will was kept in a safe deposit box or other fire-safe location. In some cases, the attorney may ask the paralegal to accompany the client in this endeavor. It is also possible that the decedent destroyed the original Will. If this is the case, that fact will need to be established, if possible.

The decedent may have a safe deposit key from a local bank. It is also possible that the attorney who drafted the Will may have been asked to retain the original. A call should be made to the firm who prepared the Will to determine if there is any indication as to where the original Will may have been kept.

Probate Code §331 (effective 1991) provides that a decedent's family member or Executor may access a safe-deposit box, if they have a key, in order to locate the Will and any other instructions with regard to the disposition of the remains of the decedent (person owning the box) even if that person's name is not listed on the box. This will be done with bank supervision and only the Will and/or disposition instructions may be removed without court order. The bank employee who supervises the opening of the safe-deposit box under these conditions will inventory the entire box, and photocopies of all documents removed will be placed in the box until the Court has authorized the removal of all of the contents from the safe-deposit box.

In the event there is evidence that a safe deposit box exists, but the Executor has not been able to locate a key, the Court may make an ex parte order to have the box drilled so that it can be opened to obtain the aforementioned documents.

Alternatively, if it has been determined that a Will does not exist, a formal probate will still need to be initiated. For the purposes of this text, most of the procedures will be the same. Where they are not, any differences in the two types of probate, testate or intestate, will be noted.

## Administrator or Personal Representative

The Court will appoint a Personal Representative or administrator in each of these situations. However, these individuals may be called by different names. If the decedent died testate (with a valid Will) naming an Executor, the Executor will most likely be the Petitioner. Once appointed by the court, the Petitioner will be called the Administrator (rather than the generic Personal Representative), when referred to in the official capacity. If the Testator did not appoint an Executor, the Petitioner will request that he/she be appointed as Administrator with Will Annexed.

If the decedent died intestate (without a Will), the Petitioner will request that he/she be appointed as Administrator. For the purposes of this book and to keep it simple, I will predominately use the term, Personal Representative, as it also includes the terms Administrator and Executor. Unless noted otherwise, whenever you see the term Personal Representative, with respect to a probate where there was a Will, it will also mean Administrator or Executor.

## Preparing the Petition and Lodging the Will

As previously indicated, the client should complete the information requested by the law office. Alternatively, the attorney or the paralegal may complete the form with input from the client. Review the Client Information (fact) Sheet provided as Appendix 4A. As you begin to prepare the Petition for Probate, it will become clear why all of the information is requested.

A word about the Judicial Council forms. These forms are very complex and can be very confusing. Always make sure the attorney has reviewed them carefully before he or she signs them. A cursory glance is not enough. If there is a question or you and/or the attorney are unclear about a particular section of the form(s) you should review the Probate Code Sections, or other sections, as applicable. Some Courts have developed a checklist to make sure that all of the boxes are checked. Check your local rules or with your local Court Clerk.

The bottom right corner of the Judicial Council forms reference the Code sections that apply to that particular form. Many of the sections on the form (particularly the Petition [Form DE-111]) also reference the Probate Code section(s) that apply. Generally, the Petition for Probate references Probate Code §§ 8002 and 10450. It also references Government Code § 26827.

The individual sections, for example Item #6, requests information as to who has survived the decedent. Item 6(a)4 references Probate Code §§ 297.5(c), 37(b), 6401(c) and 6402, as well as Family Code § 297.5, all of which define Registered Domestic Partners relative to the transfer of a decedent's property. Item 6(b) references a "stepchild or foster child or children who would have been adopted by decedent but for a legal barrier." As a new paralegal, I would carefully read Probate Code § 6450 et seq. to determine what this statement means. In the event the incorrect box is checked, the Petition will need to be amended. Refer to this code section included earlier in this chapter. In some cases, if the Petition is amended, the Notice must be given again and the Notice to Administer re-published.

Based on the language in Probate Code § 6454, if the decedent had foster or stepchildren, who were not adopted, and it is believed the decedent would have wanted the child(ren) to receive portion(s) of the estate as though they were the children, the box that is checked becomes critically important. **If you are still unclear as to the interpretation of Probate Code § 6454, discuss it with the attorney to determine if the box applies and how it should be checked.**

The Petition must include, at minimum, the following:

- The full name and any aliases of the decedent; when and where he or she died.
- The names, ages, relationship and addresses of all the decedent's heirs, and if the decedent's spouse and any heirs have predeceased the decedent.
- The approximate gross fair market value of the estate.
- The name of the proposed Administrator/Personal Representative and if the person consents to that appointment; name of person to whom the Court will issue "Letters."
- Whether a bond is required (does the Will waive bond or did the heirs waive bond).
- Any other jurisdictional facts or issues in the matter.

A sample Petition is included at the end of the chapter using a fictionalized case. The same fact pattern will be used for all of the forms and procedures throughout the probate process — from the initial Petition to the Final Distribution. It will be based on a very simple scenario. Your Instructor will discuss how to deal with difficult and/or more complex scenarios as you discuss the forms and procedures.

Once the Petition is prepared and has been reviewed by both the attorney and client for accuracy, the attorney and client (Petitioner) will need to sign the Petition and other documents which will need to accompany the form. These documents are listed at the end of this chapter. In the event the Petitioner is not located in the county or state where the probate will be filed, the attorney may verify and sign on behalf of the Petitioner. In that event, a verification will need to accompany the Petition. A sample verification is provided as Appendix 4B for your information. If the Petitioner is not a resident of California, the Petition must include a Statement of Residency.

The Petition should be as accurate and contain as much information as possible. While it is true that some property may not be valued at the time of the initial filing of the Petition, it is best that the attorney, along with the client, include all of the property and a close approximation of the gross fair market value. This is important because the court bases the filing fee on the value of the estate. The Petitioner isn't going to want to pay more fees than required to the court if the assets are over-valued. Likewise, the value will determine the amount of bond required. It may be necessary to amend the Petition at a later date to include missing asset and value information. Amending a Petition requires "Notice" of any amendments be sent to all heirs and interested parties. This could cost time and money, and may be a potential area of malpractice if the firm committed the error. This can be a bit sticky and also frustrate the Executor who is anxious to get the Petition filed and the process commenced.

At this point, the paralegal should also check the local rules for any particular filing requirements. If the paralegal is working in a County where documents are frequently filed, he/she may already have a binder containing the relevant local rules. However, if the probate will take place in an unfamiliar County, the local rules should be checked. Note, some counties will make additions, changes, or deletions to their rules bi-annually. If that is the case, the wise paralegal will know approximately when those changes are posted and double-check them before filing any documents. The Daily Recorder also provides a subscription service to Local Rules and Probate Information, which is very useful.

Many Counties require a generic Case Cover Sheet. Others such as San Francisco County require a Declaration of Real Property. It is important to know what additional forms or documents each county requires before submitting the package for filing.

The paralegal will also want to verify the current filing fee so that the client can be advised and the fees can be collected or billed to the client. The Courts frequently change their fees so it is best not to commit them to memory. Additionally, effective January 1, 2005, the probate fees are based on the value of the estate. The attorney will be able to determine the filing fee based on the value that is entered on the Petition.

The paralegal should prepare the Petition using the information provided by the client and as indicated by the attorney. Once the Petition has been signed by the Petitioner and the attorney, it is then ready for filing with the court along with the original Will. Remember, the Will must be lodged with the Court.

Copies of the Petition and any attachments should be made. The Court should receive the original and at least one copy. Many offices have a policy regarding the number of copies and that policy should be followed. Your office will also want a copy to be retained in the file until the endorsed copy(ies) is/are returned from the court. It is also a good idea to give the Petitioner a copy for his/her records. The Will must be lodged with the Court within 30 days of filing the Petition. It is usually best to do it at the same time. Local Rules will usually dictate when and how the Will must be lodged.

The original Will and any Codicils should be copied. The Petitioner should be given copies and there should be at least one copy of each document (as applicable) in the firm's file. At least one copy (again consult office policy) should accompany the original

Will (and Codicil) to the Court along with the Petition. The Court will then stamp "Lodged" on the copy, and will usually indicate the date that it was Lodged or received.

If there is no Will, this fact will be indicated on the Petition for Probate.

The copies of all of these documents will then be returned to the law office filing them. Depending upon your office's procedure, you may have a court-runner or other individual who files documents at the courthouse for you. This person may also be the paralegal, legal secretary, or law clerk. In the event you are filing documents by mail, remember always to send a self-addressed stamped envelope with the documents so that they will be returned.

## Other Documents Submitted with Petition for Probate

Notice of Hearing (DE-120)

Notice of Petition to Administration Estate (DE-121)

Duties and Responsibilities (DE-147)

Confidential Supplement (DE-147S)

In addition to filing the Petition and requesting that an Administrator be appointed and Letters issued, a Notice of Hearing and Notice of Petition to Administer Estate must also be submitted to the Court. The Notice of Hearing and Notice of Petition to Administer Estate do not require the client's signature. They do require that the Court Clerk assign a hearing date. The date, time and department in which the hearing will take place should be entered on the forms (see below). These forms will be served only after the date has been determined. The next section will discuss the calendaring and serving of the documents.

Prior to the hearing proper notice must be sent to all heirs, beneficiaries and interested persons. Additionally, a Notice must be published so that creditors and others, who have a potential claim against the estate, can become aware of the pending matter.

As an aside: The probate, once the Petition is filed, becomes public information. There will be a number of companies, creditors, bonding companies and others who will check the new filings daily in addition to checking local newspapers for publications regarding new probate filings. These people will begin sending the Petitioner, usually in care of the law firm, notices regarding the purchase of bonds, resources for searching for title and property owned by the decedent, locating potential heirs, the valuation of the decedent's property, and a host of other probate-related business propositions. These resources may be useful provided the firm does not already have preferred providers of these services. At some point, the firm may need one of these resources, such as a service that locates heirs, so it is always a good idea to have a file of these types of resources available should the attorney or client need them.

It is best, once the Petition and other documents are ready to be filed, to determine when the Court is setting probate hearings. Each County is different and sets their calendars differently. It is best to know the particular County's manner of setting the calendar so that you can review the attorney's calendar for any potential calendar conflicts. The Court may have specific days of the week and/or times of the day in which they hear probate matters. You will also want to allow enough time for the required notices to be sent, publication to be completed, and any other actions that must be taken before the matter can be heard. The matter must be heard within 30 days of filing the Petition.

For example, the Notice of Administration requires publication for four consecutive weeks. See Probate Code § 8003 for filing, publication, and notice requirements. Based on that requirement, you will want to allow enough time for the filing of the Petition, sending the filed Notice to the publication, the actual publication, the receipt of the Proof of Service of Publication from the newspaper, and the filing of same. Typically, this takes a minimum of 4 weeks (28 days). Thus, if you file your initial documents on March 1 you can anticipate a hearing date after April 1 (give or take a few days depending upon the attorney's calendar and the court's hearing dates).

For a couple of reasons, it is always a good idea to give the client a rough idea of when the hearing will occur: 1) The client's perception may be that this process takes only a few days because you are "just" filing the Petition; and 2) If the client needs to be available to attend the hearing, you don't want to schedule it for a date when the client is unavailable.

Additionally, as indicated in Chapter Three, it may be necessary to submit a Proof of Subscribing Witness or Proof of Holographic Will. In the event the subscribing witnesses have not been located, it may be necessary to prepare a Declaration re: Execution of Will. It is a pleading form, and an example is provided as Appendix 4C.

In the event a person declines to act as Executor, his/her statement should be attached to the Petition when it is filed with the Court. If there is no alternate Executor named in the Will or that person is unable or also declines to act, the person filing as Petitioner will be requesting that he/she be named Administrator With Will Annexed.

# Citation

In the event that a person needs to be "cited" to appear at the probate hearing, a Citation form (Form DE-122) must be used. This formal notice must be personally served to the party ordered to appear, the "Citee." The most common reason that a person would be ordered to appear is that they have documentation or information regarding the decedent's estate that has not been provided or disclosed to the Personal Representative after a reasonable request. The person cited may even be in possession of the original Will. The Citation can also be served any time after the Petition for Probate is filed, and the Personal Representative and/or the attorney become aware that the Citee has information that is instrumental in the probating of the estate. In that event, a separate Petition alleging the facts and need for the appearance of the Citee will be prepared and filed with the Court. (See Probate Code §§ 1240–1242 regarding Citations.) A Notice of Hearing will also be prepared. The hearing date will be set and entered on the Notice of Hearing and the Citation, and all documents will be served on the Citee, subject to Service of Process under California Code of Civil Procedure § 12, et seq. Copies of the documents should be served on all others who are required to be noticed in the matter provided. Those notices, however, may be served by mail.

# Waiver of Bond/Purchase of Bond

A bond is a type of insurance policy that guarantees that the Personal Representative will perform his/her duties as set forth in the Will, if any, and in the Duties and Liabilities (Form DE-147) that was executed along with the Petition for Probate.

The Will may waive bond. In the event the Will fails to waive bond or the decedent died Intestate, a bond may be required. The Court also has the discretion to order a bond even if the Will waived bond. Check the local rules to determine if there are any circumstances that require a bond. The Court will require a bond if the Executor resides outside of the State of California or there are minor children, even if the Will waived the bond.

The heirs or beneficiaries may waive bond if they are all adults and are competent. They must all agree to the waiver. The waivers must be in writing and must be submitted along with the Petition, as the appropriate boxes must be checked on the Petition. A sample Waiver of Bond is provided at Appendix 4D.

Bonds are obtained through surety companies who are licensed to issue such bond. Your firm may have a bonding company with whom they regularly do business. Bonding companies usually provide bonds for many different professions and types of businesses. The same company that provides the bond for a notary public will likely be able to provide the bond for the probate. You will need to provide a copy of the Petition, which indicates the gross value of the estate, along with the Order which indicates who the Court has appointed as the Personal Representative. This is the person who is being bonded.

The fee for the bond will be based on the value of the estate and will also be dependent upon whether full or limited powers were granted under the Independent Administration of Estates Act. If the powers are limited, the bond will be based on the value of the personal property of the decedent, plus any income that may accrue during the course of the probate. If the powers are unlimited (full), then the bond will be based on the **full** gross fair market value of the estate, which includes real property.

The bond company will calculate the cost of the bond and the Personal Representative must pay the fee so that the bond can be issued. The copy of the Bond must be filed with the court so that the Letters can be issued. The client should be provided with the original and a copy should be retained in the client file.

The bond is good for a period of one year from the time it is issued. In the event the matter has not been closed and the property distributed within that year, the bond will need to be renewed. The cost of the bond is an administrative expense, and the Personal Representative can request reimbursement from the estate at closing.

## The Hearing and Notice Requirements

Once the filed documents are returned from the Court and a hearing date has been set, you should immediately submit the Notice of Petition to Administer Estate to the newspaper your firm typically uses for publication. Notices must be published in a newspaper of general circulation in the County where the matter will be heard.

(Probate Code §8121.) Most large counties have a "legal" newspaper. However, if you look in your local newspaper, regardless of the size of your community, you will find that there is a "legal notice" section. The client certainly has the option of requesting that the publication occur in a smaller community newspaper, which may cost less, than in the largest newspaper in the County or the "legal," which could cost significantly more. Often the "legal" newspaper that serves the County will charge less for legal notices. The specific requirement is that the publication must be in a "newspaper of general circulation in the county which is circulated within the area of the county in which the decedent resided or the property is located." However, the Local Rules should be checked to see if there is a specific requirement for publication.

Additionally, using a smaller, more localized paper can be risky because the four-week publication requirement may be missed if, for example, the newspaper only publishes weekly and the deadline for the first week has already been missed. Your firm may also have a preference as to the publication to be used.

It is required that a copy of the Petition along with any attachments, the Notice of Hearing and the Notice of Petition to Administer be served on **all** the heirs-at-law, as well as any beneficiaries named in the Will. This can include the decedent's children, the spouse, the Executor and any persons receiving specific bequests. If the decedent died without a spouse or children, the heirs-at-law based on the degree of the relationship to the decedent should receive a notice. Consult the Table of Consanguinity, the Probate Code and Local Rules. This process is required whether the decedent died testate or intestate.

The Notice of Hearing requirements can be found at Probate Code §§ 851, 1211, 1215, 1216, 1230 and 17100. The Notice of Petition to Administer Estate notice requirements can be found at Probate Code §§ 8100, 8112, and 8121.

Probate Code § 1220 states that the hearing must be noticed 15 days prior to the hearing, plus five (5) for mailing. In most cases, since you will be mailing the notices and will need 20 days, you should mail the notice immediately after you receive it. If you are organized, you will have all of the envelopes addressed and ready for mailing as well as the Proof of Service prepared and saved on the computer. Upon receipt of the filed documents, you can then calendar the hearing, make the necessary copies, finalize the Proof of Service and mail the notices within 24 hours of receipt from the Court. Send a cover letter to the Personal Representative advising him or her of the date and any other instructions or details.

Do not forget to calendar the hearing date per the firms' calendaring system. You will also want to calendar the date so that you can follow up to make sure that the Court has received any other required documents prior to the hearing. It is also a good idea to calendar the date the Court typically has the file notes available. If the deadline for clearing the notes is missed, the matter will be continued and may cause undue delay.

In many Counties, the Court has "probate examiners (attorneys)" whose job it is to review and examine each case that is being channeled through the probate system on behalf of the Judge(s). These examiners will make sure that all Judicial Council forms have been prepared accurately and completely. They will make sure that the Petitioner and his or her attorney of record have submitted any collateral or supplemental documentation. They will also make sure that all parties who are required to receive notice have been sent the appropriate Notice(s).

For example, if the Will was not self-proving, the Proof of Subscribing Witness must be submitted prior to the hearing. The Proof of Service of all of the Notices will also need to be filed, as will the Proof of Publication of the Notice of Petition to Administer Estate. The Courts usually have local rules or internal timelines regarding the filing of these additional documents.

The Court may require that the probate examiner (or the clerk) post all file notes and deficiencies at least one week prior to the hearing. The Court may also require that any deficiencies be cleared at least two (full) court days prior to the hearing. **Check your local rules or consult with the clerk for this information**. It will then be up to the firm representing the Petitioner to access the file notes to determine if everything is in order. In other Counties, you must ask the Clerk for a copy. Many counties now have the file notes available via the internet; the notes may also be referred to as the tentative rulings. You can simply find the Department where the matter will be heard, enter the date and the time of the hearing and then look for the case number. It is always recommended that you print a copy of the notes (cut and paste so that you do not get the rulings for every case being heard on that date and/or time). This will provide a back up for the file as to the status of the case. The printed list can also be used as a checklist as the deficiencies are cleared.

Once the file is in order and any deficiencies cured, the probate attorney will recommend the Petition be approved by the Judge. In most cases, the attorney will not have to appear. If the attorney so chooses, he or she can simply submit the Order for Probate and the Letters (Testamentary or Administration) for the Judge's signature. If the attorney attends the hearing, it can speed up the process by having the documents signed, filed, and certified copies obtained at that time. Judges typically do not require the attorney to appear in routine matters due to the large volume of cases heard each day on the Court's calendar. Routine, administrative matters, in most instances, are left to the probate attorneys and the Petitioner's attorney to resolve without an appearance. The Judge may request that the attorney appear to take care of what are considered legal issues or when an Objection has been filed. Many Counties have a specific time set aside for obtaining or picking up Orders, Letters, and other documents that have been recommended for approval (RFA). Check the Local Rules or with the Clerk.

When submitting the Letters, you will also want to make sure that a check is submitted to obtain certified copies of the Letters. If the attorney attends the hearing, you should also see that he/she has a check and a return envelope with him or her. It is usually best to request at least two certified copies of the Letters. You may need more depending upon the number of assets that will need to be transferred using the Letters. Discuss the anticipated number with the attorney. With time and experience, you will be better able to gauge the number needed. Additional certified copies can be requested from the Clerk once the original has been issued. However, there will be a delay while the Court staff certifies that the document is a true and correct copy. There may be additional copying charges also. Note that most financial institutions will only honor certified copies of Letters that have been issued within the previous 60 days.

In the event there are deficiencies in the file notes, you will need to discuss how they should be cured with the attorney. Again, this is a good reason to print a copy of the notes so that the attorney can see exactly what is being requested. In most cases, the probate attorney will have referenced any Code sections that relate to the deficiency. For example, if the Proof of Service has not been filed, the appropriate code section will be referenced. If notice was not sent to all of the heirs at law, Probate Code § 1206 will be referenced. If the Proof of Subscribing Witness was not filed, Probate Code § 8220 will be referenced. Thus, the attorney will have a clear understanding of why the probate attorney determined there was a deficiency.

You should also be familiar with the local rules concerning contacting the Court's probate examiners. Some Courts will allow the attorney or his paralegal to contact the probate examiner directly and will even provide direct telephone numbers. Other Courts will require that a message be left for the probate examiner handling the matter so that he/she can call back at a more convenient time, or the Court may require that questions be faxed to them. It has been my experience that most probate examiners are very helpful and want to assist legal staff in making sure that the notes are cleared timely. They are attorneys so they are able to give legal advice, whereas a Clerk or other staff cannot.

In the event the deficiencies are not or cannot be cured in time, you will need to have the matter continued to a later date. As you can imagine continuing a hearing can be problematic and cause delay. However, there are times when it cannot be helped. The client (the Petitioner) may be upset because there is a delay in being able to move forward with taking care of matters in the estate. Bill paying or access to the decedent's funds may be impeded because the Letters have not yet been issued. In most cases, however, notice of the continued hearing is not required. (Probate Code 1205.)

As previously indicated, this can often be an area for potential malpractice. Therefore, you want to assist the attorney in making sure, to the best of your ability, that the documents are filed timely and correctly and that any deficiencies can be cleared as required.

Chapter Five will discuss the next steps in the Probate Process, which are acquiring property with the Letters, the creditor's claims period, the sale and/or transfer of property to the beneficiaries or heirs and bringing the matter to a close.

## Preparation of Judicial Council Forms

Petition for Probate (DE-111)

Notice of Hearing (DE-120)

Notice of Petition to Administer Estate (DE-121)

Duties and Liabilities of Personal Representative (DE-147)

Confidential Supplement (DE-147S)

Note: The Continuing Education of the Bar (CEB) also has several useful publications, including action guides and checklists that detail how to probate an estate, preparation of probate accountings, and transfers of property pursuant to probate.

## Key Terms

- Lodging the Will
- File Notes
- Probate Examiner/Attorney
- Bond
- Waiver of Bond

**DE-111**

| ATTORNEY OR PARTY WITHOUT ATTORNEY *(Name, State Bar number, and address)*: | FOR COURT USE ONLY |
|---|---|
| TELEPHONE NO.: FAX NO. *(Optional)*: | |
| E-MAIL ADDRESS *(Optional)*: | |
| ATTORNEY FOR *(Name)*: | |

**SUPERIOR COURT OF CALIFORNIA, COUNTY OF**
STREET ADDRESS:
MAILING ADDRESS:
CITY AND ZIP CODE:
BRANCH NAME:

ESTATE OF *(Name)*:

DECEDENT

| PETITION FOR ☐ Probate of Will and for Letters Testamentary<br>☐ Probate of Will and for Letters of Administration with Will Annexed<br>☐ Letters of Administration<br>☐ Letters of Special Administration ☐ with general powers<br>☐ Authorization to Administer Under the Independent Administration of Estates Act ☐ with limited authority | CASE NUMBER:<br><br>HEARING DATE:<br><br>DEPT.: TIME: |
|---|---|

1. Publication will be in *(specify name of newspaper)*:
   a. ☐ Publication requested.
   b. ☐ Publication to be arranged.
2. **Petitioner** *(name each)*: **requests that**
   a. ☐ decedent's will and codicils, if any, be admitted to probate.
   b. ☐ *(name)*:
      be appointed
      (1) ☐ executor
      (2) ☐ administrator with will annexed
      (3) ☐ administrator
      (4) ☐ special administrator ☐ with general powers
      and Letters issue upon qualification.
   c. ☐ full ☐ limited authority be granted to administer under the Independent Administration of Estates Act.
   d. (1) ☐ bond not be required for the reasons stated in item 3d.
      (2) ☐ $ bond be fixed. The bond will be furnished by an admitted surety insurer or as otherwise provided by law. (Specify reasons in Attachment 2 if the amount is different from the maximum required by Prob. Code, § 8482.)
      (3) ☐ $ in deposits in a blocked account be allowed. Receipts will be filed. *(Specify institution and location)*:

3. a. Decedent died on *(date)*: at *(place)*:
      (1) ☐ a resident of the county named above.
      (2) ☐ a nonresident of California and left an estate in the county named above located at *(specify location permitting publication in the newspaper named in item 1)*:

   b. Street address, city, and county of decedent's residence at time of death *(specify)*:

---

Form Adopted for Mandatory Use
Judicial Council of California
DE-111 [Rev. March 1, 2008]

**PETITION FOR PROBATE**
**(Probate—Decedents Estates)**

Probate Code, §§ 8002, 10450;
www.courtinfo.ca.gov

DE-111

| ESTATE OF (Name): | CASE NUMBER: |
|---|---|
| DECEDENT | |

3. c. **Character and estimated value of the property of the estate** (complete in all cases):
   (1) Personal property: $
   (2) Annual gross income from
       (a) real property: $
       (b) personal property: $
   (3) **Subtotal** (add (1) and (2)): $
   (4) Gross fair market value of real property: $
   (5) (Less) Encumbrances: $(           )
   (6) Net value of real property: $
   (7) **Total** (add (3) and (6)): $

d. (1) ☐ Will waives bond. ☐ Special administrator is the named executor, and the will waives bond.
   (2) ☐ All beneficiaries are adults and have waived bond, and the will does not require a bond.
       (Affix waiver as Attachment 3d(2).)
   (3) ☐ All heirs at law are adults and have waived bond. (Affix waiver as Attachment 3d(3).)
   (4) ☐ Sole personal representative is a corporate fiduciary or an exempt government agency.

e. (1) ☐ Decedent died intestate.
   (2) ☐ Copy of decedent's will dated:           ☐ codicil dated (specify for each):
       are affixed as Attachment 3e(2).
       (Include typed copies of handwritten documents and English translations of foreign-language documents.)
       ☐ The will and all codicils are self-proving (Prob. Code, § 8220).

f. **Appointment of personal representative** (check all applicable boxes):
   (1) Appointment of executor or administrator with will annexed:
       (a) ☐ Proposed executor is named as executor in the will and consents to act.
       (b) ☐ No executor is named in the will.
       (c) ☐ Proposed personal representative is a nominee of a person entitled to Letters.
           (Affix nomination as Attachment 3f(1)(c).)
       (d) ☐ Other named executors will not act because of ☐ death ☐ declination
           ☐ other reasons (specify):

           ☐ Continued in Attachment 3f(1)(d).
   (2) Appointment of administrator:
       (a) ☐ Petitioner is a person entitled to Letters. (If necessary, explain priority in Attachment 3f(2)(a).)
       (b) ☐ Petitioner is a nominee of a person entitled to Letters. (Affix nomination as Attachment 3f(2)(b).)
       (c) ☐ Petitioner is related to the decedent as (specify):
   (3) ☐ Appointment of special administrator requested. (Specify grounds and requested powers in Attachment 3f(3).)

g. Proposed personal representative is a
   (1) ☐ resident of California.
   (2) ☐ nonresident of California (specify permanent address):

   (3) ☐ resident of the United States.
   (4) ☐ nonresident of the United States.

**DE-111**

| ESTATE OF (Name): | CASE NUMBER: |
|---|---|
| DECEDENT | |

4. ☐ Decedent's will does not preclude administration of this estate under the Independent Administration of Estates Act.
5. a. Decedent was survived by (check items (1) or (2), and (3) or (4), and (5) or (6), and (7) or (8))
   (1) ☐ spouse.
   (2) ☐ no spouse as follows:
       (a) ☐ divorced or never married.
       (b) ☐ spouse deceased.
   (3) ☐ registered domestic partner.
   (4) ☐ no registered domestic partner.
       (See Fam. Code, § 297.5(c); Prob. Code, §§ 37(b), 6401(c), and 6402.)
   (5) ☐ child as follows:
       (a) ☐ natural or adopted.
       (b) ☐ natural adopted by a third party.
   (6) ☐ no child.
   (7) ☐ issue of a predeceased child.
   (8) ☐ no issue of a predeceased child.

   b. Decedent ☐ was ☐ was not survived by a stepchild or foster child or children who would have been adopted by decedent but for a legal barrier. (See Prob. Code, § 6454.)

6. (Complete if decedent was survived by (1) a spouse or registered domestic partner but no issue (only **a** or **b** apply), or (2) no spouse, registered domestic partner, or issue. (Check the **first** box that applies):
   a. ☐ Decedent was survived by a parent or parents who are listed in item 8.
   b. ☐ Decedent was survived by issue of deceased parents, all of whom are listed in item 8.
   c. ☐ Decedent was survived by a grandparent or grandparents who are listed in item 8.
   d. ☐ Decedent was survived by issue of grandparents, all of whom are listed in item 8.
   e. ☐ Decedent was survived by issue of a predeceased spouse, all of whom are listed in item 8.
   f. ☐ Decedent was survived by next of kin, all of whom are listed in item 8.
   g. ☐ Decedent was survived by parents of a predeceased spouse or issue of those parents, if both are predeceased, all of whom are listed in item 8.
   h. ☐ Decedent was survived by no known next of kin.

7. (Complete only if no spouse or issue survived decedent.)
   a. ☐ Decedent had no predeceased spouse.
   b. ☐ Decedent had a predeceased spouse who
       (1) ☐ died not more than 15 years before decedent and who owned an interest in **real property** that passed to decedent,
       (2) ☐ died not more than five years before decedent and who owned **personal property** valued at $10,000 or more that passed to decedent,
       (If you checked (1) or (2), check only the **first** box that applies):
           (a) ☐ Decedent was survived by issue of a predeceased spouse, all of whom are listed in item 8.
           (b) ☐ Decedent was survived by a parent or parents of the predeceased spouse who are listed in item 8.
           (c) ☐ Decedent was survived by issue of a parent of the predeceased spouse, all of whom are listed in item 8.
           (d) ☐ Decedent was survived by next of kin of the decedent, all of whom are listed in item 8.
           (e) ☐ Decedent was survived by next of kin of the predeceased spouse, all of whom are listed in item 8.
       (3) ☐ neither (1) nor (2) apply.

8. Listed on the next page are the names, relationships to decedent, ages, and addresses, so far as known to or reasonably ascertainable by petitioner, of (1) all persons mentioned in decedent's will or any codicil, whether living or deceased; (2) all persons named or checked in items 2, 5, 6, and 7; and (3) all beneficiaries of a trust named in decedent's will or any codicil in which the trustee and personal representative are the same person.

DE-111 [Rev. March 1, 2008]

**PETITION FOR PROBATE**
**(Probate—Decedents Estates)**

| ESTATE OF *(Name)*: | CASE NUMBER: |
|---|---|
| DECEDENT | |

**DE-111**

8. <u>Name and relationship to decedent</u>  <u>Age</u>  <u>Address</u>

☐ Continued on Attachment 8.

9. Number of pages attached: _____

Date:

▸

_____  _____
(TYPE OR PRINT NAME OF ATTORNEY)    (SIGNATURE OF ATTORNEY)*

* (Signatures of all petitioners are also required. All petitioners must sign, but the petition may be verified by any one of them (Prob. Code, §§ 1020, 1021; Cal. Rules of Court, rule 7.103).)

I declare under penalty of perjury under the laws of the State of California that the foregoing is true and correct.

Date:

▸

_____  _____
(TYPE OR PRINT NAME OF PETITIONER)    (SIGNATURE OF PETITIONER)

▸

_____  _____
(TYPE OR PRINT NAME OF PETITIONER)    (SIGNATURE OF PETITIONER)

☐ Signatures of additional petitioners follow last attachment.

DE-111 [Rev. March 1, 2008]

**PETITION FOR PROBATE**
**(Probate—Decedents Estates)**

NOTICE OF HEARING—DECEDENT'S ESTATE OR TRUST 83

**DE-120**

| ATTORNEY OR PARTY WITHOUT ATTORNEY *(Name, State Bar number, and address):* | FOR COURT USE ONLY |
|---|---|
| TELEPHONE NO.: FAX NO. *(Optional):* <br> E-MAIL ADDRESS *(Optional):* <br> ATTORNEY FOR *(Name):* | |
| **SUPERIOR COURT OF CALIFORNIA, COUNTY OF** <br> STREET ADDRESS: <br> MAILING ADDRESS: <br> CITY AND ZIP CODE: <br> BRANCH NAME: | |
| ☐ ESTATE OF *(Name):* ☐ IN THE MATTER OF *(Name):* <br> ☐ DECEDENT ☐ TRUST ☐ OTHER | |
| **NOTICE OF HEARING—DECEDENT'S ESTATE OR TRUST** | CASE NUMBER: |

**This notice is required by law.**
**This notice does not require you to appear in court, but you may attend the hearing if you wish.**

1. NOTICE is given that *(name):*
   *(representative capacity, if any):*
   has filed *(specify):*\*

2. You may refer to the filed documents for more information. *(Some documents filed with the court are confidential.)*

3. A HEARING on the matter will be held as follows:

   a. Date: Time: Dept.: Room:

   b. Address of court ☐ shown above ☐ is *(specify):*

Assistive listening systems, computer-assisted real-time captioning, or sign language interpreter services are available upon request if at least 5 days notice is provided. Contact the clerk's office for *Request for Accommodations by Persons With Disabilities and Order* (form MC-410). (Civil Code section 54.8.)

\* Do **not** use this form to give notice of a petition to administer estate (see Prob. Code, § 8100 and form DE-121) or notice of a hearing in a guardianship or conservatorship (see Prob. Code, §§ 1511 and 1822 and form GC-020).

Page 1 of 2

Form Adopted for Mandatory Use
Judicial Council of California
DE-120 [Rev. July 1, 2005]

**NOTICE OF HEARING—DECEDENT'S ESTATE OR TRUST**
**(Probate—Decedents' Estates)**

Probate Code §§ 851, 1211,
1215, 1216, 1230, 17100
www.courtinfo.ca.gov

American LegalNet, Inc.
www.USCourtForms.com

| ☐ ESTATE OF *(Name):* ☐ IN THE MATTER OF *(Name):* | CASE NUMBER: |
|---|---|
| ☐ DECEDENT ☐ TRUST ☐ OTHER | |

## CLERK'S CERTIFICATE OF POSTING

1. I certify that I am not a party to this cause.
2. A copy of the foregoing *Notice of Hearing—Decedent's Estate or Trust*
   a. was posted at *(address):*

   b. was posted on *(date):*

Date:                                                    Clerk, by _____, Deputy

## PROOF OF SERVICE BY MAIL *

1. I am over the age of 18 and not a party to this cause. I am a resident of or employed in the county where the mailing occurred.
2. My residence or business address is *(specify):*

3. I served the foregoing *Notice of Hearing—Decedent's Estate or Trust* on each person named below by enclosing a copy in an envelope addressed as shown below AND
   a. ☐ **depositing** the sealed envelope on the date and at the place shown in item 4 with the United States Postal Service with the postage fully prepaid.
   b. ☐ **placing** the envelope for collection and mailing on the date and at the place shown in item 4 following our ordinary business practices. I am readily familiar with this business's practice for collecting and processing correspondence for mailing. On the same day that correspondence is placed for collection and mailing, it is deposited in the ordinary course of business with the United States Postal Service in a sealed envelope with postage fully prepaid.

4. a. Date mailed:                    b. Place mailed *(city, state):*

5. ☐ I served with the *Notice of Hearing—Decedent's Estate or Trust* a copy of the petition or other document referred to in the Notice.

I declare under penalty of perjury under the laws of the State of California that the foregoing is true and correct.

Date:

_____          _____
(TYPE OR PRINT NAME OF PERSON COMPLETING THIS FORM)          (SIGNATURE OF PERSON COMPLETING THIS FORM)

### NAME AND ADDRESS OF EACH PERSON TO WHOM NOTICE WAS MAILED

| | Name of person served | Address *(number, street, city, state, and zip code)* |
|---|---|---|
| 1. | | |
| 2. | | |
| 3. | | |
| 4. | | |

☐ Continued on an attachment. *(You may use* Attachment to Notice of Hearing Proof of Service by Mail, *form DE-120(MA)/GC-020(MA), for this purpose.)*

* Do not use this form for proof of personal service. You may use form DE-120(P) to prove personal service of this Notice.

DE-120 [Rev. July 1, 2003]     **NOTICE OF HEARING—DECEDENT'S ESTATE OR TRUST**     Page 2 of 2
**(Probate—Decedents' Estates)**

NOTICE OF PETITION TO ADMINISTER ESTATE      85

DE-121

| ATTORNEY OR PARTY WITHOUT ATTORNEY (Name, State Bar number, and address): | FOR COURT USE ONLY |
|---|---|
| TELEPHONE NO.:        FAX NO. (Optional): | |
| E-MAIL ADDRESS (Optional): | |
| ATTORNEY FOR (Name): | |

SUPERIOR COURT OF CALIFORNIA, COUNTY OF
STREET ADDRESS:
MAILING ADDRESS:
CITY AND ZIP CODE:
BRANCH NAME:

ESTATE OF (Name):

DECEDENT

| NOTICE OF PETITION TO ADMINISTER ESTATE OF (Name): | CASE NUMBER: |
|---|---|

1. To all heirs, beneficiaries, creditors, contingent creditors, and persons who may otherwise be interested in the will or estate, or both, of (specify all names by which the decedent was known):

2. A **Petition for Probate** has been filed by (name of petitioner):
   in the Superior Court of California, County of (specify):

3. The Petition for Probate requests that (name):
   be appointed as personal representative to administer the estate of the decedent.

4. ☐ The petition requests the decedent's will and codicils, if any, be admitted to probate. The will and any codicils are available for examination in the file kept by the court.

5. ☐ The petition requests authority to administer the estate under the Independent Administration of Estates Act. (This authority will allow the personal representative to take many actions without obtaining court approval. Before taking certain very important actions, however, the personal representative will be required to give notice to interested persons unless they have waived notice or consented to the proposed action.) The independent administration authority will be granted unless an interested person files an objection to the petition and shows good cause why the court should not grant the authority.

6. **A hearing on the petition will be held in this court as follows:**

   a. Date:          Time:          Dept.:          Room:

   b. Address of court: ☐ same as noted above  ☐ other (specify):

7. **If you object** to the granting of the petition, you should appear at the hearing and state your objections or file written objections with the court before the hearing. Your appearance may be in person or by your attorney.

8. **If you are a creditor or a contingent creditor of the decedent,** you must file your claim with the court and mail a copy to the personal representative appointed by the court within the **later** of either (1) **four months** from the date of first issuance of letters to a general personal representative, as defined in section 58(b) of the California Probate Code, or (2) **60 days** from the date of mailing or personal delivery to you of a notice under section 9052 of the California Probate Code.
   Other California statutes and legal authority may affect your rights as a creditor. You may want to consult with an attorney knowledgeable in California law.

9. **You may examine the file kept by the court.** If you are a person interested in the estate, you may file with the court a *Request for Special Notice* (form DE-154) of the filing of an inventory and appraisal of estate assets or of any petition or account as provided in Probate Code section 1250. A *Request for Special Notice* form is available from the court clerk.

10. ☐ Petitioner  ☐ Attorney for petitioner (name):

    (Address):

    (Telephone):

**NOTE:** If this notice is published, print the caption, beginning with the words NOTICE OF PETITION TO ADMINISTER ESTATE, and do not print the information from the form above the caption. The caption and the decedent's name must be printed in at least 8-point type and the text in at least 7-point type. Print the case number as part of the caption. Print items preceded by a box only if the box is checked. Do not print the italicized instructions in parentheses, the paragraph numbers, the mailing information, or the material on page 2.

Page 1 of 2

Form Adopted for Mandatory Use
Judicial Council of California
DE-121 [Rev. January 1, 2013]

**NOTICE OF PETITION TO ADMINISTER ESTATE**
(Probate—Decedents' Estates)

Probate Code, §§ 8100, 9100
www.courts.ca.gov

**DE-121**

| ESTATE OF (Name): | CASE NUMBER: |
|---|---|
| DECEDENT | |

**PROOF OF SERVICE BY MAIL**

1. I am over the age of 18 and not a party to this cause. I am a resident of or employed in the county where the mailing occurred.
2. My residence or business address is (specify):

3. I served the foregoing *Notice of Petition to Administer Estate* on each person named below by enclosing a copy in an envelope addressed as shown below **AND**
   a. ☐ **depositing** the sealed envelope with the United States Postal Service on the date and at the place shown in item 4, with the postage fully prepaid.
   b. ☐ **placing** the envelope for collection and mailing on the date and at the place shown in item 4 following our ordinary business practices. I am readily familiar with this business's practice for collecting and processing correspondence for mailing. On the same day that correspondence is placed for collection and mailing, it is deposited in the ordinary course of business with the United States Postal Service, in a sealed envelope with postage fully prepaid.

4. a. Date mailed:        b. Place mailed (city, state):

5. ☐ I served, with the *Notice of Petition to Administer Estate*, a copy of the petition or other document referred to in the notice.

I declare under penalty of perjury under the laws of the State of California that the foregoing is true and correct.

Date:

▶

_____           _____
(TYPE OR PRINT NAME OF PERSON COMPLETING THIS FORM)    (SIGNATURE OF PERSON COMPLETING THIS FORM)

**NAME AND ADDRESS OF EACH PERSON TO WHOM NOTICE WAS MAILED**

| | Name of person served | Address (number, street, city, state, and zip code) |
|---|---|---|
| 1. | | |
| 2. | | |
| 3. | | |
| 4. | | |
| 5. | | |
| 6. | | |

☐ Continued on an attachment. *(You may use form DE-121(MA) to show additional persons served.)*

Assistive listening systems, computer-assisted real-time captioning, or sign language interpreter services are available upon request if at least 5 days notice is provided. Contact the clerk's office for *Request for Accommodations by Persons With Disabilities and Order* (form MC-410). (Civil Code section 54.8.)

DE-121 [Rev. January 1, 2013]

**NOTICE OF PETITION TO ADMINISTER ESTATE**
(Probate—Decedents' Estates)

DUTIES AND LIABILITIES OF PERSONAL REPRESENTATIVE   87

**DE-147**

| ATTORNEY OR PARTY WITHOUT ATTORNEY (Name, state bar number, and address): | FOR COURT USE ONLY |
|---|---|
| TELEPHONE NO.:     FAX NO. (Optional): | |
| E-MAIL ADDRESS (Optional): | |
| ATTORNEY FOR (Name): | |
| **SUPERIOR COURT OF CALIFORNIA, COUNTY OF** | |
| STREET ADDRESS: | |
| MAILING ADDRESS: | |
| CITY AND ZIP CODE: | |
| BRANCH NAME: | |
| ESTATE OF (Name):                                       DECEDENT | |
| **DUTIES AND LIABILITIES OF PERSONAL REPRESENTATIVE** and Acknowledgment of Receipt | CASE NUMBER: |

## DUTIES AND LIABILITIES OF PERSONAL REPRESENTATIVE

When the court appoints you as personal representative of an estate, you become an officer of the court and assume certain duties and obligations. An attorney is best qualified to advise you about these matters. You should understand the following:

### 1. MANAGING THE ESTATE'S ASSETS

**a. Prudent investments**
You must manage the estate assets with the care of a prudent person dealing with someone else's property. This means that you must be cautious and may not make any speculative investments.

**b. Keep estate assets separate**
You must keep the money and property in this estate separate from anyone else's, including your own. When you open a bank account for the estate, the account name must indicate that it is an estate account and not your personal account. Never deposit estate funds in your personal account or otherwise mix them with your or anyone else's property. Securities in the estate must also be held in a name that shows they are estate property and not your personal property.

**c. Interest-bearing accounts and other investments**
Except for checking accounts intended for ordinary administration expenses, estate accounts must earn interest. You may deposit estate funds in insured accounts in financial institutions, but you should consult with an attorney before making other kinds of investments.

**d. Other restrictions**
There are many other restrictions on your authority to deal with estate property. You should not spend any of the estate's money unless you have received permission from the court or have been advised to do so by an attorney. You may reimburse yourself for official court costs paid by you to the county clerk and for the premium on your bond. Without prior order of the court, you may not pay fees to yourself or to your attorney, if you have one. If you do not obtain the court's permission when it is required, you may be removed as personal representative or you may be required to reimburse the estate from your own personal funds, or both. You should consult with an attorney concerning the legal requirements affecting sales, leases, mortgages, and investments of estate property.

### 2. INVENTORY OF ESTATE PROPERTY

**a. Locate the estate's property**
You must attempt to locate and take possession of all the decedent's property to be administered in the estate.

**b. Determine the value of the property**
You must arrange to have a court-appointed referee determine the value of the property unless the appointment is waived by the court. You, rather than the referee, must determine the value of certain "cash items." An attorney can advise you about how to do this.

**c. File an Inventory and appraisal**
Within four months after Letters are first issued to you as personal representative, you must file with the court an inventory and appraisal of all the assets in the estate.

Page 1 of 2

Form Adopted for Mandatory Use
Judicial Council of California
DE-147 [Rev. January 1, 2002]

**DUTIES AND LIABILITIES OF PERSONAL REPRESENTATIVE**
(Probate)

Probate Code, § 8404

American LegalNet, Inc.
www.USCourtForms.com

| ESTATE OF (Name): | CASE NUMBER: |
|---|---|
| DECEDENT | |

**d. File a change of ownership**
At the time you file the inventory and appraisal, you must also file a change of ownership statement with the county recorder or assessor in each county where the decedent owned real property at the time of death, as provided in section 480 of the California Revenue and Taxation Code.

### 3. NOTICE TO CREDITORS
You must mail a notice of administration to each known creditor of the decedent within four months after your appointment as personal representative. If the decedent received Medi-Cal assistance, you must notify the State Director of Health Services within 90 days after appointment.

### 4. INSURANCE
You should determine that there is appropriate and adequate insurance covering the assets and risks of the estate. Maintain the insurance in force during the entire period of the administration.

### 5. RECORD KEEPING
**a. Keep accounts**
You must keep complete and accurate records of each financial transaction affecting the estate. You will have to prepare an account of all money and property you have received, what you have spent, and the date of each transaction. You must describe in detail what you have left after the payment of expenses.

**b. Court review**
Your account will be reviewed by the court. Save your receipts because the court may ask to review them. If you do not file your accounts as required, the court will order you to do so. You may be removed as personal representative if you fail to comply.

### 6. CONSULTING AN ATTORNEY
If you have an attorney, you should cooperate with the attorney at all times. You and your attorney are responsible for completing the estate administration as promptly as possible. **When in doubt, contact your attorney.**

---

**NOTICE:**
1. This statement of duties and liabilities is a summary and is not a complete statement of the law. Your conduct as a personal representative is governed by the law itself and not by this summary.
2. If you fail to perform your duties or to meet the deadlines, the court may reduce your compensation, remove you from office, and impose other sanctions.

---

## ACKNOWLEDGMENT OF RECEIPT

1. I have petitioned the court to be appointed as a personal representative.

2. My address and telephone number are *(specify):*

3. I acknowledge that I have received a copy of this statement of the duties and liabilities of the office of personal representative.

Date:

_____  ▶  _____
(TYPE OR PRINT NAME)                      (SIGNATURE OF PETITIONER)

Date:

_____  ▶  _____
(TYPE OR PRINT NAME)                      (SIGNATURE OF PETITIONER)

---

**CONFIDENTIAL INFORMATION:** If required to do so by local court rule, you must provide your date of birth and driver's license number on supplemental Form DE-147S. (Prob. Code, § 8404(b).)

| | |
|---|---|
| ESTATE OF *(Name)*: <br><br> DECEDENT | CASE NUMBER: |

**CONFIDENTIAL** — **DE-147S**

## CONFIDENTIAL STATEMENT OF BIRTH DATE AND DRIVER'S LICENSE NUMBER

(Supplement to *Duties and Liabilities of Personal Representative* (Form DE-147))

(NOTE: This supplement is to be used if the court by local rule requires the personal representative to provide a birth date and driver's license number. Do **not** attach this supplement to Form DE-147.)

This separate *Confidential Statement of Birth Date and Driver's License Number* contains confidential information relating to the personal representative in the case referenced above. This supplement shall be kept separate from the *Duties and Liabilities of Personal Representative* filed in this case and shall not be a public record.

INFORMATION ON THE PERSONAL REPRESENTATIVE:

1. Name:

2. Date of birth:

3. Driver's license number: State:

---

**TO COURT CLERK:**
THIS STATEMENT IS **CONFIDENTIAL**. DO NOT FILE
THIS CONFIDENTIAL STATEMENT IN A PUBLIC COURT FILE.

---

Form Adopted for Mandatory Use
Judicial Council of California
DE-147S [New January 1, 2001]

**CONFIDENTIAL SUPPLEMENT TO DUTIES AND LIABILITIES OF PERSONAL REPRESENTATIVE**
(Probate)

Probate Code, § 8404

PROBATE COMPLETED

DE-111

**ATTORNEY OR PARTY WITHOUT ATTORNEY** *(Name, State Bar number, and address):*
Nancy Noe-Nonsense
Law Offices of Nancy Noe-Nonsense
11111 Courthouse Plaza
Sacramento, CA 95826
**TELEPHONE NO.:** 916-xxx-xxxx  **FAX NO.** *(Optional):* 916-xxx-xxxx
**E-MAIL ADDRESS** *(Optional):* nancy@noe-nonsense.com
**ATTORNEY FOR** *(Name):* EDDY WADE SHORES, Petitioner

**SUPERIOR COURT OF CALIFORNIA, COUNTY OF** SACRAMENTO
**STREET ADDRESS:** 3341 Power Inn Road
**MAILING ADDRESS:** 3341 Power Inn Road
**CITY AND ZIP CODE:** Sacramento, CA 95826
**BRANCH NAME:** Probate Division

**ESTATE OF** *(Name):*
CORAL LEIGH SHORES, aka CORAL REDD SHORES
                                                                    DECEDENT

**PETITION FOR** [☒] **Probate of Will and for Letters Testamentary**
[ ] **Probate of Will and for Letters of Administration with Will Annexed**
[ ] **Letters of Administration**
[ ] **Letters of Special Administration** [ ] **with general powers**
[☒] **Authorization to Administer Under the Independent Administration of Estates Act** [ ] **with limited authority**

**CASE NUMBER:**

**HEARING DATE:**

**DEPT.:**   **TIME:**

1. Publication will be in *(specify name of newspaper):* ELK GROVE TRUMPET
   a. [☒] Publication requested.
   b. [ ] Publication to be arranged.
2. **Petitioner** *(name each):* EDDY WADE SHORES **requests that**
   a. [☒] decedent's will and codicils, if any, be admitted to probate.
   b. [☒] *(name):* EDDY WADE SHORES
      be appointed
      (1) [☒] executor
      (2) [ ] administrator with will annexed
      (3) [ ] administrator
      (4) [ ] special administrator [ ] with general powers
      and Letters issue upon qualification.
   c. [☒] full [ ] limited authority be granted to administer under the Independent Administration of Estates Act.
   d. (1) [☒] bond not be required for the reasons stated in item 3d.
      (2) [ ] $_____ bond be fixed. The bond will be furnished by an admitted surety insurer or as otherwise provided by law. *(Specify reasons in Attachment 2 if the amount is different from the maximum required by Prob. Code, § 8482.)*
      (3) [ ] $_____ in deposits in a blocked account be allowed. Receipts will be filed.
          *(Specify institution and location):*

3. a. Decedent died on *(date):* 5/15/2013  at *(place):* Elk Grove, California
      (1) [☒] a resident of the county named above.
      (2) [ ] a nonresident of California and left an estate in the county named above located at *(specify location permitting publication in the newspaper named in item 1):*

   b. Street address, city, and county of decedent's residence at time of death *(specify):*
      22222 WONDERFUL PLACE, ELK GROVE, CA 95624

Page 1 of 4

Form Adopted for Mandatory Use
Judicial Council of California
DE-111 [Rev. March 1, 2008]

**PETITION FOR PROBATE**
**(Probate—Decedents Estates)**

Probate Code, §§ 8002, 10450;
www.courtinfo.ca.gov

| | | DE-111 |
|---|---|---|
| ESTATE OF (Name): CORAL LEIGH SHORES, aka CORAL REDD SHORES DECEDENT | | CASE NUMBER: |

3. c. **Character and estimated value of the property of the estate** (complete in all cases):
   (1) Personal property: $ 25,000
   (2) Annual gross income from
      (a) real property: $
      (b) personal property: $
   (3) **Subtotal** (add (1) and (2)): $ 25,000
   (4) Gross fair market value of real property: $ 450,000
   (5) (Less) Encumbrances: $( 200,000 )
   (6) Net value of real property: $ 250,000
   (7) **Total** (add (3) and (6)): $ 275,000

   d. (1) ☐ Will waives bond. ☐ Special administrator is the named executor, and the will waives bond.
      (2) ☐ All beneficiaries are adults and have waived bond, and the will does not require a bond. (Affix waiver as Attachment 3d(2).)
      (3) ☐ All heirs at law are adults and have waived bond. (Affix waiver as Attachment 3d(3).)
      (4) ☐ Sole personal representative is a corporate fiduciary or an exempt government agency.
   e. (1) ☐ Decedent died intestate.
      (2) ☒ Copy of decedent's will dated: 8/2/12 ☐ codicil dated (specify for each):
         are affixed as Attachment 3e(2).
         (Include typed copies of handwritten documents and English translations of foreign-language documents.)
         ☐ The will and all codicils are self-proving (Prob. Code, § 8220).
   f. **Appointment of personal representative** (check all applicable boxes):
      (1) Appointment of executor or administrator with will annexed:
         (a) ☒ Proposed executor is named as executor in the will and consents to act.
         (b) ☐ No executor is named in the will.
         (c) ☐ Proposed personal representative is a nominee of a person entitled to Letters. (Affix nomination as Attachment 3f(1)(c).)
         (d) ☐ Other named executors will not act because of ☐ death ☐ declination
             ☐ other reasons (specify):




         ☐ Continued in Attachment 3f(1)(d).
      (2) Appointment of administrator:
         (a) ☒ Petitioner is a person entitled to Letters. (If necessary, explain priority in Attachment 3f(2)(a).)
         (b) ☐ Petitioner is a nominee of a person entitled to Letters. (Affix nomination as Attachment 3f(2)(b).)
         (c) ☐ Petitioner is related to the decedent as (specify):
      (3) ☐ Appointment of special administrator requested. (Specify grounds and requested powers in Attachment 3f(3).)
   g. Proposed personal representative is a
      (1) ☒ resident of California.
      (2) ☐ nonresident of California (specify permanent address):



      (3) ☐ resident of the United States.
      (4) ☐ nonresident of the United States.

**PETITION FOR PROBATE**
(Probate—Decedents Estates)

**DE-111**

| ESTATE OF (Name): CORAL LEIGH SHORES, aka CORAL REDD SHORES  DECEDENT | CASE NUMBER: |
|---|---|

4. ☐ Decedent's will does not preclude administration of this estate under the Independent Administration of Estates Act.
5. a. Decedent was survived by *(check items (1) or (2), and (3) or (4), and (5) or (6), and (7) or (8))*
   (1) ☐ spouse.
   (2) ☒ no spouse as follows:
      (a) ☐ divorced or never married.
      (b) ☒ spouse deceased.
   (3) ☐ registered domestic partner.
   (4) ☐ no registered domestic partner.
      *(See Fam. Code, § 297.5(c); Prob. Code, §§ 37(b), 6401(c), and 6402.)*
   (5) ☒ child as follows:
      (a) ☒ natural or adopted.
      (b) ☐ natural adopted by a third party.
   (6) ☐ no child.
   (7) ☐ issue of a predeceased child.
   (8) ☐ no issue of a predeceased child.

  b. Decedent ☐ was ☒ was not survived by a stepchild or foster child or children who would have been adopted by decedent but for a legal barrier. *(See Prob. Code, § 6454.)*

6. *(Complete if decedent was survived by (1) a spouse or registered domestic partner but no issue (only **a** or **b** apply), or (2) no spouse, registered domestic partner, or issue. (Check the **first** box that applies):*
  a. ☐ Decedent was survived by a parent or parents who are listed in item 8.
  b. ☐ Decedent was survived by issue of deceased parents, all of whom are listed in item 8.
  c. ☐ Decedent was survived by a grandparent or grandparents who are listed in item 8.
  d. ☐ Decedent was survived by issue of grandparents, all of whom are listed in item 8.
  e. ☒ Decedent was survived by issue of a predeceased spouse, all of whom are listed in item 8.
  f. ☐ Decedent was survived by next of kin, all of whom are listed in item 8.
  g. ☐ Decedent was survived by parents of a predeceased spouse or issue of those parents, if both are predeceased, all of whom are listed in item 8.
  h. ☐ Decedent was survived by no known next of kin.

7. *(Complete only if no spouse or issue survived decedent.)*
  a. ☐ Decedent had no predeceased spouse.
  b. ☐ Decedent had a predeceased spouse who
   (1) ☐ died not more than 15 years before decedent and who owned an interest in **real property** that passed to decedent,
   (2) ☐ died not more than five years before decedent and who owned **personal property** valued at $10,000 or more that passed to decedent,
     *(If you checked (1) or (2), check only the **first** box that applies):*
     (a) ☐ Decedent was survived by issue of a predeceased spouse, all of whom are listed in item 8.
     (b) ☐ Decedent was survived by a parent or parents of the predeceased spouse who are listed in item 8.
     (c) ☐ Decedent was survived by issue of a parent of the predeceased spouse, all of whom are listed in item 8.
     (d) ☐ Decedent was survived by next of kin of the decedent, all of whom are listed in item 8.
     (e) ☐ Decedent was survived by next of kin of the predeceased spouse, all of whom are listed in item 8.
   (3) ☐ neither (1) nor (2) apply.

8. Listed on the next page are the names, relationships to decedent, ages, and addresses, so far as known to or reasonably ascertainable by petitioner, of (1) all persons mentioned in decedent's will or any codicil, whether living or deceased; (2) all persons named or checked in items 2, 5, 6, and 7; and (3) all beneficiaries of a trust named in decedent's will or any codicil in which the trustee and personal representative are the same person.

DE-111 [Rev. March 1, 2008]

**PETITION FOR PROBATE**
**(Probate—Decedents Estates)**

|  | | **DE-111** |
|---|---|---|
| ESTATE OF *(Name)*: CORAL LEIGH SHORES, aka CORAL REDD SHORES  DECEDENT | CASE NUMBER: | |

8. | Name and relationship to decedent | Age | Address |
|---|---|---|
| EDDY WADE SHORES - SON | 38 | 22222 WONDERFUL PLACE, ELK GROVE, CA |
| SHELLY P. LINE - DAUGHTER | 35 | 7777 LITTLEON WAY, STOCKTON, CA |

☐ Continued on Attachment 8.

9. Number of pages attached: _____

Date:

NANCY NOE-NONSENSE
(TYPE OR PRINT NAME OF ATTORNEY)          ▶          (SIGNATURE OF ATTORNEY)*

* (Signatures of all petitioners are also required. All petitioners must sign, but the petition may be verified by any one of them (Prob. Code, §§ 1020, 1021; Cal. Rules of Court, rule 7.103).)

I declare under penalty of perjury under the laws of the State of California that the foregoing is true and correct.

Date:

EDDY WADE SHORES
(TYPE OR PRINT NAME OF PETITIONER)          ▶          (SIGNATURE OF PETITIONER)

(TYPE OR PRINT NAME OF PETITIONER)          ▶          (SIGNATURE OF PETITIONER)

☐ Signatures of additional petitioners follow last attachment.

DE-111 [Rev. March 1, 2008]

**PETITION FOR PROBATE**
**(Probate—Decedents Estates)**

**NOTICE OF HEARING—DECEDENT'S ESTATE OR TRUST COMPLETED**

---

**DE-120**

| | |
|---|---|
| ATTORNEY OR PARTY WITHOUT ATTORNEY *(Name, State Bar number, and address):*<br>Nancy Noe-Nonsense, SBN *********<br>Law Office of Nancy Noe-Nonsense<br>11111 Courthouse Plaza<br>Sacramento, CA 95826<br>TELEPHONE NO.: 916-XXX-XXXX  FAX NO. *(Optional):* 916-XXX-XXXX<br>E-MAIL ADDRESS *(Optional):* nancy@noe-nonsenselaw.com<br>ATTORNEY FOR *(Name):* EDDY WADE SHORES, Petitioner | |

SUPERIOR COURT OF CALIFORNIA, COUNTY OF SACRAMENTO
STREET ADDRESS: 3341 Power Inn Road
MAILING ADDRESS: 3341 Power Inn Road
CITY AND ZIP CODE: Sacramento, CA 95826
BRANCH NAME: Probate Division

[✓] ESTATE OF *(Name):*  [ ] IN THE MATTER OF *(Name):*
CORAL LEIGH SHORES, aka CORAL REDD SHORES
[✓] DECEDENT  [ ] TRUST  [ ] OTHER

**NOTICE OF HEARING—DECEDENT'S ESTATE OR TRUST**

CASE NUMBER:

---

**This notice is required by law.**
**This notice does not require you to appear in court, but you may attend the hearing if you wish.**

1. NOTICE is given that *(name):* EDDY WADE SHORES
   *(representative capacity, if any):* Executor
   has filed *(specify):* *

   Petition for Probate

2. You may refer to the filed documents for more information. *(Some documents filed with the court are confidential.)*

3. A HEARING on the matter will be held as follows:

   a. Date:       Time:       Dept.:       Room:

   b. Address of court [✓] shown above  [ ] is *(specify):*

---

Assistive listening systems, computer-assisted real-time captioning, or sign language interpreter services are available upon request if at least 5 days notice is provided. Contact the clerk's office for *Request for Accommodations by Persons With Disabilities and Order* (form MC-410). (Civil Code section 54.8.)

---

* Do **not** use this form to give notice of a petition to administer estate (see Prob. Code, § 8100 and form DE-121) or notice of a hearing in a guardianship or conservatorship (see Prob. Code, §§ 1511 and 1822 and form GC-020).

Page 1 of 2

Form Adopted for Mandatory Use
Judicial Council of California
DE-120 [Rev. July 1, 2005]

**NOTICE OF HEARING—DECEDENT'S ESTATE OR TRUST**
*(Probate—Decedents' Estates)*

Probate Code §§ 851, 1211, 1215, 1216, 1230, 17100
www.courtinfo.ca.gov

American LegalNet, Inc.
www.USCourtForms.com

# NOTICE OF HEARING—DECEDENT'S ESTATE OR TRUST COMPLETED 95

| ☑ ESTATE OF (Name): ☐ IN THE MATTER OF (Name): | CASE NUMBER: |
|---|---|
| CORAL LEIGH SHORES, aka CORAL REDD SHORES | |
| ☑ DECEDENT ☐ TRUST ☐ OTHER | |

## CLERK'S CERTIFICATE OF POSTING

1. I certify that I am not a party to this cause.
2. A copy of the foregoing *Notice of Hearing—Decedent's Estate or Trust*
   a. was posted at *(address)*:

   b. was posted on *(date)*:

Date: _____ Clerk, by _____, Deputy

## PROOF OF SERVICE BY MAIL *

1. I am over the age of 18 and not a party to this cause. I am a resident of or employed in the county where the mailing occurred.
2. My residence or business address is *(specify)*:
   Law Offices of Nancy No-Nonsense, 11111 Courthouse Plaza, Sacramento, CA 95826

3. I served the foregoing *Notice of Hearing—Decedent's Estate or Trust* on each person named below by enclosing a copy in an envelope addressed as shown below AND
   a. ☐ **depositing** the sealed envelope on the date and at the place shown in item 4 with the United States Postal Service with the postage fully prepaid.
   b. ☑ **placing** the envelope for collection and mailing on the date and at the place shown in item 4 following our ordinary business practices. I am readily familiar with this business's practice for collecting and processing correspondence for mailing. On the same day that correspondence is placed for collection and mailing, it is deposited in the ordinary course of business with the United States Postal Service in a sealed envelope with postage fully prepaid.

4. a. Date mailed: _____ b. Place mailed *(city, state)*: Sacramento, CA

5. ☑ I served with the *Notice of Hearing—Decedent's Estate or Trust* a copy of the petition or other document referred to in the Notice.

I declare under penalty of perjury under the laws of the State of California that the foregoing is true and correct.

Date:

Sallie Jo Smith-Allen, Paralegal
_____  _____
(TYPE OR PRINT NAME OF PERSON COMPLETING THIS FORM)   (SIGNATURE OF PERSON COMPLETING THIS FORM)

### NAME AND ADDRESS OF EACH PERSON TO WHOM NOTICE WAS MAILED

| | Name of person served | Address *(number, street, city, state, and zip code)* |
|---|---|---|
| 1. | Eddy Wade Waters | 22222 Wonderful Place, Elk Grove, CA 95624 |
| 2. | Shelley P. Line | 7777 Littleton Way, Stockton, CA 95722 |
| 3. | | |
| 4. | | |

☐ Continued on an attachment. *(You may use Attachment to Notice of Hearing Proof of Service by Mail, form DE-120(MA)/GC-020(MA), for this purpose.)*

* Do not use this form for proof of personal service. You may use form DE-120(P) to prove personal service of this Notice.

DE-120 [Rev. July 1, 2005]   **NOTICE OF HEARING—DECEDENT'S ESTATE OR TRUST**   Page 2 of 2
(Probate—Decedents' Estates)

## NOTICE OF PETITION TO ADMINISTER ESTATE COMPLETED

**DE-121**

| ATTORNEY OR PARTY WITHOUT ATTORNEY *(Name, State Bar number, and address):* | FOR COURT USE ONLY |
|---|---|
| Nancy Noe-Nonsense, SBN ******** <br> Law Offices of Nancy Noe-Nonsense <br> 11111 Courthouse Plaza <br> Sacramento, CA 95826 <br> TELEPHONE NO.: 916-XXX-XXXX   FAX NO. *(Optional):* 916-XXX-XXXX <br> E-MAIL ADDRESS *(Optional):* nancy@noe-nonsenselaw.com <br> ATTORNEY FOR *(Name):* EDDY WADE SHORES, Petitioner | |
| **SUPERIOR COURT OF CALIFORNIA, COUNTY OF** SACRAMENTO <br> STREET ADDRESS: 3341 Power Inn Road <br> MAILING ADDRESS: 3341 Power Inn Road <br> CITY AND ZIP CODE: Sacramento, CA 95826 <br> BRANCH NAME: Probate Division | |
| **ESTATE OF** *(Name):* <br> CORAL LEIGH SHORES, aka CORAL REDD SHORES              **DECEDENT** | |
| **NOTICE OF PETITION TO ADMINISTER ESTATE OF** <br> *(Name):* CORAL LEIGH SHORES, aka CORAL REDD SHORES | **CASE NUMBER:** |

1. To all heirs, beneficiaries, creditors, contingent creditors, and persons who may otherwise be interested in the will or estate, or both, of *(specify all names by which the decedent was known):* <br> CORAL LEIGH SHORES, aka CORAL REDD SHORES
2. A **Petition for Probate** has been filed by *(name of petitioner):* EDDY WADE SHORES <br> in the Superior Court of California, County of *(specify):* SACRAMENTO
3. The Petition for Probate requests that *(name):* EDDY WADE SHORES <br> be appointed as personal representative to administer the estate of the decedent.
4. ☐ The petition requests the decedent's will and codicils, if any, be admitted to probate. The will and any codicils are available for examination in the file kept by the court.
5. ☐ The petition requests authority to administer the estate under the Independent Administration of Estates Act. (This authority will allow the personal representative to take many actions without obtaining court approval. Before taking certain very important actions, however, the personal representative will be required to give notice to interested persons unless they have waived notice or consented to the proposed action.) The independent administration authority will be granted unless an interested person files an objection to the petition and shows good cause why the court should not grant the authority.
6. **A hearing on the petition will be held in this court as follows:**

    a. Date:          Time:          Dept.:          Room:

    b. Address of court: ☐ same as noted above   ☐ other *(specify):*

7. **If you object** to the granting of the petition, you should appear at the hearing and state your objections or file written objections with the court before the hearing. Your appearance may be in person or by your attorney.
8. **If you are a creditor or a contingent creditor of the decedent,** you must file your claim with the court and mail a copy to the personal representative appointed by the court within the **later** of either (1) **four months** from the date of first issuance of letters to a general personal representative, as defined in section 58(b) of the California Probate Code, or (2) **60 days** from the date of mailing or personal delivery to you of a notice under section 9052 of the California Probate Code. <br> Other California statutes and legal authority may affect your rights as a creditor. You may want to consult with an attorney knowledgeable in California law.
9. **You may examine the file kept by the court.** If you are a person interested in the estate, you may file with the court a *Request for Special Notice* (form DE-154) of the filing of an inventory and appraisal of estate assets or of any petition or account as provided in Probate Code section 1250. A *Request for Special Notice* form is available from the court clerk.
10. ☐ Petitioner   ☐ Attorney for petitioner *(name):* NANCY NOE-NONSENSE

    *(Address):* LAW OFFICES OF NANCY NOE-NONSENSE, 11111 COURTHOUSE PLAZA, SACRAMENTO, CA 95826

    *(Telephone):* 916-XXX-XXXX

**NOTE:** If this notice is published, print the caption, beginning with the words NOTICE OF PETITION TO ADMINISTER ESTATE, and do not print the information from the form above the caption. The caption and the decedent's name must be printed in at least 8-point type and the text in at least 7-point type. Print the case number as part of the caption. Print items preceded by a box only if the box is checked. Do not print the italicized instructions in parentheses, the paragraph numbers, the mailing information, or the material on page 2.

Page 1 of 2

Form Adopted for Mandatory Use <br> Judicial Council of California <br> DE-121 [Rev. January 1, 2013]

**NOTICE OF PETITION TO ADMINISTER ESTATE** <br> **(Probate—Decedents' Estates)**

Probate Code, §§ 8100, 9100 <br> www.courts.ca.gov

# NOTICE OF PETITION TO ADMINISTER ESTATE COMPLETED 97

**DE-121**

| ESTATE OF (Name): CORAL LEIGH SHORES, aka CORAL REDD SHORES DECEDENT | CASE NUMBER: |

## PROOF OF SERVICE BY MAIL

1. I am over the age of 18 and not a party to this cause. I am a resident of or employed in the county where the mailing occurred.
2. My residence or business address is (specify): LAW OFFICE OF NANCY NOE-NONSENSE
   11111 COURTHOUSE PLAZA
   SACRAMENTO, CA 95826
3. I served the foregoing *Notice of Petition to Administer Estate* on each person named below by enclosing a copy in an envelope addressed as shown below **AND**

   a. ☐ **depositing** the sealed envelope with the United States Postal Service on the date and at the place shown in item 4, with the postage fully prepaid.

   b. ☑ **placing** the envelope for collection and mailing on the date and at the place shown in item 4 following our ordinary business practices. I am readily familiar with this business's practice for collecting and processing correspondence for mailing. On the same day that correspondence is placed for collection and mailing, it is deposited in the ordinary course of business with the United States Postal Service, in a sealed envelope with postage fully prepaid.

4. a. Date mailed:      b. Place mailed (city, state): SACRAMENTO, CA

5. ☑ I served, with the *Notice of Petition to Administer Estate*, a copy of the petition or other document referred to in the notice.

I declare under penalty of perjury under the laws of the State of California that the foregoing is true and correct.

Date:

SALLIE JO SMITH-ALLEN, Paralegal
(TYPE OR PRINT NAME OF PERSON COMPLETING THIS FORM)     ▶     (SIGNATURE OF PERSON COMPLETING THIS FORM)

### NAME AND ADDRESS OF EACH PERSON TO WHOM NOTICE WAS MAILED

| # | Name of person served | Address (number, street, city, state, and zip code) |
|---|---|---|
| 1. | | |
| 2. | | |
| 3. | | |
| 4. | | |
| 5. | | |
| 6. | | |

☐ Continued on an attachment. *(You may use form DE-121(MA) to show additional persons served.)*

Assistive listening systems, computer-assisted real-time captioning, or sign language interpreter services are available upon request if at least 5 days notice is provided. Contact the clerk's office for *Request for Accommodations by Persons With Disabilities and Order* (form MC-410). (Civil Code section 54.8.)

**NOTICE OF PETITION TO ADMINISTER ESTATE**
(Probate—Decedents' Estates)

98     DUTIES AND LIABILITIES OF PERSONAL REPRESENTATIVE COMPLETED

---

**DE-147**

| ATTORNEY OR PARTY WITHOUT ATTORNEY *(Name, state bar number, and address):* <br> Nancy Noe-Nonsense, SBN ******** <br> Law Offices of Nancy Noe-Nonsens <br> 11111 Courthouse Plaza <br> Sacramento, CA 95826 <br> TELEPHONE NO.: 916-XXX-XXXX    FAX NO. *(Optional):* 916-XXX-XXXX <br> E-MAIL ADDRESS *(Optional):* nancy@noe-nonsenselaw.com <br> ATTORNEY FOR *(Name):* EDDY WADE SHORES, Petitioner | |
|---|---|
| SUPERIOR COURT OF CALIFORNIA, COUNTY OF SACRAMENTO <br> STREET ADDRESS: 3341 Power Inn Road <br> MAILING ADDRESS: 3341 Power Inn Road <br> CITY AND ZIP CODE: Sacramento, CA 95826 <br> BRANCH NAME: Probate Division | |
| ESTATE OF *(Name):* <br>     CORAL LEIGH SHORES, aks CORAL REDD SHORES    DECEDENT | |
| **DUTIES AND LIABILITIES OF PERSONAL REPRESENTATIVE** <br> **and Acknowledgment of Receipt** | CASE NUMBER: <br> 13PRXXXXX |

## DUTIES AND LIABILITIES OF PERSONAL REPRESENTATIVE

When the court appoints you as personal representative of an estate, you become an officer of the court and assume certain duties and obligations. An attorney is best qualified to advise you about these matters. You should understand the following:

### 1. MANAGING THE ESTATE'S ASSETS

**a. Prudent investments**
You must manage the estate assets with the care of a prudent person dealing with someone else's property. This means that you must be cautious and may not make any speculative investments.

**b. Keep estate assets separate**
You must keep the money and property in this estate separate from anyone else's, including your own. When you open a bank account for the estate, the account name must indicate that it is an estate account and not your personal account. Never deposit estate funds in your personal account or otherwise mix them with your or anyone else's property. Securities in the estate must also be held in a name that shows they are estate property and not your personal property.

**c. Interest-bearing accounts and other investments**
Except for checking accounts intended for ordinary administration expenses, estate accounts must earn interest. You may deposit estate funds in insured accounts in financial institutions, but you should consult with an attorney before making other kinds of investments.

**d. Other restrictions**
There are many other restrictions on your authority to deal with estate property. You should not spend any of the estate's money unless you have received permission from the court or have been advised to do so by an attorney. You may reimburse yourself for official court costs paid by you to the county clerk and for the premium on your bond. Without prior order of the court, you may not pay fees to yourself or to your attorney, if you have one. If you do not obtain the court's permission when it is required, you may be removed as personal representative or you may be required to reimburse the estate from your own personal funds, or both. You should consult with an attorney concerning the legal requirements affecting sales, leases, mortgages, and investments of estate property.

### 2. INVENTORY OF ESTATE PROPERTY

**a. Locate the estate's property**
You must attempt to locate and take possession of all the decedent's property to be administered in the estate.

**b. Determine the value of the property**
You must arrange to have a court-appointed referee determine the value of the property unless the appointment is waived by the court. You, rather than the referee, must determine the value of certain "cash items." An attorney can advise you about how to do this.

**c. File an inventory and appraisal**
Within four months after Letters are first issued to you as personal representative, you must file with the court an inventory and appraisal of all the assets in the estate.

Page 1 of 2

| Form Adopted for Mandatory Use <br> Judicial Council of California <br> DE-147 [Rev. January 1, 2002] | **DUTIES AND LIABILITIES OF PERSONAL REPRESENTATIVE** <br> **(Probate)** | Probate Code, § 8404 |

| ESTATE OF *(Name)*: CORAL LEIGH SHORES, aka CORAL REDD SHORES DECEDENT | CASE NUMBER: 13PRXXXXX |
|---|---|

**d. File a change of ownership**
At the time you file the inventory and appraisal, you must also file a change of ownership statement with the county recorder or assessor in each county where the decedent owned real property at the time of death, as provided in section 480 of the California Revenue and Taxation Code.

### 3. NOTICE TO CREDITORS

You must mail a notice of administration to each known creditor of the decedent within four months after your appointment as personal representative. If the decedent received Medi-Cal assistance, you must notify the State Director of Health Services within 90 days after appointment.

### 4. INSURANCE

You should determine that there is appropriate and adequate insurance covering the assets and risks of the estate. Maintain the insurance in force during the entire period of the administration.

### 5. RECORD KEEPING

**a. Keep accounts**
You must keep complete and accurate records of each financial transaction affecting the estate. You will have to prepare an account of all money and property you have received, what you have spent, and the date of each transaction. You must describe in detail what you have left after the payment of expenses.

**b. Court review**
Your account will be reviewed by the court. Save your receipts because the court may ask to review them. If you do not file your accounts as required, the court will order you to do so. You may be removed as personal representative if you fail to comply.

### 6. CONSULTING AN ATTORNEY

If you have an attorney, you should cooperate with the attorney at all times. You and your attorney are responsible for completing the estate administration as promptly as possible. **When in doubt, contact your attorney.**

> **NOTICE:**
> 1. This statement of duties and liabilities is a summary and is not a complete statement of the law. Your conduct as a personal representative is governed by the law itself and not by this summary.
> 2. If you fail to perform your duties or to meet the deadlines, the court may reduce your compensation, remove you from office, and impose other sanctions.

## ACKNOWLEDGMENT OF RECEIPT

1. I have petitioned the court to be appointed as a personal representative.

2. My address and telephone number are *(specify)*:
   22222 WONDERFUL PLACE, ELK GROVE, CA 95824
   916-XXX-XXXX

3. I acknowledge that I have received a copy of this statement of the duties and liabilities of the office of personal representative.

Date:

EDDY WADE SHORES
(TYPE OR PRINT NAME) ▸ (SIGNATURE OF PETITIONER)

Date:

(TYPE OR PRINT NAME) ▸ (SIGNATURE OF PETITIONER)

> **CONFIDENTIAL INFORMATION:** If required to do so by local court rule, you must provide your date of birth and driver's license number on supplemental Form DE-147S. (Prob. Code, § 8404(b)).

100 CONFIDENTIAL SUPPLEMENT TO DUTIES AND LIABILITIES COMPLETED

| | |
|---|---|
| **CONFIDENTIAL** | **DE-147S** |
| ESTATE OF *(Name)*: CORAL LEIGH SHORES, aka CORAL REDD SHORES DECEDENT | CASE NUMBER: 13PRXXXXXXX |

## CONFIDENTIAL STATEMENT OF BIRTH DATE AND DRIVER'S LICENSE NUMBER

**(Supplement to *Duties and Liabilities of Personal Representative* (Form DE-147))**

*(NOTE: This supplement is to be used if the court by local rule requires the personal representative to provide a birth date and driver's license number. Do **not** attach this supplement to Form DE-147.)*

This separate *Confidential Statement of Birth Date and Driver's License Number* contains confidential information relating to the personal representative in the case referenced above. This supplement shall be kept separate from the *Duties and Liabilities of Personal Representative* filed in this case and shall not be a public record.

INFORMATION ON THE PERSONAL REPRESENTATIVE:

1. Name: EDDY WADE SHORES

2. Date of birth: 9/1/1975

3. Driver's license number: AXXXXXXX          State: CA

> **TO COURT CLERK:**
> THIS STATEMENT IS **CONFIDENTIAL**. DO NOT FILE
> THIS CONFIDENTIAL STATEMENT IN A PUBLIC COURT FILE.

Form Adopted for Mandatory Use
Judicial Council of California
DE-147S [New January 1, 2001]

**CONFIDENTIAL SUPPLEMENT TO DUTIES AND LIABILITIES OF PERSONAL REPRESENTATIVE**
**(Probate)**

Probate Code, § 8404

# Chapter Five

# Probate Process Continued

## Probate — Part II

Once the Petition has been filed and the related Order for Probate and Letters Testamentary have been issued by the Court, the paralegal's role will become even more critical and involved.

The next steps, notifying creditors and valuation of the estate, will ultimately lead to the distribution of the decedent's estate. These basic procedures will be covered in this chapter. As with the previous chapter, you will continue to use the simple case scenario that was provided.

Each procedure will contain references to whether the same or some other procedure should be used, depending upon whether the decedent died testate or intestate and when the procedure differs. Additionally, the Instructor will provide you with information as to variations when a more complex estate is involved.

I recommend that you have a checklist to follow as the probate progresses. The firm may have already created one or customized one using information provided in a continuing education course or as part of an estate administration software package. If the firm does not have such a checklist, it would be an excellent opportunity for you to create one. The Continuing Education of the Bar (CEB) has an excellent and very complete checklist, which contains calendaring of actions and other requirements.

Upon receipt of the Order for Probate and the Letters Testamentary, it is very important that two things are determined: 1) The name of the Probate Referee appointed, if any, and, 2) the date the Letters were issued.

The appointment of the Probate Referee is discussed further in this chapter. The date the Letters are issued triggers the next important calendaring date. Four months from the first date of issuance of Letters, marks the end of the creditor's claim period. It is also the deadline for filing the Inventory and Appraisal with the court.

# Request for Special Notice

Probate Code § 1250 sets forth the requirements for seeking a Request for special notice.

Probate Code § 1250.

(a) At any time after the issuance of letters in a proceeding under this code for the administration of a decedent's estate, any person interested in the estate, whether as devisee, heir, creditor, beneficiary under a trust, or as otherwise interested, may in person or by attorney, file with the court clerk a written request for special notice.

(b) The request for special notice shall be so entitled and shall set forth the name of the person and the address to which notices shall be sent.

(c) Special notice may be requested of one or more of the following matters:

  (1) Petitions filed in the administration proceeding.
  (2) Inventories and appraisals of property in the estate, including any supplemental inventories and appraisals.
  (3) Objections to an appraisal.
  (4) Accounts of a Personal Representative.
  (5) Reports of status of administration.

(d) Special notice may be requested of any matter in subdivision (c) by describing it, or of all the matters in subdivision (c) by referring generally to "the matters described in subdivision (c) of Section 1250 of the Probate Code" or by using words of similar meaning.

(e) A copy of the request shall be personally delivered or mailed to the Personal Representative or to the attorney for the Personal Representative. If personally delivered, the request is effective when it is delivered. If mailed, the request is effective when it is received. (f) When the original of the request is filed with the court clerk, it shall be accompanied by a written admission or proof of service.

Any document, hearing or other event that requires notice must be served on the person(s) requesting special notice within the fifteen day period as prescribed in Probate Code §§ 1220–1221.

Upon receipt of a Request for Special Notice, the attorney will usually ask that the paralegal prominently note the requirement on the file and any other place the firm may require. The person or entity must receive copies of all documents requiring service as an interested party. This includes the Inventory and Appraisal, Notice of Proposed Action, any Hearing, the Preliminary and/or Final Petitions for Distribution, until such time as the person or entity withdraws or waives further notice. Often, if an entity requires special notice such as a creditor, the entity may withdraw the notice once the claim has been satisfied.

# Appointment of Probate Referee

Upon receipt of the Order for Probate, you will need to check at the bottom right of the form where the Clerk has filled in the name of the person appointed to be the Probate Referee. (Some Counties may require or have a separate form used for the appointment of Probate Referee.) The attorney and/or the paralegal will work closely with this person, particularly if there is a large estate to be valued. As indicated above, you will also want to calendar the four-month date as the deadline for completion of the Inventory and Appraisal.

Regardless of the size of the estate, unless the Court has determined it is not necessary, a Probate Referee will be appointed. For example, a Probate Referee might not be required if the decedent owned only **cash** assets such as bank, savings, CD, accounts. (**Accounts** are defined in Probate Code § 21.) Those types of accounts can have their value determined simply by looking at the bank statement or contacting the financial institution to obtain the actual value on the date the decedent died. If the decedent owned only his or her clothing and a few items of furniture and furnishings, it is unlikely that the Probate Referee will need to value those items. Real estate, stocks, bonds, mutual funds, vehicles and other assets **must** be valued by an independent, court-appointed referee. (See Probate Code §§ 8901–8902 for a list of those assets which must be appraised by the probate referee.)

In the event the decedent's only assets were cash, the Inventory is completed, reviewed and signed by the client, signed by the attorney, and submitted to the court, along with any supporting documentation.

Cash includes, but is not limited to the following:

Money, money orders, checks, wages and earnings, refunds, money market and certificate of deposit accounts, Social Security and/or Veteran's death benefits, dividends and interest, insurance proceeds

The *Daily Journal* publishes the *Probate Referees' Procedure Guide*. It is an excellent resource for the paralegal to use in learning which property simply requires an inventory by the Personal Representative, with the assistance of the attorney and/or paralegal, and which property must be appraised by the Probate Referee.

The Probate Referee is appointed by the California State Controller. The requirements and criteria for appointment can be found at Probate Code §§ 400–408. The duties and responsibilities of the Probate Referee can be found at Probate Code §§ 450–453.

The fees paid to the Probate Referee are provided in Probate Code § 8961-8963. Currently the rate is one-tenth of one percent (.1%) of the total value of the assets appraised, plus costs. The Referee cannot charge less than $75 or more than $10,000. The fees and reasonable costs charged by the Probate Referee will be included on the Inventory and Appraisal (Form DE-160) and must be approved by the court. The Personal Representative is responsible for paying the Probate Referee upon receipt of the Appraisal. In the event the Personal Representative is unable to pay these fees and costs out of the decedent's estate, the representative may request reimbursement of out of either the preliminary or the final distribution of the estate.

It is usually best to make sure that the client is aware of the fee and that it needs to be paid upon completion of the Inventory and Appraisal, so that it will be paid promptly upon receipt. Alternatively, if the Administrator is not in a position to pay the fee at that time, the attorney may agree to advance the fee and request reimbursement upon distribution if the estate. This will relieve potential ill will with any Probate Referees who deal regularly with the firm.

# Inventory and Appraisal

As stated above, much of the decedent's property will be valued by the Probate Referee. Therefore, it will be necessary to provide the Probate Referee with a list of all the decedent's assets and support documents that need to be valued. This will include legal property descriptions, statements (bank, annuity, retirement or other type of employee compensation, stock/bond accounts, etc.) and any other information that provides the Probate Referee with information that will help him or her best approximate the value as of the date of death.

The attorney may request that the court waive the appointment of the referee. This may be done by a separate petition that sets forth the facts that justify the waiver. In some instances, the attorney and Personal Representative may request that an independent appraiser be used to value the estate because it contains certain unique items. Alternatively, if the decedent did not own any real property or other items requiring a value to be determined, appointment of the referee is not necessary.

The Inventory and Appraisal form (DE-160) requires two Attachments. The first Attachment (No. One) should contain all property that is appraised by the Personal Representative and belonging to the decedent, as referenced above.

The Probate Referee will appraise all other property using Attachment No. Two. The property requiring valuation by the Probate Referee includes, but is not limited to:

Real property, promissory notes and loans (secured and unsecured), businesses, contracts, accounts receivable, cash dividends, stocks, bonds and other securities, coin collections, jewelry, vehicles, cash that is not issued by the U.S. government or which may have a value higher than its face value, insurance proceeds and annuities that are not payable in a lump sum.

The Inventory and Appraisal (Form DE-160) should be prepared, as should the Attachment Two, and both are sent to the Probate Referee. It is an excellent idea to have both the attorney and client review the list of property on Attachment Two to make sure that it is complete. The values will **not** be listed on the Attachment Two page. The Probate Referee will provide that information once he or she has valued each asset. You will note that the form indicates that a description of the property should be provided on the Attachment Two page. The **total value** on the face page (DE-160) should not be completed until the Referee has completed and returned it along with the Attachment Two page.

The Probate Referee will typically require additional information in order to complete the appraisal. For example, real property requires a "Legal Description." Some legal descriptions are quite lengthy and may include easements and other information, which may or may not be necessary for the probate referee. In addition, there is only a small space on the Judicial Council form in which to provide the information. If that is the case, it is simply better to put a short description on the form and provide the probate referee with a copy of the actual deed and/or title, and other descriptive documents. This is especially important if the property is owned with another individual and is not in joint tenancy. The manner in which the property is held is also relevant to the appraisal.

The same is true for investments and other types of non-cash accounts. For example, stocks that a person may have owned for a long period of time may be difficult to locate. The company may have merged with another company or may no longer exist. The more information that the Referee has, the more readily they will be able to locate the information they need. Providing a copy of the actual stock certificate will save time. The Referee will not have to try to track the information, find that more is needed, and then have to request it from your office. There is certain key information on stock certificates that allows brokerage firms and others involved in securities to be able to track the issuer of the certificate more easily.

Conversely, many elderly people will have original stock certificates (shares) that must be located and surrendered in order to liquidate them. As you become more involved in the probate process you will learn the nuances of stocks and bonds, and more importantly, you will learn who to contact for expert advice, clarification, and assistance in working with these types of assets.

Many individuals today do not even own stock certificates. The "shares" they own may simply be maintained in a brokerage account. The decedent could own shares of stock in a variety of companies and never have received actual certificates. The shares are maintained electronically in that person's account. If that is the case, although it is not necessary, it is certainly easier if the Referee knows where the brokerage account is maintained. Is it an E*Trade™ account or an account held with an investment company, where an account executive is involved? You will also need to learn the difference between a stocks that are privately held and those publicly traded, as they will be treated differently as well.

It is always a good idea to provide as much paper documentation as possible for the Probate Referee. Confidential information can certainly be redacted before sending it to the Referee. Copies of documents **should not** be attached to the Inventory and Appraisal when it is filed with the Court, as those documents, when filed, become public record. The documentation should be for the Probate Referee's reference only. It is always a good idea to request that the Probate Referee shred or return the documents upon completion of the Appraisal.

Always keep in mind that the Inventory and Appraisal is due four months from the **first** date the Letters were issued. In the event there are assets such as businesses, partnerships, promissory notes and contracts, the attorney may need to work closely with the Referee in order to provide additional documentation. Care must also be taken to assure that the valuation determined is consistent with what the Internal Revenue Service will find acceptable. For example, a limited partnership may require additional time, as it is not a publicly traded entity. The Referee will need information such as the initial investment of the decedent. He/she may also need to review tax returns, information about any commercial property owned by the partnership, etc.

The paralegal can be instrumental in keeping the costs of the probate referee to a minimum by providing as much documentation as possible regarding the assets the probate referee is valuing. While some costs are not flexible, other such as title searches, photocopies, and such can be avoided if the paralegal understands what documents the probate referee will need and provides them as early in the process as possible.

Upon completion of the appraisal of the property on Attachment Two, the Probate Referee will enter the fees and costs for the appraisal of the property. The Referee will sign the Declaration on the face page and return it to the law firm, usually with an invoice to be paid by the Personal Representative. The invoice should reflect the amount of the statutory commission and the expenses listed on the face page.

When preparing Attachment One, it may be necessary to contact the financial institution holding the account to request a determination of **date-of-death** value.

For example, if the client has provided a copy of the previous end of month statement, but the decedent died in the middle of the month, any actual interest accrued to that date may need to be determined by someone who has knowledge of how interest is paid on that account.

The attorney and the client can determine who will contact the financial institution and likely, it may be the paralegal that performs this work. In that event, you will need to provide a copy of the Letters that have been issued, usually within 60 days. This will provide the Institution with verification that the firm is representing the decedent's Personal Representative and that they can release the information to the law firm. Each financial institution operates differently and requires different documentation in order to release information. It may be necessary for the client (Personal Representative) to obtain the information even though the client would prefer that the law firm perform as much of the work as possible. Some firms will have created a form for the financial institution to complete and return.

After reviewing Attachment Two, the attorney and the client should sign the Inventory & Appraisal (DE-160) face page. Attachment One, which will have been completed by the attorney or paralegal, using the information provided by the client, would also be attached. The document is then ready to be filed with the Court. Again, only the general information about the inventoried property should be included in the form. Your office will certainly use the account statements in order to complete the forms. However, do not attach any of the personal statements or documents, as they are confidential. The Inventory & Appraisal should be served on any party requesting Special Notice.

See the sample completed Inventory, Appraisal, and Attachment (page one and two) forms at the end of this Chapter for reference and discussion with your Instructor.

## Creditor's Claims

Concurrently with the preparation of the Inventory & Appraisal, the law firm will want to notify all known creditors of the death of the decedent, the pending probate and the process by which the creditors will be paid, as applicable, through the pending probate.

Regardless of whether the decedent died testate or intestate, the procedure for paying creditor's claims is the same. Probate Code §§ 9000–9304 set forth the statutory procedure for the notifying the creditors.

The statutory notice requirement is as follows:

A) Creditors have four months from the first date the Letters are issued[1] to file their claim;

B) The Personal Representative must give notice to a creditor within thirty days after he or she first becomes aware of the creditor.

Notice is deemed to have been given as a result of the Notice to Administration that was published immediately after the Petition was filed. Although it is not required, a copy of the Notice of Administration to Creditors should be sent to any known creditor. A Creditor's Claim (Form DE-172) should also be sent to the creditor with the notice. (The Notice of Administration states, "You may obtain a Creditor's Claim Form from any superior court clerk." Most firms will provide the form as a courtesy.) These forms are also available to anyone through the Judicial Council website.

Probate Code § 9051 establishes the time period for acknowledgment and notice of creditors. As previously indicated, some creditors check the court clerk's filings weekly or daily to determine if any new probate filings have been made that involve potential

---

1. There can be additional "issue" dates for the Letters. Therefore, dates are based on the first date issued, rather than subsequent dates.

creditors. In that instance, it is likely the law firm will receive correspondence from the creditor directly. Alternatively, the Executor or a family member will be collecting the decedent's mail that will include bills and other debts of the decedent. The Personal Representative also has a fiduciary responsibility to determine any debts within the statutory period. However, the Personal Representative is **not required** to search for unknown creditors.

For example:

> The Personal Representative will likely know if the decedent had any treatment for illnesses before they passed away. If the decedent remained in his/her home during their final illness, there may have been hospice expenses, prescriptions, etc. Likely, there were also bills for utilities (gas, water, electricity, telephone, etc.). Even if the decedent had been in the hospital, there may still be medical bills not covered by insurance, and there will be insurance and possibly mortgage payments and utility bills, associated with the home, as well as bills for a skilled nursing facility or hospital, insurance and possibly mortgage payments.

There is, therefore, a reasonable expectation that the Personal Representative will contact creditors even though bills are not received. However, unless the Personal Representative receives credit card statements or knows that the decedent had purchased items using credit or had a loan or other debt, the Personal Representative is not required to contact every credit card company, in existence, to determine if the decedent owed them any money.

Probate Code § 9053 states that provided they acted in good faith, neither the Personal Representative nor the attorney are liable for the failure to give notice which results in a claim being unpaid. In the event a creditor is discovered after the Creditor's Claim period has expired and the estate has not been distributed, the claim may be paid. There are also mechanisms in place for the creditor to Petition the Court for payment.

The creditor is required to complete the Creditor's Claim form, sign the Affidavit, file a copy with the Court and serve a copy along with any supporting documents on the Personal Representative's attorney of record. Supporting documentation can be an itemized list on the backside of the form, a copy of a billing statement, or any other information supporting the charges incurred by the decedent. The Notice also advises the creditor to send the claim by certified mail to the court as well as to the Personal Representative. This is often **not** done.

It has been my experience, that depending upon the sophistication of the creditors, they may or may not file a copy of the Claim with the Court. Credit card companies, hospitals, and many others will most likely file the Creditor's Claim and provide reasonable documentation as to the debt. Smaller companies that have not previously been involved in the probate process may be unclear as to exactly what is expected in filing the Claim, although the information is clearly stated on the form. Despite a creditor's non-conformance to procedures, it is most likely the attorney will advise the administrator to pay the debt since the Personal Representative has a fiduciary responsibility to pay the decedent's debts in good faith.

This particular portion of the probate will most likely be completed by the paralegal. Most personal representatives will simply turn over all of the creditor information to the paralegal, who will review the information and send out the Notice to Administer with the claim forms. The paralegal will then review and process all of the Creditor's Claims received from the creditors. He or she will determine whether a claim was filed with the Court, if the supporting documentation has been provided and note any discrepancies or problems. It is also a good idea to keep a running list of all of the creditors and the various amounts due.

An Excel™ spreadsheet is an excellent tool for keeping track of the creditor's claims. It can be as detailed as your firm would like it to be. At minimum, the spreadsheet should include the name and address of the creditor, the amount due, if the creditor was sent Notice and a Claim form, when the claim form was returned, and the amount paid (at such time as payment was made). The firm may want you to keep more detailed information, and the format can be modified to meet those needs. The spreadsheet should also be able to calculate the total amount of the debts, so that the attorney and client have an idea of whether the estate will be able to pay the debts in full and to pay them in proper priority.

The Personal Representative may pay any known debt, in good faith, prior to the expiration of the creditor's claim period provided that the debt is "justly due," the amount is correct, and the estate is solvent (Probate Code §9154). It is to always best to wait until the Personal Representative has all known debt information to insure that the estate is solvent and will be able to pay the decedent's debts in full.

Once all of the creditor's claims are received, the Personal Representative may allow or reject the claim(s). The Personal Representative may allow only a portion of the claim. If a claim, or any portion, is allowed, the "allowance" is filed within thirty days. The Judge may then approve the claim. (You will want to check your local rules to determine how this action takes place in the County where your firm practices.)

A rejection of a claim must be sent to the creditor. It is advisable to send it by certified mail, with return receipt requested. The creditor whose claim is rejected has three months to file an action in the matter (Probate §9353(b)).

A creditor whose claim has been neglected or where the Personal Representative has refused to act, may file a Petition with the Court after the thirtieth day following the date the claim was due. This is equivalent to a notice of rejection (Probate Code §9256).

Creditors have recourse in the event they do not learn of the pending probate until just prior to the expiration of the four-month Creditor's Claim period. The creditor may file a Petition with the Court and request a hearing pursuant to Probate Code §1220. The Creditor must prove the following:

1) The creditor, or his attorney, had no knowledge of the administration of the estate more than fifteen days prior to the expiration of the time prescribed by Probate Code §9100, and that the creditor's petition was filed within thirty days of learning of the probate; or

2) The creditor, or his attorney, had no knowledge of the existence of a claim more than fifteen days prior to the expiration of the time prescribed by Probate Code §9100, and that the creditor's petition was filed within thirty days of learning of the probate (Probate Code §9103(a)).

There is a one-year statute of limitations on creditor's claims. The statute tolls from the date the notice is sent to the creditor either allowing or rejecting the claim.

## Payment of Creditor's Claims

As stated above, it is usually best if all of the creditor's claims are gathered and an accounting kept. Although personal representatives may pay any of the decedent's debts thirty days prior to the close of the Creditor Claim period, most attorneys will advise them **not** to do so for several reasons.

Note that in most cases, a creditor cannot assess penalties, late fees, and finance charges during the pendency of the probate. The exception would be a mortgage associated with real property. Credit card companies and other creditors can only charge interest on charges made up to the date of death.

First, although the estate may be solvent, there may not be adequate cash in the estate to pay the debts.

For example, the primary asset of the estate may be real property that must be sold. Thus, there are not adequate liquid assets to pay such debts upon the closing of the Creditor Claim period.

Second, there will be additional sums that will need to be factored into the debts of the estate before monies are dispersed.

For example, there may be reimbursements to the Executor for administration costs (publication fees, filing and certification fees, death certificates, etc.); the probate referee's fees and costs will have to be paid, statutory attorney and Executor fees will need to be paid, as well as any potential estate taxes, title transfer fees, etc. It is sometimes difficult to know the extent of all those fees and costs at this stage.

Third, although there are assets in the estate, they may not be large enough to pay all of the creditors in full once all of the other estate fees are paid. The probate code also establishes a priority scheme for payment of debts. Taxes are always the highest priority. Expenses of estate administration and funeral expenses are the next priority. The third priority is the statutory fees due to the executor and the attorney. Probate Code §§ 11420 and 11421 establish the priority in which debts are paid. Last to be paid are all other debts of the decedent.

It is possible that there will not be enough to pay the debts of the decedent. Alternatively, the debts may have to be paid *pro rata*.

For example, The decedent's home has been sold and all commissions, taxes, mortgage, and related escrow fees were paid. All of the decedent's assets are in a cash account and ready for distribution. The total amount in the account is $80,000.

The decedent's estate owes $200 in federal taxes. The executor/Personal Representative is entitled to a reimbursement of $800 for estate administration expenses. There is $5,000 in funeral expenses due. The executor and the attorney are entitled to $3,000 each for statutory fees. There are $30,000 in unpaid medical bills and last illness expenses.

The remaining amount after payment of all of these "priority" expenses is $38,000.

The decedent has the following debts: $10,000 credit card; $2,000 miscellaneous credit card debt (clothing, decorative items, furniture, etc.), $5,000 auto loan (which is due after the sale of the vehicle) and $1,000 in miscellaneous utilities and other expenses incurred while he/she was hospitalized.

The remaining amount to be divided among decedent's four children is $20,000 or $5,000 each.

The attorney and the Personal Representative have consulted and decided that the creditors will be contacted to determine if they would be willing to reduce the amount of their respective claims. The Personal Representative may contact the creditors or the attorney may have the paralegal perform this function.

It is likely that most of the creditors will be willing to negotiate, since they may feel that if they do not, the Personal Representative could simply reject the claim. In the event the claim is rejected, the creditor would have to Petition the Court, which would cost more than simply agreeing to reduce the claim. Many creditors will want to know if the other creditors are reducing their claims and to what extent, before they give their final approval.

Confirming letters or pleadings will need to be prepared for each creditor to sign indicating the agreed upon payment. The Judge will require that the documents be filed with the Court as part of the Preliminary or Final Distribution.

The Personal Representative may also simply determine the pro rata share for each creditor and allow the Claim for that amount.

Note that the above scenario does not include allowed expenses (Probate Code §§ 11420 and 11421) for family allowance and wage claims.

There are several cases that have established the expenses of administration and the priority of claims upon which the court relies. They are as follows:

*In re Jameson's Estate* (1949) 93 CalApp.2d 35; *In re Allen's Estate* (1941) 42 Cal.App.2d, 346; *In re Cornitius' Estate* (1957) 154 Cal.App.2d 422; *In Re Ockerlander's Estate* (1961) 195 Cal.App.2d 185; *Quigley v Nash* (1934) 1 Cal.2d 502.

As with a personal budget, it is best for the attorney and Personal Representative to determine the cash flow of the estate. All assets should be determined and totaled, as should the debts, the estate administration fees, taxes and burial fees, statutory fees of attorney and Personal Representative. The remaining **net** estate is what will be divided among the beneficiaries or heirs. There are several examples in Appendix 5A. It is always best to prepare at least a rough estimate for the attorney and client to review prior to paying any creditor's claim. This estimate will also be the foundation for the preparation of the Petition for Final Distribution.

# Payment of Medi-Cal Liens

As indicated in Chapter Four, the Department of Health Services (DHS) must be notified within 90 days of the date of death, if the executor, spouse, beneficiary, or any person who has knowledge of the decedent's affairs believes that the decedent or his/her spouse received any Medi-Cal benefits. Such benefits will usually be in the form of nursing home care. In some cases, the Department of Health Services may have already placed a lien on the decedent's home, particularly if benefits were provided to a previously deceased spouse.

If Medi-Cal benefits were paid to the decedent or to the spouse and the Department of Health Services has been properly notified, it is also good practice to send them a Notice of Petition to Administer along with a Creditor's Claim. Alternatively, once DHS has received notice of the decedent's death and determined that benefits were provided, DHS will most likely file a Creditor's Claim of its own.

The reimbursement of these benefits must be included in the distribution of the estate. In most cases, the Court will not allow the claim to be rejected, although it may be reduced provided the Department of Health Services and Personal Representative agree in writing.

# Sale of Property

It will be the Personal Representative's responsibility, with the assistance of the attorney (and most likely the paralegal), to sell any property in the decedent's estate to satisfy the estate's debts and distribute the proceeds to the beneficiaries or heirs.

Such property may include the decedent's home and any other real property they owned, vehicles, investments, jewelry, tools, furniture, furnishings, appliances, artwork and other items in the estate.

The property cannot be sold until it has been valued either by the probate referee as applicable, by the Personal Representative, depending upon the type of asset. It can take several weeks, if not months to liquidate certain types of assets. The person or company handling the transfer or escrow of each asset may have particular requirements to which the Personal Representative must adhere.

This is an area where the paralegal can excel, and serve as an excellent resource by keeping a file or database of information. This is also an area where extraordinary fees may be requested by the Personal Representative and/or the attorney.

There are several issues that will need to be considered regarding the sale of real property. First, make sure that the decedent's heirs wish to sell the property. Did the decedent leave a "family cabin" to all of his or her children so that they could continue to use it for family vacations? If so, the children may not want to sell the property.

Second, does one of the heirs want to keep the property and "buy out" the others? Perhaps the child lived in the house with the parent during the parent's illness and that child would like to continue to live in the house. Provided the child has the means to purchase the property or obtain a mortgage in order to give his or her siblings their distributive share and the siblings agree, the property may be distributed in that manner.

Third, property may be distributed in "cash or kind." This means that an heir may take a piece of real property while another heir takes other assets, such as bank accounts, vehicles, antiques or other property. This is acceptable as long as the property taken is equal in value. Also keep in mind that certain types of distribution may have tax consequences to the estate or the individual receiving the property. This should always be considered prior to making this type of distribution. However, the "estate" is the client and therefore the attorney will, in most circumstances, do what is best for the estate rather than an individual beneficiary. That said, the attorney should always be aware of the consequences so that the rationale behind any distribution averse to a beneficiary can be addressed as needed.

Keep in mind that regardless of how the heirs take the property, there must be enough cash in the estate to pay the decedent's debts (creditor's claims), the administration costs, taxes, attorneys fees, executor fees as well as any special distributions such as cash to charities or grandchildren which must be satisfied pursuant to the decedent's Will. Sometimes, it is impossible for an heir to take property in kind, as it must be liquidated in order to pay the debts and distribute the property equally. Alternatively, the heir must pay the estate so that the share can be distributed to the others.

Fourth, if the decedent died intestate, and depending upon whether the Personal Representative has been given full or limited authority under the Letters Testamentary, Notice may be required to be given regarding the intent to list the property for sale. The attorney will need to determine whether this notice is required prior to the listing of the property.

If Notice is required, a Notice of Proposed Action (Form DE-165) must be filed with the court and served on all required persons, as well as anyone who has requested Special Notice. After the Hearing and upon the Court issuing the Order of Proposed action, the property may be listed for sale. It may be necessary for the attorney to obtain a certified copy of this Order so that the real estate agent and the title company have verification that the Personal Representative is allowed to list the property for sale.

It is always advisable to contact a licensed real estate agent who is familiar with the probate process. Oftentimes, an heir will have a friend who is a real estate agent and to whom they want to "give the business." Possibly a family member is a real estate agent. This is rarely a good idea. A family member cannot benefit financially from the probate administration, and this must be stated when the Petition for Final Distribution is prepared. While it is always nice to have a friend of the family who is able to assist and, of course, benefit financially, there can be inherit problems.

The property should be listed with a licensed real estate agent only. The Court, especially if it is required to approve the listing for sale and the ultimate sale of the property, will require that the listing agent be licensed in the State of California. This means that they agent has been properly trained and meets certain ethical standards. The Court also limits the amount of commission that an agent can receive under a probate sale. An agent knowledgeable in the area of probate will know this from the outset and will not be disappointed when the Court does not approve the full commission.

Most important, an agent knowledgeable in probate will know that the process may take longer than most sales, especially if the Personal Representative does not have full authority. The sales contract and distribution must be approved by the Court before the property can be listed; the sale will also need to be confirmed. If the Personal Representative has full authority, then the contract and escrow closing statement will simply be provided with the Petition for Final Distribution. When the Personal Representative does not have full authority, there will be additional time needed to obtain a hearing date and Order for the sale. If the buyer of the property wants a short escrow time, the buyer may not be willing to wait for the probate process. An agent who is unfamiliar with the process will not make a quick sale and may disappoint buyers if a quick escrow is not possible. It should always be disclosed in the listing and related agreement with the agent or broker that the property is a probate sale. Many brokers use special forms created for probate sales.

## Overseeing the Estate During Administration

The Personal Representative is responsible for maintaining the estate during the pendency of the administration. This means that he or she is responsible for keeping the estate in good order.

It may be necessary for the Personal Representative to make sure that the lawn is mowed and the home otherwise maintained while it is vacant and on the market. In that event, there will be a long period of time between the commencement of the probate and the sale of the property, the property may need to be rented so that the estate will grow in value. The Personal Representative has a fiduciary responsibility to make sure that the estate's assets do not lose their value.

Your instructor will discuss this more in detail with you. However, the following are a couple of examples that will demonstrate the Personal Representative' fiduciary responsibility.

> The decedent owned a home. The attorney and Personal Representative have determined that due to various issues they anticipate a lengthy probate. The attorney ad-

vises the Personal Representative that the home should be rented during this time. This is so that the rent can be added to the value of the decedent's estate and so that it will be less likely that the vacant home will be vandalized or come to some disrepair during the pending probate. The rent can also cover the costs of mortgages, insurance, maintenance, etc. rather than depleting the estate.

The decedent has several bank accounts, mutual funds and stocks. The Personal Representative must open an interest bearing account for the estate. As each asset is liquidated, those funds must be added to the estate account so that the estate will increase in value during the pendency of the probate. It should be noted that the estate assets should be placed in a federally insured account. The Personal Representative has a fiduciary responsibility to place any funds in an account that is secure, is federally insured and is not subject to a potential loss in value.

## Petition for Final Distribution

At the conclusion of the four-month creditor's claim period, the Personal Representative may petition the Court for permission to distribute the decedent's estate. That is the soonest possible date distribution can be requested. However, it is unlikely that the estate will be ready to close at that point, especially if the decedent owned any property that must be sold or liquidated.

Consider the following scenario: It would be very ambitious to complete the probate within the four-month period. This includes paying the debts and filing the Petition for Final Distribution filed exactly four months after Letters are issued.

The decedent owned a house, stocks and bonds, a time-share in Hawaii, and a recreational vehicle. Decedent also had a mortgage on the house and the time-share and several credit card balances totaling approximately $5,000 as well as some expenses relating to last illness and burial.

The Executor is given full authority to administer the estate (there was a Will and the oldest child was named as Executor). Letters have issued and a probate referee has been appointed. The Notice has gone out to all known creditors, the Department of Health Services (re: Medi-Cal lien), and the Inventory and Appraisal was sent to the Probate Referee within one month of the Letters being issued. A licensed real estate agent has been retained and the property has been listed for sale within one month of the issuance of Letters.

Approximately, 45 days after the property is listed for sale, an offer is made. The requested escrow is for thirty days as the buyer has been pre-approved for the loan. However, the Inventory & Appraisal for the property has not been received from the Probate Referee. The property cannot be sold for less than the value listed on the Inventory & Appraisal without approval from the Court. The Probate Referee has until the conclusion of the "four month" period to submit the Appraisal. (It is generally not my experience that it usually takes the entire four months, but statutorily, the Probate Referee is allowed that amount of time.)

Time-share: The agency holding the paper on the time-share in Hawaii will have to be contacted. The contract for sale (again making sure that the agency understands this is a probate and therefore the Court limits the commission paid) will need to be prepared and sent for the Administrator's approval and signature and then sent to

Hawaii. It may take several months to sell a property such as a time-share. Once sold, the sales documents will need to be completed. Keep in mind that the loan will have to be paid off. As with the permanent home, the Probate Referee's Appraisal will also need to be completed to confirm that sales price is at least the fair market value. The time-share can certainly sell for more, unless the Court approves the sale for less.

Stocks and bonds must be liquidated. In the event the decedent owned "paper" stocks and bonds, a person who is approved by the Securities and Exchange Commission will need to begin the process of liquidating the stocks and bonds. In the event the stocks and bonds are held in "an account," the account executive or agent handling that account will need to be contacted about liquidating the account. The corporation and/or the brokerage firm will need to be contacted and a request for all documents required to liquidate the stocks and bonds will be requested. (This is a project that is often performed by the paralegal.)

There are numerous documents that will need to be completed, signed by the Personal Representative, and then processed through the brokerage account or through the authorized trust agent for the corporation named on the certificate(s). Post-September 11, there is additional documentation that must be completed, including declarations that the Personal Representative of the estate is a US Citizen. The Personal Representative's social security number, driver's license, home address and telephone, and other personal information will need to be provided to the trustee's agent or the brokerage firm, even though the personal representative is not going to "own" any of these assets him or herself. Additionally, documents signed by the Personal Representative must have a "Medallion Signature Guarantee." This is not the same as a notary and, in most cases, a notarial acknowledgment or jurat are not acceptable. The process of submitting the required documentation, liquidating the assets and placing the funds in the estate bank account may take, at minimum, two to three months. (The Medallion Signature Guarantee and this process will be discussed in greater detail in Chapter Seven.)

Has the Personal Representative contacted a CPA or other tax preparer regarding the preparation of the decedent's final personal taxes, a fiduciary tax return, and to confirm whether a Federal Estate Tax return needs to be filed? If applicable, have those taxes been paid by the Personal Representative?

If you prepare a time line for the above scenario, you can see that it may be almost impossible to achieve the goal of having the Petition for Final Distribution filed immediately upon the conclusion of the four-month period. Keep in mind that given the above scenario, the Administrator has not even received the escrow proceeds from the sale of the properties and may not have received the funds from the sale of the stocks and bonds. The recreational vehicle will also need to be sold.

All bequests of personal items should have been made by the Administrator during this time period. All personal items not made by specific bequest should be distributed to the decedent's beneficiaries as stated in the Will (e.g. in equal shares, at the discretion of the Executor, etc.) or, if intestate, equally to the decedent's heirs as provided in the Probate Code. Any property not taken by heirs should be liquidated or donated. Furniture, appliances, furnishings and other personal items may be sold at an estate sale, or if applicable, donated to charity. The proceeds of the sale will be placed in the estate account. The Personal Representative should keep a detailed inventory of the property distributed, sold and/or donated.

As indicated in earlier chapters, it is imperative that the Administrator and the heirs understand that, although the estate **can** be ready to close four months after the issuance of letters, it is highly unlikely. Additionally, the Petition for Final Distribution must be prepared only **after** all monies have been collected and deposited in the estate account, all creditors claims have been approved and paid or rejected, and the accounting prepared.

The Personal Representative will then need to schedule an appointment with the attorney, and/or his or her paralegal, to discuss the status of the estate and preparation of the Petition for Final Distribution. All receipts, inventory, bank statements, escrow accountings and pertinent documents should be brought to the appointment.

## Preparing the Petition for Final Distribution

Prior to scheduling the meeting with the client, the checklist should be reviewed to determine that all activities have been completed as prescribed by law and that the estate is ready to be closed.

Have all notices been sent to heirs, beneficiaries and those requiring special notice? If it was a creditor filing for special notice, has the creditor terminated the special notice requirement? If not, the creditor will also need to be noticed for the Final Distribution. If it is a creditor, the office might want to contact the person and request that the Withdrawal be filed prior to the filing of the Petition for Final Distribution. Otherwise, you will be required to serve notice of documents that are not necessarily pertinent. Although the Petition will be public information, it is always best to limit the distribution of information unless absolutely necessary to individuals who are not personally involved in the estate.

Check the Court file to make sure that all the Creditor's Claims (accepted or rejected) were filed with the Court. The Order approving any Proposed Action should have been filed by the court and an endorsed copy should be in the firm's file. Make sure that the Inventory and Appraisal has been received from the Probate Referee and that it has been completed, signed by the client and attorney and filed with the court. An endorsed copy should be in the file.

As indicated above, has all personal property been disbursed, sold, donated or otherwise disposed of? Has the real property been sold and the proceeds placed in an estate account or was the property distributed to an heir, the mortgage paid in full and the proceeds from the escrow placed in the estate account? Have stocks, bonds, mutual funds and other assets subject to disposition by the estate been liquidated and the funds placed in the estate account? Have the estate taxes been determined and/or paid? Have the decedent's personal taxes paid? Have all creditors been paid? Have the debts of last illness and funeral expenses been paid? Were there any liens from Medi-Cal? If so, have they been paid?

Has the Personal Representative gathered all the receipts of administration? Has he or she completed the inventory of all property and who received it? Does the Personal Representative have receipts for any other expenses he or she paid on behalf of the decedent? Has each beneficiary receiving property signed a receipt? Have any preliminary distributions of money been made? If so, have those persons signed a receipt?

Always check the local rules to determine if any other documents that were filed or that need to be filed have been completed and filed as necessary. Also, make sure that copies of same are in the file.

Once all of those items have been completed, as well as any other items that may be on your firm's checklist or are required due to the nature of the estate, it is time to meet with the client to begin preparing the Petition for Final Distribution. A sample Petition for Final Distribution is provided at Appendix 5B. (Note, this sample is for a simple distribution where all beneficiaries have waived a **full** and final accounting.)

One of the tricks I have learned is to have the template for the Petition started prior to the meeting with the client. This will help to identify any additional information that you will need for the client to bring or to assure that all tasks have been completed. You will note that some information in the template calls for dates and other information that might not be readily available in the file. For example, the Petition for Final Distribution will ask for the date the decedent died, the date the Petition for Probate was filed, the date Medi-Cal was notified, the date the Property Tax Certification was sent to the County Recorder. In most cases, that information will be in the client's file. In the event it is not and you know that the client has that information, you will want to ask that the client bring it to the meeting.

Having the Petition for Final Distribution started will also organize the information in the order it is going to be placed into the document. As you prepare the Petition, you can follow the sequence and easily find the information provided by the client and/or contained within the firm (client's) file.

During the meeting, the attorney will also want to discuss with the client the attorney's fees that will be disbursed upon approval of the Petition by the Court. The attorney will want to cover any extraordinary fees that will be due for such activities as selling real property and costs involved in liquidating other property (certified copies of documents, certified mail or overnight fees, etc.). The attorney will also want to confirm whether the Personal Representative is going to request or waive the statutorily allowed fees.

The attorney should also discuss the approximate amount of time it will take to prepare the Petition for Final Distribution and that a hearing on the matter will be set. Again, confirming with the client that in the event they need to appear at the hearing, there are no conflicting dates on the client's calendar for the anticipated hearing date.

The attorney and client should also discuss whether the heirs of the estate would be willing to waive the final accounting. In the event the heirs are willing to waive the accounting, a simplified version of the accounting may be filed with the Court. In situations where there have been contentious proceedings, it is feasible that not every heir will be willing to sign the Waiver. In that event, the Petition for Final Distribution will need to be much more detailed than the one provided in this book. You will need to check with the attorney to determine if the firm has a template for this type of Petition or, alternatively, have the attorney provide the additional information that is going to be needed for the Petition.

In the event the heirs are willing to sign the Waiver, the Petition for Final Distribution should be sent to them along with a Waiver form (a sample is included at Appendix 5C) and a self-addressed stamped envelope for the return of the Waiver. In most cases, the attorney will draft a letter to each heir explaining the procedure, include a summary of the account and proposed distribution, and request that the Waiver be returned within a certain number of days. This is so that the Petition can be filed once all Waivers have been received.

It is possible to file the Petition before having all the Waivers, but it is not advisable. It is always best to submit all supporting documentation with the documents as there is less for the court to question when the probate notes are prepared. The Court will then have all the information referenced in the Petition at their fingertips. Additionally, if one heir should forget to provide the Waiver in a timely manner, you will not be frantically trying to obtain it at the last moment and be faced with the prospect of having to continue the hearing date because the Court is missing vital information.

# Statutory Attorney and Executor Fees

Prior to finalizing the Petition for Final Distribution of an estate, the attorney and/or executor fees must be determined so that they can be paid. The probate code does allow for a preliminary distribution of some attorneys fees and/or administrative costs. We are not going to address those here. The Instructor may provide you with additional information or give you a research assignment regarding preliminary distributions. For the most part, a preliminary distribution will be made if the Court determines the estate will take more than a year to settle and provided there are funds in the estate for the proposed distribution.

The Probate Code sets forth statutory fees that an attorney is allowed to charge. Depending upon the complexity or the value of the case, some attorneys may agree to accept less, but they cannot accept more. Attorneys and Executors are, however, allowed to request extraordinary fees from the estate for work over and above the normal scope of the probate process.

## Statutory Attorney and Executor Fees

Probate Code § 10800–10810, state as follows:

Probate Code § 10800. (a) Subject to the provisions of this part, for ordinary services the Personal Representative shall receive compensation based on the value of the estate accounted for by the Personal Representative, as follows:

(1) Four percent on the first one hundred thousand dollars ($100,000).

(2) Three percent on the next one hundred thousand dollars ($100,000).

(3) Two percent on the next eight hundred thousand dollars ($800,000).

(4) One percent on the next nine million dollars ($9,000,000).

(5) One-half of one percent on the next fifteen million dollars ($15,000,000).

(6) For all amounts above twenty-five million dollars ($25,000,000),

   (a) reasonable amount to be determined by the court.

   (b) For the purposes of this section, the value of the estate accounted for by the Personal Representative is the total amount of the appraisal value of property in the inventory, plus gains over the appraisal value on sales, plus receipts, less losses from the appraisal value on sales, without reference to encumbrances or other obligations on estate property.

Probate Code § 10803. An agreement between the Personal Representative and an heir or devisee for higher compensation than that provided by this part is void.

Probate Code § 10810. (a) Subject to the provisions of this part, for ordinary services the attorney for the Personal Representative shall receive compensation based on the value of the estate accounted for by the Personal Representative, as follows:

(1) Four percent on the first one hundred thousand dollars ($100,000).

(2) Three percent on the next one hundred thousand dollars ($100,000).

(3) Two percent on the next eight hundred thousand dollars ($800,000).

(4) One percent on the next nine million dollars ($9,000,000).

(5) One-half of 1 percent on the next fifteen million dollars ($15,000,000)

(6) For all amounts above twenty-five million dollars ($25,000,000),

   (a) a reasonable amount to be determined by the court.

   (b) For the purposes of this section, the value of the estate accounted for by the Personal Representative is the total amount of the appraisal of property in the inventory, plus gains over the appraisal value on sales, plus receipts, less losses from the appraisal value on sales, without reference to encumbrances or other obligations on estate property.

The attorney and executor fees are based on the gross value of the estate. This means that even if the decedent had a mortgage against their real property and/or a lot of credit card debt, the fees will still be based on the gross value, and not the net value—based on the property less liens, encumbrances and other debts. The attorney and the executor are entitled to the same fees.

The following is an example of how the fees are calculated if the gross value of the estate is $524,000, if the decedent had two children who would each receive one-half.

When calculating the net estate for the final distribution, the fees need to be doubled, provided the Executor has not waived his or her fees. The following are two examples:

The net estate to be distributed to the heir (if the Executor took his or her fee), if there are two children, would be:

| $100,000 x 4% | 4,000 |
| $100,000 x 3% | 3,000 |
| $324,000 x 2% | 6,480 |
| | 13,480 x 2 (Executor & Attorney) $26,960 |
| $524,000 | $489,040 |
| >26,960 | >98,040 (liens, creditors claims, etc.) |
| $498,040 | 400,000 |

$200,000 each ($400,000 ÷ 2 = $200,000)

The net estate to be distributed to the heirs, (if the Executor does not take his or her fee), if there are two, would be:

| $100,000 x 4% | 4,000 |
| $100,000 x 3% | 3,000 |
| $324,000 x 2% | 6,480 |
| | 13,480 |
| $524,000 | $510,520 |
| >13,480 | >98,040 (liens, creditors claims, etc.) |
| $510,520 | 412,480 |

$206,240 each ($412,480 ÷ 2 = $206,240)

Remember also, that the Executor can certainly waive fees. This means that the Executor may appear to receive less (using the above scenario of two children) but their sibling will get more than he/she would have if the Executor had taken the fees. The children will each receive equal shares if the Executor waives his or her fees. However, the Executor's fees are taxable (the inherited estate is, in most simple cases not) and that may be the most significant reason why many Executors waive their fee. The amount the Executor receives (if no taxes are paid) may actually be almost the same. This is certainly a judgment call on the part of the Executor and there is no right or wrong answer. The Executor will want to discusss these options with the attorney and his or her tax preparer.

## Extraordinary Fees

The following are the probate codes that relate to **Extraordinary Fees** on the part of both the Personal Representative and the attorney, respectively:

Probate Code § 10801.

(a) Subject to the provisions of this part, in addition to the compensation provided by Section 10800, the court may allow additional compensation for extraordinary services by the Personal Representative in an amount the court determines is just and reasonable.

(b) The Personal Representative may also employ or retain tax counsel, tax auditors, accountants, or other tax experts for the performance of any action which such persons, respectively, may lawfully perform in the computation, reporting, or making of tax returns, or in negotiations or litigation which may be necessary for the final determination and payment of taxes, and pay from the funds of the estate for such services.

The California Rules of Court—Rule 7.703(e) specifically—also provide for the recovery of paralegal fees for extraordinary services. Please review these rules to determine the current fee structure and rules governing these fees.

For example, California Courts use the paralegal hourly rate for determining the amount to be paid to the attorney for extraordinary fees. Thus, an attorney whose hourly billing rate is $400 per hour may only receive $130–$150 per hour. As a result, since most of the work involving extraordinary fees, such as working with real estate agents, financial institutions, and others to liquidate and transfer property, is more task oriented than a matter of legal interpretation. The Court has, therefore, determined that this work is highly suitable for the paralegal to participate in this area of the practice.

## Special Considerations When Preparing the Petition for Final Distribution

Prior to preparing the Petition for Final Distribution there are a few things of which you should know.

First, the Final Distribution is very much like a balance sheet. Just like a personal account, the value of the estate at the decedent's death should balance at the time the property is going to be disbursed with what has been sold, received and accrued by the estate during the administration against what has been paid for creditor's claims, administration expenses, attorneys and executor fees, preliminary distributions, taxes and any other estate expenses.

The estate accounting should include any gains or losses on property. If the home was sold for more than the value placed on it by the Probate Referee, then that is considered a gain. Interest on accounts and investments after the date of death are income as is rent that was received if the home was rented. Likewise, if the property experienced a loss, that information also must be included. Did stock or bond values decline during the period of time from the decedent's death until they could be liquidated? Were there any expenses paid by the estate for losses such as insurance claims? Insurance claims could include property that was stolen from the decedent's residence during the last illness or after death while the property was vacant. It might be a wrongful death action against the decedent. **All** of these assets and debts must appear in the accounting and it must balance. The end result will be the **net** value of the estate to be dispersed to the decedent's heirs.

## Hearing on Petition for Final Distribution

When the Petition for Final Distribution is completed, the attorney will carefully review the document to assure that it is accurate and complete. Once the attorney (and any other person in the firm required to do so) has reviewed the document, the client should be provided with a copy for review. The attorney may want you to send a copy to the client for review, or he or she may prefer that the client be scheduled for an appointment to review it in the office with the attorney and/or paralegal. Once the client has reviewed and signed the document, it will need to be filed with the court. The client's signature must be verified and the appropriate verification should be attached or included in the pleading.

A Notice of Hearing will also need to be submitted to the Court in order to obtain a hearing date. As previously indicated, all supporting documents such as Waivers from the heirs, escrow documents, and any other local court-mandated documents should be submitted with the Petition for Final Distribution. The date should be set according to dates available on the attorney's calendar as well as when the client will also be available, if necessary.

Upon the filing of the Petition for Final Distribution and a hearing date being obtained, the Petition and Notice should be mailed to all heirs, as required, as well as any persons who still require Special Notice. The date should be calendared on all appropriate firm calendars as should the date when the anticipated file notes will be available.

At this time, the paralegal should also prepare receipts for each heir who will receive his or her distributive share once the Order has been obtained from the Court. A sample Receipt is provided at Appendix 5D. These same receipts may be modified for use when making a Preliminary Distribution.

## Order for Final Distribution

An Order for Final Distribution will need to be prepared which mirrors the Petition. A sample is provided for you at Appendix 5E. Check the Local Rules to determine if the Order must be submitted prior to the Hearing. If the Order does not need to be submitted early, the attorney should take the Order with him or her to the hearing, if attendance is required. If the file notes indicate that all items are in order and that the matter is recommended for approval, the Order may be submitted as per local rules. If the attorney will attend the hearing, he or she should have several copies of the order, a self-addressed stamped envelope for the return of the filed documents and a check to obtain a certified copy. The attorney will determine if more than one certified copy is needed in the event there is any property that must be transferred or accounts created as a result of the Order. For example, if there are minor children for who trust or custodial (UTMA) accounts must be created, the bank may require a certified copy of the Order to open such accounts.

# Distribution to Heirs/Beneficiaries

Upon receipt of the Order, the client should be notified that he or she could make any disbursements as set forth in the Order. The Personal Representative will pay all debts that remain unpaid, will pay the attorney's fees, and repay him or herself, if necessary, as provided in the Order. The Personal Representative will also pay any specific bequests, not previously made, (e.g. $5,000 to the SPCA or to a specific person) and will finally make distributions to the heirs or as otherwise set forth in the decedent's Will.

The Personal Representative will need to calculate any additional sums that the heir(s) will receive due to any interest or income earned during the period of time from when the Petition was prepared until the final distribution. You will note that both the Petition and the Order indicate that this gain will be disbursed based on each person's distributive share.

The following is an example of how the property would be disbursed:

Decedent had two adult children. The Will stated that each child should receive one-half of the decedent's estate. Upon liquidation of the estate and after payment of all fees and costs associated with the estate, there is $100,160 remaining in the estate account. Therefore, each child will receive $50,080 upon distribution. However, there has been a gain of $80 in interest since the date the Petition for Final Distribution was prepared. Thus, the Personal Representative will actually write a check to each child in the amount of $50,120, or $40 more for each child.

The Personal Representative will send a check for the appropriate amount to each person and/or entity along with a receipt. It is always best to include a self-addressed, stamped envelope so that the person can immediately sign the receipt and return it. In the event there are custodial (UTMA) accounts required, the trustee or custodian of those accounts will need to provide verification that the accounts were created, so the funds can be deposited and confirmation provided.

It is most likely that this process will be handled by the law firm. The client will write the checks and provide them to the attorney. The attorney or paralegal will then send the checks along with the receipts, instructions, and other documents to the applicable person(s) or entity(ies).

Once the checks have been written, the Personal Representative will close the estate account. The account should be closed as soon as the Personal Representative knows that the checks have been cleared. In fact, he or she should let the beneficiaries know that the checks should be cashed or deposited immediately upon receipt. The account will have been an interest-bearing account, but the bank may begin charging maintenance fees from the account. In order to avoid this occurrence, any checks drawn should be immediately acted upon by the recipient so that the Personal Representative may close the account without incurring additional charges to the estate.

If a bond was issued, the bonding company should be contacted and the bond discharged.

All receipts and/or other documentation required by the Court will then be filed with the Court. At the same time, a Discharge of Representative should be filed with the Court. This document is usually a local form. The purpose of this form is to notify the Court that all distributions have been made, the estate is closed, and that the Personal Representative has fulfilled all of his or her responsibilities.

Transfers on any property that have title can be made using the procedures to be discussed in Chapter Six.

## Preparation of Judicial Council Forms

Order for Probate (DE-140)
Letters (DE-150)
Inventory & Appraisal and Attachments (DE-160 and DE-161)
Notice of Administration to Creditors (DE-157) and Creditor's Claims (DE-172)
Notice of Petition to Administer Estate (DE-121)

## Key Terms

- Petition for Final Distribution
- Petition for Preliminary Distribution
- Notice of Proposed Action
- Allowance or Rejection of Creditor's Claims
- Request for Special Notice
- Executor Fees
- Attorney Fees
- Extraordinary Fees
- Discharge of Representative
- Custodial Account
- Uniform Transfer to Minors Act

**DE-140**

| ATTORNEY OR PARTY WITHOUT ATTORNEY *(Name, state bar number, and address)*: | TELEPHONE AND FAX NOS. | |
|---|---|---|
| ATTORNEY FOR *(Name)*: | | |

**SUPERIOR COURT OF CALIFORNIA, COUNTY OF**
STREET ADDRESS:
MAILING ADDRESS:
CITY AND ZIP CODE:
BRANCH NAME:

ESTATE OF *(Name)*:

DECEDENT

**ORDER FOR PROBATE**

**ORDER APPOINTING**
☐ Executor
☐ Administrator with Will Annexed
☐ Administrator   ☐ Special Administrator
☐ Order Authorizing Independent Administration of Estate
☐ with full authority   ☐ with limited authority

CASE NUMBER:

**WARNING: THIS APPOINTMENT IS NOT EFFECTIVE UNTIL LETTERS HAVE ISSUED.**

1. Date of hearing:        Time:        Dept./Room:        Judge:

**THE COURT FINDS**
2. a. All notices required by law have been given.
   b. Decedent died on *(date)*:
      (1) ☐ a resident of the California county named above.
      (2) ☐ a nonresident of California and left an estate in the county named above.
   c. Decedent died
      (1) ☐ intestate
      (2) ☐ testate
      and decedent's will dated:        and each codicil dated:
      was admitted to probate by Minute Order on *(date)*:

**THE COURT ORDERS**
3. *(Name)*:
   is appointed **personal representative**:
   a. ☐ executor of the decedent's will             d. ☐ special administrator
   b. ☐ administrator with will annexed                (1) ☐ with general powers
   c. ☐ administrator                                  (2) ☐ with special powers as specified in Attachment 3d(2)
                                                       (3) ☐ without notice of hearing
                                                       (4) ☐ letters will expire on *(date)*:
   and letters shall issue on qualification.
4. a. ☐ **Full authority** is granted to administer the estate under the Independent Administration of Estates Act.
   b. ☐ **Limited authority** is granted to administer the estate under the Independent Administration of Estates Act (there is no authority, without court supervision, to (1) sell or exchange real property or (2) grant an option to purchase real property or (3) borrow money with the loan secured by an encumbrance upon real property).
5. a. ☐ Bond is not required.
   b. ☐ Bond is fixed at: $        to be furnished by an authorized surety company or as otherwise provided by law.
   c. ☐ Deposits of: $        are ordered to be placed in a blocked account at *(specify institution and location)*:
      and receipts shall be filed. No withdrawals shall be made without a court order.   ☐ Additional orders in Attachment 5c.
   d. ☐ The personal representative is not authorized to take possession of money or any other property without a specific court order.
6. ☐ *(Name)*:        is appointed probate referee.

Date:

JUDGE OF THE SUPERIOR COURT
7. Number of pages attached: ____        ☐ SIGNATURE FOLLOWS LAST ATTACHMENT

Form Approved by the
Judicial Council of California
DE-140 [Rev. January 1, 1998]

**ORDER FOR PROBATE**

Probate Code, §§ 8006, 8400

**DE-150**

| ATTORNEY OR PARTY WITHOUT ATTORNEY *(Name, state bar number, and address)*: | TELEPHONE AND FAX NOS.: | |
|---|---|---|
| ATTORNEY FOR *(Name)*: | | |

**SUPERIOR COURT OF CALIFORNIA, COUNTY OF**
STREET ADDRESS:
MAILING ADDRESS:
CITY AND ZIP CODE:
BRANCH NAME:

**ESTATE OF** *(Name)*:

DECEDENT

**LETTERS**
☐ **TESTAMENTARY** ☐ **OF ADMINISTRATION**
☐ **OF ADMINISTRATION WITH WILL ANNEXED** ☐ **SPECIAL ADMINISTRATION**

CASE NUMBER:

### LETTERS

1. ☐ The last will of the decedent named above having been proved, the court appoints *(name)*:
   a. ☐ executor.
   b. ☐ administrator with will annexed.

2. ☐ The court appoints *(name)*:
   a. ☐ administrator of the decedent's estate.
   b. ☐ special administrator of decedent's estate
      (1) ☐ with the special powers specified in the *Order for Probate.*
      (2) ☐ with the powers of a general administrator.
      (3) ☐ letters will expire on *(date)*:

3. ☐ The personal representative is authorized to administer the estate under the Independent Administration of Estates Act ☐ with full authority
   ☐ with limited authority (no authority, without court supervision, to (1) sell or exchange real property or (2) grant an option to purchase real property or (3) borrow money with the loan secured by an encumbrance upon real property).

4. ☐ The personal representative is not authorized to take possession of money or any other property without a specific court order.

WITNESS, clerk of the court, with seal of the court affixed.

(SEAL) Date:

Clerk, by
_____ (DEPUTY)

### AFFIRMATION

1. ☐ **PUBLIC ADMINISTRATOR:** No affirmation required (Prob. Code, § 7621(c)).

2. ☐ **INDIVIDUAL: I solemnly affirm** that I will perform the duties of personal representative according to law.

3. ☐ **INSTITUTIONAL FIDUCIARY** *(name)*:

   **I solemnly affirm** that the institution will perform the duties of personal representative according to law. I make this affirmation for myself as an individual and on behalf of the institution as an officer.
   *(Name and title)*:

4. Executed on *(date)*:
   at *(place)*:                            , California.

▶ _____
(SIGNATURE)

### CERTIFICATION

I certify that this document is a correct copy of the original on file in my office and the letters issued the personal representative appointed above have not been revoked, annulled, or set aside, and are still in full force and effect.

(SEAL) Date:

Clerk, by
_____ (DEPUTY)

Form Approved by the
Judicial Council of California
DE-150 [Rev. January 1, 1998]

**LETTERS**

Probate Code, §§ 1001, 8403, 8405, 8544, 8545;
Code of Civil Procedure, § 2015.6

# INVENTORY AND APPRAISAL

**DE-160/GC-040**

ATTORNEY OR PARTY WITHOUT ATTORNEY *(Name, state bar number, and address):*

TELEPHONE NO.:     FAX NO. *(Optional):*
E-MAIL ADDRESS *(Optional):*
ATTORNEY FOR *(Name):*

**SUPERIOR COURT OF CALIFORNIA, COUNTY OF**
  STREET ADDRESS:
  MAILING ADDRESS:
  CITY AND ZIP CODE:
  BRANCH NAME:

ESTATE OF *(Name):*

☐ DECEDENT    ☐ CONSERVATEE    ☐ MINOR

**INVENTORY AND APPRAISAL**

☐ Partial No.:      ☐ Corrected
☐ Final      ☐ Reappraisal for Sale
☐ Supplemental      ☐ Property Tax Certificate

CASE NUMBER:

Date of Death of Decedent or of Appointment of Guardian or Conservator:

## APPRAISALS

1. Total appraisal by representative, guardian, or conservator (Attachment 1): $
2. Total appraisal by referee (Attachment 2): $
                                                     TOTAL: $

## DECLARATION OF REPRESENTATIVE, GUARDIAN, CONSERVATOR, OR SMALL ESTATE CLAIMANT

3. Attachments 1 and 2 together with all prior inventories filed contain a true statement of ☐ all ☐ a portion of the estate that has come to my knowledge or possession, including particularly all money and all just claims the estate has against me. I have truly, honestly, and impartially appraised to the best of my ability each item set forth in Attachment 1.
4. ☐ No probate referee is required ☐ by order of the court dated *(specify):*
5. **Property tax certificate.** I certify that the requirements of Revenue and Taxation Code section 480
   a. ☐ are not applicable because the decedent owned no real property in California at the time of death.
   b. ☐ have been satisfied by the filing of a change of ownership statement with the county recorder or assessor of each county in California in which the decedent owned property at the time of death.

I declare under penalty of perjury under the laws of the State of California that the foregoing is true and correct.
Date:

_____     ▶     _____
(TYPE OR PRINT NAME; INCLUDE TITLE IF CORPORATE OFFICER)            (SIGNATURE)

## STATEMENT ABOUT THE BOND
*(Complete in all cases. Must be signed by attorney for fiduciary, or by fiduciary without an attorney.)*

6. ☐ Bond is waived, or the sole fiduciary is a corporate fiduciary or an exempt government agency.
7. ☐ Bond filed in the amount of: $      ☐ Sufficient    ☐ Insufficient
8. ☐ Receipts for: $      have been filed with the court for deposits in a blocked account at *(specify institution and location):*

Date:

_____     ▶     _____
(TYPE OR PRINT NAME)            (SIGNATURE OF ATTORNEY OR PARTY WITHOUT ATTORNEY)

Form Adopted for Mandatory Use
Judicial Council of California
DE-160/GC-040 [Rev. January 1, 2003]

**INVENTORY AND APPRAISAL**

Probate Code, §§ 2610–2616, 8800–8980;
Cal. Rules of Court, rule 7.501

American LegalNet, Inc.
www.USCourtForms.com

| ESTATE OF (Name): | CASE NUMBER: |
|---|---|
| ☐ DECEDENT ☐ CONSERVATEE ☐ MINOR | |

## DECLARATION OF PROBATE REFEREE

9. I have truly, honestly, and impartially appraised to the best of my ability each item set forth in Attachment 2.
10. A true account of my commission and expenses actually and necessarily incurred pursuant to my appointment is:

    Statutory commission:   $
    Expenses (specify):     $
            TOTAL: $

I declare under penalty of perjury under the laws of the State of California that the foregoing is true and correct.

Date:

_____  ▶  _____
(TYPE OR PRINT NAME)                       (SIGNATURE OF REFEREE)

## INSTRUCTIONS

(See Probate Code sections 2610–2616, 8801, 8804, 8852, 8905, 8960, 8961, and 8963 for additional instructions.)

1. See Probate Code section 8850 for items to be included in the inventory.

2. If the minor or conservatee is or has been during the guardianship or conservatorship confined in a state hospital under the jurisdiction of the State Department of Mental Health or the State Department of Developmental Services, mail a copy to the director of the appropriate department in Sacramento. (Prob. Code, § 2611.)

3. The representative, guardian, conservator, or small estate claimant shall list on Attachment 1 and appraise as of the date of death of the decedent or the date of appointment of the guardian or conservator, at fair market value, moneys, currency, cash items, bank accounts and amounts on deposit with each financial institution (as defined in Probate Code section 40), and the proceeds of life and accident insurance policies and retirement plans payable upon death in lump sum amounts to the estate, except items whose fair market value is, in the opinion of the representative, an amount different from the ostensible value or specified amount.

4. The representative, guardian, conservator, or small estate claimant shall list in Attachment 2 all other assets of the estate which shall be appraised by the referee.

5. If joint tenancy and other assets are listed for appraisal purposes only and not as part of the probate estate, they must be separately listed on additional attachments and their value excluded from the total valuation of Attachments 1 and 2.

6. Each attachment should conform to the format approved by the Judicial Council. (See *Inventory and Appraisal Attachment* (form DE-161/GC-041) and Cal. Rules of Court, rule 201.)

# INVENTORY AND APPRAISAL ATTACHMENT

**DE-161, GC-041**

| ESTATE OF *(Name)*: | CASE NUMBER: |
|---|---|

**INVENTORY AND APPRAISAL
ATTACHMENT NO.:** _____

*(In decedents' estates, attachments must conform to Probate Code section 8850(c) regarding community and separate property.)*

Page: _____ of: _____ total pages.
*(Add pages as required.)*

| Item No. | Description | Appraised value |
|---|---|---|
| 1. | | $ |

Form Approved by the Judicial Council of California
DE-161, GC-041 [Rev. January 1, 1998]

**INVENTORY AND APPRAISAL ATTACHMENT**

Probate Code, §§ 301, 2610-2613, 8800-8920

# NOTICE OF ADMINISTRATION TO CREDITORS

**DE-157**

**NOTICE OF ADMINISTRATION OF THE ESTATE OF**

_____
(NAME)

**DECEDENT**

**NOTICE TO CREDITORS**

1. (Name):
   (Address):

   (Telephone):
   is the **personal representative** of the **ESTATE OF** *(name):* _____, who is deceased.

2. The personal representative HAS BEGUN ADMINISTRATION of the decedent's estate in the
   a. **SUPERIOR COURT OF CALIFORNIA, COUNTY OF** *(specify):*
      STREET ADDRESS:
      MAILING ADDRESS:
      CITY AND ZIP CODE:
      BRANCH NAME:
   b. Case number *(specify):*

3. You must FILE YOUR CLAIM with the court clerk (address in item 2a) AND mail or deliver a copy to the personal representative before the **last to occur** of the following dates:
   a. **four months** after *(date):* _____, the date letters (authority to act for the estate) were first issued to a general personal representative, as defined in subdivision (b) of section 58 of the California Probate Code, **OR**
   b. **60 days** after *(date):* _____, the date this notice was mailed or personally delivered to you.

4. LATE CLAIMS: If you do not file your claim within the time required by law, you must file a petition with the court for permission to file a late claim as provided in Probate Code section 9103. Not all claims are eligible for additional time to file. See section 9103(a).

**EFFECT OF OTHER LAWS:** Other California statutes and legal authority may affect your rights as a creditor. You may want to consult with an attorney knowledgeable in California law.

**WHERE TO GET A CREDITOR'S CLAIM FORM:** If a *Creditor's Claim* (form DE-172) did not accompany this notice, you may obtain a copy of the form from any superior court clerk or from the person who sent you this notice. You may also access a fillable version of the form on the Internet at www.courts.ca.gov/forms under the form group Probate—Decedents' Estates. A letter to the court stating your claim is *not* sufficient.

**FAILURE TO FILE A CLAIM:** Failure to file a claim with the court and serve a copy of the claim on the personal representative will in most instances invalidate your claim.

**IF YOU MAIL YOUR CLAIM:** If you use the mail to file your claim with the court, for your protection you should send your claim by certified mail, with return receipt requested. If you use the mail to serve a copy of your claim on the personal representative, you should also use certified mail.

**Note:** To assist the creditor and the court, please send a blank copy of the *Creditor's Claim* form with this notice.

(Proof of Service by Mail on reverse)

Form Adopted for Mandatory Use
Judicial Council of California
DE-157 [Rev. January 1, 2013]

**NOTICE OF ADMINISTRATION TO CREDITORS**
**(Probate—Decedents' Estates)**

Probate Code, §§ 9050, 9052
www.courts.ca.gov

# NOTICE OF ADMINISTRATION TO CREDITORS

**DE-157**

| ESTATE OF (Name): | CASE NUMBER: |
|---|---|
| DECEDENT | |

**[Optional]**
**PROOF OF SERVICE BY MAIL**

1. I am over the age of 18 and not a party to this cause. I am a resident of or employed in the county where the mailing occurred.
2. My residence or business address is *(specify)*:

3. I served the foregoing *Notice of Administration to Creditors* ☐ and a blank *Creditor's Claim* form* on each person named below by enclosing a copy in an envelope addressed as shown below AND
    a. ☐ **depositing** the sealed envelope with the United States Postal Service with the postage fully prepaid.
    b. ☐ **placing** the envelope for collection and mailing on the date and at the place shown in item 4 following our ordinary business practices. I am readily familiar with the business's practice for collecting and processing correspondence for mailing. On the same day that correspondence is placed for collection and mailing, it is deposited in the ordinary course of business with the United States Postal Service in a sealed envelope with postage fully prepaid.

4. a. Date of deposit:            b. Place of deposit *(city and state)*:

I declare under penalty of perjury under the laws of the State of California that the foregoing is true and correct.

Date:

_____           ▶  _____
(TYPE OR PRINT NAME)                              (SIGNATURE OF DECLARANT)

**NAME AND ADDRESS OF EACH PERSON TO WHOM NOTICE WAS MAILED**

| | Name of person | Address *(number, street, city, state, and zip code)* |
|---|---|---|
| 1. | | |
| 2. | | |
| 3. | | |
| 4. | | |
| 5. | | |
| 6. | | |
| 7. | | |
| 8. | | |

☐ List of names and addresses continued in attachment. *(You may use form POS-30(P) to show additional persons to whom a copy of this notice was mailed. Do not use page 2 of this form or form POS-030(P) to show that you personally delivered a copy of this notice to a creditor. You may use forms POS-020 and POS-020(P) for that purpose.)*

* **NOTE:** To assist the creditor and the court, please send a blank copy of the Creditor's Claim *(form DE-172)* with the notice.

DE-157 [Rev. January 1, 2013]    **NOTICE OF ADMINISTRATION TO CREDITORS**
(Probate—Decedents' Estates)

# CREDITOR'S CLAIM

**DE-172**

| ATTORNEY OR PARTY WITHOUT ATTORNEY *(Name, state bar number, and address)*: | TELEPHONE AND FAX NOS.: | FOR COURT USE ONLY |
|---|---|---|
| ATTORNEY FOR *(Name)*: | | |

**SUPERIOR COURT OF CALIFORNIA, COUNTY OF**
STREET ADDRESS:
MAILING ADDRESS:
CITY AND ZIP CODE:
BRANCH NAME:

ESTATE OF *(Name)*:

DECEDENT

| **CREDITOR'S CLAIM** | CASE NUMBER: |
|---|---|

> You must file this claim with the court clerk at the court address above before the LATER of (a) four months after the date letters (authority to act for the estate) were first issued to the personal representative, or (b) sixty days after the date the *Notice of Administration* was given to the creditor, if notice was given as provided in Probate Code section 9051. You must also mail or deliver a copy of this claim to the personal representative and his or her attorney. A proof of service is on the reverse.
> **WARNING:** Your claim will in most instances be invalid if you do not properly complete this form, file it on time with the court, and mail or deliver a copy to the personal representative and his or her attorney.

1. Total amount of the claim: $
2. Claimant *(name)*:
   a. ☐ an individual
   b. ☐ an individual or entity doing business under the fictitious name of *(specify)*:
   c. ☐ a partnership. The person signing has authority to sign on behalf of the partnership.
   d. ☐ a corporation. The person signing has authority to sign on behalf of the corporation.
   e. ☐ other *(specify)*:
3. Address of claimant *(specify)*:

4. Claimant is ☐ the creditor ☐ a person acting on behalf of creditor *(state reason)*:

5. ☐ Claimant is ☐ the personal representative ☐ the attorney for the personal representative.
6. I am authorized to make this claim which is just and due or may become due. All payments on or offsets to the claim have been credited. Facts supporting the claim are ☐ on reverse ☐ attached.

I declare under penalty of perjury under the laws of the State of California that the foregoing is true and correct.

Date:

▶

_____       _____
(TYPE OR PRINT NAME AND TITLE)                     (SIGNATURE OF CLAIMANT)

**INSTRUCTIONS TO CLAIMANT**

A. On the reverse, itemize the claim and show the date the service was rendered or the debt incurred. Describe the item or service in detail, and indicate the amount claimed for each item. Do not include debts incurred after the date of death, except funeral claims.
B. If the claim is not due or contingent, or the amount is not yet ascertainable, state the facts supporting the claim.
C. If the claim is secured by a note or other written instrument, the original or a copy must be attached *(state why original is unavailable.)* If secured by mortgage, deed of trust, or other lien on property that is of record, it is sufficient to describe the security and refer to the date or volume and page, and county where recorded. *(See Prob. Code, § 9152.)*
D. Mail or take this original claim to the court clerk's office for filing. If mailed, use certified mail, with return receipt requested.
E. Mail or deliver a copy to the personal representative and his or her attorney. Complete the *Proof of Mailing or Personal Delivery* on the reverse.
F. The personal representative or his or her attorney will notify you when your claim is allowed or rejected.
G. Claims against the estate by the personal representative and the attorney for the personal representative must be filed within the claim period allowed in Probate Code section 9100. See the notice box above.

(Continued on reverse)

Form Approved by the
Judicial Council of California
DE-172 [Rev. January 1, 1998]

**CREDITOR'S CLAIM**
**(Probate)**

Probate Code, §§ 9000 et seq., 9153

American LegalNet, Inc.
www.USCourtForms.com

# CREDITOR'S CLAIM

| ESTATE OF (Name): | CASE NUMBER: |
|---|---|
| DECEDENT | |

**FACTS SUPPORTING THE CREDITOR'S CLAIM**
☐ See attachment (if space is insufficient)

| Date of item | Item and supporting facts | Amount claimed |
|---|---|---|
| | | |
| | **TOTAL:** | $ |

**PROOF OF** ☐ **MAILING** ☐ **PERSONAL DELIVERY** **TO PERSONAL REPRESENTATIVE**
*(Be sure to mail or take the original to the court clerk's office for filing)*

1. I am the creditor or a person acting on behalf of the creditor. At the time of mailing or delivery I was at least 18 years of age.
2. My residence or business address is *(specify)*:

3. I mailed or personally delivered a copy of this *Creditor's Claim* to the personal representative as follows *(check either a or b below)*:
   a. ☐ **Mail**. I am a resident of or employed in the county where the mailing occurred.
      (1) I enclosed a copy in an envelope AND
         (a) ☐ **deposited** the sealed envelope with the United States Postal Service with the postage fully prepaid.
         (b) ☐ **placed** the envelope for collection and mailing on the date and at the place shown in items below following our ordinary business practices. I am readily familiar with this business' practice for collecting and processing correspondence for mailing. On the same day that correspondence is placed for collection and mailing, it is deposited in the ordinary course of business with the United States Postal Service in a sealed envelope with postage fully prepaid.
      (2) The envelope was addressed and mailed first-class as follows:
         (a) Name of personal representative served:
         (b) Address on envelope:

         (c) Date of mailing:
         (d) Place of mailing *(city and state)*:
   b. ☐ **Personal delivery**. I personally delivered a copy of the claim to the personal representative as follows:
      (1) Name of personal representative served:
      (2) Address where delivered:

      (3) Date delivered:
      (4) Time delivered:

I declare under penalty of perjury under the laws of the State of California that the foregoing is true and correct.
Date:

▶

_____ _____
(TYPE OR PRINT NAME OF CLAIMANT)          (SIGNATURE OF CLAIMANT)

DE-172 [Rev. January 1, 1998]

**CREDITOR'S CLAIM**
(Probate)

DE-140

| ATTORNEY OR PARTY WITHOUT ATTORNEY (Name, state bar number, and address): | TELEPHONE AND FAX NOS.: | FOR COURT USE ONLY |
|---|---|---|
| Nancy Noe-Nonsense, ********* <br> Law Offices of Nancy Noe-Nonsense <br> 11111 Courthouse Plaza <br> Sacramento, CA 95826 | ***_***_**** | |
| ATTORNEY FOR (Name): EDDY WADE SHORES, Petitioner | | |

SUPERIOR COURT OF CALIFORNIA, COUNTY OF SACRAMENTO
STREET ADDRESS: 3341 Power Inn Road
MAILING ADDRESS: 3341 Power Inn Road
CITY AND ZIP CODE: Sacramento, CA 95826
BRANCH NAME: Probate Division

ESTATE OF (Name):
CORAL LEIGH SHORES aka CORAL REDD SHORES
DECEDENT

**ORDER FOR PROBATE**

ORDER APPOINTING
- [✓] Executor
- [ ] Administrator with Will Annexed
- [ ] Administrator
- [ ] Special Administrator
- [✓] Order Authorizing Independent Administration of Estate
  - [✓] with full authority
  - [ ] with limited authority

CASE NUMBER:
07PR555599

**WARNING: THIS APPOINTMENT IS NOT EFFECTIVE UNTIL LETTERS HAVE ISSUED.**

1. Date of hearing:      Time:      Dept./Room:      Judge:

**THE COURT FINDS**
2. a. All notices required by law have been given.
   b. Decedent died on (date):
      (1) [✓] a resident of the California county named above.
      (2) [ ] a nonresident of California and left an estate in the county named above.
   c. Decedent died
      (1) [ ] intestate
      (2) [✓] testate
      and decedent's will dated: 11/1/2000      and each codicil dated:
      was admitted to probate by Minute Order on (date):

**THE COURT ORDERS**
3. (Name): EDDY WADE SHORES
   is appointed **personal representative**:
   a. [✓] executor of the decedent's will      d. [ ] special administrator
   b. [ ] administrator with will annexed      (1) [ ] with general powers
   c. [ ] administrator      (2) [ ] with special powers as specified in Attachment 3d(2)
        (3) [ ] without notice of hearing
        (4) [ ] letters will expire on (date):
   and letters shall issue on qualification.
4. a. [✓] **Full authority** is granted to administer the estate under the Independent Administration of Estates Act.
   b. [ ] **Limited authority** is granted to administer the estate under the Independent Administration of Estates Act (there is no authority, without court supervision, to (1) sell or exchange real property or (2) grant an option to purchase real property or (3) borrow money with the loan secured by an encumbrance upon real property).
5. a. [✓] Bond is not required.
   b. [ ] Bond is fixed at: $      to be furnished by an authorized surety company or as otherwise provided by law.
   c. [ ] Deposits of: $      are ordered to be placed in a blocked account at (specify institution and location):
      and receipts shall be filed. No withdrawals shall be made without a court order. [ ] Additional orders in Attachment 5c.
   d. [ ] The personal representative is not authorized to take possession of money or any other property without a specific court order.
6. [✓] (Name):      is appointed probate referee.

Date:

JUDGE OF THE SUPERIOR COURT
[ ] SIGNATURE FOLLOWS LAST ATTACHMENT

7. Number of pages attached: _____

Form Approved by the
Judicial Council of California
DE-140 [Rev. January 1, 1998]

**ORDER FOR PROBATE**

Probate Code, §§ 8006, 8400

American LegalNet, Inc.
www.USCourtForms.com

**DE-150**

| ATTORNEY OR PARTY WITHOUT ATTORNEY (Name, state bar number, and address): | TELEPHONE AND FAX NOS.: | FOR COURT USE ONLY |
|---|---|---|
| Nancy Noe-Nonsense, ********<br>Law Offices of Nancy Noe-Nonsense<br>11111 Courthouse Plaza<br>Sacramento, CA 95826 | ***-***-**** | |
| ATTORNEY FOR (Name): EDDY WADE SHORES, Petitioner | | |

SUPERIOR COURT OF CALIFORNIA, COUNTY OF SACRAMENTO
STREET ADDRESS: 3341 Power Inn Road
MAILING ADDRESS: 3341 Power Inn Road
CITY AND ZIP CODE: Sacramento, CA 95826
BRANCH NAME: Probate Division

ESTATE OF (Name):
CORAL LEIGH SHORES aka CORAL REDD SHORES
DECEDENT

**LETTERS**
[✓] TESTAMENTARY [ ] OF ADMINISTRATION
[ ] OF ADMINISTRATION WITH WILL ANNEXED [ ] SPECIAL ADMINISTRATION

CASE NUMBER: 07PR555599

**LETTERS**

1. [✓] The last will of the decedent named above having been proved, the court appoints (name):
   a. [✓] executor.
   b. [ ] administrator with will annexed.

2. [✓] The court appoints (name):
   EDDY WADE SHORES
   a. [✓] administrator of the decedent's estate.
   b. [ ] special administrator of decedent's estate
      (1) [ ] with the special powers specified in the Order for Probate.
      (2) [ ] with the powers of a general administrator.
      (3) [ ] letters will expire on (date):

3. [✓] The personal representative is authorized to administer the estate under the Independent Administration of Estates Act [✓] with full authority
   [ ] with limited authority (no authority, without court supervision, to (1) sell or exchange real property or (2) grant an option to purchase real property or (3) borrow money with the loan secured by an encumbrance upon real property).

4. [ ] The personal representative is not authorized to take possession of money or any other property without a specific court order.

WITNESS, clerk of the court, with seal of the court affixed.

| (SEAL) | Date:<br><br>Clerk, by<br><br><br>(DEPUTY) |
|---|---|

**AFFIRMATION**

1. [ ] PUBLIC ADMINISTRATOR: No affirmation required (Prob. Code, § 7621(c)).

2. [✓] INDIVIDUAL: **I solemnly affirm** that I will perform the duties of personal representative according to law.

3. [ ] INSTITUTIONAL FIDUCIARY (name):
   **I solemnly affirm** that the institution will perform the duties of personal representative according to law. I make this affirmation for myself as an individual and on behalf of the institution as an officer.
   (Name and title):

4. Executed on (date):
   at (place): SACRAMENTO , California.

▶ _____
(SIGNATURE)

**CERTIFICATION**
I certify that this document is a correct copy of the original on file in my office and the letters issued the personal representative appointed above have not been revoked, annulled, or set aside, and are still in full force and effect.

| (SEAL) | Date:<br><br>Clerk, by<br><br><br>(DEPUTY) |
|---|---|

Form Approved by the
Judicial Council of California
DE-150 [Rev. January 1, 1998]

**LETTERS**
**(Probate)**

Probate Code, §§ 1001, 8403,
8405, 8544, 8545;
Code of Civil Procedure, § 2015.6

134 INVENTORY AND APPRAISAL COMPLETED

**DE-160/GC-040**

ATTORNEY OR PARTY WITHOUT ATTORNEY (Name, state bar number, and address):
Nancy Noe-Nonsense, SBN ********
Law Offices of Nancy Noe-Nonsense
11111 Courthouse Plaza
Sacramento, CA 95826

TELEPHONE NO.: ***-***-****  FAX NO. (Optional): ***-***-****
E-MAIL ADDRESS (Optional):
ATTORNEY FOR (Name): EDDY WADE SHORES, Petitioner

SUPERIOR COURT OF CALIFORNIA, COUNTY OF SACRAMENTO
STREET ADDRESS: 3341 Power Inn Road
MAILING ADDRESS: 3341 Power Inn Road
CITY AND ZIP CODE: Sacramento, CA 95826
BRANCH NAME: Probate Division

ESTATE OF (Name):
CORAL LEIGH SHORES aka CORAL REDD SHORES
[✓] DECEDENT  [ ] CONSERVATEE  [ ] MINOR

**INVENTORY AND APPRAISAL**
[ ] Partial No.:          [ ] Corrected
[✓] Final                 [ ] Reappraisal for Sale
[ ] Supplemental          [ ] Property Tax Certificate

CASE NUMBER: 07PR555599
Date of Death of Decedent or of Appointment of Guardian or Conservator: 1/15/07

**APPRAISALS**
1. Total appraisal by representative, guardian, or conservator (Attachment 1): $ 28,333.00
2. Total appraisal by referee (Attachment 2): $
TOTAL: $

**DECLARATION OF REPRESENTATIVE, GUARDIAN, CONSERVATOR, OR SMALL ESTATE CLAIMANT**

3. Attachments 1 and 2 together with all prior inventories filed contain a true statement of
   [✓] all  [ ] a portion of the estate that has come to my knowledge or possession, including particularly all money and all just claims the estate has against me. I have truly, honestly, and impartially appraised to the best of my ability each item set forth in Attachment 1.
4. [ ] No probate referee is required  [✓] by order of the court dated (specify): xx/xx/2006
5. **Property tax certificate.** I certify that the requirements of Revenue and Taxation Code section 480
   a. [ ] are not applicable because the decedent owned no real property in California at the time of death.
   b. [✓] have been satisfied by the filing of a change of ownership statement with the county recorder or assessor of each county in California in which the decedent owned property at the time of death.

I declare under penalty of perjury under the laws of the State of California that the foregoing is true and correct.
Date:

EDDY WADE SHORES  ▶
(TYPE OR PRINT NAME; INCLUDE TITLE IF CORPORATE OFFICER)   (SIGNATURE)

**STATEMENT ABOUT THE BOND**
(Complete in all cases. Must be signed by attorney for fiduciary, or by fiduciary without an attorney.)

6. [✓] Bond is waived, or the sole fiduciary is a corporate fiduciary or an exempt government agency.
7. [ ] Bond filed in the amount of: $          [ ] Sufficient   [ ] Insufficient
8. [ ] Receipts for: $          have been filed with the court for deposits in a blocked account at (specify institution and location):

Date:

NANCY NOE-NONSENSE  ▶
(TYPE OR PRINT NAME)   (SIGNATURE OF ATTORNEY OR PARTY WITHOUT ATTORNEY)

Page 1 of 2

Form Adopted for Mandatory Use
Judicial Council of California
DE-160/GC-040 [Rev. January 1, 2007]

**INVENTORY AND APPRAISAL**

Probate Code, §§ 2610-2616, 8800-8980;
Cal. Rules of Court, rule 7.501
www.courtinfo.ca.gov

American LegalNet, Inc.
www.FormsWorkflow.com

INVENTORY AND APPRAISAL COMPLETED                    135

DE-160/GC-040

| ESTATE OF *(Name)*: | CASE NUMBER: |
|---|---|
| CORAL LEIGH SHORES aka CORAL REDD SHORES  [✓] DECEDENT  [ ] CONSERVATEE  [ ] MINOR | 07PR555599 |

**DECLARATION OF PROBATE REFEREE**

9. I have truly, honestly, and impartially appraised to the best of my ability each item set forth in Attachment 2.
10. A true account of my commission and expenses actually and necessarily incurred pursuant to my appointment is:
    Statutory commission:    $
    Expenses *(specify)*:    $
    TOTAL: $

I declare under penalty of perjury under the laws of the State of California that the foregoing is true and correct.

Date:

_____          ▶          _____
(TYPE OR PRINT NAME)                             (SIGNATURE OF REFEREE)

**INSTRUCTIONS**
(See Probate Code sections 2610-2616, 8801, 8804, 8852, 8905, 8960, 8961, and 8963 for additional instructions.)

1. See Probate Code section 8850 for items to be included in the inventory.

2. If the minor or conservatee is or has been during the guardianship or conservatorship confined in a state hospital under the jurisdiction of the State Department of Mental Health or the State Department of Developmental Services, mail a copy to the director of the appropriate department in Sacramento. (Prob. Code, § 2611.)

3. The representative, guardian, conservator, or small estate claimant shall list on Attachment 1 and appraise as of the date of death of the decedent or the date of appointment of the guardian or conservator, at fair market value, moneys, currency, cash items, bank accounts and amounts on deposit with each financial institution (as defined in Probate Code section 40), and the proceeds of life and accident insurance policies and retirement plans payable upon death in lump sum amounts to the estate, except items whose fair market value is, in the opinion of the representative, an amount different from the ostensible value or specified amount.

4. The representative, guardian, conservator, or small estate claimant shall list in Attachment 2 all other assets of the estate which shall be appraised by the referee.

5. If joint tenancy and other assets are listed for appraisal purposes only and not as part of the probate estate, they must be separately listed on additional attachments and their value excluded from the total valuation of Attachments 1 and 2.

6. Each attachment should conform to the format approved by the Judicial Council. *(See Inventory and Appraisal Attachment* (form DE-161/GC-041) and Cal. Rules of Court, rules 2.100—2.119.)

INVENTORY AND APPRAISAL ATTACHMENT COMPLETED

DE-161, GC-041

| ESTATE OF (Name): CORAL LEIGH SHORES, aka CORAL REDD SHORES | CASE NUMBER: 13PRXXXXX |
|---|---|

**INVENTORY AND APPRAISAL**
**ATTACHMENT NO.: ONE**

*(In decedents' estates, attachments must conform to Probate Code section 8850(c) regarding community and separate property.)*

Page: 2 of: 3 total pages.
*(Add pages as required.)*

| Item No. | Description | Appraised value |
|---|---|---|
| 1. | 2010 BUICK CENTURY | $5,000 |
| 2 | GOLDEN ONE CREDIT UNION | 1,158 |
| 3 | BANK OF AMERICA CD | $20,235 |
| 4 | 1994 TOYOTA PICK UP | $1,000 |
| 5 | Personal Effects: Clothing and Jewelry | $2,000 |
| 6 | CD Account | |

**INVENTORY AND APPRAISAL ATTACHMENT**

INVENTORY AND APPRAISAL ATTACHMENT COMPLETED 137

| | DE-161, GC-041 |
|---|---|
| ESTATE OF (Name): CORAL LEIGH SHORES, aka CORAL REDD SHORES | CASE NUMBER: 13PRXXXXX |

**INVENTORY AND APPRAISAL
ATTACHMENT NO.: TWO**

*(In decedents' estates, attachments must conform to Probate Code section 8850(c) regarding community and separate property.)*

Page: 3 of: 3 total pages.
*(Add pages as required.)*

| Item No. | Description | Appraised value |
|---|---|---|
| 1. | 22222 WONDERFUL PLACE ELK GROVE, CA | $ |

**INVENTORY AND APPRAISAL ATTACHMENT**

| | DE-121 |
|---|---|
| ATTORNEY OR PARTY WITHOUT ATTORNEY *(Name, State Bar number, and address):*<br>NANCY NOE-NONSENSE, SBN *******<br>Law Offices of Nancy Noe-Nonsense<br>11111 Courthouse Plaza<br>Sacramento, CA  95826<br>TELEPHONE NO.: ***-***-****   FAX NO. *(Optional):* ***-***-****<br>E-MAIL ADDRESS *(Optional):*<br>ATTORNEY FOR *(Name):* EDDY WADE SHORES, Petitioner | FOR COURT USE ONLY |
| SUPERIOR COURT OF CALIFORNIA, COUNTY OF  SACRAMENTO<br>STREET ADDRESS: 3341 Power Inn Road<br>MAILING ADDRESS: 3341 Power Inn Road<br>CITY AND ZIP CODE: Sacramento, CA  95826<br>BRANCH NAME: PROBATE DIVISION | |
| ESTATE OF *(Name):*<br>CORAL LEIGH SHORES, aka CORAL REDD SHORES<br>DECEDENT | |
| **NOTICE OF PETITION TO ADMINISTER ESTATE OF**<br>*(Name):* CORAL LEIGH SHORES aka CORAL REDD SHORES | CASE NUMBER:<br>07PR555599 |

1. To all heirs, beneficiaries, creditors, contingent creditors, and persons who may otherwise be interested in the will or estate, or both, of *(specify all names by which the decedent was known):*
   CORAL LEIGH SHORES aka CORAL REDD SHORES

2. A **Petition for Probate** has been filed by *(name of petitioner):* EDDY WADE SHORES
   in the Superior Court of California, County of *(specify):* SACRAMENTO

3. The Petition for Probate requests that *(name):* EDDY WADE SHORES
   be appointed as personal representative to administer the estate of the decedent.

4. [✓] The petition requests the decedent's will and codicils, if any, be admitted to probate. The will and any codicils are available for examination in the file kept by the court.

5. [✓] The petition requests authority to administer the estate under the Independent Administration of Estates Act. (This authority will allow the personal representative to take many actions without obtaining court approval. Before taking certain very important actions, however, the personal representative will be required to give notice to interested persons unless they have waived notice or consented to the proposed action.) The independent administration authority will be granted unless an interested person files an objection to the petition and shows good cause why the court should not grant the authority.

6. **A hearing on the petition will be held in this court as follows:**

   a. Date:           Time:           Dept.:           Room:

   b. Address of court: [✓] same as noted above   [ ] other *(specify):*

7. **If you object** to the granting of the petition, you should appear at the hearing and state your objections or file written objections with the court before the hearing. Your appearance may be in person or by your attorney.

8. **If you are a creditor or a contingent creditor of the decedent**, you must file your claim with the court and mail a copy to the personal representative appointed by the court within four months from the date of first issuance of letters as provided in Probate Code section 9100. The time for filing claims will not expire before four months from the hearing date noticed above.

9. **You may examine the file kept by the court.** If you are a person interested in the estate, you may file with the court a *Request for Special Notice* (form DE-154) of the filing of an inventory and appraisal of estate assets or of any petition or account as provided in Probate Code section 1250. A *Request for Special Notice* form is available from the court clerk.

10. [ ] Petitioner   [✓] Attorney for petitioner *(name):* NANCY NOE-NONSENSE

    *(Address):* 1111 Courthouse Plaza, Sacramento, CA  95826

    *(Telephone):* ***-***-****

**NOTE:** If this notice is published, print the caption, beginning with the words NOTICE OF PETITION TO ADMINISTER ESTATE, and do not print the information from the form above the caption. The caption and the decedent's name must be printed in at least 8-point type and the text in at least 7-point type. Print the case number as part of the caption. Print items preceded by a box only if the box is checked. Do not print the italicized instructions in parentheses, the paragraph numbers, the mailing information, or the material on page 2.

Page 1 of 2

Form Adopted for Mandatory Use
Judicial Council of California
DE-121 [Rev. January 1, 2006]

**NOTICE OF PETITION TO ADMINISTER ESTATE**
**(Probate—Decedents' Estates)**

Probate Code, § 8100
www.courtinfo.ca.gov

American LegalNet, Inc.
www.USCourtForms.com

NOTICE OF PETITION TO ADMINISTER ESTATE COMPLETED  139

**DE-121**

| ESTATE OF *(Name):* CORAL LEIGH SHORES, aka CORAL REDD SHORES  DECEDENT | CASE NUMBER: 13PRXXXXXX |
|---|---|

### PROOF OF SERVICE BY MAIL

1. I am over the age of 18 and not a party to this cause. I am a resident of or employed in the county where the mailing occurred.
2. My residence or business address is *(specify):* 11111 Courthouse Plaza, Sacramento, CA 95826

3. I served the foregoing *Notice of Petition to Administer Estate* on each person named below by enclosing a copy in an envelope addressed as shown below **AND**
   a. ☐ **depositing** the sealed envelope with the United States Postal Service on the date and at the place shown in item 4, with the postage fully prepaid.
   b. ☑ **placing** the envelope for collection and mailing on the date and at the place shown in item 4 following our ordinary business practices. I am readily familiar with this business's practice for collecting and processing correspondence for mailing. On the same day that correspondence is placed for collection and mailing, it is deposited in the ordinary course of business with the United States Postal Service, in a sealed envelope with postage fully prepaid.

4. a. Date mailed:          b. Place mailed *(city, state):* Sacramento, CA

5. ☑ I served, with the *Notice of Petition to Administer Estate*, a copy of the petition or other document referred to in the notice.

I declare under penalty of perjury under the laws of the State of California that the foregoing is true and correct.

Date:

Sallie Jo Smith-Allen
(TYPE OR PRINT NAME OF PERSON COMPLETING THIS FORM)                                    ▶          (SIGNATURE OF PERSON COMPLETING THIS FORM)

### NAME AND ADDRESS OF EACH PERSON TO WHOM NOTICE WAS MAILED

| Name of person served | Address *(number, street, city, state, and zip code)* |
|---|---|
| 1. | |
| 2. | |
| 3. | |
| 4. | |
| 5. | |
| 6. | |

☐ Continued on an attachment. *(You may use form DE-121(MA) to show additional persons served.)*

Assistive listening systems, computer-assisted real-time captioning, or sign language interpreter services are available upon request if at least 5 days notice is provided. Contact the clerk's office for *Request for Accommodations by Persons With Disabilities and Order* (form MC-410). (Civil Code section 54.8.)

DE-121 [Rev. January 1, 2013]    **NOTICE OF PETITION TO ADMINISTER ESTATE**
(Probate—Decedents' Estates)

140 NOTICE OF ADMINISTRATION TO CREDITORS COMPLETED

**DE-157**

# NOTICE OF ADMINISTRATION
# OF THE ESTATE OF

__CORAL LEIGH SHORES, aka CORAL REDD SHORES__
(NAME)

## DECEDENT

**NOTICE TO CREDITORS**

1. *(Name):* EDDY WADE SHORES
   *(Address):* c/o Law Offices of Nancy Noe-Nonsense
   11111 Courthouse Plaza, Sacramento, CA 95826

   *(Telephone):*

   is the **personal representative** of the ESTATE OF *(name):* Coral Leigh Shores, who is deceased.

2. The personal representative HAS BEGUN ADMINISTRATION of the decedent's estate in the
   a. **SUPERIOR COURT OF CALIFORNIA, COUNTY OF** *(specify):* SACRAMENTO
      STREET ADDRESS: 3341 Power Inn Road
      MAILING ADDRESS: 3341 Power Inn Road
      CITY AND ZIP CODE: Sacramento, CA 95826
      BRANCH NAME: Probate Division
   b. Case number *(specify):*

3. You must FILE YOUR CLAIM with the court clerk (address in item 2a) AND mail or deliver a copy to the personal representative before the **last to occur** of the following dates:
   a. **four months** after *(date):* xx/xx/2013, the date letters (authority to act for the estate) were first issued to a general personal representative, as defined in subdivision (b) of section 58 of the California Probate Code, OR
   b. **60 days** after *(date):* _____, the date this notice was mailed or personally delivered to you.

4. LATE CLAIMS: If you do not file your claim within the time required by law, you must file a petition with the court for permission to file a late claim as provided in Probate Code section 9103. Not all claims are eligible for additional time to file. See section 9103(a).

EFFECT OF OTHER LAWS: Other California statutes and legal authority may affect your rights as a creditor. You may want to consult with an attorney knowledgeable in California law.

WHERE TO GET A CREDITOR'S CLAIM FORM: If a *Creditor's Claim* (form DE-172) did not accompany this notice, you may obtain a copy of the form from any superior court clerk or from the person who sent you this notice. You may also access a fillable version of the form on the Internet at www.courts.ca.gov/forms under the form group Probate—Decedents' Estates. A letter to the court stating your claim is *not* sufficient.

FAILURE TO FILE A CLAIM: Failure to file a claim with the court and serve a copy of the claim on the personal representative will in most instances invalidate your claim.

IF YOU MAIL YOUR CLAIM: If you use the mail to file your claim with the court, for your protection you should send your claim by certified mail, with return receipt requested. If you use the mail to serve a copy of your claim on the personal representative, you should also use certified mail.

Note: To assist the creditor and the court, please send a blank copy of the *Creditor's Claim* form with this notice.

(Proof of Service by Mail on reverse)

Form Adopted for Mandatory Use
Judicial Council of California
DE-157 [Rev. January 1, 2013]

**NOTICE OF ADMINISTRATION TO CREDITORS**
**(Probate—Decedents' Estates)**

Probate Code, §§ 9050, 9052
www.courts.ca.gov

# NOTICE OF ADMINISTRATION TO CREDITORS COMPLETED

141

**DE-157**

| ESTATE OF (Name): CORAL LEIGH SHORES, aka CORAL REDD SHORES DECEDENT | CASE NUMBER: |

**[Optional]**
**PROOF OF SERVICE BY MAIL**

1. I am over the age of 18 and not a party to this cause. I am a resident of or employed in the county where the mailing occurred.
2. My residence or business address is (specify):

   Law Offices of Nancy Noe-Nonsense, 11111 Courthouse Plaza, Sacramento, CA 95826

3. I served the foregoing *Notice of Administration to Creditors* [✓] and a blank *Creditor's Claim* form* on each person named below by enclosing a copy in an envelope addressed as shown below AND
   a. ☐ depositing the sealed envelope with the United States Postal Service with the postage fully prepaid.
   b. [✓] placing the envelope for collection and mailing on the date and at the place shown in item 4 following our ordinary business practices. I am readily familiar with the business's practice for collecting and processing correspondence for mailing. On the same day that correspondence is placed for collection and mailing, it is deposited in the ordinary course of business with the United States Postal Service in a sealed envelope with postage fully prepaid.

4. a. Date of deposit:      b. Place of deposit (city and state): Sacramento, CA

I declare under penalty of perjury under the laws of the State of California that the foregoing is true and correct.

Date:

_____Sallie Jo Smith-Allen, Paralegal_____  ▶  _____
(TYPE OR PRINT NAME)                            (SIGNATURE OF DECLARANT)

**NAME AND ADDRESS OF EACH PERSON TO WHOM NOTICE WAS MAILED**

| | Name of person | Address (number, street, city, state, and zip code) |
|---|---|---|
| 1. | | |
| 2. | | |
| 3. | | |
| 4. | | |
| 5. | | |
| 6. | | |
| 7. | | |
| 8. | | |

☐ List of names and addresses continued in attachment. (You may use form POS-30(P) to show additional persons to whom a copy of this notice was mailed. Do not use page 2 of this form or form POS-030(P) to show that you personally delivered a copy of this notice to a creditor. You may use forms POS-020 and POS-020(P) for that purpose.)

*** NOTE:** To assist the creditor and the court, please send a blank copy of the Creditor's Claim (form DE-172) with the notice.

DE-157 [Rev. January 1, 2013]        **NOTICE OF ADMINISTRATION TO CREDITORS**        Page 2 of 2
(Probate—Decedents' Estates)

# Chapter Six

# Transfer of Property Without Estate Administration

There are numerous ways to avoid probate and/or transfer property without the need for a formal probate.

Property held in joint tenancy may be transferred upon death to the surviving joint tenant. This is true for real property, vehicles, bank accounts and other types of assets where there is "title."

Assets to which a beneficiary is designated also avoid probate. Insurance policies, annuities, retirement and employee benefit plans, Individual Retirement Accounts, just to name a few, are contractual in nature and require that a beneficiary be named when establishing the account. Upon the death of the "owner" of the asset, the named beneficiary(ies) will receive the value of the asset. There are some exceptions and those will be discussed later in the chapter.

Property, which is owned with a spouse or a Registered Domestic Partner, may be transferred directly to the surviving spouse or domestic partner. (Note: Within this chapter, for ease of information and unless otherwise stated, surviving spouse and registered domestic partner will be used synonymously.) Registered Domestic Partnerships will be discussed in greater detail in Chapter 12.

The property may also be transferred by an Affidavit procedure to a surviving spouse or heirs if the decedent's assets (excluding real property) are less than One Hundred Fifty Thousand ($150,000).

In the event the decedent died intestate and there is a question as to the inheritance rights of the spouse and children of the decedent, a Petition for Probate or a Petition to Determine Succession to Real Property may be filed, depending upon whether the decedent had other assets.

The attorney will need to meet with the client, review the documents and related assets, and then determine the best course of action for the client. The attorney should first determine whether the decedent had a Will or died intestate.

If the decedent had a Will, the attorney will interpret the decedent's wishes as to how the property should be transferred. The Will may have specified, for example, "I leave my entire estate to my spouse." In that event, the property may be transferred without a formal probate. However, if the Will specifies that someone other than the spouse will receive either all or part of the separate property, probate will be required. Keep in mind that the decedent's community property, unless otherwise agreed, in writing, with the spouse, will be distributed to the spouse. The characterization of property may need to be considered and will be discussed in the next section.

The estate may be of a small enough value and/or property is held in such a manner that the property may qualify for a summary probate procedure, a spousal property petition, and/or an affidavit procedure. A critical determination, particularly with real property, is whether the title of the property is held in joint tenancy, as community property, owned solely by the decedent and/or some other manner of holding title. If there are other assets, such as bank accounts, stocks, bonds, mutual fund accounts, it will be necessary to provide the company "holding" those assets with the proper documentation in order to effectuate any transfer to the heirs and beneficiaries. The attorney will need to determine whether the documentation is best obtained through a formal probate proceeding, a summary procedure, an affidavit or in some cases with simply a copy of the decedent's death certificate.

In most cases, a surviving spouse will have little difficulty acquiring the assets of the decedent when the property is simply furniture and personal effects. However, as you may have personally seen with today's blended families, these items can also be a source of acrimony between the natural children and a new spouse. There will be more formality when the decedent has assets which are titled or over which another person, corporation, or other business organization has control. Such entities include but are not limited to, financial institutions, title companies, investment firms, insurance companies, retirement plans, and other similar accounts.

Also of concern to the attorney, when transferring property without formal administration, is whether the decedent's spouse has predeceased him or her. The problem is compounded when the attorney determines that after the death of the first spouse none of the assets were transferred to the surviving spouse, which made the surviving spouse the sole owner of those assets. In the event this occurs, the attorney may need to work with the decedent's heirs to create the documents needed to transfer the property posthumously to "a then" surviving spouse. Either the assets will then be transferred to the heirs using the affidavit or summary procedures, or the decedent's estate will undergo probate.

The attorney may also need to consider any tax consequences that may be involved and which may be affected by the method of transfer. For example, there may be federal and/or state taxes incurred by transferring property through probate or conversely taxes may be avoided by probate. The attorney may need to research this issue and weigh the pros and cons with the Administrator and/or heirs to determine the best way to proceed. The attorney may need to bring in a CPA or tax attorney to give an opinion of the best course of action as well. What may be best for the estate may not be bests for an individual heir or beneficiary so the attorney will need to put all the cards on the table **and** do his or her best to avoid a conflict of interest or potential malpractice by giving advice that is adversarial depending upon whom he or she represents.

# Community Property, Surviving Spouse, Domestic Partner, Joint Tenancy

Community and quasi-community property may be disposed of by the surviving spouse or Personal Representative forty days **after** the death of the decedent. (Probate Code § 13540.) A Spousal Property Petition may be filed, provided a Petition for Probate is not currently pending. In the event both types of administration are filed concurrently, the actions may be joined. (Probate Code § 13653.)

The attorney and client must discuss whether this is the best avenue for the surviving spouse as he or she is **personally** liable for all of the decedent's debts regardless of when the claims are made. Whereas when filing a formal probate, the estate rather than the surviving spouse, is liable for the decedent's debts and only for those claims made during the creditor's claim period. If there are significant debts owed by the decedent, it may be best to prepare and file a Petition for Probate. However, a Petition for Probate will require certain formalities, including administration fees and costs (publication fees, probate referee, etc.) and the statutory attorney fees. A summary procedure will only require an initial filing fee, and the fees to be paid to the attorney will be by agreement between the client and the attorney. The client will have to weigh these factors as to which are best for their personal circumstances as well as for the estate.

The attorney will mostly likely want to confirm whether property is community, quasi-community, or separate property before making a final recommendation as to the proper method of administering the decedent's estate. This is an issue that must be considered whether or not a surviving spouse is entitled to inherit the property.

## Community Property

In order to have community property a person must be married. For the purposes of probate, the "surviving spouse" must have been legally married to the decedent at the time of the decedent's death.

Community property may be transferred to the surviving spouse, provided the decedent had a Will and stated that the surviving spouse was to receive the entire estate. If the Will states that any other person should receive any portion of the property, a formal probate will be required.

At any time **after** the forty day "waiting period" the surviving spouse may transfer any property to which the title indicates the property was "community property" or held as "husband and wife." In California, this can be accomplished by recording an Affidavit—Death of Spouse with the County Clerk/Recorder where the property is located. The document is signed before a notary public and a death certificate must be attached. (A sample Affidavit—Death of Spouse is provided at Appendix 6A.) The County Assessor may also require that a Death of Spouse form be filed alerting them to a potential change in ownerships. (A sample of this form is provided at Appendix B.)

In most cases, a spouse is exempt from paying Documentary Transfer Tax in California subject to Revenue and Tax Code §§ 62-63. If the transfer is exempt, the Change of Ownership Report (which must be submitted with all property transfers in California) should indicate that the transfer is exempt and the appropriate box(es) should be checked. (A sample Change of Ownership Report is provided as Appendix 6C.) Consult R&T §§ 62-63 for additional information.

Married couples or domestic partners may hold title to the property as "community property, with right of survivorship." This means that the surviving spouse or partner will receive the property even if the Will indicated that the spouse and children were to receive the decedent's estate. The manner in which title is held is controlling in the State of California.

A surviving spouse also has the ability to collect compensation from the decedent's employer. This includes wages, unused vacation, and any other sums due to the decedent upon death. The amount cannot exceed $15,000, and the surviving spouse must be entitled to the compensation either under the decedent's Will or under the rights of intestate succession. (Probate Code § 13600.)

The surviving spouse can execute a Declaration for Collection of Compensation Owed a Deceased Spouse (a sample is provided at Appendix 6D) and present it to the employer.

# Separate Property

Separate property typically means that property owned by one individual. The person can be married or single. That person is solely responsible for the mortgage, insurance, and taxes. He or she personally enjoys the benefits of the property ownership.

For example, if Jon owned a 1955 Chevrolet Bel Air prior to his marriage to Jane, it is his separate property. He will enjoy the benefit of driving it. In most cases, he will retain ownership by keeping the "title" through the Department of Motor Vehicles solely in his name.

Thus, a married person may own separate property. Property acquired prior to marriage, during marriage by gift, bequest, or inheritance, or after the date of separation remains the separate property of the person acquiring it, unless the person chooses to transfer the property by adding the spouse's name to the property. (This is referred to as transmutation.) The parties may also execute an agreement, typically a pre-marital or post-marital agreement, wherein they agree that certain property, including income, is the sole and separate property of one party. In the State of California, this agreement **cannot** be verbal, it must be written. This has been a source of much litigation over the years, both in probate and family law. This topic was previously covered in Chapter One.

It is possible for a married person to have separate property, particularly a home, and provide for a Life Estate or Life Tenancy for their spouse. Typically, the life tenancy is created so that a spouse can use the property for the remainder of his or her life. Upon the spouse's death, the property would be distributed to the decedent's heirs.

The following is a typical example:

Wife was previously married and has two biological children from that marriage. She has remarried and her husband does not have any children. The parties married when they were in their sixties and Wife owned a house. Wife has specified in her Will that if she predeceases Husband, Husband will have a life estate in the property. Upon his death, the property will be distributed to her two children.

# Types of Ownership

For the purpose of this course, there are three primary types of ownership: Joint Tenancy, Tenancy in Common, and Community Property. You will recall that Joint Tenancy means that upon the death of a tenant, there is an automatic right to inherit the property from the decedent.

Property owned as Tenants in Common does not enjoy the automatic right to inherit. The decedent's portion of the property will be distributed to his or her heirs, unless there was an agreement between the tenants in common which otherwise provides for the disposition of that person's factional interest. Again, the agreement **must** be in writing, otherwise, the Court is required to distribute the decedent's property as set forth in his or her Will or as set forth in the laws of intestate succession. Whenever title to a property **does not** specify the manner in which title is to be held (joint tenants, community property with right of survivorship, etc.) then it is presumed to be owned as tenants in common.

Property owned as Community Property does not absolutely give the surviving spouse the right to "inherit" the property, unless there is a Will that specifies that the property should be distributed to the surviving spouse. Absent the Will, the matter of property ownership and transfer to the surviving spouse will have to be determined by the Court. Title may specify Community Property with Right of Survivorship. In that event, the surviving spouse will inherit the decedent's one-half without the need for Probate. It is important that the surviving spouse transfer the 1/2 received to him or herself as sole owner on the title by recording the Affidavit Death of Spouse to eliminate confusion and additional steps to clear title upon their death (see community property).

As indicated above, one party may also retain separate ownership of property and give a spouse a life estate in the property.

## Joint Tenancy

In most cases, property held in a joint tenancy may be transferred by the same Affidavit method discussed under community property. Real property that is held in joint tenancy can be transferred to the surviving joint tenant by preparing an Affidavit—Death of Joint Tenant and attaching a copy of the decedent's Death Certificate. The document is then recorded with the County Recorder in the County where the property is located. The surviving joint tenant is then afforded all rights as the owner of the property. There is no waiting period for transferring the property, as there is for community property.

An example of an Affidavit—Death of Joint Tenant is provided at Appendix 6E. The surviving tenant must sign the Affidavit, having sworn before a notary pubic that the information in the document is true and correct. There will be a recording fee assessed by the County Recorder.

The attorney will need to determine if a transfer tax must be paid. In most cases, a surviving joint tenant is exempt from paying Documentary Transfer Tax in California subject to Revenue and Tax Code §§ 62-63. If the transfer is exempt, the Change of Ownership Report must, as indicated in the above section, "Community Property," be prepared and submitted to the County Clerk. Additionally, if the transfer is being made to a child of the decedent, even if that child is a joint tenant, an Exclusion of Reassessment (form) must also be submitted to the County Assessor where the property is located. Property that is not "excluded" will incur taxes when the beneficiary sells the property. The county assessor's website should be reviewed to confirm what information and/or documentation needs to be provided with the deed and other title transfer documents.

The attorney will want to explain to the client why this is important. For the purposes of this text, I will briefly identify the concept known as "basis." You will want to, however, ask your instructor or the attorney for whom you work, to provide you with more detail on the concept of basis. You may want to conduct some additional research on your own about this topic as well.

## Basis

Basis is defined as the value of the property at the time it was acquired. When a person owns property, particularly real estate and stocks, the property will usually acquire increased value as the years pass. When a person inherits property, it is usually worth more than the decedent paid for it. Thus, a child who receives the parent's home as part of an estate has, theoretically, received a home that has increased in value from the time it was purchased until the time it is received. What if the child turns around and sells the inherited property? The child has then made a "profit." Such a profit would normally incur capital gains taxes and the person would have to report the gain on their personal income taxes.

Both Federal and California tax laws allow property acquired by inheritance to receive a "stepped-up" basis. This means that the beneficiary receives a one-time opportunity to have the property valued as of the date of the decedent's death and not the value at the time the decedent acquired the property. For Federal Estate Tax purposes, this is also referred to as an "alternate valuation date."

Essentially, the beneficiary does not have to pay personal income taxes on the difference between the original purchase price and the current fair market value of the property. In order to be able to be entitled to the stepped up basis or alternate valuation" the proper steps must be documented. One means of documenting the change in basis is to complete the Exclusion from Reassessment form and submit it to the County Assessor at the time the property is transferred to the child or spouse.

## Petition to Determine Succession to Real Property

When the decedent has left real property and the **gross** fair market value of the property is less than $150,000, the property may be distributed by using the summary procedure known as a Petition to Determine Succession to Real Property. Judicial Council form (Form DE-310) must be completed and filed with the Court, not sooner than 40 days after the decedent's death. In most cases the person who wishes to have the property transferred to him/her (such as a sole child—frequently called the successor in interest), the person named as Executor, or a person who would be qualified as a Personal Representative will be the person filing the Petition to Determine Succession.

This action may also be referred to as a "small estate set-aside."

Probate Code §13150 et seq. provides the specific guidelines for a determination of succession to real property as follows:

Probate Code §13150. The procedure provided by this chapter may be used only if one of the following requirements is satisfied:

(a) No proceeding is being or has been conducted in this state for administration of the decedent's estate.
(b) The decedent's Personal Representative consents in writing to use of the procedure provided by this chapter to determine that real property of the decedent is property passing to the petitioners.

Probate Code § 13151 provides the qualifying circumstances for filing a Petition to Determine Succession, as follows:

Probate Code § 13151. Exclusive of the property described in Section 13050, if a decedent dies leaving real property in this state and the gross value of the decedent's real and personal property in this state does not exceed one hundred thousand dollars ($150,000) and 40 days have elapsed since the death of the decedent, the successor of the decedent to an interest in a particular item of property that is real property, without procuring letters of administration or awaiting the probate of the will, may file a petition in the superior court of the county in which the estate of the decedent may be administered requesting a court order determining that the petitioner has succeeded to that real property. A petition under this chapter may include an additional request that the court make an order determining that the petitioner has succeeded to personal property described in the petition.

Probate Code Sections 13152 through 13158 provide the detailed instructions for filing and obtaining an Order for Succession. Note that an Inventory and Appraisal (DE-160) will need to be prepared; the Probate Referee will need to complete the appraisal of the property and the document will then be filed with the Court. The same procedures should be followed as in Chapter Five as in the formal probate procedure.

## Small Estates Set-Aside

Probate Code § 6600 et seq. outline the circumstances under which an estate that is valued at less than $50,000 may be distributed or transferred upon the death of the decedent.

Specifically, Probate Code § 6600 defines the decedent's estate subject to small estate set aside as follows:

"[D]ecedent's estate" means all the decedent's personal property, wherever located, and all the decedent's real property located in this state.

(b) For the purposes of this chapter:

(1) Any property or interest or lien thereon which, at the time of the decedent's death, was held by the decedent as a joint tenant, or in which the decedent had a life or other interest terminable upon the decedent's death, shall be excluded in determining the estate of the decedent or its value.

(2) A multiple-party account to which the decedent was a party at the time of the decedent's death shall be excluded in determining the estate of the decedent or its value, whether or not all or a portion of the sums on deposit are community property, to the extent that the sums on deposit belong after the death of the decedent to a surviving party, P.O.D. payee, or beneficiary. As used in this paragraph, the terms "multiple-party account," "party," "P.O.D. payee," and "beneficiary" have the meanings given those terms in Article 2 (commencing with Section 5120) of Chapter 1 of Part 2 of Division 5.

Probate Code § 6602: A petition may be filed under this chapter requesting an order setting aside the decedent's estate to the decedent's surviving spouse and minor children, or one or more of them, as provided in this chapter, if the net value of the decedent's estate, over and above all liens and encumbrances at the date of death and over and above the value of any probate homestead interest set apart out of the decedent's estate under Section 6520, does not exceed fifty thousand dollars ($50,000).

Note that the above language states that the value of the estate is net, as determined **after** all liens, encumbrances and applicable homestead are deducted. In addition, the language in Section 6600 states that the portion of any asset that is subject to joint tenancy or some other joint ownership is also deducted and not included in the decedent's estate.

Most estates in California will not qualify for this type of administration if the decedent owned any real property. There are always exceptions to every rule. Based on property values in California alone, a decedent owning a home in which there is any equity will not likely qualify as an estate whose value is less than $50,000, once the value of the real property is combined with the other assets subject to administration.

The legislature has also determined that a decedent's family and heirs should have the ability to make transfers and distributions after the decedent's death based on certain qualifying factors. This is referred to as the Transfer of Small Estates Without Administration. The Probate Code commencing at § 13000 to § 13606 governs the various mechanisms and criteria that must be met in order to be able to use the small estate transfers.

These types of transfers include: Affidavits for Real Property valued at less than $50,000, Small Estates Set-Aside for property valued at less then $50,000, Order Determining Succession to Real Property (valued under $150,000), Collection by Affidavit of Compensation Owned to Deceased Spouse, and Affidavit pursuant to Probate Code § 13100, et seq. for personal property valued at under $150,000.

Estates that have a total value under One Hundred Fifty Thousand Dollars ($150,000) may be passed to the decedent's surviving spouse or heirs without formal probate. (Probate Code §§ 13000, et seq.).

## Transfer of Small Estates Without Administration

Note the difference between the Petition for Determination of Succession and this type of estate administration. The Petition for Determination states that the **gross fair market value of the estate must be under $150,000**. The Transfer of Small Estates Without Administration states that the **fair market value less liens and encumbrances** must be under $150,000.

This process is an Affidavit procedure. Forty days must have elapsed since the decedent's death. It should only be used once an attorney has determined that no probate is necessary and it is clear to whom the property should be transferred. For example:

Decedent has no spouse, the real property is held in joint tenancy with the only child. The only assets are a 1970 pickup (FMV $800), bank account ($1,500), savings account ($10,200), CD account ($20,450), cash ($180), furniture, furnishings and personal belongings, all of which were purchased at least 10 years ago. There is a credit card debt of $900. The decedent also had an insurance policy and a retirement account. The only child was named as beneficiary on those accounts/policies, which are not subject to this administration and do not contribute to the fair market value of the estate.

Using the above scenario, the attorney will likely advise the client that a probate is not necessary because the total value of the personal property is less than $150,000.

Note that the real property is exempt. However, keep in mind that if the real property was held in joint tenancy, one-half belonged to the decedent and one-half to the surviving joint tenant. In the event it was necessary to value the real property, only the share (one-half) belonging to the decedent would be considered part of the estate. The decedent did not own the other half—his or her child did, even if it was a "gift" when the child's name was placed on the title as a joint tenant. Older people will often make these kinds of transfers in order to avoid probate, especially if they do not have a Will.

This section of the probate code also determines who may be considered a successor and/or a beneficiary for the purposes of using this code section to transfer or obtain property.

Probate Code § 13006. "Successor of the decedent" means:

(a) If the decedent died leaving a will, the sole beneficiary or all of the beneficiaries who succeeded to a particular item of property of the decedent under the decedent's will. For the purposes of this part, a trust is a beneficiary under the decedent's will if the trust succeeds to the particular item of property under the decedent's will.

(b) If the decedent died without a will, the sole person or all of the persons who succeeded to the particular item of property of the decedent under Sections 6401 and 6402....

A sample Affidavit Regarding Personal Property Under Probate Code Sections 13100–13106 is provided at Appendix 6F.) Note that the Affidavit provides the Code Sections referenced within the document. If there is any question as to whether this document may be used, those Probate Code sections should be reviewed. Form DE-221 should be used for Domestic Partnership transfers as well.

# Spousal Property Petition

There will be situations that will require a Court determination as to the ownership of property, where even though there is a surviving spouse or a *registered* Domestic Partnership, the title of the property is not clear. For example if the title to the family home is held as follows: Jon Doe and Jane Doe, a Court determination will need to be made as to ownership of the decedent's share and to whom it should be transferred.

A clearer way to hold title would be Jon Doe and Jane Doe, husband and wife, as joint tenants, Jon Doe and Jane Doe, husband and wife, as community property, or Jon Doe and Jane Doe, husband and wife, with right of survivorship. As you have seen from the sections above concerning community property and joint tenancy, such language leaves little question as to the ownership and to whom the decedent's share should be disbursed. A title company that is transferring title on real property using any of the above examples will have a clear understanding of the intent of the parties regarding who will own the property upon the death of the first person to die. If the title company, or the County Recorder, has any question as to the ability of a surviving spouse or "tenant" to transfer property to the survivor, they will request that the person requesting the transfer obtain a Court order.

The following are some additional examples of the manner in which title is held on frequently owned assets, and which will require that a Spousal Property Petition be filed:

- Motor vehicles where only the decedent's name was on the title or where the names of the spouses are not connected by "or" (Jon Doe or Jane Doe);
- Bank accounts in the decedent's name alone or where the names of the spouses appear as community property or as tenants in common (rather than as joint tenants);
- Stocks, bonds, mutual funds, money market accounts, and other securities listed in the decedent's name alone or where the names of spouses appear as community property or as tenants in common;
- Tangible personal property that is in the possession of a third party or property which is subject to a partnership or business interest;
- Real property held in the name of the decedent alone, or held as a tenant in common with either the spouse or another individual or entity.

The Spousal Property Petition is a Judicial Council form (Form DE-221) that is used to confirm that property owned by the decedent should be transferred to the surviving spouse. This form is used primarily when the decedent died intestate. However, it can be used when there was a Will and in lieu of the formal probate process where there is only a question as to the inheritance of the specific item of property (bank account, stocks, bonds, motor vehicle, real property, etc.). The following is a common scenario wherein a Spousal Property Petition may be needed or in lieu of the formal probate.

For example, if Jon and Jane Doe owned their home together. They both have Wills that indicate that they will each inherit the entire estate of each other. Approximately one year prior to Jane's death, the couple refinanced the property. Due to Jon's poor credit from a failed business, they agreed that they would refinance the property only in Jane's name. All other property (vehicles, bank accounts, etc.) where held in joint tenancy. When the deed was recorded after the refinance, the title was held **only** in Jane's name. The title company informed Jane that she could put Jon's name back on the property once the loan was funded and the deed recorded. They had intended to do so, but never got around to it. Jane was killed in an automobile accident.

As you can see from the above, all of the couple's assets were held jointly except their home. All of the other assets can be transferred by providing the person or entity with a copy of Jane's death certificate and an affidavit, if required, in order to transfer the property to Jon. The attorney has determined that there is no need to file a formal probate. The only debts due are those which were jointly acquired such as utilities, credit cards, etc. which were in both Jon and Jane's names. Therefore, the attorney advises that the appropriate procedure needed in this instance is a Spousal Property Petition. The attorney has advised Jon that the Petition can be filed, a hearing date obtained, and that it should be a fairly routine matter to have the Court issue the Order for Spousal Property Petition. Once the Order is received, a certified copy can be obtained and the Order can then be recorded. Upon the recording of the Order, Jon will become the legal owner of the property. The attorney has quoted Jon a flat fee for this process and Jon has agreed to pay that amount along with the required Court filing fee.

It is always a good idea to check with the person or entity that is holding the title to the property (the financial institution, stock or bond company, Department of Motor Vehicles) to determine if a Court Order is required. Some may only require a copy of the death certificate and an affidavit or others may want their own "internal" documentation to be used to transfer the property to the surviving spouse. This is especially true post-9/11, due to the Patriot Act, wherein the Securities and Exchange Commission (SEC) and other federal regulations require additional documents for any transaction related to stock, bonds, or other federally regulated assets. Additionally, some of these forms require a Medallion Signature Guarantee rather than a notary. It is important to understand the difference and where to send a client who needs this service.

For example, a financial institution where the couple has had a bank account for 25 years and on which both have them have signed checks, made deposits and withdrawals, and may even have loans, may not require anything more than a death certificate because they are readily familiar with both parties personally. There are still others that regardless of how familiar the bank may be with the decedent and the surviving spouse, due to the bank policies or concerns for potential liability, the bank will not take any action without a Court Order.

The most critical information to be provided on the Spousal Property Petition is covered by Item Nos. 7(a) and 7(b), which is the **legal description** of the property along with the statement of (1) that the surviving spouse is entitled to receive the one-half of the community property belonging to the decedent, and (2) that the surviving spouse owns the other one-half of the property. (Samples of attachments 7(a) and 7(b) are provided at Appendix 6G.)

A Notice of Hearing must be submitted to the Court along with the Petition. The Notice must be served on persons listed in item numbers 7 and 8 of the Petition at least 15 days prior to the hearing. Remember to add 5 days for mailing.

As with a formal probate, the probate examiner (attorney) will review the Petition and supporting documentation and confirm that the Petition is in order and that it should be recommended for approval by the Judge. In the event there are any deficiencies, those will have to be cured prior to the hearing date, or the hearing date will have to be continued. It is the same process as the formal probate hearing, and you should review that section again if your firm is going to use this procedure. Remember that the hearing date must be calendared, along with the date the file notes are expected to be available.

Once the probate examiner has recommended the Petition for approval the Order may be submitted or the attorney may choose to take the Order to the hearing and have it signed immediately. Check the local Court Rules to determine if there is a specific date for submission of the proposed Order. The attorney should bring along a return, postage-paid, self-addressed envelope in the event the Order cannot be signed immediately, as well as a check so that a certified copy (or more if needed) can be obtained.

Anytime it is anticipated that an Order or other document will need to be recorded with the County Recorder, a certified copy will be required. Other agencies or financial institutions may also require a certified copy when the Spousal Property Petition also includes motor vehicles, securities, promissory notes, bank accounts, money market, mutual funds, or tangible property in the possession of a third party, and/or any other assets, which may be transferred by this method. It is always wise to check with the agency or financial institution ahead of time to determine what documentation is required in order to transfer the property to the surviving spouse. You will find that each agency and institution has its own specific requirements. This will save a lot of time and frustration.

If there is real property and the Order for Succession must be recorded, a Title cover sheet will be required. As always, a Change of Ownership Report will also need to be submitted along with the required recording fees. The attorney will confirm that this transfer is exempt from Documentary Transfer Tax and that those taxes do not have to be paid at the time of the recording.

# Information Regarding Property Transfers

Now that you are familiar with the different methods of transferring assets without formal administration of the decedent's estate, it is helpful to understand some of the nuances of actually making the transfers of property to the successor(s) of the decedent.

This is also an area where the paralegal can greatly assist the client. Many of the agencies and companies who handle these transfers have their own unique documents and requirements for making transfers. As a probate paralegal, I keep a file containing copies of the many collateral documents that would be needed for these types of transfers, particularly for agencies within the State of California. Each financial institution often has its own "in-house" forms that you will be unable to access. However, as you learn of different requirements, it is a good idea to keep a file or a list on the computer of some of the things you have learned. This will give you the ability to give the client a "heads up" as to what he/she will need to take to the financial institution or the types of additional documentation that is going to be required. You will be the client's hero, as you will save them much time and frustration as they begin the process of making the transfers and obtaining the property.

As previously indicated, once the Court has entered an Order or the appropriate small estate affidavits, joint tenancy transfers, and other documents have been executed by the successor, the property will need to be acquired.

## Real Property

As previously stated, any documents that have been prepared regarding real property will need to be recorded with the county recorder where the property is located. A Preliminary Change of Ownership Report (PCOR) will also need to be submitted. In the event the property is being transferred to a child or grandchild, the appropriate Parent-Child Exclusion form will also need to be provided to the County Assessor. The Attorney should review these forms to confirm that the successor is entitled to the exemption(s) requested in these documents. Remember also that the County Clerk may require a Cover Page (title page) if any documents are being recorded.

The above-described transfer of real property example is inferring, however, that the successor wishes to retain the property. What if the successor wants to sell the property? Alternatively, there are two siblings and they need to sell the house so that they can each receive their share. On the other hand, there are two siblings, but one wants to keep the house and "cash" the other one out.

In any of those events, the successor(s) should contact a licensed Real Estate Agent, Broker, or Financial Company and provide the Agent/Broker with copies of the documents (Deeds, Affidavit, or Order) so that the property can be listed for sale. The originals should be retained until the property is sold. At that time, the Title Company will need to have the **original** for recording the documents.

## Motor Vehicles

The Department of Motor Vehicles (DMV) lists most of the information and forms needed to transfer motor vehicles on the DMV website. Most of the forms can be downloaded from the internet and completed prior to going to DMV to make the transfers. The client should make sure that he/she has the form that indicates the transfer is pursuant to a transfer at death and is "not a sale." Otherwise, the client may be assessed California Sales Tax, from which they are exempt. Only the actual processing fee would need to be paid so that a new "pink slip" can be issued showing the successor as the new owner. The same is true for boats, recreational vehicles, motorcycles, quads, and any type of vehicle that may operate on a road or highway. Copies of the Order or Affidavit and a Death Certificate, plus any internal forms are the primary documents required by the California DMV. The client should easily be able to transfer the vehicle to either himself or herself or a new owner in the event the vehicle has been sold when prepared with this information.

## Mobile Homes

Although they are called mobile homes, they are not "vehicles" in the true sense of the word. They cannot operate independently on roads or highways. Mobile homes are living quarters that may be moved from location to another. In most cases, if the decedent lived in a mobile home park, he/she owned the mobile home (may be 1 to 3 units) and rented the space on which the mobile home sits. Prior to 1980 titles were kept by the Department of Motor Vehicles. Transfers must now be made through the Department of Housing and Urban Development (HUD). There are a number of forms that must accompany these transfers, including a certification that the unit(s) contains smoke detector(s). The HUD website should be consulted for the forms that will be needed to complete these transfers. HUD can also be called and the forms will be mailed. The client will need to make sure that he/she has located the current registration that should have been previously provided in order to obtain the Order or to prepare the Affidavit Under Probate Code § 13100.

If the successor is not the spouse, he/she may want to sell the unit. The mobile home park is a good source for determining a licensed real estate agent who is familiar with the sale of such residences as there are a number of specific issues that relate to such a sale. The agent will also need to have copies of the title papers and the Order or Affidavit in order to list the mobile home for sale. The successor also needs to be aware that he/she will have to continue to pay the rental on the space while the property is listed until it is sold. The client should take these items to the bank with him/her and complete the transaction with the bank personnel.

## Bank, Savings & CD Accounts

For the most part, financial accounts are the most easily transferred assets. A copy of the certified Order or Affidavit and a copy of the death certificate will usually allow the successor to transfer the ownership of the account or to remove the assets from the bank.

## Stocks and Bonds

The Securities and Exchange Commission has some very specific requirements as to the documentation that is required to transfer stocks and bonds. This information does not apply to Subchapter S or privately owned corporations. Additionally, subsequent to the Patriot Act, which was enacted because of 9/11 has added an entirely new level of paperwork required to transfer stocks and bonds. The successor will be required to complete that particular company's forms that will require the successor's social security number, driver's license, and other personal data. In most cases, the company will also require a document called an Affidavit of Domicile. The successor will sign under penalty of perjury that they are the decedent's heir and that the decedent resided (and worked, if applicable) and died in the location set forth in the Order or the Affidavit. The company will be happy to send you the required form with the other information. That Affidavit will also need to be notarized. The company may also request that the successor submit a W-9, which provides his/her tax identification or social security number. That information will be sent to the Internal Revenue Service as reported income.

Numerous stocks were issued during the early "dot-com" development. Some of those companies no longer exist, some have been absorbed by other companies, and some have less value then when they were issued. Most stocks and bonds will have to be mailed by certified mail and the transfer agent will require a fee for issuing the new certificate or bond. It may take several hours of research to find the company and determine the transfer agent. It is always a good idea to call and confirm that the listed transfer agent is still the current agent. You will also serve the client well if you ask the current transfer agent to send **all** the forms, required documentation, and information needed to transfer the stock or bond certificate.

The client may also have to take into consideration that the stocks or bonds have little value and are not worth the fees and time it is going to take to transfer the stocks and bonds. The client may also want to decide whether he/she wants an actual certificate or if it would be better to place the shares in a "paperless" account. Some companies now charge to issue paper stock certificates. As seen in this section also, future transactions and transfers may be more cumbersome than paperless transactions.

The Securities and Exchange Commission (SEC) also requires a Medallion Signature Guarantee. This is similar to a notary, but is not as easily obtainable. The SEC will **not** accept a notary acknowledgment. The client will, in most cases, have to contact a person who has the ability to do a Medallion Signature Guarantee. Many investment firms and some banks may provide this service. Always confirm that the investment firm can provide the Signature Guarantee to someone who is **not** currently a client.

In some cases, the client may find it less complicated to retain an investment firm or counselor to assist with the liquidation of the stocks and bonds. The proceeds can be then kept in an investment account rather than have new stocks or bonds issued.

## Mutual Funds and Money Market Accounts

The information provided in the previous section with regard to stocks and bonds should be followed for most mutual funds and money market accounts. In most instances, the company that administers the mutual fund or money market account will have the same or similar requirements, especially as they relate to the Privacy Act. Since the company is the administrator of the fund, there should be no problem with the signature guarantee, unless the company does not have an office where the client is located.

Additionally, most fund administrators will no longer allow the successor to liquidate the account. The successor will need to open a separate account and have the funds transferred from the decedent's account into the "new" account. Once that procedure is accomplished, the successor may liquidate the account or do whatever they choose.

This requirement has caused an extra step and may delay the successor's ability to immediately utilize those funds to pay the decedent's debts or to disburse the funds to the heirs.

## Savings and Treasury Bonds

The U.S. Department of Treasury website contains information and forms needed for changing the ownership of Savings and Treasury Bonds. If you have had an experience previously of negotiating and/or liquidating bonds, you will find that the process has completely changed and you will need to review the information on the U.S. Treasury site. The following is some general information, however this information should not be relied upon as it may have changed recently and/or continuously.

Treasurer (EE) bonds are no longer issued in paper form effective 2012. For any bonds purchased or transferred, an electronic account must first be created. Once an account has been created, the purchaser may purchase new bonds through the on-line system. For those individuals wishing to transfer the bonds, forms are available for download on-line. The forms must be completed, there must be a Medallion Signature Guarantee, and the original bonds sent to the Department of Treasury for surrender. The value of the bonds will then be transferred into the on-line account. The sender should send the bonds by certified mail and the package should be insured for the full value of the bonds. Alternatively, the bonds can be sent by registered mail to make sure the bonds are not lost and are received by the Department of Treasury for processing. There are other methods of delivery also available. You will want to work with the client to determine how much they want to spend on shipping as it can be quite expensive depending upon the value of the bonds and the method of delivery confirmation. It is important to stress, however, that going the least expensive route for this procedure may not be the best course of action.

## Other Personal Property

Personal property, a business, or other property that does not fit into any of the above categories can usually be obtained by presenting a certified copy of the Order to the third party in possession of the property.

## Preparation of Judicial Council Forms

Spousal Property Petition (DE-221) with Attachments (Appendix 6G)

Notice of Hearing (DE-120)

Spousal Property Order (DE-226)

## Key Terms

- Small Estate Set Aside
- Spousal Property Petition
- Joint Tenancy
- Right of Survivorship

- Community Property
- Separate Property
- Affidavit (Declaration) Under Probate Code § 13100
- Tenants in Common
- Tenants in Common with Right of Survivorship
- Medallion Signature Guarantee
- Affidavit of Domicile

# SPOUSAL PROPERTY PETITION

**DE-221**

| ATTORNEY OR PARTY WITHOUT ATTORNEY *(Name, State Bar number, and address)*: | FOR COURT USE ONLY |
|---|---|
| TELEPHONE NO.:      FAX NO. *(Optional)*: | |
| E-MAIL ADDRESS *(Optional)*: | |
| ATTORNEY FOR *(Name)*: | |

**SUPERIOR COURT OF CALIFORNIA, COUNTY OF**
STREET ADDRESS:
MAILING ADDRESS:
CITY AND ZIP CODE:
BRANCH NAME:

ESTATE OF *(Name)*:

DECEDENT

| CASE NUMBER: |
|---|
| HEARING DATE: |
| DEPT.:    TIME: |

☐ **SPOUSAL** ☐ **DOMESTIC PARTNER** **PROPERTY PETITION**

1. **Petitioner** *(name)*:                                                               **requests**
   a. ☐ determination of property passing to the surviving spouse or surviving registered domestic partner without administration (Fam. Code, § 297.5, Prob. Code, § 13500).
   b. ☐ confirmation of property belonging to the surviving spouse or surviving registered domestic partner (Fam. Code, § 297.5, Prob. Code, §§ 100, 101).
   c. ☐ immediate appointment of a probate referee.
2. **Petitioner is**
   a. ☐ surviving spouse of the decedent.
   b. ☐ personal representative of *(name)*:                               , surviving spouse.
   c. ☐ guardian or conservator of the estate of *(name)*:                  , surviving spouse.
   d. ☐ surviving registered domestic partner of the decedent.
   e. ☐ personal representative of *(name)*:                       , surviving registered domestic partner.
   f. ☐ conservator of the estate of *(name)*:                          , surviving registered domestic partner.
3. Decedent died on *(date)*:
4. Decedent was
   a. ☐ a resident of the California county named above.
   b. ☐ a nonresident of California and left an estate in the county named above.
   c. ☐ intestate ☐ testate and a copy of the will and any codicil is affixed as Attachment 4c.
   *(Attach copies of will and any codicil, a typewritten copy of any handwritten document, and an English translation of any foreign-language document.)*
5. a. *(Complete in all cases)* The decedent is survived by
   (1) ☐ no child. ☐ child as follows: ☐ natural or adopted ☐ natural, adopted by a third party.
   (2) ☐ no issue of a predeceased child. ☐ issue of a predeceased child.
   b. Decedent ☐ is ☐ is not survived by a stepchild or foster child or children who would have been adopted by decedent but for a legal barrier. *(See Prob. Code, § 6454.)*
6. *(Complete only if no issue survived the decedent. Check only the first box that applies.)*
   a. ☐ The decedent is survived by a parent or parents who are listed in item 9.
   b. ☐ The decedent is survived by a brother, sister, or issue of a deceased brother or sister, all of whom are listed in item 9.
7. Administration of all or part of the estate is not necessary for the reason that all or a part of the estate is property passing to the surviving spouse or surviving registered domestic partner. The facts upon which petitioner bases the allegation that the property described in Attachments 7a and 7b is property that should pass or be confirmed to the surviving spouse or surviving registered domestic partner are stated in Attachment 7.
   a. ☐ Attachment 7a[1] contains the legal description *(if real property add Assessor's Parcel Number)* of the deceased spouse's or registered domestic partner's property that petitioner requests to be determined as having passed to the surviving spouse or partner from the deceased spouse or partner. This includes any interest in a trade or business name of any unincorporated business or an interest in any unincorporated business that the deceased spouse or partner was operating or managing at the time of death, subject to any written agreement between the deceased spouse or partner and the surviving spouse or partner providing for a non pro rata division of the aggregate value of the community property assets or quasi-community assets, or both.

[1] See Prob. Code, § 13658 for required filing of a list of known creditors of a business and other information in certain instances. If required, include in Attachment 7a.

Page 1 of 2

Form Adopted for Mandatory Use
Judicial Council of California DE-221
[Rev. January 1, 2005]

**SPOUSAL OR DOMESTIC PARTNER PROPERTY PETITION**
**(Probate—Decedents Estates)**

Family Code, § 297.5;
Probate Code, § 13650

American LegalNet, Inc.
www.USCourtForms.com

| ESTATE OF (Name): | CASE NUMBER: |
|---|---|
| DECEDENT | |

7. b. ☐ Attachment 7b contains the legal description *(if real property add Assessor's Parcel Number)* of the community or quasi-community property petitioner requests to be determined as having belonged under Probate Code sections 100 and 101 and Family Code section 297.5 to the surviving spouse or surviving registered domestic partner upon the deceased spouse's or partner's death, subject to any written agreement between the deceased spouse or partner and the surviving spouse or partner providing for a non pro rata division of the aggregate value of the community property assets or quasi-community assets, or both.

8. There ☐ exists ☐ does not exist a written agreement between the deceased spouse or deceased registered domestic partner and the surviving spouse or surviving registered domestic partner providing for a non pro rata division of the aggregate value of the community property assets or quasi-community assets, or both. *(If petitioner bases the description of the property of the deceased spouse or partner passing to the surviving spouse or partner or the property to be confirmed to the surviving spouse or partner, or both, on a written agreement, a copy of the agreement must be attached to this petition as Attachment 8.)*

9. The names, relationships, ages, and residence or mailing addresses so far as known to or reasonably ascertainable by petitioner of (1) all persons named in decedent's will and codicils, whether living or deceased, and (2) all persons checked in items 5 and 6

☐ are listed below ☐ are listed in Attachment 9.

| Name and relationship | Age | Residence or mailing address |
|---|---|---|

10. The names and addresses of all persons named as executors in the decedent's will and any codicil or appointed as personal representatives of the decedent's estate ☐ are listed below ☐ are listed in Attachment 10 ☐ none

11. ☐ The petitioner is the trustee of a trust that is a devisee under decedent's will. The names and addresses of all persons interested in the trust who are entitled to notice under Probate Code section 13655(b)(2) are listed in Attachment 11.

12. A petition for probate or for administration of the decedent's estate
    a. ☐ is being filed with this petition.
    b. ☐ was filed on *(date):*
    c. ☐ has not been filed and is not being filed with this petition.

13. Number of pages attached: _____

Date:

▶

_____ _____
(TYPE OR PRINT NAME)        (SIGNATURE OF ATTORNEY)

I declare under penalty of perjury under the laws of the State of California that the foregoing is true and correct.

Date:

▶

_____ _____
(TYPE OR PRINT NAME)        (SIGNATURE OF PETITIONER)

DE-221 [Rev. January 1, 2005]

**SPOUSAL OR DOMESTIC PARTNER PROPERTY PETITION**
**(Probate—Decedents Estates)**

# NOTICE OF HEARING

**DE-120**

| ATTORNEY OR PARTY WITHOUT ATTORNEY *(Name, State Bar number, and address)*: | FOR COURT USE ONLY |
|---|---|
| TELEPHONE NO.: FAX NO. *(Optional)*: | |
| E-MAIL ADDRESS *(Optional)*: | |
| ATTORNEY FOR *(Name)*: | |
| **SUPERIOR COURT OF CALIFORNIA, COUNTY OF** | |
| STREET ADDRESS: | |
| MAILING ADDRESS: | |
| CITY AND ZIP CODE: | |
| BRANCH NAME: | |
| ☐ ESTATE OF *(Name)*:   ☐ IN THE MATTER OF *(Name)*: | |
| ☐ DECEDENT   ☐ TRUST   ☐ OTHER | |
| **NOTICE OF HEARING—DECEDENT'S ESTATE OR TRUST** | CASE NUMBER: |

**This notice is required by law.**
**This notice does not require you to appear in court, but you may attend the hearing if you wish.**

1. NOTICE is given that *(name)*:
   *(representative capacity, if any)*:
   has filed *(specify)*:*

2. You may refer to the filed documents for more information. *(Some documents filed with the court are confidential.)*

3. A HEARING on the matter will be held as follows:

   a. Date:           Time:           Dept.:           Room:

   b. Address of court   ☐ shown above   ☐ is *(specify)*:

Assistive listening systems, computer-assisted real-time captioning, or sign language interpreter services are available upon request if at least 5 days notice is provided. Contact the clerk's office for *Request for Accommodations by Persons With Disabilities and Order* (form MC-410). (Civil Code section 54.8.)

* Do **not** use this form to give notice of a petition to administer estate (see Prob. Code, § 8100 and form DE-121) or notice of a hearing in a guardianship or conservatorship (see Prob. Code, §§ 1511 and 1822 and form GC-020).

Page 1 of 2

Form Adopted for Mandatory Use
Judicial Council of California
DE-120 [Rev. July 1, 2005]

**NOTICE OF HEARING—DECEDENT'S ESTATE OR TRUST**
**(Probate—Decedents' Estates)**

Probate Code §§ 851, 1211,
1215, 1216, 1230, 17100
www.courtinfo.ca.gov

American LegalNet, Inc.
www.USCourtForms.com

# NOTICE OF HEARING

| ESTATE OF *(Name)*: ☐   IN THE MATTER OF *(Name)*: ☐ | CASE NUMBER: |
|---|---|
| ☐ DECEDENT   ☐ TRUST   ☐ OTHER | |

## CLERK'S CERTIFICATE OF POSTING

1. I certify that I am not a party to this cause.
2. A copy of the foregoing *Notice of Hearing—Decedent's Estate or Trust*
   a. was posted at *(address)*:

   b. was posted on *(date)*:

Date: _____  Clerk, by _____, Deputy

## PROOF OF SERVICE BY MAIL *

1. I am over the age of 18 and not a party to this cause. I am a resident of or employed in the county where the mailing occurred.
2. My residence or business address is *(specify)*:

3. I served the foregoing *Notice of Hearing—Decedent's Estate or Trust* on each person named below by enclosing a copy in an envelope addressed as shown below AND
   a. ☐ **depositing** the sealed envelope on the date and at the place shown in item 4 with the United States Postal Service with the postage fully prepaid.
   b. ☐ **placing** the envelope for collection and mailing on the date and at the place shown in item 4 following our ordinary business practices. I am readily familiar with this business's practice for collecting and processing correspondence for mailing. On the same day that correspondence is placed for collection and mailing, it is deposited in the ordinary course of business with the United States Postal Service in a sealed envelope with postage fully prepaid.

4. a. Date mailed:          b. Place mailed *(city, state)*:

5. ☐ I served with the *Notice of Hearing—Decedent's Estate or Trust* a copy of the petition or other document referred to in the Notice.

I declare under penalty of perjury under the laws of the State of California that the foregoing is true and correct.

Date:

_____  _____
(TYPE OR PRINT NAME OF PERSON COMPLETING THIS FORM)   (SIGNATURE OF PERSON COMPLETING THIS FORM)

### NAME AND ADDRESS OF EACH PERSON TO WHOM NOTICE WAS MAILED

| | Name of person served | Address *(number, street, city, state, and zip code)* |
|---|---|---|
| 1. | | |
| 2. | | |
| 3. | | |
| 4. | | |

☐ Continued on an attachment. *(You may use* Attachment to Notice of Hearing Proof of Service by Mail, *form DE-120(MA)/GC-020(MA), for this purpose.)*

* Do not use this form for proof of personal service. You may use form DE-120(P) to prove personal service of this Notice.

DE-120 [Rev. July 1, 2005]   **NOTICE OF HEARING—DECEDENT'S ESTATE OR TRUST**
(Probate—Decedents' Estates)

# SPOUSAL PROPERTY ORDER

**DE-226**

ATTORNEY OR PARTY WITHOUT ATTORNEY (Name, State Bar number, and address):
After recording return to:

TELEPHONE NO.:
FAX NO. (Optional):
E-MAIL ADDRESS (Optional):
ATTORNEY FOR (Name):

**SUPERIOR COURT OF CALIFORNIA, COUNTY OF**
STREET ADDRESS:
MAILING ADDRESS:
CITY AND ZIP CODE:
BRANCH NAME:

FOR RECORDER'S USE ONLY

ESTATE OF (Name):

DECEDENT

CASE NUMBER:

☐ SPOUSAL ☐ DOMESTIC PARTNER PROPERTY ORDER

FOR COURT USE ONLY

1. Date of hearing: Time:
   Dept.: Room:

**THE COURT FINDS**

2. All notices required by law have been given.
3. Decedent died on (date):
   a. ☐ a resident of the California county named above.
   b. ☐ a nonresident of California and left an estate in the county named above.
   c. ☐ intestate. ☐ testate.
4. Decedent's ☐ surviving spouse ☐ surviving registered domestic partner
   is (name):

**THE COURT FURTHER FINDS AND ORDERS**

5. a. ☐ The property described in Attachment 5a is property passing to the surviving spouse or surviving registered domestic partner named in item 4, and no administration of it is necessary.
   b. ☐ See Attachment 5b for further order(s) respecting transfer of the property to the surviving spouse or surviving registered domestic partner named in item 4.
6. ☐ To protect the interests of the creditors of (business name):
   an unincorporated trade or business, a list of all its known creditors and the amount owed each is on file.
   a. ☐ Within (specify): days from this date, the surviving spouse or surviving registered domestic partner named in item 4 shall file an undertaking in the amount of $
   b. ☐ See Attachment 6b for further order(s) protecting the interests of creditors of the business.
7. a. ☐ The property described in Attachment 7a is property that belonged to the surviving spouse or surviving registered domestic partner under Family Code section 297.5 and Probate Code sections 100 and 101, and the surviving spouse's or surviving domestic partner's ownership upon decedent's death is confirmed.
   b. ☐ See Attachment 7b for further order(s) respecting transfer of the property to the surviving spouse or surviving domestic partner.
8. ☐ All property described in the *Spousal or Domestic Partner Property Petition* that is not determined to be property passing to the surviving spouse or surviving registered domestic partner under Probate Code section 13500, or confirmed as belonging to the surviving spouse or surviving registered domestic partner under Probate Code sections 100 and 101, shall be subject to administration in the estate of decedent. ☐ All of such property is described in Attachment 8.
9. ☐ Other (specify):

☐ Continued in Attachment 9.

10. Number of pages attached: _____

Date: _____

JUDICIAL OFFICER
☐ SIGNATURE FOLLOWS LAST ATTACHMENT

Page 1 of 1

Form Adopted for Mandatory Use
Judicial Council of California
DE-226 [Rev. January 1, 2005]

**SPOUSAL OR DOMESTIC PARTNER PROPERTY ORDER**
**(Probate—Decedents Estates)**

Family Code, § 297.5;
Probate Code, § 13656

American LegalNet, Inc.
www.USCourtForms.com

# Chapter Seven

# Trusts

## Inter Vivos or Living Trusts

As you have seen in previous chapters, there are number of ways a person may reduce and/or eliminate the need to have a probate or to reduce their probate estate, whether or not they have a Will.

A Trust is another mechanism for avoiding probate, which has gained in popularity in recent years. You have probably heard and/or read about trusts. You might even have a parent or other family member who has created a trust. If you have, you have probably heard such trusts referred to as Living Trusts or Inter Vivos Trusts. Sometimes the term Family Trust is also used. Inter Vivos means "between the living" in Latin. The basic definition of an Inter Vivos Trust is a Trust that is created and the gift given during the lifetime of the creator or the Trust. This means that an individual or a married couple may create a Trust, for their own benefit, during their lifetime. They gift the property to him or herself (or to the couple) to be used as they see fit during their lifetime. Upon the death, the Trust property is transferred to their beneficiaries as set forth in the Trust.

As referenced in Chapter Three, Testamentary Trusts are those set forth within a Will and are created upon the testator's death; thus they are different than the stand-alone Trusts discussed in this chapter. The attorney may include testamentary language within the pour-over Will that will be executed at the same time as the Trust to assure continuity and confirm the testator/settlor's wishes should the Trust be revoked or challenged for any reason.

There are several reasons, besides avoiding probate, why people create a Trust. The primary reasons (not listed in any order of importance) are:

- Avoid administration expenses associated with probate
- Avoid or reduce attorney and executor fees
- Confidentiality
- Reduce taxes
- Flexibility
- Protection from creditors
- Distribution to beneficiaries more expeditiously

A Trust is not always the only remedy for a client's estate planning needs. Trusts, coupled with other related documents, are a useful technique. However, a Will along with

Durable Powers of Attorney and an Advance Health Care Directive may also meet the client's needs.

The client must carefully consider the benefits of a Trust along with the costs of creating the estate planning documents, administration, and transfer costs versus the costs of a Will and probate. The client may also consider that as the net worth or estate grows, he/she/they may want or need to reduce federal estate tax liabilities.

## Trust Administration Overview

The Trust estate is distributed to the heirs of the creator(s) of the Trust. A Trustee is named and he or she performs the same functions as an Executor would under a Will. The Trustee does not require Court supervision to administer and distribute the Trust Estate. There may be some fees associated with the administration of a Trust, but no statutory fees are required as with a probate administration.

The Trust may provide for compensation of the Trustee within certain parameters. For example, the Trustee may have allocated an annual set fee and/or an amount "not to exceed." This is especially true if the Trustee is not a family member. In the event a fiduciary Trustee (financial institution trustee) is named, compensation is mandated. As in probate, a family member who is appointed Trustee will often waive the fee unless the Administration will take several years, is very complex, or will require an extraordinary amount of time on the part of the Trustee. Despite whether the Trustee will receive compensation, usually he or she will be entitled to reimbursement of out-of-pocket costs incurred on behalf of the estate. Such costs might include certified copies of documents, shipping of personal property to heirs, transfer fees, postage, etc.

The Trustee may need to retain the services of an attorney, a certified public accountant, an appraiser, etc. The fees for these services will be paid out of the estate or reimbursed to the Trustee in the event he or she has paid those fees out-of-pocket. Additionally, there is no bond required as there is no probate proceeding. This means, however, that the settlor(s) must carefully consider who will be the successor trustee after the survivor's death or upon the withdrawal of the original trustee(s) as there is a great deal of fiduciary responsibility placed on the person given this role. Not everyone is willing and/or able to meet the high standard of care and fiduciary responsibility which could cause problems with the administration of the estate and the eventual distribution to the beneficiaries. If the trustee should not properly administer the trust assets, then there could be negligence and liability issues that will need to be addressed under the probate code or subject to civil remedies. This role and related responsibilities will be discussed in greater detail later in the chapter.

## Attorney and Executor Fees

Statute does not require attorney fees for a Trust. The person creating the Trust will pay the attorney to create the Trust. Most attorneys will explain to client(s) wishing to create a Trust that the fees for developing the Trust and related documents will be far less than the statutory fees that the Executor and Attorney would receive as the result of a probate. Thus, the attorney fees are primarily paid during the person's lifetime and not upon death. Any attorney fees subsequent to the administration of the Trust will be by agreement between the Trustee and the Attorney. In most cases, the attorney will quote the Trustee a flat rate and/or an hourly fee for the work performed.

It is usually advisable that the Trustee contact an attorney to review the Trust and to make sure that all is in order for the administration. The attorney will usually want to confirm that the Trust was properly "funded." This means that all of the decedent's property is held in the name of the Trust. However, there are exceptions. As discussed in Chapter Six, insurance policies, retirement accounts, etc. that have a named beneficiary will likely be exempt from trust administration. In the event the Trust was named the beneficiary of any of those assets, the Trustee will also be responsible for administering those assets. The attorney will likely provide the Trustee with a checklist and time line for performing the duties as Trustee in the event one was not provided with the Trust Agreement and related documents.

The attorney may also provide the Trustee with examples of funding letters and other documentation that will be needed. Alternatively, the Trustee may request that the attorney provide these services and bill the estate at the hourly or a flat rate. Many Trustees are very well informed and able to administer an estate with little or no assistance after an initial meeting with an attorney. Others will not be comfortable performing certain duties and/or creating certain documents (such a deed, affidavit, etc.) and may require the attorney and his or her paralegal to be more involved with the administration of the estate. A Trust allows the creator of the Trust the maximum amount of flexibility in determining any fees to be paid to the Trustee, since there is no statutory requirement.

## Confidentiality

A probate estate is public information. Upon the lodging of the Will and the filing of a Petition for Probate, Petition for Succession, or a Spousal Property Petition anyone can ask the Court Clerk to review the decedent's probate file. Many companies check the Probate Court's records daily to learn the names of persons who have died, who is administering their estate, and what assets that person owned.

A Trust administration is not typically filed with the Court. In the event any of the property was not transferred into the Trust, a Petition for Instructions will need to be filed with the court regarding the specific items of property. Additionally, the Will must be lodged with the Court. (This will be discussed in Chapter Ten, Trust Administration.)

The information contained in the Petition for Instructions is less detailed than Petition for Probate. It will usually only reference the assets not held in the name of the Trust, rather than listing all estate assets. The Petition is also not published, as is the Notice to Administer the Estate, as required in Probate. While the Will is lodged with the Court clerk, this type of Will is a "Pour-Over" Will and does not contain the full extent of the property owned by the decedent or the manner in which the property will be distributed. In most cases, the Pour-Over Will simply states that the Will should be distributed as set forth in the Trust, even if the Trust has been revoked.

Confidentiality as discussed in this section is strictly related to "public" information rather than attorney-client confidentiality, which was discussed in Chapter One.

## Reduce Taxes

Some trusts are created to minimize the amount of Federal Estate Taxes which would be payable by the estate upon the decedent's death. This is a very complex area of law. It will be covered more specifically later in the chapter. Suffice it to say, individuals and/or married couples who are wealthy use Trusts to reduce their taxable estate. Transferring *income-producing* property to a Trust whose beneficiary is in a lower tax bracket than the Settlor(s) may reduce income taxes.

## Flexibility

A Trust is considered by many to be more flexible than a Will due to the ability to be amended numerous times. Although a Will may be amended by Codicil, most attorneys will recommend that a person who wishes to change their Will have it completely rewritten, particularly if there has already been one Codicil to that Will. A Trust can be amended numerous times and can actually be totally rewritten and/or restated by an Amendment. The Amendment must be done formally. As with a Will, it is never advisable for a person to simply cross out portions of a Trust, nor should notations be made on the document. An Amendment should be prepared by an Attorney, should be signed, notarized, and kept with the original Trust.

Additionally, the Trust allows more flexibility because property can be acquired or sold without having to modify the Trust. Since the property is acquired in the name of the Trust, when the Trustees purchase another home, vacation property, mutual funds, vehicles, etc., those properties will be purchased in the name of the Trust. A Schedule of Trust Assets is kept with the trust and incorporated by reference. However, that Schedule can be changed as the property and assets change.

## Protection from Creditors

Property that was owned by an individual(s) prior to the creation of the trust may be subject to creditors. A person cannot use a Trust to avoid having to pay a creditor. There is case law that establishes the period for transfers to avoid potential creditors. A person cannot make transfers from their deathbed in order to avoid paying a creditor.

Property distributed to or held in trust for a beneficiary will, in most cases, be protected from the decedent's creditors. There are exceptions, which are included under the "Spendthrift" section in this Chapter.

## Distribution to Beneficiaries Is Expedited

In most cases, the Trustee will be able to administer and distribute the Trust estate more expeditiously than he/she would during the administration of a probate estate. As discussed in Chapter Four, the soonest possible date a probate estate can be distributed is four months after the date the Letters were first issued.

A Trustee, however, may begin distributing trust property as soon as he or she is in a position to do so. In most cases, the Trustee will still need to gather information about the decedent's assets, determine what bills are due by the estate, determine if taxes must be paid, etc. As with a probate, this process will take some time. The Trustee will need to make sure he/she has all information before making any distributions.

If needed, there is more flexibility in making preliminary distributions, as there is no judicial oversight. If the Trust provides discretion on the part of the Trustee and the

Trustee feels it is in the best interests to distribute property, including money, he or she may do so and will not need permission.

The Trustee is required to give notice to all beneficiaries of the administration of the trust as well as its administration. Probate Code § 16060. The beneficiaries must be notified within 60 days of certain occurrences pursuant to Probate Code § 16061.7. There is no set judicial period under which the Trustee must function beyond the initial notice requirements and the requirements to keep the beneficiaries informed of the administration of the estate, unless a beneficiary should make a specific request for notice. In the event the entire estate is ready to distribute within a few months of the decedent's death, the Trustee may distribute the property.

## Grantor, Settlor, Trustor, Trustee

The Grantor is the person creating the Trust and granting the transfer of property into the Trust along with the management of the Trust by the Trustee.

The Settlor is the same as the Grantor, the terms are synonymous. It is usually only a matter of preference of the attorney and/or the software program utilized in drafting the Trust. Many older Trusts referred to the grantor. However, Settlor has become the more commonly used term.

Trustor is the person having control over the trust property. The Trustor will be the one who transfers the trust property over to the Trustee for him or her to manage. In most cases, the Settlor and Trustor is the same person. There may be situations where they are different individuals depending upon the type of trust or the specific powers that were given to the Trustee by the Settlor.

The Trustee is the person who will manage the Trust property that has been transferred into the Trust. The Trustee may be the Settlor. He or she could also be a trusted individual or even a financial institution who is appointed by the Settlor to manage the Trust. In most situations, that you will encounter within an estate planning firm, these individuals will be the same. However, occasionally an elderly or terminally ill client may wish to appoint another individual to act as Trustee because the person is unable, or will soon be unable, to perform the duties required. Care must be taken by the attorney in assuring that a person appointing another individual as Trustee has the mental capacity to make the appointment. A person who is incompetent may not be able to even create the Trust, let alone appoint someone to act on his/her behalf.

Additionally, the Trustee may be the person who administers the Trust upon the death of the initial Trustee or the surviving Trustee. This person may also be referred to as the Successor Trustee. The Successor Trustee may also be the person who is appointed to act upon the Notice of Withdrawal as Trustee by the initial Trustee, during his/her lifetime.

There are primarily two types of Trusts: Irrevocable and Revocable.

## Irrevocable Trust

California Probate Code § 15400 provides that a voluntary trust is revocable unless expressly made irrevocable by the Trust instrument. In order for a Trust to be irrevocable, it must contain the following language, "This trust is irrevocable and shall not be altered, amended, or revoked by any person."

Probate Code §§ 15401–15412 have established the rules for amendment, modification and/or termination of an irrevocable trust. The Trust cannot be terminated if it contains a spendthrift clause (which will be discussed later in this chapter). Nor can it be amended or terminated unless all the beneficiaries consent. The Court does have the ability to determine that the termination of the Trust outweighs the purpose of the Trust.

An Irrevocable Trust will have the same objective as a Revocable Trust. The Settlor must transfer legal ownership and management of the property to the Trustee. The Settlor is making a gift or gifts to the Trust, with the primary objective of reducing taxes (inheritance, income, inheritance, or gift).

While the Settlor(s) could certainly make an outright gift of the property to heirs, it could incur any, or all, of the above types of taxes resulting in taxes due to the Trustee, the estate and the heirs. The Settlor may also have concerns about the heirs' ability to manage the trust property. The Settlor will also appoint a Trustee who has no interest in the estate. The Settlor cannot act as Trustee.

Once the property is transferred to the Irrevocable Trust, it cannot be undone. Therefore, the Settlor(s) must be sure that they will not need the property. It will have been given over to the Trust and a Trustee to manage until death. There are administrative costs associated with the creation and maintenance of an Irrevocable Trust. A tax identification number will be obtained and income taxes must be filed.

Depending upon the powers given to the Trustee, he or she may have been given the authority to make occasional gifts to the beneficiaries, usually at his or her discretion. Beneficiaries may be unhappy about the manner in which the Trustee is making distributions. This may cause animosity between the beneficiaries and the Trustee.

An Irrevocable Trust must be carefully written so that the intention of the Settlor(s) will be properly met. For instance, income should be clearly defined. A layperson's definition of income could be vastly different from the Internal Revenue Service's (IRS) definition of income.

For the purposes of the IRS, a gift tax exclusion of $13,000 per annum (for 2013) is allowed per beneficiary (otherwise called a donee).[1] A gift tax return does not have to be filed provided the gift is under the $13,000 limit. The federal government may change this amount annually, so always check for the allowable maximum amount. The trustee may gift less than the maximum allowable gift. He or she will want to work with the attorney and most likely a CPA to make sure the proper amount is gifted or in the case of an irrevocable trust is set aside as per the terms of the trust agreement.

A gift to an Irrevocable Trust must be considered a "present" interest and not a "future" interest. Present interest is defined as a gift that is made outright and the donee must have absolute present control of the money or property given. (Reg. § 25.2503-3.) A future interest is defined under Regulation § 25.2503 3(a).

The Irrevocable Trust must specify that the income from the Trust is either paid, credited, or distributed to the beneficiary. The Trust may also state that only the principal (and not the interest) be distributed to the beneficiary.

---

1. This figure is for the tax year 2013; $14,000 for 2014; and subject to ratification or change for subsequent years.

## Revocable Trust

This type of Trust is the most common Trust created in California. In many ways, it resembles a contract made between the Settlor(s) and the Trustee(s) regarding the delivery of property, the receipt of the property, and the management of the property.

The Settlor(s) are the people who own the property and wish to create a Trust "Agreement," transferring that property into the Trust. The Trustee(s) are those persons appointed by the Settlor's to manage the property once the Trustee acknowledges receipt of the property. The Settlor is going to give the Trustee powers (limited or unlimited) to manage the property that will usually be enumerated within the Trust. In most cases, for the purposes of a Revocable Trust, the Settlor(s) and Trustee(s) will be the same person(s).

(Note: you will often see the terms "under" *trust agreement (UTA), trust document (UTD)*, and *trust instrument* used interchangeably when referring to a revocable trust.)

A Revocable Trust, in most cases, may be amended, restated, or revoked, at any time, pursuant to the terms of the Trust and provided that one, or both, of the Trustee(s) wishes to do so.

A Revocable Trust can transfer a future interest, whereas in the Irrevocable Trust the Settlor does not have that ability. For example, the Settlor may grant a life estate to a spouse, a child or to any particular individual they wish. As discussed previously under the Will provisions, the property would only transfer upon the death of the person having the life estate; thus, this is a testamentary trust.

A Revocable Trust most commonly will provide for a future interest, known as a *remainder*. A typical Trust created by a husband and wife may provide for the Trust to be divided into two parts upon the death of the first spouse. (These will be discussed later in the chapter under marital deduction and by-pass trusts.) The property, including the principal and interest, in the decedent's share, may be used by the surviving spouse during his/her lifetime. Once the surviving spouse passes away the decedent's share of the estate passes to those who were to receive the property as set forth in the Trust. Thus, a future interest is created, as the decedent's named beneficiaries do not receive the estate upon the decedent's death; this would be a testamentary trust.

The revocable Trust allows the Settlor the most options in creating, dispersing, and managing the trust, particularly during his/her lifetime.

## Advantages of a Revocable Trust

The assets of a revocable trust are not subject to probate, provided the assets have been transferred into the Trust. As previously indicated under the probate process, a decedent's estate becomes public through the Court system. A Trust will remain private between the Trustee and the beneficiaries. There are exceptions such as when an asset was not transferred into the Trust and the Court must be asked for Instructions (as indicated in the previous section) or if a beneficiary contests the Trust. Typically, however, a Trust is more difficult to contest.

A Trust can also include *wealth management* techniques that may help the Settlor (and/or their spouse) and their children delay or completely avoid certain types of taxes. The Settlors have much more flexibility when creating a Trust in determining how their assets will be distributed, setting aside money, providing a future interest for an heir, particularly a child who is mentally incompetent or who is disabled and receiving some type of public assistance. A Trust, and its related documents, can provide protection from conservatorship of the Settlor(s) should he and/or she become incompetent. The Settlor(s) may wish to create a Trust(s) for their minor children and/or grandchildren. These are referred to as sub-trusts. The sub-trusts created by Revocable Trust, even for a minor child, do not normally require judicial oversight, as would an account created under a Guardianship of the Estate, a custodial or UTMA.

Additionally, the assets of the Trust are protected because they are not owned by an individual. The Trust is the owner of the property and the Trustee is the person named to represent the Trust and to carry out Trust business. This, however, may also be cumbersome to some individuals as there are additional steps required each time a person needs to alter the property in some manner. As you have learned, stocks, bonds, mutual funds, real and even some personal property may be transferred only after certain documentation is provided. It is essential that the Settlor(s) property be transferred into the Trust to be afforded this protection.

For example, if you own paper stocks and are frequently selling and purchasing stocks, each time a transaction is made, you are going to be required to complete certain formalities. However, if you own a brokerage account or mutual fund and can trade, purchase, or sell stocks and/or bonds though that account, you will not have to complete the formalities for each transaction. Once the account is set, unless it is completely liquidated, you have greater flexibility. The person who owns paper stocks is going to hesitate creating a Trust and then funding the Trust with his or her stocks and bonds if they understand the "paper trail" that is going to be required with each transaction. This critical step is an often neglected one, unfortunately.

The same is true if you plan to buy and sell your home every few years or if you buy and sell income-producing property. Each time you purchase property you will have to complete the second step of placing the property into the Trust. Many title companies will not provide this service upon the closing of the loan. Some may, but for an extra fee. Additionally, if you refinance your home and the property is owned by the Trust, the lender or title company may require that the Trustee transfer the property out of the Trust prior to the loan funding. Once the loan is funded, the property will need to be transferred back into the Trust. This critical step is often a neglected one, unfortunately.

Although it is a fairly simple process, some individuals cite this as a reason for not creating a Trust. Others state that it is too expensive to have an attorney draft a Trust and the related documentation. For some individuals this may be true and as previously indicated, he/she may be able to accomplish the transfer of property to heirs by other means, or the estate may be so small that it does not warrant the expenditure.

The average Californian (aged 25–50) who owns a medium priced home, has a good job with a pension, has a spouse and a couple of children, two automobiles, the usual furniture, bank, and/or savings accounts may not feel they need to create a Trust. That may be true. However, the issues become more complex as this family acquires more assets and potentially inherits property from their respective parents. Once the family begins to accumulate wealth, they may need to discuss tax-planning issues with an attorney so that the estate will lessened in value before the children ultimately inherit the estate.

Using the above scenario, the attorney can, upon review of the assets and circumstances determine whether the couple may need protection on two fronts: 1) protection from federal estate taxes, and 2) protection for the children from requiring judicial oversight of custodial accounts if both parents die when the children are still minors. The attorney can also recommend whether the creation of a Trust, transfer costs, and future administration outweigh the lesser costs of creating a Will and the future costs of probate. A Trust will typically include provisions, or additional documents that provide for a conservatorship and/or agent for property management should the Trustee become incapacitated.

## Protection from Federal Estate Taxes

Each United States citizen may give (transfer) a total of Five Million Dollars ($5,000,000) to their beneficiaries upon their death (effective January 1, 2012) without incurring federal estate tax. This is commonly referred to as the **unified credit** or **applicable exclusion amount**. (Internal Revenue Code §§ 2505 and 2010(c).) For your reference, a chart is provided at Appendix 7A showing the applicable exclusion amount for previous and future years.

There are numerous ways in which a single individual and/or a married couple may choose to reduce their potential federal estate taxes. First, the attorney will want to work with the client to determine their current and potential assets (net worth). He or she will also need to know the ages of the client and the children.

# Custodial Accounts

Using the above scenario, imagine that both parents work. They both have jobs where they accumulate a pension and contribute to an IRA or some other retirement or educational type of fund. They have also purchased life insurance so their children will be cared for if something happens to them.

As discussed in Chapter Six, pensions, IRAs and life insurance are "contractual" agreements and have a named beneficiary. Upon the death of the person owning the account, the beneficiary receives the money in those assets. In most cases, married persons will name each other as primary beneficiary and their children as secondary beneficiaries. What happens if both parents die in a tragic automobile accident? The child receives the retirement and insurance proceeds ... right? Only if the children are eighteen years of age. A child who is under the age of eighteen would not receive those funds. The funds would have to be put into a custodial account with judicial oversight. This means that a person would have to be appointed as custodian. Every two years, the custodian will have to report to the court on the status of on the account for each child. This will cost time and money for the custodian and will usually, tie up the money until the child is eighteen. (This will be discussed in more detail in Chapter Eleven.)

By creating a Revocable Trust, the Settlors (parents) can name the Trust as the secondary beneficiaries of any retirement and insurance accounts. If both parents should die and they have minor children, the monies from those accounts will be transferred into the Trust. The successor Trustee will then oversee the Trust estate created for the children without judicial oversight. The Trust may provide that the Trustee can distribute money from the Trust for the children's education and welfare while they are minors. The custodian does not have that ability. Thus, if a child needs to have special equipment (books, sports equipment, computer, etc.) while they are in high school and the Trustee feels it is warranted, the Trustee can provide it for the child. The Trustee does not have to wait until the child is eighteen to make the money available. The Trustee does not have to ask permission from the Court, as would a custodian or guardian. This is very important to a lot of families and a good reason to create a Trust, even if the client does not feel he or she has much in the way of assets.

## Ability to Amend Trust

A Trust as a "living" document during the Trustee(s) lifetime may evolve with the family. A Trustee may inherit property from a parent or other person and wish to keep that property separate and/or want to assure that the property is distributed in a specific manner. The Trustee may have grandchildren that he or she now wishes to provide for by creating a sub-trust.

Rather than completely re-write the Trust instrument each time a change occurs or is needed, the Trustee(s) may execute an amendment addressing the changes. The Trustee(s) can also revoke a Trust and execute an entirely new Trust in order to make significant changes that are clearly understood. The Trustee may also amend and/or re-state the Trust to change or clarify the document, particularly if laws change that may affect taxes and/or distributions.

The following is typical language in a trust (created by a married couple) that either trustee may amend or revoke the trust at any time. This or other standard language regarding this topic is required in a **revocable** trust:

> Settlors' Rights to Amend, Change or Revoke the Trust Agreement. Either Settlor may, during the joint lives of the Settlors, by signed instruments delivered to the Trustee: (1) withdraw the joint estate from this Trust in any amount and at any time upon giving reasonable notice in writing to the Trustee and to the other Settlor; provided, however, that all or any part of the joint estate withdrawn by either Settlor shall be conveyed and delivered to both Settlors as tenants in common; (2) withdraw the separate estate contributed by such Settlor from this Trust in any amount and at any time upon giving reasonable notice in writing to the Trustee; (3) add separate property to the Trust.

# Types of Trusts

There are as many different Trust documents as there are individuals. A Trust is considered a "living document" that evolves with each individual and/or married couple. As indicated under the Wills section, estate planning is unique to each individual person or couple. As you become more familiar with trust drafting, you will the hear names for many **types** of Trusts:

- Power of Appointment
- Disclaimer
- Sprinkling
- Marital Deduction
- By Pass
- Survivor's
- Spendthrift
- Five-by-Five Power
- Charitable Remainder Trust
- Minor's Trust
- Special Needs
- Crummey

- Generation Skipping
- Dynasty

For the most part, the above "types" of Trust relate to specific provisions that will be included within the trust agreement of a particular client. (These Trust provisions will be discussed in greater detail later in this Chapter.) In fact, some Trusts will contain more than one of the provisions listed above. Thus, it will depend upon what the client hopes to accomplish in creating his or her estate planning documents.

The following are some typical questions the attorney will need to ask each client to evaluate his or her specific needs and goals:

- Is the client simply trying to avoid probate?
- Do they wish to minimize their estate taxes? If so, what is the net worth?
- Do they want to make sure that their minor children's inheritance is properly protected and that they have a Trustee rather than a court-appointed custodian?
- Do they want or need for their grandchildren to receive all of their estate, rather than have the estate go directly to their children who may not need it?
- Do they have an adult child who has disabilities and is receiving benefits and they want those benefits to be protected?

In many instances, the client is going to be trying to accomplish one or more of the above by creating an estate plan.

## Revocable Life Insurance Trust

In some instances, a Settlor will create a Revocable (Life Insurance) Trust for the benefit of their beneficiaries. This type of Trust is especially useful when the person(s) has minor children and does not want to create a standard Revocable Trust. An Insurance Trust may be changed or terminated at any time. An independent Trustee must be appointed to manage the Trust. The Trustee may be given powers to invade the principal in the event the beneficiary has an emergency, such as for an illness or for educational purposes.

The proceeds of the "policy" are paid directly to the named beneficiaries and are therefore not a part of the insured's estate, provided the insured has not made the estate the beneficiary. The Trustee will oversee the management of the investment and other financial matters for the children.

In most cases, the Grantor/Settlor is creating a Trust, while minimizing taxes for the estate. The Grantor would prefer that the beneficiaries wait until their death to receive the proceeds of the insurance trust (policy). Thus, each year the Trustee must advise the beneficiary(ies) that they have thirty (30) days to request the distribution of shares of the trust. This is referred to as a Crummey election or a Crummey letter. (Crummey v. Commissioner (1978) 397 F.2d 82 (9th Circuit). This type of revocable (insurance) trust is best created for adult children as beneficiaries, only after the parents have discussed this type of estate planning mechanism with the children. The children should agree that they will elect to wait to receive their derivative share upon the death of the Settlor (or the surviving Settlor) as the case may be.

An Insurance Trust allows the Settlor(s) to contribute up to the annual exclusion ($13,000) per beneficiary[2] into an Insurance policy for the benefit of the children upon death (or the second death, if married). Even though any person may make an annual gift to as many individuals as they choose, the Grantor may wish to delay the transfer of wealth, while maximizing the allowable federal estate tax reduction. The Insurance Trust allows the opportunity to do so.

## Other Estate Planning

Estate planning is the area of legal practice that includes the creation and administration of the many different types of trusts. Most legal practitioners, however, consider estate planning to encompass not just trusts, but the many other collateral documents that they recommend a client execute in order to create the most effective manner of managing their estate. These include, but are not limited to, Pour-Over Wills, Durable Powers of Attorney for Property Management, Durable Powers of Attorney for Health Care, Advance Health Care Directives, Deeds, Assignments of Property, Transmutation Agreements, and Certified Abstracts of Trusts. These various documents are considered an **entire** Estate Planning package.

The majority of the above listed documents will be discussed in Chapters Eight and Nine.

## Pour-Over Wills

Regardless of whether the client wishes to have the attorney create and prepare an entire estate plan package, the attorney will prepare a Pour-Over Will in conjunction with a Trust that is created. It is potentially malpractice if the attorney does not create a Pour-Over Will for each Settlor/Trustee.

The Pour-Over Will is similar in almost all aspects to the Will as discussed in Chapter Three. The Will provides the information as to the Testator, his or her family, nomination of Executor, as well as guardianship provisions for any minor children. The primary difference will be the manner in which property is to be distributed.

A Pour-Over Will contains a provision or provisions that state that the Testator has created a Trust. The provision(s) will provide the name of the Trust and state when it was created. In many cases, the provision will state that the Trust was created on the same day as the Will and executed immediately before the Will. Some software programs will require the insertion of the actual date. The attorney may prefer to include a date specific or only the reference to the signing of the documents. You will prepare the drafts based on that preference.

The Pour-Over Will becomes a receptacle for: 1) property that was not transferred into the Trust; 2) the Testator's property in the event the Trust was revoked; or 3) property which is to be received via insurance, retirement, or some other beneficiary designation.

The Pour-Over Will usually states that if any portion of the Testator's estate is not disposed of by the Trust, the Executor should distribute the property in the same manner as set forth in the Trust. Thus, the term "pour-over."

---

2. The amount should be verified annually as Congress has not determined an annual exclusion amount past 2014 for which the exclusion is $14,000.

Common reasons people need a Pour-Over Will are as follows:

1) Real property was refinanced and the property was not transferred back into the trust upon completion of the mortgage documents and title transfers.

2) Testator received a windfall (inheritance, lottery winnings, etc.) and did not have an opportunity to place the property into the Trust prior to death.

In either of the two above events, when the decedent dies and the property is not held by the Trust, the property will require probate. The Court will be required to provide instructions as to who will receive the property. This can be accomplished by a summary procedure known as a Petition for Instructions, rather than a full probate. The Petition for Instructions will be discussed further in Chapter Ten.

Thus, if the Settlor stated that his or her estate should be distributed in equal shares to his/her two adult children; the Court will instruct the Executor/Trustee to distribute the estate to the two adult children pursuant to the Trust.

The following is an example of "pour-over" provisions:

Gift of Entire Estate. I give all of my property to the trustee of the _____ **Family Trust**, created under the declaration of trust executed on the same date as, but immediately before, the execution of this will, by _____, as settlors and trustees. The trustee of that trust shall add the property disposed of under this will to the trust principal and hold, administer, and distribute the property in accordance with the provisions of that declaration of trust, including any amendments of that declaration of trust that have been made before or after execution of this will.

Disposition of Residue Disposition of Residue. If the _____ **Family Trust** has been revoked, terminated, or declared invalid for any reason, I give the residue of my estate to the executor of this will, as trustee, who shall hold, administer, and distribute the property under a testamentary trust, the terms of which shall be identical to the terms of the _____ **Family Trust** that are in effect on the date of execution of this will or such later date on which this will is republished.

Without a Pour-Over Will and in the event the Trust was not funded and/or property was not properly transferred into the Trust, the entire purpose of the Trust (avoiding probate, taxes, etc.) would be lost.

## Creating a Trust

As with a Will, the first step is for the attorney to meet with the client(s) to discuss their needs, evaluate their circumstances and estate, and to reach an understanding as to how to best accomplish the goals for transfer of their wealth upon their death. Once the clients decide to create a Trust, the attorney will also want to discuss the various other types of documents that should be created at the same time: Pour-Over Will(s), Durable Powers of Attorney for Property Management and/or Health Care, Advance Heath Care Directive, and any other documents the attorney typically uses to create an estate planning package for a client. The attorney will also want to discuss with the clients the pros and cons of creating a Trust and impress upon the clients some of the formalities that accompany creating this type of estate plan. The clients will also need to be aware that as the family changes and/or their net worth increases, decreases, or other life changes occur such as an illness, they will likely need to reevaluate the estate planning documents and needs.

Just as with a Will, the attorney is going to want the client(s) to complete a questionnaire. Typically, these questionnaires are at least 10–12 pages long. There is a great amount of detail that will be needed by the attorney. You will find that many clients do not like to do paperwork. They will return the questionnaire, or come to the next meeting without having completed much of the information. It may be necessary for the attorney or paralegal to sit down with the client, go through the questions, and fill out the form for them. Although somewhat time-consuming, it will save the paralegal and/or the attorney many follow up telephone calls to obtain the information. The most critical information needed is as follows:

- Full name(s) of client(s)
- Current address and telephone numbers
- Social Security Numbers
- Dates of Birth
- Names of all children
- Birth dates of all children
- Names of deceased children
- Name of child's other parent (if spouse is not the natural parent)
- Name(s) of persons to be appointed as Trustee, Executor, Agent for Power of Attorney and Health Care Directive, Guardian if minor children
- List of assets and their approximate values (residence and/or vacation property, automobiles, recreational vehicles, retirement, mutual fund accounts, annuities, IRAs, insurance, antiques, collectibles and other items of value
- If anyone has "special needs"
- Proof of citizenship

The client may have also failed to bring in copies of important papers such as deeds, insurance policies, vehicle title/registration, IRA, retirement accounts, mutual fund accounts, etc. It is imperative that the firm receive this documentation so that any assets that will need to be transferred into the Trust can be completed prior to the execution of the Trust Agreement. The attorney must be able to review all of the documents to determine which must be "owned" by the Trust and the correct instrument for making said transfer. As indicated in Chapter Six, with regard to transfers of property, you will have noted that often it takes a few days, if not weeks to obtain a financial institutions forms and/or a list of the required information in order to make a transfer. The same will be true with Trust transfers.

For example, if a married couple has minor children, the attorney will most likely recommend that their respective insurance policies be changed to name the Trust as the secondary beneficiary. It will likely be the paralegal who will contact the insurance company to obtain the required forms for the client to execute.

Note: Some attorneys will have the client(s) perform this function while others will have their paralegal (or other office staff) request the information and complete the forms. That way, the attorney knows the forms have been completed, reviewed, and signed and that the changes were sent to the appropriate person or entity to be changed. Obviously, you will need the name of the company and a telephone number to contact to obtain the forms. This is not possible until the client has provided the firm with the required information.

As a reliable and organized paralegal, you will learn how to best facilitate the various ways of getting this information in a timely manner from the clients. This will allow you to have the work completed, reviewed by the attorney, and ready for the clients' signatures when they come in to sign their estate planning documents.

## The Nuts and Bolts of the Trust (Mandatory and/or Boilerplate Language)

As with the Will, the Trust will likely have a specific format that the attorney will use based on the type of software package he or she uses or templates that have been created by the firm. There are many specific provisions that must be included in a valid Trust. However, there is often discretion as to the exact language. The following sections contain some of that information.[3]

The initial paragraph of the Trust is usually referred to as the *Declaration of Trust*. This is where the Settlor(s) declares him and/or herself as the Trustee(s) of the Trust property. The attorney will need to determine, with the client's input and preferences, the name of the Trust, which will be referenced within the *Declaration*. There are many variations for naming the trust.

The following are a few examples:

The Sam E. Fellow, Jr. and Marci Fellow Revocable Trust

The Sam and Marci Fellow Revocable Trust

The Sam and Marci Fellow Family Trust

The 2012 Fellow Family Trust

In addition, some attorneys like to put the exact date the Trust was created on the first page under the "Declarations of Trust." Others will only make reference to the "date of execution" which then requires that anyone reviewing the Trust look at the signature page to determine the date of execution and thus creation of the Trust. One reason some attorneys prefer to have the date of execution within the declaration is so that anyone asking for verification of the Trust, for example the bank where the client will be renaming a money market or similar account, will only need to have a copy of the first and last pages of the Trust. Since the Trust is a confidential document, in most cases, a bank or other financial institution does not need to see and know the contents of the trust in its entirety. The execution may be the need to see the *powers* of the trustee, however again only those provisions need to be provided. Alternatively, a Trust Certification, which will be discussed later, will serve the same purpose. The Trust Certification will be discussed in Chapter Eight.

The second section of the Trust is used to identify the Settlor(s), Trustor, and Trustee(s). It may also identify any children of each Settlor, as well as whether there are any deceased children. In the event there are children of "blended" families, the attorney may want to indicate the child's other natural parent.

A note about estate planning software and/or templates. As previously indicated in Chapters Two and Three, almost every situation is unique in some way. Therefore, many estate planning software packages include generic provisions. It will be up to the attorney to determine how each document is created for the client and which provisions will

---

3. The language provided in this section is **not** meant to be legal advice. These provisions are for the purpose of illustration only.

need to be added, deleted, or modified to achieve the client's situation, goals, and needs. It will be to your advantage to keep some type of file, spreadsheet, or other document that will provide you with a quick reference as to some of the unique and/or often used language to be included in Trusts for other clients.

The order of the Trust, from this point forward, will be dependent upon the type of software and/or the attorney's preference. Some software will list the names of the Successor Trustees immediately after the first two sections. Others will place the Trustee information later in the document. Regardless of where it is placed, the name(s) of the Successor Trustee(s) should be prominently noted; it will usually be set within a separate article or section.

Another important section is the identification of property to be included in the Trust with the statement that the property owned by the Settlor(s) is being transferred into the Trust and will be held and administered by the Trustee(s). The following is an example of a standard transfer of property language for a married couple's Trust:

> The Settlors have paid over, assigned, granted, conveyed, transferred and delivered, and by this Agreement do hereby pay over, assign, grant, convey, transfer and deliver unto the Trustee the property described in Schedule A, annexed hereto and made a part hereof, and have caused or will cause the Trustee to be designated as beneficiary of those life insurance policies described in Schedule B, annexed hereto and made a part hereof. These insurance policies, and any other insurance policies that may be delivered to the Trustee hereunder or under which the Trustee may be designated as beneficiary, the proceeds of all such policies being payable to the Trustee, and any other property that may be received or which has been received by the Trustee hereunder, as invested and reinvested (hereinafter referred to as the "Trust Estate"), shall be held, administered and distributed by the Trustee as hereinafter set forth.

> Any property designated by the Settlors as Joint Property and transferred to the Trustee by the Settlors, as invested and reinvested, together with the rents, issues and profits therefrom (hereinafter referred to as "the joint estate") shall be deemed to be property held as tenants in common and shall retain its characteristics as property held as tenants in common during the joint lifetimes of the Settlors, subject, however, to the provisions of this Agreement.

> Separate property (defined as property owned by one Settlor) transferred to the Trustee, as invested and reinvested, together with the rents, issues and profits therefrom (hereinafter referred to as "the separate estate") shall retain its character as separate property of the Settlor who transferred such property to the Trustee, subject, however, to the provisions of this Agreement.

The Trust must also provide the Trustees with the power to perform certain acts and duties during their lifetime(s). The following is sample language that allows the Trustee to use any of the Trust property during the lifetime of the Settlor(s) for the Settlor's benefit. This provision provides the Trustee with broad discretion as to how the property may be used.

> The Trustee shall hold, manage, invest and reinvest the joint estate (if any requires such management and investment) and shall collect the income, if any, therefrom and shall dispose of the net income and principal during the joint lives of the Settlors as follows:

> The Trustee shall pay to or apply for the benefit each of the Settlors an undivided one-half of all the net income of the joint estate.

The Trustee may pay to or apply for the benefit of each of the Settlors such sums from the principal of the joint estate as in its sole discretion shall be necessary or advisable from time to time for the medical care, education, support and maintenance in reasonable comfort of the Settlors, taking into consideration to the extent the Trustee deems advisable, any other income or resources of the Settlors known to the Trustee. Any payment made shall be to both Settlors.

Either Settlor may at any time during the joint lives of the Settlors and from time to time withdraw all or any part of the principal of the joint estate, free of trust, by delivering an instrument in writing duly signed by him or her to the Trustee and to the other Settlor, describing the property or portion thereof desired to be withdrawn. Upon receipt of such instrument, the Trustee shall thereupon convey and deliver to the Settlors, free of trust, the property described in such instrument. Such conveyance from the joint estate shall be made to the Settlors as tenants in common.

The Trustee shall hold, manage, invest and reinvest the separate estate of each Settlor (if any requires such management and investment) and shall collect the income, if any, therefrom and shall dispose of the net income and principal during the joint lives of the Settlors as follows:

The Trustee shall pay to or apply for the benefit of the Settlor who contributed such separate estate all of the net income of such Settlor's separate estate.

The Trustee may pay to or apply for the benefit of the Settlor who contributed such separate estate such sums from the principal thereof as in its sole discretion shall be necessary or advisable from time to time for the medical care, education, support and maintenance in reasonable comfort of such Settlor, taking into consideration to the extent the Trustee deems advisable, any other income and resources of such Settlor known to the Trustee.

The Trustee and/or successor Trustee must be defined. The successor Trustee will also need to be given certain powers, both during the lifetime of the Settlors, as well as after the Settlor's (or second Settlor's) death.

The Settlor(s) may also appoint joint successor Trustees. In that event, the Trustee provision should also include consideration for who will act as Trustee if one of the co-Trustees is unable or unwilling to act.

The following is sample language for a joint trust:

**Naming Individual Successor or Substitute Trustee.** If the Surviving Spouse and the initial successor individual Trustee should fail to qualify as Trustee hereunder, or for any reason should cease to act in such capacity, the successor or substitute Trustee who shall also serve without bond shall be _____ and _____

If for any reason is either unable or unable to serve as Trustee the remaining one of them shall serve.

**Final Succession If Individual Successor Trustee Cannot Act Final Succession If Individual Successor Trustee Cannot Act.** If the individual successor Trustee should fail to qualify as Trustee hereunder, or for any reason should cease to act in such capacity, then the successor or substitute Trustee who shall also serve without bond shall be_____.

Following the naming of the successor trustee(s), the Trust should contain provisions for who may be named the Trustee. This provision should also include any limitations, if any. Such language would be similar to the following:

Definition of Trustee. Whenever the word "Trustee" or any modifying or substituted pronoun therefore is used in this Trust, such words and respective pronouns shall include both the singular and the plural, the masculine, feminine and neuter gender thereof, and shall apply equally to the Trustee named herein and to any successor or substitute Trustee acting hereunder, and such successor or substitute Trustee shall have all the rights, powers and duties, authority and responsibility conferred upon the Trustee originally named herein.

The Trust must also provide language that sets forth the powers being given to the Trustee(s) and successor Trustee(s). The following is "boilerplate" type language:

Powers for Trustee. The Trustee is authorized in its fiduciary discretion (which shall be subject to the standard of reasonableness and good faith to all beneficiaries) with respect to any property, real or personal, at any time held under any provision of this Trust Agreement and without authorization by any court and in addition to any other rights, powers, authority and privileges granted by any other provision of this Trust Agreement or by statute or general rules of law:

To retain in the form received any property or undivided interests in property donated to, or otherwise acquired as a part of the Trust Estate, including residential property and shares of the Trustee's own stock, regardless of any lack of diversification, risk or nonproductivity, as long as it deems advisable, and to exchange any such security or property for other securities or properties and to retain such items received in exchange, although such property represents a large percentage of the total property of the Trust Estate or even the entirety thereof.

To invest and reinvest all or any part of the Trust Estate in any property and undivided interests in property, wherever located, including bonds, debentures, notes, secured or unsecured, stocks of corporations regardless of class, interests in limited partnerships, limited liability companies or similar entities, real estate or any interest in real estate whether or not productive at the time of investment, interests in trusts, investment trusts, whether of the open and/or closed fund types, and participation in common, collective or pooled trust funds of the Trustee, insurance contracts on the life of any beneficiary or annuity contracts for any beneficiary, without being limited by any statute or rule of law concerning investments by fiduciaries.

To sell or dispose of or grant options to purchase any property, real or personal, constituting a part of the Trust Estate, for cash or upon credit, to exchange any property of the Trust Estate for other property, at such times and upon such terms and conditions as it may deem best, and no person dealing with it shall be bound to see to the application of any monies paid.

To hold any securities or other property in its own name as Trustee, in its own name, in the name of a nominee (with or without disclosure of any fiduciary relationship) or in bearer form.

To keep, at any time and from time to time, all or any portion of the Trust Estate in cash and uninvested for such period or periods of time as it may deem advisable, without liability for any loss in income by reason thereof.

To sell or exercise stock subscription or conversion rights.

To refrain from voting or to vote shares of stock which are a part of the Trust Estate at shareholders' meetings in person or by special, limited, or general proxy and in general to exercise all the rights, powers and privileges of an owner in respect to any securities constituting a part of the Trust Estate.

To participate in any plan of reorganization or consolidation or merger involving any company or companies whose stock or other securities shall be part of the Trust Estate, and to deposit such stock or other securities under any plan of reorganization or with any protective committee and to delegate to such committee discretionary power with relation thereto, to pay a proportionate part of the expenses of such committee and any assessments levied under any such plan, to accept and retain new securities received by the Trustee pursuant to any such plan, to exercise all conversion, subscription, voting and other rights, of whatsoever nature pertaining to such property, and to pay any amount or amounts of money as it may deem advisable in connection therewith.

To borrow money and to encumber, mortgage or pledge any asset of the Trust Estate for a term within or extending beyond the term of the trust, in connection with the exercise of any power vested in the Trustee.

To enter for any purpose into a lease as lessor or lessee with or without option to purchase or renew for a term within or extending beyond the term of the trust.

To subdivide, develop, or dedicate real property to public use or to make or obtain the vacation of plats and adjust boundaries, to adjust differences in valuation on exchange or partition by giving or receiving consideration, and to dedicate easements to public use without consideration.

To make ordinary or extraordinary repairs or alterations in buildings or other structures, to demolish any improvements, to raze existing or erect new party walls or buildings.

To continue and operate any business owned by the Settlors or either of them at such Settlor's death and to do any and all things deemed needful or appropriate by the Trustee, including the power to incorporate the business and to put additional capital into the business, for such time as it shall deem advisable, without liability for loss resulting from the continuance or operation of the business except for its own negligence; and to close out, liquidate or sell the business at such time and upon such terms as it shall deem best.

To collect, receive, and receipt for rents, issues, profits, and income of the Trust Estate.

To insure the assets of the Trust Estate against damage or loss and the Trustee against liability with respect to third persons.

In buying and selling assets, in lending and borrowing money, and in all other transactions, irrespective of the occupancy by the same person of dual positions, to deal with itself in its separate, or any fiduciary capacity.

To compromise, adjust, arbitrate, sue on or defend, abandon, or otherwise deal with and settle claims in favor of or against the Trust Estate as the Trustee shall deem best.

To employ and compensate agents, accountants, investment advisers, brokers, attorneys-in-fact, attorneys-at-law, tax specialists, realtors, and other assistants and advisors deemed by the Trustee needful for the proper administration of the Trust Estate, and to do so without liability for any neglect, omission, misconduct, or default of any such agent or professional representative provided such person was selected and retained with reasonable care.

To determine what shall be fairly and equitably charged or credited to income and what to principal.

To hold and retain the principal of the Trust Estate undivided until actual division shall become necessary in order to make distributions; to hold, manage, invest, and account for the several shares or parts thereof by appropriate entries on the Trustee's books of account; and to allocate to each share or part of share its proportionate part of all receipts and expenses; provided, however, the carrying of several trusts as one shall not defer the vesting in title or in possession of any share or part of share thereof.

To make payment in cash or in kind, or partly in cash and partly in kind upon any division or distribution of the Trust Estate (including the satisfaction of any pecuniary distribution) without regard to the income tax basis of any specific property allocated to any beneficiary and to value and appraise any asset and to distribute such asset in kind at its appraised value; and when dividing fractional interests in property among several beneficiaries to allocate entire interests in some property to one beneficiary and entire interests in other property to another beneficiary or beneficiaries.

In general, to exercise all powers in the management of the Trust Estate which any individual could exercise in his or her own right, upon such terms and conditions as it may reasonably deem best, and to do all acts which it may deem reasonably necessary or proper to carry out the purposes of this Trust Agreement.

To purchase property, real or personal, from either Settlor's general estate upon such terms and conditions as to price and terms of payment as the Settlor's executor or administrator and the Trustee shall agree, to hold the property so purchased as a part of the Trust Estate although it may not qualify as an authorized trust investment except for this provision, and to dispose of such property as and when the Trustee shall deem advisable. The fact that the Settlor's executor or administrator and the Trustee are the same shall in no way affect the validity of this provision.

To lend funds to either Settlor's general estate upon such terms and conditions as to interest rates, maturities, and security as the Settlor's executor or administrator and the Trustee shall agree, the fact that they may be the same in no way affecting the validity of this provision.

To receive property bequeathed, devised or donated to the Trustee by either Settlor or any other person; to receive the proceeds of any insurance policy that names the Trustee as beneficiary; to execute all necessary receipts and releases to Executors, donors, insurance companies and other parties adding property to the Trust Estate.

To combine assets of two or more trusts if the provisions and terms of each trust are substantially identical, and to administer them as a single trust, if the Trustee reasonably determines that the administration as a single trust is consistent with the Settlors' intent, and facilitates the trust's administration without defeating or impairing the interests of the beneficiaries.

To divide any trust into separate shares or separate trusts or to create separate trusts if the Trustee reasonably deems it appropriate and the division or creation is consistent with the Settlors' intent, and facilitates the trust's administration without defeating or impairing the interests of the beneficiaries.

To divide property in any trust being held hereunder with an inclusion ratio, as defined in section 2642(a)(1) of the Internal Revenue Code of 1986, as from time to time amended or under similar future legislation, of neither one nor zero into two separate trusts representing two fractional shares of the property being divided, one to have an inclusion ratio of one and the other to have an inclusion ratio of zero, to create trusts to receive property with an inclusion ratio of either one or zero and if this cannot be done to refuse to accept property which does not have a matching inclusion ratio to the receiving trust's ratio, all as the Trustee in its sole discretion deems best.

If the Trustee shall act as the Executor of either Settlor's estate, to elect to allocate any portion or all of such Settlor's generation-skipping transfer exemption provided for in Code section 2631 or under similar future legislation, in effect at the time of such Settlor's death, to any portion or all of any other trusts or bequests in such Settlor's Will or any other transfer which such Settlor is the transferor for purposes of the generation-skipping tax. Generally, the Settlors anticipate that each Settlor's Executor will elect to allocate this exemption first to direct skips as defined in Code section 2612, then to *[the name of] Family Trust*, unless it would be inadvisable based on all the circumstances at the time of making the allocation; and to make the special election under section 2652(a) (3) of the Code to the extent such Settlor's Executor deems in the best interest of the Settlor's estate.

## Trustee Powers

One important note regarding Trustee powers. The powers may need to be different for someone who will be the initial Settlor/Trustee than the Successor Trustee who may not be a spouse, trusted family member or friend. A Trustee who is a financial institution or other fiduciary or even an individual with whom the Settlor does not have complete confidence and trust who will be named as Trustee or Successor Trustee may need to have more restricted powers. The Settlor/Trustee may even feel that requiring a bond is warranted. The attorney will need to make sure that these provision and powers are clearly stated in order to avoid potential abuse of power at such time as that Trustee begins to act and fulfill his or her duties.

## Discretionary Provisions

Most Trusts, including sub-trusts, will include provisions for the Trustee to use his/her discretion while administering the estate. This includes successor Trustees. It is difficult to predict exactly what beneficiaries might need at some future date. Children and/or grandchildren may need extensive medical treatment and care, they may wish to attend college or technical school, or need funds for lessons, training, and/or extracurricular activities such as being a member of an athletic or Olympic team.

The Settlor(s) typically will provide that the Trustee use his or her judgment (discretion) to make decisions as to what is best for the needs of the child provided there are adequate funds in the estate, rather than make a mandatory requirement.

For example, the Settlor may request the inclusion of provisions similar to the following:

> At any time or times during the trust term, the trustee shall pay to or apply for the benefit of the child so much, or all, of the net income and principal of the trust as the trustee deems proper for the child's health, education, support, and maintenance. In exercising discretion, the trustee shall give the consideration that the trustee deems proper to all other income and resources that are known to the trustee and that are readily available to the beneficiaries for use for these purposes. All decisions of the trustee regarding payments under this subsection, if any, are within the trustee's discretion and shall be final and incontestable by anyone. The trustee shall accumulate and add to principal any net income not distributed.

## Revocation and Amendment

As previously indicated there should be language that allows the Trustee(s) to revoke or amend the Trust. There should also be a provision that allows the Trustee to resign and appoint a Successor to act while the Trustee is still alive.

## Taxes

Most well written Trusts will also include language that references the Internal Revenue Codes that apply to the transfer of property subject to a Trust. Below is an example of such language:

**Definition of Words Relating to the Internal Revenue Code.** As used herein, the words "gross estate," "adjusted gross estate," "taxable estate," "unified credit" ("unified credit" shall also mean "applicable credit amount"), "state death tax credit," "maximum marital deduction," "marital deduction," "pass," and any other word or words which from the context in which it or they are used refer to the Internal Revenue Code shall have the same meaning as such words have for the purposes of applying the Internal Revenue Code to a deceased Settlor's estate. For purposes of this Trust Agreement, such Settlor's "available generation-skipping transfer exemption" means the generation-skipping transfer tax exemption provided in section 2631 of the Internal Revenue Code of 1986, as amended, in effect at the time of such Settlor's death reduced by the aggregate of (1) the amount, if any, of such Settlor's exemption allocated to lifetime transfers of such Settlor by such Settlor or by operation of law, and (2) the amount, if any, such Settlor has specifically allocated to other property of the such Settlor's gross estate for federal estate tax purposes. For purposes of this Trust Agreement if at the time of such Settlor's death such Settlor has made gifts with an inclusion ratio of greater than zero for which the gift tax return due date has not expired (including extensions) and such Settlor has not yet filed a return, it shall be deemed that such Settlor's generation-skipping transfer exemption has been allocated to these transfers to the extent necessary (and possible) to exempt the transfer(s) from generation-skipping transfer tax. Reference to sections of the Internal Revenue Code and to the Internal Revenue Code shall refer to the Internal Revenue Code amended to the date of such Settlor's death.

Generation-Skipping Transfer Tax (GSTT)—The California Revenue & Tax Code also governs the application of GSTT qualifications at R&T §§ 16800 et seq. that may need to be considered and, if necessary, incorporated within the Trust agreement.

## Provisions for Distribution of the Trust Estate

Of primary importance are the provisions that relate to how the Trust will be administered and distributed upon the Settlor's death. If the Trust is for a married couple, then the Trust will need to contain language directing the administration and distribution upon the death of the first Settlor, as well as upon the death of the Surviving Settlor.

These provisions are those that will be the most complex within the Trust Agreement. The language may need to be modified (if using a software program or a template) to incorporate the client's specific needs. Those needs may include, but are not limited to, the following:

- distribution to lawful beneficiaries
- distribution to a blended family
- tax planning
- gifting (reduction of estate)
- disclaimer of property

- generation skipping transfers
- distribution of specific items of property
- distribution of separate property
- minor children
- adult child(ren) with special needs

The attorney will need to determine the client's needs with regard to the distribution of the property. The following are several relatively simple scenarios that may affect the manner in which the trust is distributed.

Husband and Wife are in their seventies and have both retired. They have three adult children. They own a 3 Bedroom, 2.5 Bath home that they own outright in joint tenancy in Merced, California. They receive retirement and social security. They have two automobiles, a recreational vehicle, and a boat. They have a time-share in Hawaii and a mutual fund account. The total estate is valued at $950,000.

Husband and Wife are in their seventies and have both retired. They have three adult children. They own a 3 Bedroom, 2.5 Bath home that they own outright in joint tenancy in Merced, California. They receive retirement and social security. They have two automobiles, a recreational vehicle, and a boat. They have a time-share in Hawaii and a mutual fund account. Husband and Wife own a small business that was incorporated and which they previously ran. Their oldest child has taken over running the business and pays them an annual stipend. The total estate is valued at $2,300,000.

Husband and Wife are in their seventies and have both retired. They have three adult children. They own a 5 Bedroom, 3.5 Bath home that they own in joint tenancy, located in San Diego, California. They have a 3 Bedroom, 2.5 Bath home in Lake Tahoe, California and a time-share in Hawaii. They own a commercial building in San Francisco, which was inherited by Wife during marriage and which is revenue generating. (The attorney needs to determine if this is maintained as separate property or it has been commingled.) They own four automobiles, a recreational vehicle, and a motorcycle. The couple owns numerous stocks and bonds, mutual funds and other investments. Their estate is valued at $6,000,000.

Husband and Wife are in their forties and both work. They have two adult children and one minor child. The two adult children are in college. They own a 3 Bedroom, 2.5 Bath home in joint tenancy, with a mortgage, located in Fresno, California. They have 2 automobiles and a motorcycle. They have a time-share in Hawaii and a mutual fund account. The value of their estate is $1,250,000.

Husband and Wife are in their forties and both work. Each was previously married. They each have two adult children from their previous marriages and have two minor children from their current marriage to each other. They own a 4 Bedroom, 3 Bath home in Sacramento, California, with a mortgage. They own 4 automobiles (2 for the college-age children) and a recreational vehicle. They have an IRA and a mutual fund account. The value of their estate is $900,000.

Husband and Wife are in their early sixties and ready to retire within the next 1–2 years. They have four adult children, one of whom receives social security due to a disability. They own a 4 Bedroom, 3 Bath house in San Jose, California, held in joint tenancy and with no mortgage. They own a cabin at Lake Isabelle, California. They own a time-share in Hawaii and have a Thousand Trails membership. They own three automobiles, a recreational vehicle, and a motorcycle. They each have an IRA, retirement, deferred compensation, and a joint mutual fund account. Their estate is valued at $3,200,000.

Husband and Wife are in their early sixties and ready to retire within the next 1–2 years. Wife has one adult child from a previous marriage. Husband has no children. They own a 4 Bedroom, 3 Bath house in San Jose, California, held in joint tenancy and with no mortgage. They own a cabin at Lake Isabelle, California. They own a time-share in Hawaii and have a Thousand Trails membership. They own three automobiles, a recreational vehicle, and a motorcycle. They each have an IRA, retirement, deferred compensation, and a joint mutual fund account. Wife received an inheritance and maintains that inheritance as her separate property. She also has numerous items of personal property such as family heirlooms and Civil War memorabilia that belonged to her grandfather. The couple's joint estate is valued at $4,000,000.

Some of these scenarios may seem straightforward. The attorney will work with the clients to determine what they wish to accomplish with the estate plan (as listed previously). Are they making a simple distribution of all of their property in equal shares to their lawful heirs? On the other hand, do they wish that their beneficiaries receive disproportionate shares? Do they want items of specific property to go to an individual or do they want any or all of their estate to go to charity? Do they wish to gift some of their property now in order to reduce the size of their estate or do they wish to reduce their federal estate tax liability upon the survivor's death? Do they have minor children for whom they wish to set aside money for support and/or education? Alternatively, is there an adult child who receives government assistance and that assistance would be lost through an inheritance?

These are all issues to be considered and discussed with the clients, in even the most basic estate planning.

The sections that follow provide some of the basic information related to the above issues and scenarios. These will give you a feel for some of the basic trust provisions you will encounter as a probate and estate planning paralegal. Keep in mind that there are many more complex and diverse manners in which to transfer a Trust Estate beyond that which is covered in this text. As you become more experienced as a probate and estate planning paralegal you will become more knowledgeable in tax planning and transfers of wealth that are beyond the basic scope of estate planning.

## Outright Distribution to Beneficiaries

The most common distribution, which is similar to property distributed by Will, is to give your Trust Estate to your spouse, your children, and/or other beneficiaries. In fact, the Settlor may simply state that their estate should be "distributed as set forth in Probate Code §246." Many Trusts will default to Probate Code §246 in the event there are no named beneficiaries who remain living at the time of distribution.

For example, a Trust distribution may state the following:

The Trust Estate shall be distributed to the surviving Settlor upon the first Settlor's death. Upon the surviving Settlor's death, the Trust Estate will be distributed in equal shares to the surviving children of the Settlors. If any of the Settlors' children have predeceased them, that child's share shall be distributed to their issue by right of representation. If the deceased child has no living issue, that child's share shall lapse.

In the event all of the Settlors' children should predecease the surviving Settlor, the trust property shall be distributed to as follows: one-half to the heirs of [husband] and one-half to the heirs of [wife] as set forth in Probate Code Section 246.

The client may specify, however, that another individual, such as a brother or sister, parent, niece or nephew, close family friend or even a charity rather than the default language in the second paragraph above.

## Distribution of Specific Items of Property

Oftentimes people will want to leave certain specific items of property to a certain individual. For example: a male parent might want to leave his fishing or hunting gear to his male child(ren) and a female parent might want to leave her jewelry to female children. Alternatively, in blended families a parent might want to assure that a relic or certain memorabilia be "kept in the family" and therefore state that his/her child should receive that item.

Some attorneys will utilize language that incorporates a "memorandum" of personal property that is kept with the Trust, but is not specifically incorporated within the Trust. This allows the Settlor to make a list of items later. It also allows the Settlor to change the list without having to make formal changes in the Trust itself. These requests are precatory rather than mandatory.

This type of memorandum, which will be referenced within the Trust document, is used for items such as jewelry, furniture, antiques, sporting equipment, and other types of personal items. However, if a person wishes to make a bequest of money, or of a piece of real property, (items that have "title") it must be so stated within the Trust Agreement. Specifically, any references to real property should also contain the address and "legal description" within the document. It is also recommended by most attorneys that other items of significant value be listed within the Trust Agreement as well. This could include a business, jewelry that has been appraised, automobiles, or recreational vehicles.

The attorney should determine which type of language should be used for any of these types of specific gifts, especially since many of the software packages do not include the ability to include these types of bequests or may not utilize the specific language preferred by the attorney. In addition, software may allocate gifts after the distribution of the general estate. Most attorneys prefer that specific bequests be made before the general Trust estate, so that the general estate only contains the remainder.

## Distribution with Tax Planning

In the event the attorney determines the value of the estate will be large enough to incur federal estate taxes, there are several mechanisms allowed by the Internal Revenue Service, which may defer, reduce, or potentially eliminate the federal estate tax liability, using the allowable annual exclusion amount.

One of the most common means of transferring property between married individuals and reducing federal estate taxes is referred to as a Marital Deduction or Bypass Trust. There are several requirements that must be met in order to qualify for the Marital Deduction (see PC§§ 21520 et seq. which provides definition and requirements under IRC§ 2523 that must be met in order to qualify for the marital deduction). Some of the requirements are as follows:

1) The deceased spouse must have been a United State citizen or legal resident at the time of their death;

2) The surviving spouse must be a United States citizen (there are some exceptions);

3) The spouse must have been legally married at the time of his/her death;

4) The property subject to the deduction must be included in the decedent's gross estate;

5) The property must pass from the deceased spouse to the surviving spouse either through a trust, by will, through intestate succession or by a qualified non-probate transfer.

6) The property cannot be considered a non-deductible terminable interest (the interest may end due to the lapse of time or occurrence of a certain event, such as a life estate or conditional gift).

The transfer of the property through marital deduction may be outright which allows the surviving spouse unlimited flexibility in the use of the property. Alternatively, the bypass provisions may contain restrictive language, such as the "surviving spouse must survive by ninety days.

The Trust may also provide for the Trustee to create a Qualified Terminable Interest Trust (Q-TIP) upon the death of the first spouse. A Q-TIP is governed by Internal Revenue Code Section §2056(b)(7). A Q-TIP allows the surviving spouse to benefit from the property while preserving it for the heirs of the decedent. This is a popular mechanism when there are blended families or when the Settlors want to make sure that if the surviving spouse remarries, the heirs will receive the property rather than the new spouse.

In some cases, the Q-TIP will also include a Power of Appointment Trust. The power of appointment allows the survivor to decide which trust property will qualify for the marital deduction. (IRC§ 2056(b)(5).) There are certain requirements that must be met to qualify for the power of appointment. An attorney who creates estate planning documents will be well aware of these requirements. If you would like to know more about these types of trusts, you should read the appropriate IRC sections. The following are some of the requirements:

1) The surviving spouse must be entitled to all income from the property and that income interest must last for the surviving spouse's lifetime and the income must be distributed at least once per year.

2) The surviving must have a general power of appointment over the trust *corpus*. There can be no restrictions or limitations placed on the power of appointment by the deceased spouse.

3) The surviving spouse must have the right to exercise the power of appointment without consent or permission from any other person. No other person can have the power over the surviving spouse's interest, including a trustee that would allow that person to appoint the property to a person other than the surviving spouse.

## Disclaimer Trust

Another form of transferring wealth, without incurring taxes, is a Disclaimer Trust. The language in this type of trust provision is utilized by individuals who wish to decrease their tax liability by transferring a portion of their estate to a child or children rather than to their spouse. A spouse, as beneficiary, may disclaim an inheritance; the disclaimed property then passes pursuant to the terms of the Trust as though the beneficiary had predeceased the Settlor.

There are certain federal requirements that must be met in order to receive the tax benefits of a disclaimer. California has some of its own requirements; however, most of them mirror the federal laws. For the requirements of disclaimed property, see Appendix 7B.

## Separate Share Trust

The language used in Separate Share Trust provisions allows the Trustee to distribute Trust property to minor children. Usually a separate Trust is created for each minor child and often the Trust is named for that child. For example, if the Trustee(s) has three minor children (this mechanism can also be used for grandchildren, nieces, nephews, etc.) there might be three Trusts created which are named: The Sandy Smith Trust, The Robert Smith Trust, and The Jeffrey Jones Trust.

Each separate Trust will state how that child's Trust will be administered and distributed. This type of trust allows the Trustee to stipulate if the child should receive his/her entire share (plus accumulated interest) on a certain date, such as the eighteenth birthday. Alternatively, the Trustee could state that the child would receive his/her share at different times, such as on the twenty-first, twenty-fifth, and thirtieth birthdates. The Successor Trustee may also be given discretion to give property, principal and/or interest, for educational, and health needs. Thus if the child wishes to attend college, but he/she would not ordinarily receive any portion of the trust estate until he/she were twenty-five. The Trustee would have the ability to pay the child's tuition. Books and living expenses could also be paid out of the Trust.

## Special Needs Trust

The *Special Needs* Trust is language that is used within the Trust that provides for an adult child or other beneficiary who is receiving some type of government assistance. This tool is particularly useful for children who have disabilities and who are receiving Social Security Disability. The inheritance of a large sum of money and/or property may affect the benefits to which a disabled "child" is entitled. The attorney will draft these provisions so that the child may receive his/her distributive share in payments that will not cause a reduction or loss of those benefits.

Most software programs will come with a type of template that may be incorporated or the firm may have already created language that is preferred. In the event you are asked to draft such language, you should ask the attorney if there is already a template created or if the formbooks that accompany the software package contain sample language.

## Spendthrift Trust Provisions

Almost all Trusts include a spendthrift clause that protects the manner in which the Trust is administered in two ways, 1) By stating that a beneficiary cannot give away, sell, or transfer their interest in Trust property, and 2) By preventing the beneficiary's creditors from accessing the Trust property. A spendthrift clause essentially protects a beneficiary, who cannot adequately manage his/her affairs, from putting the Trust estate in jeopardy, while still allowing the beneficiary the benefit of the property.

There are exceptions to a spendthrift clause. Some common exceptions are:

(1) a creditor has provided the beneficiary with "necessities of life" such as food and shelter;

(2) the former spouse and/or children of a beneficiary who has not provided support; and,

(3) tort claimants (e.g. wrongful death action) may be able to collect on a Judgment in instances where the beneficiary committed a crime. These exceptions are based on public policy which says: (1) a creditor may provide the necessities of life to an individual without fear of being repaid; (2) a beneficiary should not be able to evade support obligations through a spendthrift clause; and (3) where the tort claimant was innocent of any wrongdoing, there is financial hardship on the part of the claimant, and the beneficiary's conduct was illegal.

## The Conclusion

The Trust must be signed by the Settlor(s) and Trustee(s). Most Trusts will contain a signature line for each capacity. The signature(s) must be notarized using a typical California *Acknowledgment*. (See California Civil Code § 1189.)

## Transfers of Property and Other Documents

Of primary importance once the Trust has been created and executed is to assure that the Settlor(s)' assets are transferred into the Trust. This is an area where the paralegal's skills and knowledge can be particularly useful. As discussed in Chapter Six transfers of property as the result of a probate or as a probate, avoidance tool will be similar in nature.

Paralegals may be asked to assist in assuring that Trust Transfer Deed(s) is/are executed and recorded with the appropriate County Recorder(s) or even the appropriate entity in another state for each piece of property owned by the Settlor(s), assisting the client in obtaining Beneficiary Designation change forms for life insurance policies, annuities, IRAs, and other assets is essential, as well as the knowledge of how to complete them. Letters of Instruction to banks, financial institutions, and mutual fund companies will be needed. Additionally, knowing how to obtain the information, keeping a database and/or file of previously used documents and information to make such transfers will make the attorney's life easier. It will also help assure that the client's Trust has been properly funded, which reduces the risk of potential malpractice.

Understanding the manner in which stocks and bonds are transferred as well as, the documents and detail required is critical. A basic knowledge of what circumstances other property should be transferred and how it is transferred is very important. The attorney may provide you with a checklist of types of property, the manner in which title should be held, and any other pertinent information so that all documents can be ready for the client's signature provided your office will be assisting the client with those transfers. The attorney should also provide a checklist and/or instructions to the client about funding the Trust.

## Key Terms

- Remainder
- Revocable Trust
- Irrevocable Trust
- Grantor
- Settlor
- Trustor
- Trustee
- Residue
- Gross Estate
- Net Estate
- Generation Skipping Transfer Tax
- Generation Skipping Trust
- Unified Credit
- Applicable Credit Amount
- Gift Tax
- Disclaimer Trust
- Qualified Terminable Interest Trust (Q-TIP)
- Marital Deduction
- Crummey Trust
- Separate Share Trust
- Power of Appointment
- Sprinkling Trust
- Survivor's Trust
- By Pass Trust
- Clifford Trust
- Spendthrift Trust
- Five-by-Five Power
- Special Needs Trust
- Precatory

# Chapter Eight

# Collateral Documents

In addition to creating and executing a Trust and/or Will, most law firms will prepare most, if not all, collateral documents for the client. These documents may include, but are not limited to, Certified "Abstract" of Trust, Assignment of Property, Transmutation Agreement, and a Memorandum of Personal Property. A paper trail is as important in estate planning as it is in the corporate domain. Attorneys, Successor Trustees, family members, and the Courts need to know that certain matters were handled properly.

Most law firms will prepare a formal Letter of Instruction ("funding" letter) to the client. This letter will memorialize the formality of the Trust. It will likely confirm what assets the client has transferred into the Trust, whether the client or the firm will complete any additional transfers, the manner in which title should be held for assets of the Trust, information on amending the Trust, and any other information the attorney feels the client may need to keep the Trust in good order. The attorneys also usually include instructions for the client about assets transfers, where to keep the trust "binder," and where to keep other documents such as insurance policies, deeds, and other estate related papers.

The firm may have created many documents as templates for the paralegal or other staff to "fill-in the blanks" with the pertinent information. The attorney may also prefer to create drafts of the documents using the estate planning software. He or she may also have created his or her own customized language from a variety of sources. As you prepare the final drafts for the attorney's review, you should ask whether there are collateral documents already created, provided you have not previously been made aware of them and where they can be found.

The collateral documents can serve several purposes. Often they will be a continuation of the Trust. They may also provide instructions to the Trustee, a third party, or even the Court regarding the Trustee's intentions.

## Certified Abstract

The Certified "Abstract" of Trust is a document that the Trustee may use for financial institutions, insurance companies, and other entities that do not need to be privy to the actual provisions of the Trust. For example, knowing to whom the Trustee is leaving his or her estate is not necessary for a bank or other financial institution. The bank simply needs to know the name of the Trust, the date that it was executed, the name(s) of the Trustee(s), the powers of the Trustee, and the Tax Identification Number (if applicable). An Abstract, properly drafted, will contain that pertinent information.

A third party may also require the Abstract for persons refinancing property, insurance, retirement, and annuities to confirm that a Trust exists. A person cannot simply walk into a bank and open an account in the name of the Trust. The bank will need to confirm that the Trust indeed exists. This may be a CYA "attitude" on the part of the financial institution; however, it is not without merit or legitimate concern. The client needs to be prepared to provide the Abstract. The Abstract may also be referred to as a Certification. However, if a bank, financial institution or other entity requests a copy of the **entire** trust, the client should request that they contact the attorney to clarify the need for the document. Banks have different procedures due to the Patriot Act.

The firm attorneys will most likely have a template they prefer to use for the Abstract. Some estate planning software programs can create the Abstract while creating the Trust. This is the most reliable way to create the Abstract, as the Abstract language, particularly the Trustee powers, will be taken directly from the Trust document as the attorney drafts it. In the event the firm has neither, the California Continuing Education of the Bar has a suggested format that can be used. The publication is called *CEB—Funding Revocable Trusts*.

Often the format for the Abstract provides a space on the upper right corner so that the document can be recorded with the County Recorder where the Settlor resides or where the property is located. Usually the Abstract is not recorded until after the Settlor dies or after the first Settlor dies, if it is a joint Trust. The attorney will determine if there is a need to have the Abstract recorded upon the execution the Trust. The recording of the Abstract will be discussed further in Chapter Nine, *Trust Administration*.

## Assignment of Property

An Assignment of Property is typically a "catch-all" for property owned by the Settlors for which there is no formal title. For example, a person's furniture, furnishings, household appliances, jewelry, books, clothing, collectibles, etc. do not usually have a title or certificate of ownership. A person's home, vehicle(s), bank accounts, bonds, etc. do have "ownership" attached to them; they have a "title."

There must be some mechanism to identify the ownership of property without title owned by the Settlor(s). That method is the Assignment of Property. An example is provided as Appendix 8A.

When properly drafted, the Trust should contain a statement as to the transfer of this type of property, and the Assignment will become a reciprocal document by referencing the same property. This makes it clear that the Settlor(s) fully intended to transfer the property to the Trust unless otherwise stated in the Trust; the Trustee will distribute the referenced property as though it were part of the Trust estate.

## Transmutation Agreement

In the event a Settlor has separate property and he or she wishes to now make that property part of the Trust and subject to "community" property, a Transmutation Agreement should be prepared by the attorney and executed by the person owning the property. A Transmutation Agreement may also be used to convert property to joint tenancy as a form of "correcting" title, such as under a spousal property petition. In the case of real property, an Interspousal Transfer Deed will suffice to transfer title between married persons and provide a paper trail.

It is no longer good enough to have oral "pillow talk" agreements between spouses as to the transfer of their personal or separate property. Case law has made it clear that the courts look to written agreements as to the ownership of property as well as the transfer of ownership. The "he said–she said" verbal agreements no longer have any legal standing. Most California statutes—both probate and family law—have recognized the need to codify the requirement for written agreements as a result of these cases. Additionally, the paralegal should be aware of the presumption of title which provides that if title to property is held in a specific manner, for example Joe Doe, as his sole and separate property, that the courts presume the property belongs to Joe, not Joe and his wife, Joan. Thus, if Joe intended that he and his wife, Joan, were to be joint tenants, that presumption must be disproved. The paper trail is essential to proving that the manner in which the title is held (presumed to be held) was inadvertent or an error.

For example, Wife has inherited lakefront property in Lake Tahoe, California and has maintained it as separate property for a number of years. However, now the couple is in their 60's. The couple wants to create a Trust for the benefit of their children and Wife has decided that the property should be jointly owned and should be distributed to the children upon the second spouse's death.

The attorney will likely recommend that a Transmutation Agreement be executed between the parties acknowledging that Wife now wants to make the property community property. The attorney will also likely recommend that Wife execute an Interspousal Transfer Deed transferring the property to the couple as Husband and Wife. That Deed would be recorded just prior to the Trust Transfer Deed transferring the property into the Trust, with husband and wife as Trustees.

These two documents serve as a paper trail of the Wife's intentions as to the ownership of the property. There would be no question by a Court that Wife fully intended to transfer one-half of the property to her husband.

In the event the client lists any separate property on the Client Information Questionnaire, the paralegal will want to confirm with the attorney how this property is to be transferred, if at all. It may be evident based on the terms of the Trust. The paralegal will want to be sure whether it should be transferred to the sole owner of the property as Trustee or if there going to be a transmutation involved. If so, the attorney will determine the correct course of action for the property and advise the paralegal as to which documents to prepare. As you become more experienced, you will better be able to anticipate the attorney's wishes.

## Revocation of Trust

Another collateral document may be the revocation of a Trust previously executed by the client? For example, if one of the spouses was previously married and had a Trust with their former spouse, you will want to insure that the previous Trust has been revoked. As indicated in Chapter One, a dissolution or legal separation of marriage will affect a Will or Trust. Most attorneys will err on the side of caution and have the Revocation prepared so that the client can execute the document to assure that any future claim to the client's estate may not be made by the former spouse.

## Other Collateral Documents

The attorney may also be preparing Durable Powers of Attorney, an Advance Health Care Directive (Living Will), or similar documents for the client. These documents will be discussed in greater detail in Chapter Nine.

In most cases, these documents will be prepared and executed at the same time as the Trust. In the event the attorney has not provided the drafted documents or made a notation in the file as to the preparation of these documents, you should confirm whether they must be prepared. There are occasions when a client does not wish to have the attorney prepare these documents. On the other hand, perhaps, the client has just executed them due to a recent hospitalization. It is always wise to confirm whether the documents are required or already exist. The attorney should also review the documents to make sure they do not contradict any of the provisions in the newly created estate plan. Otherwise, they will all need to be redone. If it was just the attorney's oversight, he or she can then draft the documents or advise the paralegal if he or she should use a template or some other method for drafting the documents.

It is also a good idea, if the attorney is **not** preparing any collateral documents that this fact be clearly noted in the file. In the event, the client already has those documents; it is also wise to request a copy for the file so that the attorney will have a copy for future reference. Family members may look to the attorney to determine whether Durable Powers of Attorney and/or Advance Health Care Directives were executed if the person becomes incapacitated.

## Funding Trusts

Once the Trust has been drafted and executed, it is critical that the Trustee(s)' property is transferred or "funded" into the Trust. Property that is not transferred into the Trust may be subject to Probate. Often the reason for having a Trust is probate avoidance. Not funding or improperly funding the Trust can then result in exactly the situation the client was trying to avoid. The attorney will want to take great care in explaining the importance of making the transfers and maintaining the property in the Trust.

Much like a corporation or other business entity a certain level of due diligence must be followed and maintained. The client must understand the importance of maintaining the "corporate" trail and guard against the intent of the estate plan being misconstrued or challenged.

Remember also that Trusts that have not been properly funded are a primary reason for legal malpractice. Not only does the Trust need to be funded, but it must also be done properly. Trust funding is considered routine in most law firms and is likely to be the responsibility of the paralegal. As with all legal matters, the paralegal will want to confirm with the attorney the assets transfers that will be handled by the firm. He or she will then confirm that the documents have been prepared, executed, and submitted to the appropriate financial institution, company, or agency who administers that asset. This is typically best accomplished by requesting that the documentation be returned to the law office and then sent to the client after the documents have been copied and placed in the client's file.

The transfer of the property to a Trust is, in most cases, a "non-taxable event." There are exceptions and those are beyond the scope of this text. An attorney will be able to determine whether the "funding" is a taxable event under the Internal Revenue Code and will have counseled the client as to any financial ramifications.

Most Trusts, on which you will be working as a paralegal, are transfers that are considered "non-taxable events." Non-taxable events are those transfers made where the Trustee is not paying the Settlor for the property; and there is no "consideration." Most transfers will, therefore, not require a (tax) fee that would typically be assessed in a sale of property. There may be, however, a transfer (recording) fee. These will be discussed under the subsections below.

For example, transferring the Settlors' residence to the Trustee of the Trust is not a "sale." The Trustee is not paying the Settlor any money for the property.

It has been my experience that once the client has retained the office to prepare estate planning documents, the paralegal should create a checklist of documents to be drafted and property to be transferred. The firm may have already created such a checklist.

The checklist can then be discussed with the attorney to assure that all the documents will be drafted and ready to be executed at the client meeting. It will also provide the paralegal with the foundation for obtaining information regarding the client's assets. It is often necessary to contact financial institutions, corporations, insurance companies, retirement plans, and others to obtain instructions and required forms for transferring assets into a Trust. As previously indicated, often corporations and companies will have their own "in-house" forms and require that they be completed and submitted in order to make any ownership or beneficiary changes.

The client will be very appreciative when all of the documents and information is ready for them at the time they execute their estate planning documents. It will make the firm look professional and detail oriented if everything is prepared in advance. It will also reduce the risk of assets not being transferred into the Trust, especially if they will be the client's responsibility.

The following are the most common types of asset transfers you will encounter as an estate planning paralegal. This is not an all-inclusive list. There will be other types of assets you will encounter, particularly if you work in a larger firm or as you become more experienced. Some of this information was also covered in Chapter Six. However, the information below is specific to the transfer of assets into a trust rather than after a death.

## Real Property

As an estate planning paralegal, real property will likely to be the asset that you will most commonly be involved in transferring. It is, in most cases, a simple process; however, you should not take for granted that it can be more complex. Some of those situations will be noted below. Your instructor will provide you with other circumstances.

The first item needed in order to transfer real property into a Trust is a copy of the current Deed. This can be confusing for many clients. They will have a one-inch stack of escrow documents they received from the title company when they purchased or refinanced the property, but they are not sure if they have "the deed."

It is essential that the client's file have a copy of the current recorded deed for two reasons: 1) to confirm who owns the property, how the title is held, and for the legal description to the property; and, 2) so that the attorney has a record of the ownership of the property prior to it being transferred into the Trust.

The attorney will want to confirm the actual owner of any property. Is it only one of the clients in a situation where the firm is preparing a joint Trust? Is there another person, such as a sibling, parent, or other individual listed as an owner of the deed? Is the property held as joint tenants, as tenants in common, as sole and separate property, or in some other manner?

Situation #1—Married clients wish to create a marital trust. They have both been married previously. They bring a copy of the deed to their first client meeting. The attorney reviews the deed and determines that the vesting is stated as follows:

Jane F. Doe, Wife, transfers of all her interest to John Q. Doe, as his sole and separate property. The deed is an "Interspousal Transfer Deed." and indicates that the transfer is pursuant to a marital settlement agreement. When the clients married, husband did not transfer the property he received from his former wife to make his new wife a joint tenant or make the property community. The attorney will need to discuss this with the clients to determine husband's intent. Was it simply an oversight or does he want the property to remain his sole and separate property?

Situation #2—A single client wishes to create a Trust. The attorney reviews the deed to her condominium. The deed shows the title held as follows: Sally A. Smith, an unmarried woman, and Edna Jones, an unmarried woman, as joint tenants. Who is Edna Jones the attorney asks the client? "She is my Mother," replies the client. She is on the deed because the client was unable to finance the property herself, and Mother co-signed on the loan. The title company put both names on the deed so that in the event Mother passed away the property would be automatically the daughter's. The attorney asks the client if her Mother will sign a "Quitclaim Deed" transferring the property to client (daughter) so that the property can then be transferred to client as Trustee of the Trust.

Situation #3—A widower with no children wishes to create a Trust. The attorney reviews the deed and determines that the property is held as tenants in common with his brother and two sisters. The attorney determines, based on the conversation with the client, that this is a vacation property that was inherited from the client's parents. The property is only in the names of the heirs and is held as tenants in common so that each sibling's issue will inherit that person's share upon death. The attorney advises the client that a deed will have to be prepared showing that the client's share will be transferred into the Trust. All other vesting for the other siblings will remain the same.

Based on the above situations, you can see how important it is that the attorney be able to obtain a copy of the actual recorded deed. Each person who purchases property should have a copy of the deed that was recorded at the time the property was purchased or refinanced. In the event the client cannot find a copy of the deed, they can go to the country recorder and pay a fee to obtain a duplicate copy. Some law firms have a relationship with a title company that allows them to request a copy of the recorded deed by simply providing the address. Some counties also have basic property ownership information available on the County Recorder's website. Note, however, you will most likely still need an actual copy of the recorded deed as the parcel number, legal description, and full title information may not be included under the public information.

Oftentimes, the client will bring their entire escrow file to the office and ask the paralegal which papers are actually the deed. You will become familiar, as you gain experience, with a deed versus lending and escrow documents. Until this time, you should ask the attorney to review the client's real estate documents.

Additionally, if there are any situations similar to the above, the deed preparation may be a two-step process. It may be necessary to prepare a deed transferring the property (Situation #1 and Situation #2) to the individual. This is often referred to as clearing the title. Then a Trust Transfer Deed (or whatever your firm calls it) can be prepared transferring the property to the Trust, with the Settlor(s) as Trustee(s).

Just as you must create a paper trail for a Transmutation of property, it is necessary to create the same chain of title (paper trail) for the changes in vesting of real property. The County Clerk/Recorder, the County Assessor and title companies may need to know the "chain of title" for the property at some point in the future. It has been my experience that if you do not create this chain of title, the Recorder and/or the Assessor may question the transfer. They may request that the title be cleared or may require that the property be reassessed or a fee paid as there is a question as to whether the transfer is indeed a non-taxable event. A sample Trust Transfer Deed showing a **simple** transfer to a marital Trust is provided as Appendix 8B.

The Clerk/Recorder in each County in the State of California requires that a document called a Preliminary Change of Ownership Report (PCOR) be submitted with **all** deeds submitted for recording. These forms are available through most County Recorder's website. The firm's Judicial Council software may also contain the form. The form is primarily to inform the County Assessor that the property should not be reassessed, as it is not a sale. It also informs the Recorder that it is not a sale and therefore is exempt from Documentary Transfer Tax pursuant to California Revenue and Tax Code § 62.

The Country Recorder's website will also contain information regarding the Recording Fee, which will need to be submitted for **each** deed. Most California counties currently (2013) charge either $10 or $12 for the first page ($8^{1/2}$ x 11) and $3 or $5 for each additional page. Always confirm these fees before submitting the deeds.

## Financial Institutions

Most attorneys will recommend that the client go to the local branch of his or her bank, savings or credit union and complete a new signature card. This is a routine matter and one that the client can easily handle. In the event the client has an account that is out of the area or web based, he/she may need some handholding. The client should simply call the financial institution and inform the institution he/she has created a Trust and will need a new signature card sent to him/her.

A new signature card should be completed for each account. Many clients will have checking, savings, and Certificate of Deposit accounts. They may also have accounts at several different institutions.

Occasionally the attorney may advise the client that he or she does **not** need to change the household checking account that is used for the day-to-day finances. Typically, people do not have a great deal of money in those accounts. In the event the account is not in the name of the Trust and as long as there is less than $150,000 in the account, the funds in the account can be transferred via the Probate Code § 13100 affidavit procedure. Additionally, if the estate planning is for a married couple the account is probably already in joint tenancy and would transfer to the survivor automatically upon death anyway. Oftentimes, elderly people will put a child's name on the account so that he or she can pay bills or assist them if needed. Thus, any monies in the account would also pass by right of survivorship simply by providing the financial institution with a copy of the death certificate. The disadvantage of this would be if the owner of the account had several children and the monies should be disbursed among the children rather than ago directly to one child. This will be a situation that the attorney and client will want to discuss to determine the best method of handling the checking account relative to the estate plan and the client's intentions.

## Motor Vehicles, Etc.

Automobiles can be transferred into the Trust by taking the current title ("pink slip") to the Department of Motor Vehicles and making the transfer. In the event there is a lien on the vehicle, the change will have to be made through the lender.

The attorney may advise the client that their old clunker does not need to be transferred into the Trust. As indicated above under "Financial Institutions" the vehicle may pass to the joint tenant or pass by affidavit if it is valued under $150,000.

If the client has a recreational vehicle, motorcycle(s), boat with trailer, valuable collector's vehicles, etc., then the attorney will likely recommend that these vehicles be transferred into the Trust.

The Department of Motor Vehicles will charge a fee for a new title. The client should complete the applicable forms and check the boxes that indicate that the transfer is **not** a sale so that sales tax and other taxes will not be assessed.

## Stocks and Bonds

Stocks and bonds can be the most complex assets to transfer into a Trust. The complexity is not because of the Trust. It is due to the rules imposed by the Securities and Exchange Commission. There are also additional regulations and restrictions regarding transfers, due to the events surrounding 9-11.

The easiest stocks to transfer are those for privately owned or Sub-Chapter S corporations. Clients who own and operate their own business, and where that business entity is designated as a corporation, can simply transfer and issue new stock certificates to the name of the Trust. The attorney will provide specific instructions. Often the client will ask the attorney (read: the paralegal) to prepare the new certificates.

As discussed in Chapter Six, most Treasury Bonds must be purchased on-line effective January 1, 2013. An account must be created and the bonds, particularly EE bonds, must be liquidated or transferred following the steps on the "Treasury Direct Account" website. The URL is: http://www.treasurydirect.gov. You or the client will need to download the forms required to be submitted for liquidating or transferring the bonds. As previously indicated, the estate administrator will need to have his or her signature *guaranteed* through an agent who is authorized to provide a Medallion Signature Guarantee. It is always best to check the website for new and updated procedures as they are subject to change, especially since as of the writing of this text the entire process for purchasing bonds and subsequent transactions are new and evolving. As indicated in Chapter Six, you will want to work with the client to determine the best method of shipping the bonds for their surrender to make sure they arrive at the proper location.

Refer back to Chapter Six or forward to Chapter Eleven regarding specific information and instructions in transferring "paper" stocks and public bonds that are publicly traded. These transfers will require specific documentation for each individual stock or bond. Additionally, the documentation will require a Medallion Signature Guarantee.

There may also be fees assessed to make the transfers. The attorney is likely to encourage the client to transfer the stocks and bonds into an account rather than have new certificates issued.

In the event there are stock certificates for a Closely Held (small/family) or Subchapter S corporation, those stock certificates will need to be reissued. The paralegal should work with the client, who may or may not be an officer of the corporation, and any officers of the corporation to return and void the existing stock certificates and then prepare new certificates. This transaction will need to be properly recorded within the Corporation documents to reflect the change of ownership of the stock from an individual or a married couple to the Trustee of the Trust.

## Mutual Funds

The mutual fund company should be contacted to obtain any instructions and specific forms required. Mutual funds are governed by the rules and regulations of the Securities and Exchange Commission. Therefore, certain formalities will be required, although, in most cases, an account fund can be easier to transfer than stocks and bonds.

Most mutual fund companies routinely work with clients to transfer their funds into the Trust. They are very helpful and will usually promptly send the forms and information to the attorney or client. Some mutual funds provide the forms via the internet. The forms can be downloaded by the client and then the firm can assist the client as needed.

As indicated under the stocks and bonds, most mutual funds will require a Medallion Signature Guarantee on forms rather than a notary.

## Insurance & Annuities

It has been my experience that most companies who provide insurance and/or annuities will have their own "in-house" forms that must be completed. They will not, in most cases, take generic forms. It is a good idea for the client to request the "Change of Beneficiary" forms from the company as soon as they have decided to create a Trust. These forms can be confusing, and the client may want the attorney's assistance in filling out the form(s).

## Retirement Accounts

As with insurance accounts, retirement accounts are contractual. The retirement plan should be contacted to obtain the "Change of Beneficiary" forms and any other forms required by that entity. This applies to employee benefit retirement plans, deferred compensation plans, Individual Retirement Plans (IRA), SEP IRA, KEOGH, or any accounts governed by Federal ERISA regulations.

## Mobile Homes

As indicated in Chapter Six, the transfer of Mobile Homes is not necessarily complicated, but it can be a lengthy process. The paralegal should contact the Department of Housing and Urban Development (HUD) to obtain the required forms. You will also want to make sure that the client has the original title(s) to the unit(s) for reference as to the manufacturer, model, year of manufacturer, the serial number(s) and the State Registration forms.

All other applicable forms must be completed, signed, and sent along with the registration forms to HUD along with the required fees. The client should be advised that it might take at least six (6) months to receive the new title.

In the event the client intends to sell the mobile home within the period, the attorney may recommend that the client refrain from placing the property into the Trust.

## Promissory Notes

Persons who have a promissory note ("Note") from another individual or individuals will want to "assign" the Note to the Trust. This document is very similar to the Assignment of Property, but it is specific to this type of asset. Check with the attorney to see if the firm has previously created such a document. If you cannot find one in the firm's files, you should use a resource such as the Continuing Education of the Bar Action Guide, titled, *Funding a Revocable Trust*. There is a sample in that publication. Once the client has executed the Assignment of Promissory Note, a copy should be mailed to the person responsible for paying the "Note." The original should be inserted in the Trust binder.

## Trust Amendments and Restatements

As indicated in Chapter Seven, a Revocable Trust can be amended at any time the Settlor(s) and Trustee agree to amend the Trust or as specified in the Trust Agreement. There are numerous reasons an individual or married couple may want to amend the Trust. The following is a list of some of the most common reasons.

- Marital status has changed
- Birth or death of a child, grandchild or other issue
- Change the Successor Trustee (and Executor, if applicable)
- Laws have changed (Probate Code, Tax Laws, Transfer of Property, etc.)
- Change of distributions

Another reason may be that the Trust was improperly drafted and/or collateral documents were not prepared and executed. As a paralegal in a law firm, I observed that numerous clients brought in Trust documents that had been prepared by a so called "trust mill." Those documents were often incomplete or did not protect the Trustee(s) from probate, taxes, and other consequences.

The attorney and client will need to discuss the changes needed. If there are numerous, sweeping changes, the attorney may recommend that the Trust be revoked and a new one prepared. Alternatively, because the revocation may affect the other documents previously executed, as well as the assets that were funded into the original Trust (such as recording a Trust Transfer Deed), the attorney may recommend that an amendment be prepared, which will completely restate the Trust. Essentially, this will be a completely new Trust using the original name of the Trust and the date of execution (creation) of same. The Amendment will commence by stating, that this instrument is an Amendment and that the previous Trust is amended "in its entirety."

# Conclusion

There can be numerous other documents unique to the client that will need to be prepared or with which the client will need assistance. Clients are often hesitant to complete and submit documents for fear the information will be done incorrectly. This is an area at which the paralegal can excel and for which both the attorney and client will be thankful. A paralegal who takes continuing education courses about funding a trust and who maintains a folder or database of information regarding transferring assets to a Trust will find him/herself in much demand and held in high esteem.

The primary focus for any funding into a Trust should be making sure all assets requiring transfer have been successfully transferred by either the firm or the client.

I highly recommend obtaining a copy of the Continuing Education of the Bar Action Guide, titled, *Funding a Revocable Trust* if your firm does not already have this publication. It contains a great deal of useful information, sample forms, and documents, instructions on how to complete the forms, and to whom to send them to properly fund the client's Trust.

## Key Terms

- Certified Abstract
- Assignment of Property
- Assignment of Promissory Note
- Transmutation Agreement
- Housing & Urban Development
- Revocation of Trust
- Trust Transfer Deed
- Preliminary Change of Ownership Form
- Revenue & Tax Code §§ 62-63
- Documentary Transfer Tax
- Securities and Exchange Commission
- Medallion Signature Guarantee
- Clearing Title
- Chain of Title
- Amendment of Trust
- Restatement of Trust

# Chapter Nine

# Powers of Attorney

This chapter will discuss some additional documents that the paralegal is likely to prepare when developing an estate plan for a client, whether it is a Will or a Trust. The two most common related documents are Durable Powers of Attorney and Advance Health Care Directives.

First, we will review the types of powers of attorney a person might grant to another. You will also become familiar with the powers and/or limitation of powers that can be granted in a power of attorney, and how long the power of attorney is effective.

The other documents that you will learn about are Advance Health Care Directives. These documents are primarily used for providing instructions to health care providers in the event a person needs medical treatment in an emergency or due to a near-fatal illness. The Advance Health Care Directive may also be referred to as the Durable Power of Attorney for Health Care, Advance Directive or a "Living Will." (See Chapter Twelve for additional information regarding appointment of a Health Care Surrogate.)

## Powers of Attorney

Powers of attorney are often referred to as "disability" planning. There are, however, several types of Powers of Attorney. The various types are outlined in this chapter. For the purposes of this text and estate planning, we will focus on Powers of Attorney for Property Management and/or Health Care. As with all other documents in this text, any specific language included is for clarity and understanding only. They are not to be construed as legal advice.

A power of attorney is a document that allows one person to act for another. The person who grants the authority for another to act on his or her behalf is called the Principal. The person given the authority to act is the Attorney-in-Fact, or may also be referred to as an Agent. This will be true regardless of the type of power of attorney that is granted.

### Limited or Specific Power of Attorney

A principal may execute this special type of power of attorney so that another person may be able to perform certain duties or responsibilities for a specified period.

For example, a person in the armed forces is being sent for active duty. While they are gone, they may need someone to pay bills, sell property, or perform other specific functions in their absence.

In that event, the soldier may name a spouse, family member, or trusted friend to act as their Agent. He or she may specify the exact duties to be performed or they may convey general type powers. The duties should be broad enough, rather than be so specific in nature that it will restrict the agent's ability to act. He or she will not want to say, for example, that the agent can only pay bills, when it may be necessary for the agent to transfer funds between bank accounts, collect rent or other monies, and make deposits.

The length of time and/or any restrictions as to the Principal's capacity is also a consideration. Is the Agent only to act while the person is out of the country, while he/she is undergoing surgery, or more generally as long as it is determined he/she are unable to act. Moreover, what is the standard to measure the person's incapacity or his/her inability to act? The standard, if applicable, should be stated within the document.

The Principal may want his/her Agent to be able to sell a car, and only the car. Thus, he or she may want to limit the Agents capacity to only the car and state that the Agent may not sell any of the Principal's other assets. The Principal may simply need to appoint someone to act as Guardian of a child or another person over whom he or she has custody or guardianship, during the subsequent absence. A parent having sole legal custody of a child may need to provide another person with the ability to care of the child. This may include not only the "physical" custody, such as making sure the child attends school, does homework, receives medical treatment, etc; the agent may also need to access funds for the child's care such as paying for day care, school supplies and activities, clothing, and anything else relating to the child's health, welfare, and education.

Alternatively, the Principal may want to grant broad powers to the Agent so that he or she can "take any action the principal would take." These types of powers are vast and in the wrong hands could detrimental to the Principal. The Principal will want to make sure that if he/she gives broad powers to a person, it is a person who is trustworthy; a person who will not sell everything the Principal owns while he/she is absent or incapacitated, and then take the money and run.

There are a number of "Form" powers of attorney that can be purchased at stationary or office supply stores. There are also services on the internet where a person can purchase a power of attorney. Most of these forms are created under the Uniform Statutory Form Power of Attorney Act. The Act allows the Principal to authorize powers for the boxes checked on the form. Any writing on the form, other than the person's signature, may cause the power of attorney to be void. The person accessing the form over the internet may choose the incorrect form and/or complete the form incorrectly. Care should be taken when using this resource. (See Probate Code §§ 4400 et seq. for additional information and requirements for using a power of attorney form.)

The powers granted should be carefully considered by the person. The document must be properly executed either before witnesses or before a notary public.

Care must be taken by the paralegal who may be asked to notarize the form, particularly if he/she is a notary public in California. In such capacity, the paralegal may be asked by the person executing the power of attorney to assist him or her in completing the form. The person may also ask the paralegal, "If I check this box will my Agent be able to sell my car?" or the paralegal may be asked to interpret a certain provision. This is crossing the line into the area of the Unauthorized Practice of Law (UPL) and should be avoided. It can be very frustrating for the person to be told that as a notary and/or paralegal you cannot tell them whether the document is correct or incorrect. As a notary, you can only notarize the person's signature and not comment on any aspect of the form's language or accuracy. As a paralegal, you must refer the person to the attorney about the actual contents of the document.

The above would also be a violation of the California Notary Public laws. When acting in the capacity of a notary, the document must be complete before it can be notarized. (Government Code § 8205.) The person must understand what he or she is signing, and the document must be completed. In the event the person is unclear as to any provision of the power of attorney and is hesitant to sign it, the notary will not be able to notarize the person's signature until the form is completed.

The above section reviewed some of the aspects of general or limited powers of attorney. A durable power of attorney, however, allows the Principal to designate his/her Agent and to provide that Agent with those powers even if the Principal is disabled, incompetent, or incapacitated, unless those qualifications have not been included in the document. A person executing a Durable Power of Attorney needs to carefully consider the "what ifs" and worse case scenarios when specifying the powers given to the Agent. These should be addressed by an attorney.

## Durable Powers of Attorney

In most cases, in the estate planning environment, a paralegal will be involved in drafting durable powers of attorney. The firm may have software programs that will draft the powers of attorney based on the information entered into the program. These software programs are usually tied with the estate planning software that drafts Trusts and Wills. Alternatively, the firm may have standard templates they use for preparing the durable powers of attorney.

There is a great deal of standard, boilerplate language within the durable power of attorney. There will be many aspects of the document, however, that are customized for the client and/or where the Principal must determine the extent of the powers to be given to the Agent.

## Naming of Agent/Attorney-in-Fact

As with the Trust or Will, the validity of the document and the authority must first be established. The introduction of the document will usually include language similar to the following:

> "I, _____ (Principal) appoint _____ (Agent), as my attorney-in-fact. The agent shall have the power and authority to perform or undertake any action I could perform or undertake if I were personally present or able to do so."

The introductory section should also state that the person designated as the agent might decline to serve. Therefore, most attorneys will also encourage the Principal to appoint a second person, or successor, to act if the first-named Agent declines to serve or, for any reason, is unable to act. A person appointed as an Agent must be at least 18 years of age.

As with the naming of a Trustee or an Executor, the person being appointed as the Agent should be a person the Principal trusts, especially if the Agent is given broad powers. There are some instances, such as when the person has no family or close friends on whom they can rely or trust to act on their behalf, when it may be necessary to appoint a corporate fiduciary as Agent.

The attorney will discuss this in detail with the client prior to drafting the documents. Again, the Principal will need to convey enough power for the Agent to act on his or her behalf without trying to tie the Agent's hands in certain activities.

## Springing Powers

The introduction may also establish whether the document is a springing durable power of attorney. A springing provision allows the Principal to delay the time the document becomes effective, usually upon the incapacity or disability of the Principal. The Principal may choose to make the document immediately effective upon execution. Most clients who are in good health do not have an immediate need to have another individual act on their behalf, as they are still able and competent to act on their own. Married couples may, however, choose to grant immediate powers so that they do not have to go through the procedure of proving incapacity, while others feel it is not necessary due to the nature of how title is held. Therefore, the client may wish to delay the ability of the Agent to act until a future date. This may be accomplished by creating a springing durable power of attorney.

The springing provision should indicate the manner in which the principal's incapacity will be determined. Such determination will usually be made by a physician (or the Principal may specify two physicians) who will state, in writing, that the Principal is unable to manage his or her own affairs. This authority, once established, will also allow the Agent to seek guardianship or conservatorship (subject to the specific provisions in the durable power of attorney) in the event the Principal is considered incompetent.

Care must be taken when drafting Powers of Attorney as well as any other estate planning documents to make sure the principal is capable of making the required appointments, knowing the extent of the powers to be given, and executing the documents. As with a Will and/or a Trust the principal/testator/settlor must be of sound mind. The attorney and his or her staff must make sure that the client has the mental capacity to make those decisions and especially to decide whether the power of attorney should be effective immediately or later. As people age and there is an increase occurrence of dementia, Alzheimer's, or other similar mental incapacity; there may be a very fine line in knowing whether the client is able to make these decisions.

The attorney and staff must also be aware of any efforts by family, care-givers, and other interested individuals who may be attempting to gain control of the person—personally as well as property—by appointing him or herself as custodian or guardian without the right to do so. The client may be accompanied to the appointment and state that he or she wants to make the power of attorney effective immediately which could be contradictory to the wishes of the client. What happens if the attorney feels the client may be walking the fine line between being able to make decisions on his or her own and needing the assistance of an agent? The agent may be pressing for immediate power, but he or she is not the client and thus the attorney must follow the wishes of the client. An attorney working in this area of law must carefully weigh all of the information and facts in helping the client decide what type of power of attorney should be created and especially how those powers should be allocated and when they will become effective.

Depending upon the type of software or template used by the law firm, the springing provision may appear at the beginning within the introduction, or it may be a separate section of its own at either the beginning or the end of the document.

The following are some of the many decisions a client must make with respect to their durable power of attorney. Keep in mind, this is not an exhaustive list, nor are they in any specific order.

> Compensation for Agent. The principal may state whether the Agent should receive any type of compensation for performing his or her duties. Most people will not provide compensation for a spouse or child. They may consider paying a close family friend, especially if they anticipate there will be a great deal of time involved in acting as Agent. In the event a corporate fiduciary is named, the document should include compensation, as the fiduciary would be acting in that capacity only upon being paid. In most cases, the Principal will allow the agent to be reimbursed for any expenses.
>
> Ability to modify and amend trusts and/or create trusts or sub-trusts. The Principal may direct that the Agent have the ability to modify or amend an existing trust. He or she may also provide the Agent with the power to create additional trusts or sub-trusts, including but not limited to, Custodial Trusts or minor children.
>
> Property Management. The Principal will provide the agent with certain powers as to how the estate should be managed and to what extent. As previously indicated, many principals give broad (almost unlimited) authority to the Agent, especially if that Agent is their spouse. An example of the types of broad powers that may be given to an Agent can be found at Appendix 9A. Particularly important are the powers to change beneficiary designations and the preparation and filing of tax returns.
>
> Care and Control of the Person. The Principal will provide the Agent with certain powers as to how they should care from them personally. An example of the types of powers can be found at Appendix 9B.
>
> Guardian or Custodian. The Principal may provide instructions for the creation of a guardianship or appointment of a custodian for him or herself and under what conditions. The Principal will also need to specify whether the named Agent would be the guardian or custodian, of the person and/or estate, or if another individual is named in this capacity. The Principal may also make provisions for guardianship for a child and for any other person over whom the Principal may have been made a guardian or custodian.
>
> Medical Treatment and Records. The principal may provide authority for the Agent to authorize medical treatment, as well as to request records and information regarding the principal's past and current medical treatment. The document may also include reference to treatment in certain types of medical facilities such as a hospital, nursing home, rehabilitation facility, hospice or other in-home treatment, etc. The attorney may be drafting a separate Durable Power of Attorney for Health Care or an Advance Health Care Directive for the client that will also address these issues with more specificity. This provision, if included, should be consistent with the other document and the client's wishes.[1]

---

1. Note: The Health Insurance Portability & Accountability Act of 1996 (HIPAA) requires specific language within documents or as a separate document that relates to the release of medical records. In the event the firm is using any type of old template or software, the attorney should confirm that the current and appropriate HIPAA language is included in the Durable Power of Attorney or it may be ineffective when using for document to obtain medical records for the principal.

Health Care. The Principal may enumerate specific types of treatment within the Durable Power of Attorney for Property Management, although most attorneys will prefer to do a separate document for health care or prepare an Advance Health Care Directive, especially when it relates to whether a person wishes to be resuscitated and/or being placed on life support and under what circumstances.

Anatomical Gifts. The Principal may direct in this document or in another document whether he or she wishes to make any anatomical gifts. He or she may specify under what type of conditions the anatomical gifts may be made. For example, the Principal may state the anatomical gifts may only be for transplant purposes or he/she may not have a preference and give the Agent discretion as to whether the organs can be used for scientific or research purposes as well as transplant along with other restrictions if organ donation is allowed.

Disposition of Remains. The Principal may direct the Agent as to the disposition of his or her remains. This could include the type of funeral arrangements that the person wishes or may have already made. It may include reference to cremation or other types of disposition. The provision can be as specific as the Principal wishes or may be generic and give the Agent the power of his or his discretion. In the event the Principal has made any previous arrangements, such as prepaid cremation or burial arrangements, those should be noted in this section. It is also a good idea for the Agent to know where the Principal has put any documents relating to the previous arrangements that have been made, or they should be kept with the other estate planning documents so that the Agent can find them easily at the time the documents are needed.

Incidental Provisions. There is often a section within the document that is a catchall for powers that are not appropriate in another section. An example of these types of powers can be found at Appendix 9C. This section may include the power to care for pets, provide social, recreational, and religious activity for the conservatee.

Third Party Reliance. A provision will usually be included by the attorney regarding third parties relying upon the document. An Agent cannot force a third party to accept the authority of the Agent. An indemnification clause is included to provide for such an event.

It is very important that these documents be reviewed periodically to assure that not only are the powers current and applicable, but that the laws have not changed and/or the wishes and needs of the principal have not altered. A principal who is fairly young and in good health may have a different perspective after numerous life changes and situations once he or she reaches retirement, faces death, or some other life-changing circumstance.

# Durable Powers of Attorney and Advance Health Care Directives

## Durable Power of Attorney for Health Care

Prior to 1982, a Power of Attorney for Health Care was not allowed by law. Although this particular document is still used today, the Advance Health Care Directive ("Advance Directive") is the document preferred by most health care providers. The attorney and client will need to discuss whether it is necessary to have both documents and whether the client prefers one and in what format. The Advance Directive is also preferred over simply naming a surrogate, as it is more formal and considered a more binding document by health care practitioners.

It has been my experience, that an elderly client is more likely to prefer the Durable Power of Attorney for Health Care because it is more detailed. It is also used at times when a client may have children or other family members who do not agree on the care of the parents. The Durable Power of Attorney for Health Care may be specifically tailored to detail the client's exact wishes, leaving little or no room for interpretation. In such cases, it would make it more difficult for a family member to go against the wishes of the client when this document exists and, particularly, when the family members have been provided with copies. The attorney may recommend the Principal provide copies to family members, especially where there may be persons who disagree with the explicit wishes of the client.

The Durable Power of Attorney for Health Care will have a similar format to the Durable Power of Attorney for Property Management. The introduction will include the particulars as to the name of the Principal, the Agent, and any successor Agents.

The document should also state whether it is a springing power of attorney. Again, an elderly client, or one who has a terminal illness, is more likely to make the document effective upon execution (immediate), rather than wait for a later date.

A client may choose to name a different person to provide for their health care needs. For example, a child who is not fiscally responsible enough to take care of the client's estate (property) may have excellent judgment as to the health care needs and quality of life decisions. A particular child may have more similar religious beliefs and/or philosophies about life as the parent. Such a child may, therefore, be more suited to making decisions relating to life and death situations.

The Durable Power of Attorney for Health Care will contain more specific details as to the Principal's requests with respect to health care wishes such as a treatment, payment of medical bills, obtaining medical records, etc. Usually, there will also be boilerplate language such a specific powers, guardianship or conservatorships, anatomical gifts, disposition of remains, etc. that may duplicate the provisions in the Durable Power of Attorney for Property Management. The document should also include incidental provisions. The document should also be executed with the same formality as any other power of attorney

Sample language for the Health Care Powers is included as Appendix 9D.

# Advance Health Care Directive

California was the first state (1976) to authorize a person with the ability to state, in writing, his/her wishes regarding life-sustaining procedures. This document was often called a "living will." It was also called a directive to physicians or advance directive. The person (Principal) is able to state, in writing, that he/she wishes to refuse treatment, such as nutrition and hydration, when he/she has a terminal condition and is unable to communicate those wishes verbally. The Principal may also state the types of treatment he or she wants, or does not want to receive.

Many states adopted similar language shortly after California. The Uniform Rights of Terminally Ill Action § 2(b) (1989) states as follows:

> If I should have an incurable and irreversible condition that, without the administration of life-sustaining treatment, will, in the opinion of my attending physician, cause my death within a relatively short time, and I am no longer able to make deci-

sions regarding my medical treatment, I direct my attending physician, pursuant to [state] to withhold or withdraw treatment that only prolongs the process of dying and is not necessary for my comfort or to alleviate pain.

California was also the first state to enact legislation (1983) providing for a statutory, fill-in-the-blank durable power of attorney for health care form. Many states rapidly followed suit. This legislation allowed the person to appoint an agent to make decisions on his/her behalf. California went a step further than the original advance directive.

The Uniform Health Care Decisions Act of 1993 created more standard decision-making among principals, agents, and health care providers. In 2000 the Act was amended to include registered Domestic Partners who may act as a surrogate when no document has been created and executed appointing a surrogate to act should a person become incapacitated.

Some attorneys will use a template they have created within the firm's document system. Many estate planning software programs will include an advance directive. The statutory form can be found within Probate Code § 4701. Probate Code § 4700 states:

The form provided in Section 4701 may, but need not, be used to create an advance health care directive. The other sections of this division govern the effect of the form or any other writing used to create an advance health care directive. An individual may complete or modify all or any part of the form in Section 4701. Thus, the attorney may choose to use the statutory form in its entirety or may wish to adapt specific language to customize it to meet the client's needs and wishes.

The attorney will want to carefully review all of the options with the client. In some cases, the specific sections or choices must be initialed by the client so that anyone relying on the document in the future will have a clear understanding of the person's wishes.

The Principal must have legal capacity and be competent when he or she completes the form. The form must be witnessed or notarized. The designated Agent must be over the age of 18. A client who has a child who is under the age of 18 would be discouraged from appointing that child as Agent. However, some attorneys will provide for a child to be a successor and will add language stating, "If the child is 18 at the time of appointment."

The attorney should encourage clients to complete the applicable forms with the Department of Motor Vehicles if he or she wished to be an organ donor. A client should also provide a copy of the Advance Health Care Directive to their doctor, the Agent, and family members, if applicable, so that each knows the Principal's wishes, should an event occur requiring the use of the document.

The document should incorporate a statement that a photocopy or other copy is valid. The pre-printed form does not have this statement. This is important in the event that it is needed and the original cannot be located quickly.

# Importance of Advance Health Care Directives

The importance of having an Advance Health Care Directive or a Durable Power of Attorney for Health Care cannot be overstated.

Most attorneys will encourage their estate planning clients to execute these documents regardless of their age. In an estate-planning practice, clients will frequently want to have a "living will" done because they are going in for surgery. Most hospitals in California will not perform surgery unless the patient has executed an Advance Health Care

Directive. If the patient does not have one, one will likely be presented by the hospital staff when the patient checks in.

These documents, however, are not just for the elderly or persons who have a medical condition requiring treatment or surgery. Most attorneys who work in this area of law will tell you how frustrating it is to have a client's spouse or family member call and want to have a "living will" done because the client is in the hospital because of a serious accident.

As with all legal documents, the person executing the document must know what he/she is signing. The execution of estate planning documents (trusts, wills, durable powers of attorney and advance health care directives), in particular, require that the person "be of sound mind" or not signing under "coercion or duress." Thus a person who is in the hospital in a coma, under anesthetic, or some other severe condition that inhibits cognitive powers cannot sign an advance health care directive or, for that matter, any other legal document. The attorney will be unable to help the client.

Remember also, that a notary cannot witness the signature of a person who they believe to be incapable of understanding what they are signing. This is often an ethical issue for the paralegal who is also a notary. The attorney may want you to notarize a document under his or her direction, which as a notary you feel may jeopardize your notary oath.

Most large hospitals, having been faced with several of these issues, have review boards that will follow the family's wishes, even if the patient has not executed an advance health care directive. However, what if the family members cannot agree? You are all familiar with recent "famous" cases where parents and spouses of patients have not agreed on whether the patient should be kept alive by artificial means. In those cases, the hospital's hands are tied and medical personnel will have to rely on the decision of the courts when the family cannot agree.

An Advance Care Directive will not make the decision easier, but it will help the family and the medical staff to know the patient's wishes with respect to life support and treatment. It will simplify the process and reduce the anguish of the family in having to make a decision for the patient.

There are special procedures that must be followed if an Advance Directive is to be executed in a hospital-like setting. An Ombudsman must be present when the Principal signs the Advance Directive. The Ombudsmen must also sign the document stating that the Principal understands the document he or she is signing. A hospital, nursing home, or health care employee cannot witness the signing of the document for the Principal.

# Key Terms

- Agent
- Attorney-in-Fact
- Durable Power of Attorney
- Principal
- Power of Attorney
- General Power of Attorney
- Limited or Specific Power of Attorney
- Springing Power of Attorney
- Advance Health Care Directive

- Living Will
- Directive to Physicians
- Health Insurance Portability & Accountability Act (HIPAA)

# Chapter Ten

# Trust Administration

Trust administration will occur after a Settlor or Trustee has died. A trust administration can be very simple or highly complex. As a probate/estate planning paralegal, most of the Trusts requiring administration will be simple and straightforward. This does not mean that attention to detail is not important. Just as in a probate or the creation of the estate planning documents, the successor Trustee must account for and deal with all assets of the decedent.

Trust administration, in most cases, will be similar to business transactions—the business of the Trust. Transactions and transfer of assets to beneficiaries, in some cases liquidating assets and/or the sale of property, payment of debts and expenses of last illness, and preparation of final tax returns for the individual, and if necessary for the estate, are just some of the *business* transactions that must occur. Each Successor Trustee will be different in determining the complexity and therefore the amount of assistance that may be needed in administering the estate.

Complex trust administrations will occur for several reasons. One of the most common reasons is that the Trustee did not properly fund the Trust; assets will have to be transferred posthumously via a summary probate procedure known as a Petition for Instructions. This specific procedure will be discussed in more detail later in this Chapter.

Other reasons for complex trust administration:

- Tax considerations
- Sub-trusts or generation skipping trusts
- Charitable donations and creation of charitable trust
- Types and/or value of assets
- Later discovered assets

This section will start with a simple trust administration and follow with some more complex issues.

Refer to Chapter Four regarding probate for the general information on the initial client meeting. Trust administration is a similar process in that much of the same information and documents will need to be gathered to commence the procedure.

The potential "client" will likely be the decedent's spouse, successor or co-trustee and/or a close family member or friend. It is a good idea to have the client bring as many documents as possible with them to the first meeting with the attorney. One advantage of creating a trust is that people have a better awareness of the documents involved and what the attorney will need. They will often keep important estate planning documents together in one place and may bring the entire "binder" or file with them to the meeting. Another advantage is, if the firm created the estate plan for the decedent, the attorney can review the file before the meeting and have an understanding of exactly what will need to be done and what information he or she will need to get started.

The client should bring with them the following documents to the first meeting (this is not meant to be an all-inclusive list):

- Original Trust
- Original Will
- Death Certificate
- Deed(s) if real property was owned
- Insurance Policy(ies)
- Retirement or Other Benefit Information
- Names of all person(s) listed in the Trust and Will, dates of birth, and their current addresses
- List of all assets and how held (joint tenancy, in trust, etc.)
- List of debts of the decedent as of that date

At the initial meeting, the attorney should discuss with the client the duties and responsibilities of fulfilling his/her duties as Executor and successor Trustee. He or she should also discuss any potential conflict of interest, especially if the attorney drafted the estate planning documents and is now being asked to assist with the administration of the estate. There may also be a potential conflict if the spouse is the Trustee. The attorney should discuss that conflict with the client/spouse. If necessary, a conflict waiver should be executed.

## Acceptance to Appointment of Trustee

The nominated person must first accept the appointment as Trustee. A person named a successor does not **have** to serve. He or she can decline. Perhaps the named successor Trustee does not feel able to administer the Trust. That person may have personal and/or health issues that preclude acting in such a capacity, especially if the Trust will need to be administered over a long period.

If a person declines to act, he or she will need to sign a statement saying that he/she declines. At that point, the person would appoint the named alternate. If no alternate has been named in the Trust or the named alternate also declines, the Trust provisions will need to be reviewed by the attorney and then followed as to the appointment of the Trustee. For example, the Trust may state that the Court must appoint a corporate fiduciary, or it may state that the named successor Trustee appoint the next person to serve. The Court may need to be involved in this event.

A Settlor and/or their spouse, as Trustee, or a person named a successor Trustee, may decide that he/she no longer wishes to act as Trustee and chooses to appoint a successor. For example, an elderly person diagnosed with a terminal condition or perhaps the early stages of Alzheimer's may wish to have a child, who has been named a Trustee or successor Trustee, to take over the administration, while the person is still able to make the appointment. This will make for a smooth transition so that the resigning Trustee can "hand over the reins," and reduce the need to have two doctors verify the person is no longer able to take care of personal affairs under the Durable Power of Attorney. It often gives the Trustee a feeling of having more control over the estate and its administration.

# Beginning the Administration Process

Once the Trustee agrees to retain the attorney, the attorney should discuss his or her fees with the Trustee, as the client. As indicated earlier, probate fees are paid pursuant to the statutory amount based on the value of the estate. Estate administration will usually be paid at the attorney's hourly rate or a flat rate. The attorney can give the client an estimate of the number of hours and the potential costs (if any) to the estate. The attorney will want to have the client sign a fee agreement and may request a retainer.

The attorney will review the documents to make sure that he or she understands what projects need to be completed. At this point, it is an excellent idea for the attorney and the paralegal to sit down with the Trustee and outline the various tasks and who will complete each of them. The attorney may provide an approximate time line for the client. The administration of a simple trust estate will usually take much less time than the average probate.

The next step is to "lodge" the original Will with the probate court. Although the Will does not undergo the formal probate process, the law requires that the Court receive and document that they have received the decedent's original Will. (Follow the same procedure as outlined in Chapter Four.)

The third step is to list all of the assets and debts of the decedent. It is a great idea to create a spreadsheet so that the information can be entered and will be easily accessible to the attorney and the paralegal. It can also be provided to the client for reference, to a CPA, a third party as required, or even a beneficiary, if necessary.

Remember that the decedent, if married, only owns one-half of the trust property.

For example, if the family home is valued at $400,000, the decedent's property is worth $200,000. If the property is valued at $400,000 but there is a $200,000 mortgage, the decedent's estate value is $100,000 ($400,000–$200,000 = $200,000 ÷ 2).

The primary reason for the spreadsheet is so that the attorney can make sure that the decedent's estate will not incur federal estate taxes. If there is any question as to the possibility the estate will incur federal estate taxes, the client should be referred to a Certified Public Accountant (CPA) who is familiar with estate administration. Most small to mid-size law offices will have a CPA to whom they regularly refer probate and estate planning clients. The CPA firm is also likely to refer clients to the law firm for their estate planning needs. Larger firms may have a "tax section." In that event, the attorney should schedule a meeting with an attorney in that department and the client to discuss any tax consequences. The attorney and perhaps a senior paralegal should also attend the meeting so that everyone is working toward the same goal.

The spreadsheet will also help in determining the commingling of any trust property for a married couple. As indicated above, one-half of the property belongs to each spouse. A spreadsheet showing the "division" of trust assets, even if the entire estate will go to the surviving spouse/trustee and may protect the surviving spouse from potential creditors.

Second, the Trustee has a fiduciary responsibility to the decedent. That responsibility includes making sure all bills are paid. However, the Trustee need only pay the bills from the decedent's one-half of the estate. If the decedent's one-half of the estate is not sufficient to pay all of the creditors, the Trustee will need to advise the creditors of the situation. In the event the Trustee has commingled assets, the creditor may try to make the surviving Settlor responsible for paying the decedent's debts. The Trustee could also be held responsible in the event he or she destroys any property or loses its date of death value.

The Trustee has a responsibility to make sure that any beneficiaries receive their property. Any breach in the Trustee's fiduciary responsibility in this respect may result in the Trustee being held accountable and liable.

The third reason for the spreadsheet is that if this is a more complex trust administration and sub-trusts will be created, the debts can be allocated to the different trusts to reduce the possibility of a taxable event.

The final reason is so that the firm can assist the client in making sure that all debts have been timely paid. During this stressful time, the client may appreciate that there is someone to help with "little" things. A client can certainly take care of this aspect of the estate, but the attorney will want to be able to confirm, without a doubt, that the administration has been carried out properly and completely.

The accounting should be considered a balance sheet for the estate's assets. All income or gain and debts, losses and deductions must be included. The balance sheet will also help with the preparation of any the decedent's personal and/or estate tax returns.

The third step is to give notice to all beneficiaries. Probate Code §§ 16060–16064 requires that all beneficiaries be given notice of the pending trust administration. The beneficiaries will also be advised that they may request a copy of the Trust document and may request an accounting of the Trust property by the Trustee, pursuant to the terms of the Trust. Some law firms will prepare the notice and enclose a copy of the Trust, rather than wait to see if any beneficiary requests a copy. This also reduces the need to wait the prescribed period to make distributions if they can be made sooner.

## Trustee Powers

The attorney should carefully review the powers that have been given to the Trustee to administer the Trust. The Trustee should understand the standard of care and his or her fiduciary responsibility. Some Trusts will give the Trustee a broad standard of discretion that allows him or her to do anything the decedent would have, if the decedent were still alive. This type of unlimited power is usually bestowed upon a spouse or other trusted family member.

The original Trustee may choose, however, to limit the power of the successor Trustee, especially if the named Trustee is not a spouse or immediate family member. The attorney should explain exactly what duties the Trustee can or cannot perform and let the Trustee know that if he/she has any questions about the powers granted, he/she should ask before acting. Many firms have created a form letter and/or Trustee instructions to give the client. The Continuing Education of the Bar (CEB) *Trust Administration Practice Guidelines* is also an excellent resource.

The Trustee should also clearly understand the distribution provisions of the Trust. The attorney should discuss with the Trustee how the distributions should be made, particularly if any liquidation of property needs to take place to satisfy a specific bequest. The Trust may require the Trustee to provide accountings to beneficiaries. The attorney should advise the Trustee at what intervals any accountings are required, e.g., quarterly, annually, or at the close of the administration.

Distributions are also subject to the laws governing distribution to minors—See Chapter Three regarding UTMA bequests. Additionally, if distributions are subject to discretionary or sprinkling distributions, the Trustee will need to be advised as properly setting up these accounts, which may or may not be dictated within the terms of the Trust.

## Making Distributions

It is the Trustee's duty to make any and all Trust distributions as set forth in the Trust. Thus the Trustee cannot decide to **not** distribute Child A's share to that person because he/she has started using drugs and, therefore, the Trustee does not think Child A should have the money he/she is entitled to under the Trust agreement. It is not within the Trustee's discretion to decide, unless the Trust specifically states that the Trustee has that discretion.

Examples of trust distributions (simple administrations):

A) The Trustee is either the surviving Trustee or if the person is single, the named successor-Trustee, and the Trust states: "The trustee shall distribute my personal effects as listed on the memorandum prepared and that is attached to this Trust ... The remaining trust estate will be distributed to the trustee's 'living' children in equal shares." There are three adult children.

The Trustee must account for all of the estate property, which includes: a home valued at $400,000 with no debt; a 2012 Yukon Denali with no debt, valued at $26,000; a bank account with $2,000, mutual fund account valued at death at $84,000, an insurance plan valued at $100,000, who names the trust as secondary beneficiary (the deceased spouse was the primary beneficiary) and miscellaneous furniture, furnishings, appliances, and personal effects.

1) The first step after preparing an inventory of the property would be to confirm the value of the estate and confirm whether any federal estate taxes will be due from the estate.
2) The Trustee should obtain a Tax Identification Number (TIN) for the estate. The paralegal or the CPA office may perform this function.
3) The Trustee should distribute the personal effects to the three children as set forth in the memorandum.
4) The Trustee should also check with the children to see if there is any remaining property (furniture, furnishings, appliances, etc.) that a specific child wishes to have.
5) The Trustee should contact Social Security, the decedent's retirement plan, if any, and any other persons from whom the decedent received benefits that will need to be terminated. Any overpayments must be returned, as required.
6) The Trustee should contact the bank, provide a copy of the death certificate, collect the proceeds in the account, and open an interest-bearing account in the name of the Trust, with the successor Trustee as the named signatory, provided it is a Trust asset and not held in joint tenancy.

Note this is a very simplified process reflected here. Many financial institutions will have their own specific forms and/or documents required for the Trustee in order to take control of the account. The Trustee should be prepared to initially contact the financial institution to determine what is required and then take the steps to fulfill those requirements.

7) The Trustee should sell the real property and the vehicle and place the proceeds in the interest-bearing account unless a beneficiary chooses to take the home as an "in kind" distribution.

8) The Trustee should contact the mutual fund company and the insurance company; provide each with a copy of the death certificate, and any other information required by that particular entity, to obtain the sums payable to the estate. Once those items have been liquidated, the proceeds should be placed in the interest-bearing account.

9) The Trustee should sell the decedent's remaining furniture, furnishings, appliances, etc. at an estate or yard sale (depending upon which is most appropriate). Any property that is not in a condition to be sold or which remains after the sale, should be donated, or hauled away. Receipts for these should be kept and records maintained.

10) The Trustee should pay any debts, funeral expenses, or expenses of last illness from the interest-bearing account. The Trustee should work with decedent's health insurance provider, Medicare, or any supplemental health plan to assure that all forms have been properly submitted and all claims properly paid. If the decedent received any Medi-Cal benefits, the proper notification will need to be sent, as these will likely need to be reimbursed or if a lien has been placed on the property it will need to be satisfied.

11) The Trustee should work with a CPA to prepare the decedent's final personal tax return, determine if any taxes are due, and pay as necessary.

12) The Trustee should pay him or herself any administrative costs due and any compensation allowed by the Trust. The law firm should be paid for any agreed-upon fees and costs incurred. Those deductions should be reflected on the spreadsheet. Likewise, the CPA or any other third party providing services to the estate should be paid.

13) The Trustee should prepare an accounting detailing all of the above transactions. Much as a probate accounting should balance upon completion, so should be the Trust accounting. All monies coming in and out of the estate should be reflected in the accounting (spreadsheet). A sample spreadsheet is provided at Appendix 10A.

The Trustee should then write checks to each of the decedent's three children. Children should sign a receipt stating he/she has received their distributive share of the decedent's estate. (See the Probate Receipt referenced in Chapter Five that can be modified for a Trust). The Trustee may want to provide an accounting to each child. It is his or her discretion unless the Trust states that the Trustee **must** provide an accounting. It is certainly a good idea as it will show each child that he/she received the same share as the others and also reflect how the "net" value of the estate was determined. A beneficiary must object to the accounting within three years. Therefore, it is best to provide the accounting to stop or shorten the time to object.

Once the checks written, based on the accounting (see Appendix 10A) have cleared the bank (the children should be encouraged to deposit their check immediately) the account may be closed. Some beneficiaries will be waiting anxiously to receive their share. Surprisingly, others will have difficulty receiving or depositing the funds as it makes things final; they are not emotionally ready to end that chapter. At this point, the Trustee has completed the job as the administrator of the estate.

The above list has been provided as "instructions for the trustee." It is a good idea to create a document that provides the successor trustee with a similar checklist of tasks that will need to be accomplished. The Trustee may want the attorney (or paralegal) to perform some, or even most, of the above-listed tasks. The Trustee may prefer to pay the law firm to perform these administrative details, provided the estate has adequate funds to do so.

This list will serve as a reference point to indicate who will perform each of the tasks. Of course, more detail can be added to customize each estate as necessary or as you become more experienced in this area of practice.

## Trust Accountings

A well-drafted Trust Agreement will, in most cases, determine the need for accountings to be prepared. A Trust Agreement stating that the surviving spouse receives all of the property of the Settlor, who is the first to die, will likely not require an accounting. In most instances, the surviving Settlor/Spouse, will not need a formal accounting, as he/she will know exactly what has been transferred and/or received from the decedent's estate.

A Trust for a single person containing distributions of personal property to various individuals, charitable donations to various organizations, with the balance going to several different family members may state that a beneficiary may request an accounting. In this instance, the spreadsheet that has been created is a useful tool for preparing the accounting. It is good practice to provide an accounting in this type of situation even if it is not requested.

As indicated in the section above, a spreadsheet is included at Appendix 10A for the example provided. There are a few additional spreadsheets included for your reference.

## Compensation

The Trustee may be entitled to some form of compensation. The Trust should specify what type of compensation the Trustee is to receive: administration costs and/or a fee for performing the services as the Trustee.

If the Trustee is the surviving spouse, he/she will most likely waive any compensation, including administrative costs. As previously stated, a Trustee might want to include administrative costs to be reimbursed in the event it will reduce any taxes payable by the estate.

If the Trustee is not a spouse or child and the Trust provides that compensation will be paid, the Trustee may make said payments. Those payments should be reflected in the accounting that is prepared.

A Trust may provide, for example, that the Trustee be paid $1,000 per year plus administrative costs. If it takes the Trustee two years to complete the administration process, the Trustee can be paid $2,000, plus any administrative costs (recording fees, shipping, postage, office supplies, long distance telephone calls, etc.). Some Trusts will state that the Trustee may receive a percentage of the value of the estate. In that case, the Trustee's compensation is usually based on the gross value, unless otherwise indicated. The Trustee, in that event, will definitely need to prepare an accounting that shows the value of the estate, including any gains or losses since the date of death, in order to determine the amount of compensation he or she is to receive. The Trustee should also sign a receipt acknowledging payment of the compensation and applicable costs. As with any business transaction, a paper trail is important. In the event the fiduciary Trustee has been appointed, costs of administration and related fees **will** have to be paid out of the Trust assets.

## Winding up the Simple Estate Administration

The simple estate administration is now ready to be closed. That was quick! Once the Will is lodged, all debts have been paid, the tax ramifications considered, and the notice has been given to all heirs, the successor Trustee has completed the liquidation of any property, and made transfers of all property pursuant to the terms of the Trust, the successor Trustee may now "wind up" the estate's affairs.

The following is another scenario for a very simple trust administration:

The Trustee and his/her spouse created a marital trust five years ago. They own a house, two vehicles, a time-share in Hawaii, a bank account and a savings account totaling $5,000 and each has a $100,000 life insurance policy. Each spouse has created a memorandum for distribution of personal effects to be distributed to their two adult children. The house is worth $400,000 and has a mortgage balance of $150,000. The time-share value is approximately $15,000. There are also mutual funds valued at $20,000 in the name of the Trust.

The Wife is the first to die. Husband has retained the law firm that prepared the Trust to assist with the administration. The house and the time-share were properly funded into the Trust. The life insurance policy names husband as beneficiary and the Trust as the secondary beneficiary, and all vehicles are owned in joint tenancy.

The attorney has met with Husband and discussed the particulars of the trust administration. The attorney has explained to the Husband his powers and fiduciary responsibility as successor Trustee of the Trust. He has also discussed the various procedures that will be used to make the appropriate transfers. The attorney has confirmed that the real property was transferred into the Trust, as there are copies of the recorded deeds in the client's file.

"Distributions" above gives a general summary of the process that is required to determine the actual distribution of the decedent's property. Below, is a more detailed list.

As the paralegal, you have been included in the meeting and the attorney has provided a list of "things to do."

- Client will obtain 10 copies of the death certificate and will bring them to the office
- Client will bring copies of all bills for last illness and funeral expenses to the office
- Client will bring a copy of the insurance policy to the office
- Client will bring in copy of mutual fund statement with date of death values
- Client will bring a copy of Wife's memorandum of personal property to the office
- Client will bring copies of both pink slips to the office
- Client will notify Social Security Administration of Wife's date of death (Wife was retired and receiving Social Security by direct deposit)

The paralegal has been instructed to prepare the following documents.

- Notice pursuant to Probate Code §§ 16060 et seq. and two copies of trust

- Affidavit Death of Trustee for real property located in California
- Preliminary Change of Ownership form for California Property
- Affidavit Death of Trustee for Hawaii timeshare
- Declaration for Tax Exemption for Hawaii
- Letter to Insurance Company with copy of Death Certificate
- Letter to Mutual Fund with copy of Death Certificate
- Receipts for children to sign
- Letter to Wife's pension plan with copy of Death Certificate.

At the next meeting, the attorney, client, and paralegal will do the following:

- Husband will review and sign the Notice; paralegal will mail copies of the notice along with a copy of the trust and a proof of service to each child
- Husband will review and sign the Affidavit Death of Trustee, with death certificate attached, and Preliminary Change of Ownership form for the California property; Paralegal will notarize his signature and send the documents to the Clerk/Recorder for recording
- Husband will review and sign the Affidavit Death of Trustee, with death certificate attached, and Declaration for Tax Exemption for Hawaii timeshare; Paralegal will notarize his signature and send the documents to the Office of Conveyances in Hawaii
- Husband will review and sign the letter to the insurance company instructing them to pay the insurance pursuant to the terms of the contract to the beneficiary
- Husband will review and sign letter to mutual fund company instructing them to change the name on the account to his as surviving Trustee
- Husband will confirm that he has notified Social Security and that they have removed the pro-rated Social Security benefits from the checking account
- Review the list of personal effects to be distributed to the children
- Review the Department of Motor Vehicle (DMV) forms that have been obtained via the DMV internet site
- Husband will contact tax preparer/CPA to advise them a "final" tax return will need to be filed at the appropriate time. He may also need to discuss whether Federal Estate Taxes may be due and an IRS Form 706 prepared

The attorney will instruct Husband to do the following:

- Husband will go to the DMV, taking a death certificate and the applicable forms and transfer the vehicles into his name
- Husband will go to the bank, taking a death certificate, and have all accounts reflect that he is the sole owner of the account; the attorney may encourage the Husband to place the account in the name of the Trust at this time since it is no longer a joint tenancy account with right of survivorship
- Husband will distribute the personal effects of Wife to the children as set forth in her memorandum; the children will sign receipts for this property

The paralegal will prepare the estate spreadsheet for all property, debts to be paid, and distributions to be made.

At such time that all transfers have been made, bequests distributed, bills paid, insurance and final retirement distributions have been received, and confirmed the mutual fund account has been changed, the Husband will need to have a final meeting with the attorney. He will also bring in the receipts from the children, unless they have already been received by the firm.

The attorney and client will review the spreadsheet. They will confirm that no federal estate taxes are due by the estate. They will also confirm that the receipts are in order, all property has been successfully transferred, and that insurance and retirement proceeds have been received by Husband. They will also confirm that no accounting has either been requested or due to the beneficiaries. The file may now be closed.

# Complex Estate Administration

A complex estate administration may involve any of the following:

- Property that was not transferred into the trust and is valued at over $100,000.
- Wealth Transfers and Federal Tax Consequences
- Trusts with specific and/or unequal distributions and/or distributions to charitable organizations and others
- Creation of children's, grandchildren's or special needs trusts
- Disclaimer or By-Pass Trust allocations and Trusts with appropriate transfers and documents

The above is not a complete list, but will be the types of complex trust administration you are most likely to encounter as an estate planning paralegal.

## Property Not Transferred into the Trust

Property that has not been transferred into the Trust and which is valued under $150,000 can be transferred using the Declaration Under Probate Code § 13100 procedure. (See Chapter Six, *Transfers of Property Without Probate*.) Property that is valued over $150,000 and not held in the name of the Trust will need to be administered by Petition for Instructions, which is covered in the next section of this chapter.

# Federal Tax Consequences and Wealth Transfers

Trusts created for those clients who anticipate their estate will be close to or will exceed the federal allowable transfers upon their death will include, within the Trust Agreement, estate planning techniques to reduce those federal taxes. There may still be federal taxes due, but the client, with the attorney's assistance, will have utilized every advantage to reduce the tax liability. Those subjects were discussed in Chapter Seven, "Trusts."

Trusts created to reduce federal estate taxes include sub-trusts such as By-Pass, Disclaimer, Marital Deduction, or Q-TIP Trusts. Wealthy clients may have provided for Charitable Remainder or Charitable Deduction Trusts to be created upon their death. The client may have also created other entities that have been funded, based on the ability to distribute wealth over and above the annual exclusions while they are alive. These distributions must be well documented in order to qualify under the Internal Revenue Code. Distributions that include Family Limited Partnership (FLP) and Corporations are beyond the scope of this textbook.

Care must be taken to determine the status of current state and federal laws. Federal taxation laws are constantly changing. Do not rely solely on this text for information on federal tax laws. As an entry level paralegal, you will want to have the attorney, along with a CPA, make any determinations as to the federal tax implications. This information is to give you general understanding of the process and the factors that will influence the administration of the Trust estate.

The following are some of the steps involved in complex trust administration. For the purposes of this textbook, only the most common and easily understandable have been included. There are many more types of estate planning techniques that can be used either in preparation of the estate plan or after the Trustee's death to reduce taxes. A paralegal working in the estate planning firm should regularly attend continuing education courses and/or obtain the numerous publications and guides available through the Continuing Education of the Bar (CEB), The Rutter Group, and other providers.

## Federal Estate Tax Consequences

This area of law is very complex and there are multiple charts and examples that illustrate the methods of determining the **Applicable Exclusion Amount,** the **Applicable Credit Amount**, and **Federal Gift Taxes**. For the purposes of this section, we will keep it simple even though we are discussing complex estate administration. Overall, you will be learning about the documents needed to begin the administration of a large estate in order to reduce, defer, and/or eliminate federal estate taxes.

The Economic Growth and Tax Relief Reconciliation Act of 2001 (EGTRRA) released the estate and generation-skipping transfer taxes as of January 1, 2010. It also allowed for lower rates and greater exclusions for the preceding ten-year period. The allowable federal exemption (exclusion) was to sunset in 2010, but Congress voted to extend it one more year. Effective January 1, 2011, Congress voted to return the federal estate tax exemption. However, only estates under $5 million at death in 2011 were exempt. Estates over $5 million were to be taxed at 35%. The return of the Federal Estate Tax (FET) also returned the application of *stepped-up basis* on inherited property, which may affect those who received wind-falls and capital gains on inherited assets into later years. There are potentially carry-over taxes for individuals that inherited property from decedents in 2010.

The American Tax Relief Act of 2012 increased the FET exemption to $5,250,000 for 2013; however, the amount over the exemption will be taxed at 40%. The allowable FET will likely be adjusted from the 2013 amount, plus inflation factors. These current laws do not "sunset" as they did in the past, leaving uncertainty about the estate tax exemptions going into future years. Congress can still vote to change or terminate the FET and any exemptions in the future without warning and based on the political nature of Congress.

The most critical thing that the attorney and paralegal can do is review the Unified Credit and Annual Exclusion information annually to determine what effect it will have upon the decedent's estate. If there is any question a tax attorney and/or CPA should be consulted.

## Applicable Exclusion Amount

The **Applicable Exclusion Amount** is the total amount of property that an individual may pass upon death without incurring federal estate tax. Remember that if the person is married, that is **his/her** share of the marital property or one-half of the community property in California, as it is a community property state. The IRC should be reviewed annually, at least, to determine the allowable exemption for the year the person died.

The IRC also makes an allowance for the payment of state estate taxes. California, however, does not **currently** have an inheritance tax, so this allowance cannot currently be considered in the adjusted credit amount.

## Federal Gift Tax

Federal **gift** taxes must be considered in order to compute federal estate taxes. All gifts that have been made during the Settlor's lifetime should be listed. The list should include the person who received the gift, their relationship to the donor, the date, the value, and how the gift was to be used. The donor cannot give a gift he or she intends to take back, or upon which conditions were made for receiving the property.

Three types of property are subject to federal gift tax:

(1) property made as an irrevocable gift;
(2) a gift that is less than the full consideration (value of what it is worth); and
(3) a power of appointment.

There are exclusions to federal gift taxes. They are:

**Annual Exclusion**—Each person may give to another person up to $13,000 per calendar year (2012–2013). There is no limit to the number of people to whom a person can gift and the beneficiary of the gift does not have to be a child. Any amount over the $13,000 would be subject to federal gift taxes. The annual gift tax for 2014 has been set at $14,000. Like the Annual Exclusion referenced above, the IRC should be checked each year if the client is in a position to do any gifting from their estate.

In most cases, a future interest in property will not be considered for exclusion. There is one exception and that is a person may create a "minor's trust" for a child who is under the age of 21 at the time the trust is created. Certain requirements must be met in order to create the minor's trust and receive the federal gift tax exclusion. The applicable IRS codes should be reviewed to determine the criteria. These gifts and exclusions should have been considered at the drafting stage to give the client the greatest benefit.

**Crummey Trust**—Annual contributions to a Crummey Trust are excluded from federal gift taxes. (See Chapter Eight—Irrevocable Trusts.) The maximum allowable annual exclusion, as noted above, must be followed for each year; note however, the amount may be less than what is allowed, it just cannot be more.

**Educational & Medical Expense Exclusion**—The payments made to another for their personal education or medical expenses are exempt from federal gift tax. (I.R.C. §2503(e)) The payments must be made directly to the educational institution or the medical provider. The person who benefits does not have to be related and there is no limit as to the number of these gifts or the amount that may be paid.

**Marital Deduction Exclusion**—There is no limit to the value of property one can give their spouse and there will be no federal **gift** taxes incurred. **Note this is not the same as federal estate taxes that may be incurred.** The Marital Deduction with respect federal estate taxes will be covered in the next section.

**Charitable Deduction**—Gifts made to charitable and educational foundations or religious organizations are deductible. (I.R.C. §2522)

Internal Revenue Service Code §2001(c) governs the amount of gift tax incurred. This code section provides a table of "tentative" tax due based on the amount gifted. Additional adjustments are made under EGTRRA for the various tax years in which a gift is made.

A gift tax return should have been prepared for each year in which a gift was made, even if no tax is owed. The Trustee(s) should keep copies of these returns with their estate planning documents so that when a Federal Estate Tax return may have to be prepared, there will be a paper trail of the gift tax returns and any taxes paid.

## Distributions and Creation of Sub-Trusts

As indicated under the section for administration of simple trusts, most property will be distributed outright to the beneficiaries. Under a marital trust, the property was simply transferred to the surviving spouse and the surviving spouse had total control over all of the property received. This also meant, however, that the surviving spouse received one-half of the **adjusted** value of the estate, because he/she already owned one-half.

## Marital Deduction Trust

Prior to 1976, the one-half that the surviving spouse received was taxed. In 1976, the surviving spouse was able to deduct **up to** the **first** $250,000 of the "gift." Commencing in 1982 (enacted by Congress in 1981) the **unlimited marital deduction** was applied to "inter vivos" gifts and/or transfers upon the death of a spouse. The rate has increased significantly since that time. (See Federal Estate Tax consequences, EGTRAA and the American Tax Relief Act of 2012 referenced earlier in this chapter.) A trust that is not properly written runs the risk of having Federal Estate Tax applied at the current tax rate after the allowed exemption. This could cause severe tax consequences for a surviving spouse or children inheriting property.

The marital deduction provisions should specify the types of trusts based on the IRS Code sections and the manner in which the clients wish to have the property protected from Federal Estate Taxes. Such marital deductions can be called, Qualified Terminable Interest Property (Q-TIP), Power of Appointment, or Disclaimer Trusts.

Chapter Seven, Trusts, set forth the qualifications of a Marital Deduction under the IRS Code §2056. The US Treasury does, however, still want to collect any federal estate taxes that are due. Therefore, the initial tax planning is critical in estate planning. The attorney, and most likely the clients' CPA, want to reduce the amount of taxes the client will have to pay upon the death of the first spouse. The taxes incurred by the beneficiaries upon the death of the second spouse are also important, but not the primary focus at this point.

## Bypass Trusts

Many marital trusts will also consider "bypass planning." That means that the couple has planned for what will happen to the property upon the second spouses death. It also, in effect, bypasses the surviving spouse during his or her lifetime and is not considered part of the estate. The surviving spouse will still have access to the principal and income if needed. That access will be determined by the type of Trust created and the amount of control and standards that are included in the bypass Trust. A Bypass Trust may be called by that name or it may also be referred to as a **Credit Shelter Trust**, or a **Survivor's Trust**. Alternatively, the Marital Deduction Trust may have been referred to as the "A Trust" and the bypass trust may be called the "B Trust." There will be some Trusts that create three different and distinct Trusts. Each firm may have its own preference on the creation of these "sub" Trusts. The important factor is that the language of the Trust(s) created to meet the IRS qualifications and requirements. The same rules will apply as to the manner in which the property should be treated with respect to tax purposes and transfers of ownership.

## Charitable Deductions and Charitable Remainder Trusts

Transfers to **qualified** charities are completely deductible for both federal estate and federal gift tax purposes. I.R.C. §§ 2055 and 2522 set forth the definition of a qualified charitable organization and also specify the purposes for which the donation cannot be used.

A **Charitable Remainder Trust** is a Trust that is created so that the estate will pass to the charity upon the death of the surviving spouse. The Trust, when it is created, must state that the surviving spouse has a "life estate" in the property if it is a residence or other real property. The Trustee will not have any control over the principal of the property during his or her lifetime. These types of Trusts are very technical and must be carefully drafted. They must also be carefully administered. A paper trail of all transactions is imperative.

## Creating and Funding Sub-Trusts

Any sub-trusts that may be created will be dictated by the terms of the Trust Agreement. An attorney will have created the Trust using specific terminology and types of trusts to accomplish the various goals of the client. In most cases where there is a married couple creating an estate plan, the Trust will provide for a Marital Deduction Trust. The Trust may also allow for a Power of Appointment, a Disclaimer or Bypass Trust, and/or a Qualified Terminable Interest Property Trust. The client's needs may also determine if Trusts are to be created for minor children or grandchildren and the manner in which those Trusts should be created.

## Funding the Sub-Trusts

The client will need to work with the attorney and CPA to determine what property should be included in the Marital Deduction Trust, which will be exempt up to the maximum allowable amount. The property to be distributed to the Bypass Trust will also need to be identified. This is crucial otherwise, the I.R.S. will apply federal taxes to property that should be considered exempt. The I.R.S. will carefully review the documentation submitted to make sure all is in order and that, the Trust has been administered properly and more specifically, that no additional taxes are due.

Similar to preparing the probate or trust accounting, a spreadsheet works well for determining how to distribute the marital property and to which Trust it should be allocated. An actuary or appraiser may need to be retained to value certain property. Remember that the allocation is based on the "net" value of the estate less all debts of the decedent, last funeral expenses, administration costs (CPA, attorney, filing fees, transfer fees, death certificates, actuaries, and appraisers used to value property, final personal tax return, etc.)

Once the property has been allocated, the Trust should be given specific names. For example if you have the Sam E. Fellow, Sr. and Marci Fellow Family Trust, and Marci Fellow has passed away, the number of trusts or sub-trusts will need to be determined. For the sake of simplicity, let us say that an "A" and a "B" Trust are provided for in the Fellow Family Trust. One trust would be called the Sam E. Fellow and Marci Fellow "A" Trust, created on _____ [date] (it would be the Marital Deduction Trust and could also be identified as the Sam E. Fellow, Sr. and Marci Fellow Marital Deduction Trust, created on _____ [date]. The second trust, which would be the Sam E. Fellow, Sr. And Marci Fellow "B" Trust, created on _____ [date]. A Tax Identification Number should then be obtained for **each** newly created trust.

The property that is to go into each Trust would then be transferred as such. Most firms will also create a document called an Allocation Agreement for the client to sign. Using the spreadsheet that has been created to identify the allocation of the property the document will state to which Trust each asset is allocated. This also becomes a paper trail for the IRS and beneficiaries, if an accounting is required or requested. It also provides the attorney with written documentation that the client understands which assets are being transferred to each specific Trust.

If the family home is going to be transferred to Trust "A" a new deed should be prepared transferring the real property to the surviving spouse [name] as Trustee of the Sam E. Fellow, Sr. and Marci Fellow "A" Trust, created _____ [date]. If the condominium (time share) in Hawaii is going to be transferred to Trust "B" a new deed should be prepared transferring the condominium to _____ [name] as trustee of the Sam E. Fellow, Sr. and Marci Fellow "B" Trust, created _____ [date]; and so on. Any other property having title, as well as bank accounts, stocks, mutual funds, etc. will likewise be transferred to the appropriate Trust. As with an Assignment (Chapter Eight), the Allocation Agreement will identify all other property that does not have title.

# Generation Skipping Transfer Tax (GST)

This mechanism has been used by individuals to reduce federal estate taxes by transferring property to a grandchild through a Trust. The premise is that only one taxable event will occur rather than two. The "first" event is a transfer to child upon the parent's death; the "second" event is the transfer from child to grandchild upon the child's death.

The GST is a "flat" rate tax that is added to the federal gift or federal estate tax (whichever is applicable) under the I.R.C. §§ 2601–2663.

The Federal Estate Tax Returns (IRS form No. 706 or "706") should indicate the GST and a Gift Tax Return must be filed. Generation Skipping Transfers should be carefully reviewed by the attorney and a CPA to insure that all IRC sections have been properly complied with. These transfers should be done by an attorney and/or experience paralegal.

# Federal Estate Tax Returns

My recommendation—let a professional do it! That being said, you may at some point in your career feel you have the skills and knowledge to prepare Federal Estate Tax Returns (otherwise referred to as 706s). I do recommend, however, that as an entry level paralegal, you go to the IRS website and download the 706 form so that you can see, and begin to understand, the complexity of filing this document. It will also give you a better appreciation as to why so many people include tax planning with the estate plan, so that they do not have to ever file this form, let alone pay federal estate taxes and try to understand the allowable exemptions, fair market value, and the other aspects of the return that can impact the estate and cause tax consequences which the Settlor had been trying to avoid.

The paralegal may be called upon to assist the client in obtaining valuations of property, obtaining documentation regarding various assets and items of property. The paralegal may also be the person keeping the spreadsheet with all of the assets listed as well as the debts and expenses. It would be helpful if the paralegal understands what documents the CPA will need in order to complete the 706 so he or she can work closely with the client and the attorney to collect all of the documentation. This same information will be reflected in any final accounting that is required of the Trustee.

The following is a brief synopsis of what is needed in order to prepare a 706, which is approximately 25 pages long and contains numerous schedules.

Three things are vitally important in addition to accuracy, in completing a 706. They are:

1) The Federal Estate Tax return must be filed within nine months of the date of death of the decedent; or an extension must be requested. Payment of anticipated taxes owed must be sent with the request for an extension.
2) A Tax Identification Number (TIN) must have been obtained for the estate and/or for each sub-Trust created.
3) All supporting documentation about all sub-trusts, date of death valuations, descriptions of property, etc. must be included with the 706 when it is submitted to the IRS.

The Federal Tax Return must contain all of the property and items belonging to the decedent and their gross value. Those things include, but are not limited to, real property (including property held in joint tenancy), jewelry, collections, stocks, bonds, bank accounts, business interests, annuities and other death benefits (retirement, pension, etc.), any type of pay-on-death account, insurance if the trust was the beneficiary, powers of appointment, potential inheritances, and any potential settlement for a tort claim. This means that **all** the decedent's property must be included, even that property that is otherwise considered exempt for the probate or administration procedure (transfers not subject to probate).

Personal property may be "grouped" provided it does not have a value of more than $500. Treasury Regulation § 20.2031-6(b) provides that items having an artistic or intrinsic value of more than $5,000 (such as silverware, jewelry, furs, guns, paintings, engravings, rugs, coin or stamp collections or other collectibles, antiques, etc.) must be appraised by an expert.

Real estate, stocks certificates, bonds (paper), businesses, and other such assets must also be valued by an expert.

# Trusts with Specific and/or Unequal Distributions and/or Distributions to Charitable Organizations or Others

Trusts that provide for unequal distributions or for gifts to charitable organizations are not particularly difficult or complex, especially when compared to creating sub-trusts or other entities. These types of distributions are included in this section because care should be taken to make sure the distributions are done correctly.

As with the simple Trust, the same procedures must be followed for collecting the Trust assets, making distributions of specific personal effects, liquidating any assets as necessary, paying the decedent's debts, taxes, administrative costs, etc, and preparing a final accounting that reflects a balance sheet. The amount to be distributed to each beneficiary can then be calculated.

Examples incorporating specific distributions and/or unequal distributions could be any of the following types of distributions:

A) The following distributions shall be made from the trust estate:

   1) $1,000 to the Trustee's niece, Ida Rather;
   2) $1,000 to the Trustee's niece, Selma Rather;
   3) $1,000 to the Trustee's nephew, Bill E. Club;

The balance of the trust estate shall be distributed to the Trustee's children in equal shares.

B) The following distributions shall be made from the trust estate:

   1) $10,000 to the American Cancer Society, _____ (local) chapter or its successor in interest;
   2) $10,000 to the American Diabetes Association, _____ (local) chapter or its successor in interest;
   3) $2,000 to the SPCA, _____ (local) chapter or its successor in interest

The balance of the trust estate shall be distributed to the Trustee's children in equal shares.

C) The balance of the trust estate shall be distributed outright as follows:

   1) One-Third to Sam E. Fellow;
   2) One-Third to Sue M. High;
   3) One-Sixth to Emma Jean Cole; and,
   4) One-Sixth to Anne D. High

D) The balance of the trust estate shall be distributed as follows:

   1) One-Third outright and free of trust to Sam E. Fellow;
   2) One-Third outright and free of trust to Sue M. High; and,
   3) One-Third to Anne D. High, in trust until she has reached 62 years of age, as set forth in Article \*\*, Trust for Anne D. High.

E) The Trustee shall distribute the real property and home located at 1000 Fellows Hall Lane, Piney Woods, California, whose legal description is _____ to Sue M.

High. The property should be valued at the time of Settlor's death and that child's share shall be deducted from the share she is to receive from the trust estate. By way of example: If the total net estate is valued at $750,000 and the property is valued at $300,000 then Sue M. High will receive $75,000. ($750,000 ÷ 2 = $375,000 > $300,000 = $75,000), of the balance of the estate.

The balance of the trust estate shall be distributed outright to Anne D. High.

*Note that the above examples should not be construed as appropriate trust language. An attorney will make sure that other language is incorporated to so there is no ambiguity. The simple language above is provided simply for illustration.*

As you should be able to ascertain, the above examples are not extremely complicated. However, they do require some special considerations when preparing the accounting. Specific bequests are made first, and then the balance of the "net" estate is distributed. Additionally, you should note that a Trustee might also value a certain item of personal property that could be deducted from the net value of the estate as in the example of the real property and house. This is normally done for a piece of tangible property that is of high value such as artwork, antiques, or collections of some sort. The Trustee may want to make sure that a particular child or person receives the property while making sure that all distributees receive their "equal" share.

The balance of the trust estate shall be distributed as follows:

1) One-Third to Sue M. High after deducting the sum of $100,000 advanced to him as set forth in the Promissory Note dated 3/1/2013;
2) One-Third to Sam E. Fellows; and
3) One-Third to Anne D. High

The above example of gifting the house could also be used to forgive a loan that was made to a child or other beneficiary.

## Creation of Children's, Grandchildren's or Special Needs Trusts

Clients will, for various reasons, specifically create children's or grandchildren's Trusts within their Trust, to take effect upon the single Settlor's death or the death of the second Settlor. A Special Needs Trust, as discussed in Chapter Seven, can be set up for a child, grandchild, or any individual to whom the Trustee(s) wishes to leave the estate property.

In the event it is necessary to set up a Trust for a child or grandchild, the attorney will need to advise the client of the conditions of the Trust. The following are some considerations that should be discussed with the client:

- Did the Trust appoint a different person to be the Trustee of a child or grandchild's Trust? (That person could be the child's parent.)
- Can Trusts, if there are more than one, be combined?
- Are there staged distributions or is distribution outright at a particular age? (For example at 25, 30 and 35; or outright at the age of 40, with no prior distributions)
- Are distributions allowed from principal and/or interest?
- Are distributions allowed for only certain things (health and education) or does the Trustee have discretion?

The attorney should make sure that the Trustee understands how these Trusts are to be administered, the standard of care, and any specific management requirements to which the Trustee will have to adhere.

## Final Distributions and Termination of the Complex Trust

The Trustee may terminate the Trust upon the completion of all estate assets being disbursed to the beneficiaries of the Trust. The Trustee may also terminate the Trust when the assets have been expended. If the Trust lacks property, the Trustee may provide a final accounting and wind up the trust administration.

## Final Accounting

The accounting for a complex Trust should follow the same steps indicated in the administration section above with respect to the simple trust administration.

The difference with a complex Trust is that the administration, and therefore, the accounting period will likely be longer over a longer period. Although the Trust may not require the Trustee to prepare an accounting, it is recommended by most attorneys, certified public accountants, and other estate planning professionals that an accounting be prepared annually, at least for internal purposes. This will make the preparation of a complete accounting when it is required much simpler. For example, if the Trust, or sub-trusts, continue for a period of five years, it would be more difficult for the accounting to be prepared for the entire five-year period, than for annual accountings to be prepared and combined into the five-year accounting period. Note: The attorney may recommend balancing the accounting every month to insure there are no surprises and to avoid missing assets, income, and distributions that the Trustee may forget to write down if the accounting is done annually. This will allow the person doing the accounting to be aware of any problems and bring them to the attorney's attention.

Although the accounting may not be required to be provided to the beneficiaries on an annual (or any other) basis, it is recommended for a couple of reasons. One is that the beneficiaries are less likely to challenge the administration of the estate if they are "in the know." It may also be more likely that the beneficiaries will waive the final accounting, if required because they have already been provided with the on-going information. The Trustee will still need to prepare the first accounting. However, it would not need to be formally served on the beneficiaries if the accounting is waived. Additionally, one beneficiary may be willing to waive the final accounting, but another may not. The date the accounting is served also tolls the statute and will protect the Trustee if there is any future litigation regarding the accountings.

## Petition for Instructions

A Petition for Instructions is the summary procedure used when tangible property (property having title showing ownership) has not been transferred into a person's Trust.

The most common occurrences are: (1) the Settlor passed away before they could place the asset(s) into the Trust, or (2) the Settlor(s) took the property out of the Trust, most often to refinance, and did not put the property back into the Trust.

This procedure is essentially asking the court for an Order (permission) to treat the asset as though it had been transferred into the Trust.

In most cases, you will have evidence of the Settlor(s) intention to place the property into the Trust. Most Trusts contain a "schedule of assets" that is incorporated by reference into the Trust. A paper trail of transactions will also provide evidence of the Trustee's intent for the property to be considered a Trust asset.

For the purpose of illustration, we will presume that the Settlor(s) did not transfer the home back into the Trust after having refinanced the property. (This is common, as most title/escrow companies require that the property be removed from the Trust during the refinancing process as they are offering the loan to the individuals and not the Trust.) Once the refinancing process is complete, many title/escrow companies do not offer, or charge extra for, the service of returning the property to the Trust. It becomes the Settlor(s)'s responsibility to complete that last step.

The following is a typical scenario:

Upon the death of one of the Settlor/Trustee's the surviving Settlor/Trustee comes to the law firm to discuss what is needed to administer the Trust. Upon review of the documents, the attorney notices that the last recorded deed shows the title listed as "husband and wife, joint tenants." When asked the client explains that the couple refinanced the property 6 months ago and forgot they needed to transfer the property back into the Trust.

The attorney confirms that the Schedule of Assets was completed and lists the real property in question. The attorney confirms that the file contains a copy of the deed recorded by the law firm transferring the property into the Trust when the trust was initially created.

The attorney advises the client that a Petition for Instructions will need to be filed with the Court requesting that the Judge make orders stating that the property should be treated as though it were in the Trust.

The attorney will need to decide whether this final step is necessary. If the property was in joint tenancy and the property will be transferred to the surviving joint tenant (spouse), the attorney may not feel that it is necessary to file a Petition for Instructions and obtain an Order. However, if the property is being transferred to a child, another individual or entity, it may be necessary to file the Petition to not only provide the paper trail but to also avoid tax consequences for the decedent's estate and/or the person receiving the property.

The Petition for Instructions (an example is provided at Appendix 10B) will need to contain the following information:

- The names of the Settlors and Trustees.
- The names, ages, and addresses of all beneficiaries.
- The provisions of the Trust that give the Settlor/Trustees the power to petition the Court.
- The provisions that state how the property is to be transferred, e.g. "all property is to be distributed outright and free of trust to the surviving spouse."
- A statement that there is a Will and that the Will has/will be lodged with the Court and that the Will states the Trust is the controlling document.

- The legal description of the property, including a copy of the deed.
- A statement as to why the property was not in the trust at the time of the decedent's death (and/or evidence of the paper trail documenting the changes in the title, if applicable).
- The Petition should contain the prayer (what is the Petitioner requesting).

The Petition will need to be signed by the client (Petitioner) under penalty of perjury (verified). It will also be signed by the attorney.

A hearing date will need to be obtained and calendared, and the original Will must be lodged with the Court.

All documents will be served on all persons listed in the Trust and/or Will as potential beneficiaries and/or family members who have an interest in the outcome of the Petition.

The Order on Petition for Instructions (the "Order") will be prepared. It must contain the legal description and address of the property and the manner in which title needs to be changed. e.g. the title should be "Sam E. Fellow, Sr. and Marci Fellow, Trustees of the Fellow Family Trust, dated _____."

The Court's file notes should be checked on the tentative rulings before the hearing, or pursuant to the Local Rules, to make sure that the Proof of Service has been received and filed by the Court and that the probate attorney has "Recommended for Approval" the signing of the Order by the Judge and that all else is in order. Deficiencies should be resolved before the hearing.

The Order is then submitted or the attorney may wish to appear at the hearing and have the Order signed. A certified copy should be obtained, as the Order will need to be recorded with the County Recorder, if it is real property. Alternatively, if it is another type of property to be transferred it would be forwarded to the appropriate agency for transfer. The Trust estate can then be administered as set forth earlier in this Chapter.

A cover page should be prepared so that the Order can be recorded, if necessary. A copy of the certified Order is then attached and the document is submitted, along with the appropriate recording fee, and the Preliminary Change of Ownership Report to the Clerk/Recorder in the County where the property was located.

# Property Located in Another State

The attorney will need to determine if any specific procedures are involved in administering property located in another state. If the property was previously transferred into the Trust, as with other trust administration transfers, it should simply be a matter of preparing the appropriate deed or other document and having it recorded in the proper jurisdiction.

However, if the property was not transferred into the Trust and/or the property was removed from the Trust (as discussed in the previous section) the attorney will need to determine if an ancillary procedure is required in the state where the property is located, if a Petition for Instructions can be filed in California, or another type of procedure is required.

## Key Terms

- Petition for Instructions
- Order for Instructions
- Lodging the Will
- Final Trust Accounting
- Trustee Compensation
- Federal Estate Tax
- Annual Exclusion
- Marital Deduction Trust
- Federal Estate Tax Return
- IRS Form 706 ("706")
- Qualified Terminable Interest Property Trust
- By Pass Trust
- Credit Shelter Trust
- Charitable Remainder Trust

# Chapter Eleven

# Guardianships and Conservatorships

The California Probate Code governs many other matters in addition to estate planning and administration. This text has covered the most common areas of wills, trust, and their administration in the previous ten chapters.

Two other areas in which probate and estate planning attorneys are often involved are guardianships and conservatorships. These two areas, while similar in many respects, require some differing procedures and fulfill different needs of the client. The primary differences are:

Guardianship involves minor children

Conservatorship involves adults

As a probate/estate planning paralegal, you should be familiar with these areas of practice. Some firms will prefer to avoid work in these areas, especially conservatorships. Instead, they may refer some clients to fiduciaries who specialize in this area of work. Probate Code § 2340–2344 governs registration of Private Professional Conservators and Private Professional Guardians. Guardianships and conservatorships can often be labor intensive and last many years. The Court often limits the fees earned in these types of cases. However, this also makes it an excellent area of work for a paralegal in the law firm. The paralegal may perform most of the work, which is task oriented, while keeping the billing rate within the fee structure that the Court must approve.

Many local Courts offer guardianship and/or conservatorship classes. It is an excellent idea to attend one of these classes or workshops as courses will provide information regarding the Judicial Council forms, as well as the local rules, forms and procedures that must be followed in the County, and more particularly, by the Judges who are hearing the matters.

A Guardian Ad Litem is the appropriate procedure for an adult to be appointed as the guardian of a child Ad Litem (pending litigation) in a civil matter. A paralegal in a law firm that does litigation may find it necessary to prepare the Petition and Order to Appoint a Guardian Ad Litem for a child who will receive a civil settlement. Thus, you do not have to be a probate/estate planning paralegal to be exposed to this procedure and area of law.

# Guardianship

Probate Code §§ 1500–1502 provide an overview of the nomination of a guardian
1500. Subject to Section 1502, a parent may nominate a guardian of the person or estate, or both, of a minor child in either of the following cases:

(a) Where the other parent nominates, or consents in writing to the nomination of, the same guardian for the same child.

(b) Where, at the time the petition for appointment of the guardian is filed, either
   (1) the other parent is dead or lacks legal capacity to consent to the nomination or
   (2) the consent of the other parent would not be required for an adoption of the child.

1501. Subject to Section 1502, a parent or any other person may nominate a guardian for property that a minor receives from or by designation of the nominator (whether before, at the time of, or after the nomination) including, but not limited to, property received by the minor by virtue of a gift, deed, trust, will, succession, insurance, or benefits of any kind.

1502.

(a) A nomination of a guardian under this article may be made in the petition for the appointment of the guardian or at the hearing on the petition or in a writing signed either before or after the petition for the appointment of the guardian is filed.

(b) The nomination of a guardian under this article is effective when made except that a writing nominating a guardian under this article may provide that the nomination becomes effective only upon the occurrence of such specified condition or conditions as are stated in the writing, including but not limited to such conditions as the subsequent legal incapacity or death of the person making the nomination.

(c) Unless the writing making the nomination expressly otherwise provides, a nomination made under this article remains effective notwithstanding the subsequent legal incapacity or death of the person making the nomination.

Probate Code §§ 1419.5–1431 state the following with respect to the definitions used in guardianship:

1419.5. "Custodial parent" means the parent who either (a) has been awarded sole legal and physical custody of the child in another proceeding, or (b) with whom the child resides if there is currently no operative custody order. If the child resides with both parents, then they are jointly the custodial parent.

1420. "Developmental disability" means a disability which originates before an individual attains age 18, continues, or can be expected to continue, indefinitely, and constitutes a substantial handicap for such individual. As defined by the Director of Developmental Services, in consultation with the Superintendent of Public Instruction, this term includes intellectual disability, cerebral palsy, epilepsy, and autism. This term also includes handicapping conditions found to be closely related to mental retardation or to require treatment similar to that required for intellectually disability individuals, but does not include other handicapping conditions that are solely physical in nature.

1424. "Interested person" includes, but is not limited to:

(a) Any interested state, local, or federal entity or agency.
(b) Any interested public officer or employee of this state or of a local public entity of this state or of the federal government.

1430. "Petition" includes an application or request in the nature of a petition.

1431. "Proceedings to establish a limited conservatorship" include proceedings to modify or revoke the powers or duties of a limited conservator.

## Guardian Ad Litem

A Petition for Guardian Ad Litem will be, in most cases, submitted with an Order in a pending legal matter. For example, if the parties have reached a settlement in a personal injury case, in which a child was injured, the Court will require that a Guardian be appointed to handle the child's settlement until he/she turns 18. The Court will not approve the settlement without first appointing a guardian. In that event, the child's guardian will likely be the parent. There are situations, however, when it would not be appropriate for a parent to be appointed as the guardian and another family member or a trusted person would be appointed. Alternatively, the Court may deem it necessary to appoint a private professional guardian.

Once appointed, the Court may approve the settlement of the civil matter and will issue an Order. The Order will set forth the conditions under which the child will receive his or her settlement. Usually, the settlement will state the child's current age, and the amount to be received by the guardian on behalf of the child. The Order will also state the type of account into which the funds will be deposited. It must be an interest-bearing account and a manager for the financial institution will sign a receipt stating the funds have been deposited. The receipt will need to be filed with the Court.

The Order will also specify at what age the child can receive the funds. Usually it will be the age of majority, which is eighteen (18) in California. It will also likely state that no funds may be withdrawn before the child's eighteenth birthday for any reason. This is called a "Blocked Account." The Court will sometimes make an exception and will allow an early withdrawal for medical or educational reasons. However, those withdrawals will have to be approved by the Court. The Order should also specify that the child can withdraw all of the funds upon his/her eighteenth birthday without Court approval.

The Court will only allow withdrawals from a minor's account under very specific circumstances and for very specific needs. For example, if the child wants to buy a car on his or her 16th birthday, the Court will most likely deny the early Petition for Withdrawal. A Petition for Withdrawal that shows a need for items or services related to education or a medical need may be allowed by the Court to withdraw a limited amount of funds. An example would be as follows: the child's eighteenth birthday is on October 1. The child has been admitted to a four-year college. The school term begins on September 15 and the tuition is due on September 1. There are ample funds in the blocked account and there is a provision in the Order that allows for expenses of education.

The Court may require periodic accountings and/or status reports if no accounting is filed. These specific requirements would be included in the Order. You will want to check the Local Rules and for other requirements. The Court retains jurisdiction over the funds until they are disbursed.

## Judicial Council Forms (Guardian Ad Litem)

Petition for Guardian Ad Litem (GC-100)

Notice of Taking Control of Assets of a Minor (GC-050)

Order Appointing Guardian Ad Litem (DE-351/GC-101)

## Guardian of the Person and the Estate

An adult may also need to be appointed as a "guardian of the estate" of a child if that child inherits money or other property. In that event, the appropriate Judicial Council forms will need to be completed, a hearing scheduled and an Order obtained.

A guardian of the person will most commonly occur as the result of two things: a parent has died or a parent is unable to care for a child.

As discussed in Chapter Three (Wills), a parent who has a minor child(ren) will want to appoint a person or persons to act as guardian for their child(ren) if they pass away before the child is an adult. The Will should state whether the guardian is being appointed as guardian for the person and/or the estate. If the Will does not specify, the Court usually interprets it as guardianship of both the person and the estate.

Alternatively, it may be necessary for a person to be granted guardianship of a child for other reasons. A parent who must leave the state or country due to active military service may need to appoint a guardian for the child. A parent who is unable to care for the child because he/she is incarcerated or in another type of institution (mental, drug rehab, etc.) may need to appoint someone to care for the child and have authority to make decisions on the child's behalf while the parent is unable to do so. There are any number of reasons why a person may relinquish rights to another adult to provide for the care of a minor child. There are still other situations where the minor child is in jeopardy with the natural parent, and the Court will determine that a guardian should to be appointed for the child.

A person appointed as guardian under the provisions of a Will and/or by consent of a parent will likely be given much broader powers and greater discretion as to the care and control of the child's "estate," if applicable. As noted under the Guardian Ad Litem appointment, the Guardian and the child are unable to access funds for most situations once the monies are placed in a blocked account. Any funds withdrawn must be by Court approval.

A properly drafted Will should provide for the powers and/or discretion given the guardian as to the child's estate. The guardian will have broader powers and discretion that will allow them to have access to the child's money for all aspects of the child's health, education, and care. A person with limited powers may only have access to the funds for the necessities of life. The same will be true for a person, such as a grandparent or other family member, appointed to act as guardian, while the parent is unable to perform parental duties. The consenting parent may give broad powers and discretion to the guardian. Conversely he or she may limit the powers by allowing the guardian access to funds for only medical attention and the necessities of life. The parent may require that any withdrawal take place only upon approval of the Court. This could be very cumbersome and time-consuming. Wills with guardianship provisions should include broad enough powers so that the person appointed to care for children of another will not have the additional burden of judicial oversight.

The Court, on its own motion, may determine that a guardian must be appointed for a child who has been made a ward of the Court. Depending upon the circumstances, this may be the result of a family law matter or a juvenile proceeding. Specific rules must be followed in the event a Court-Appointed Attorney is made for the child. This is beyond the scope of this text. See Probate Code §§ 1456-1474 for more information on these guardianships, as well as the California Rules of Court.

The Court will also need to determine whether the guardian is required to post a bond. In most cases, the Will should address whether a bond is required of a person nominated as a guardian. In the event there is no Will or the child has inherited money or other property to be controlled by a guardian, the Court will determine if there is a need for a bond. In most cases, if the Petitioner/proposed guardian is a parent, the Court can waive the bond requirement. The Petition must request the waiver of bond, and there should be information provided to the Court as to why the Court should order the bond waived. See Probate Code § 2300 et seq. for information regarding bond requirements.

## Petition for Guardianship (Person and/or Estate)

A Petition for Guardianship is filed with the Superior Court and the Probate Department will hear the matter. The Petitioner, the person named on the Will as the appointee, will provide the Court with a copy of the decedent's Will as evidence that he or she be appointed as Guardian.

Though this appointment is related to a probate, it is considered a separate matter. The Court may verify that the matter is being submitted to the Court for action. However, there is the possibility that the person appointed as Executor is not the same person requesting appointment as Guardian. If so, then the Petition for Guardianship may only be asking to be appointed as Guardian of the person. The person appointed as Executor may be the person named Guardian or Trustee of the child's estate.

If the parent died intestate, then the process will be more formal and similar to a guardianship where a person is no longer able to care of the child. If there is a probate matter pending, that should be noted in the Declaration Under Uniform Child Custody Jurisdiction Act (UCCJEA form FL-105/GC-120) that must be submitted with the Petition.

A Petition prepared for a child, when the parent is still living, requires a consent or a hearing to decide why a guardian should be appointed to a minor child without the parent's consent.

The Judicial Council forms for this process will be provided by your instructor or may be obtained online. It cannot be stressed enough that the local Rules should be reviewed to determine any specific procedures and/or forms that must be submitted along with the Guardianship documents.

## Judicial Council Forms

Petition for Appointment of Guardian of a Minor(s) (GC-210)

Declaration Under Uniform Child Custody Jurisdiction Act (FL-105/GC-120)

Confidential Guardian Screening (GC-212)

Consent of Proposed Guardian (GC-211)

Duties of Guardian (GC-248)

Notice of Hearing (GC-020)

Order Appointing Guardian (GC-240)

Letters of Guardianship (GC-250)

The Petition, Confidential Guardian Screening and Duties of Guardian are filed with the Court to commence the action. A hearing date will be set, and the Notice of Hearing is sent to all interested persons, along with a copy of the Petition. The Notice of Hearing is then filed with the Court.

It is always advisable to try to obtain the Consent(s) from the natural parent(s) and/or person who has legal control of the child before setting the matter for hearing. In the event the Consent(s) is not obtained, the hearing could be reset for a later date. In the event the Consent is not signed by the parent and the parent files an Objection, the matter may be set for trial. It will be within the Judge's discretion who will keep the child between the time of the hearing and the trial. Usually, the Judge will maintain the status quo. Thus, if the child is residing with the Petitioner at the time the Petition is filed, the Judge may issue temporary orders giving the proposed Guardian (Petitioner) temporary custody. The appropriate forms should be prepared and the attorney should have them with him or her at the hearing should that event occur.

## Other Applicable Forms

Notice of Taking Possession or Control of Assets of a Minor (GC-050)

Order Prescribing Notice (Probate) (DE-200/GC-022)

Order Dispensing with Notice (GC-021)

Order Terminating Guardianship (GC-260)

Confidential Guardian Status Report (GC-251)

The Petition and Order should address the issue of bond requirement as well as whether the guardian and the attorney should receive compensation. Compensation is addressed at Probate Code §§ 2640-2647.

# Conservatorship

A conservatorship is a procedure required to maintain the care and/or control over an adult person. The following are the initial probate codes sections that relate to conservatorship. These should be reviewed carefully before commencing the petition for conservatorship.

Probate Code § 1810. If the proposed conservatee has sufficient capacity at the time to form an intelligent preference, the proposed conservatee may nominate a conservator in the petition or in a writing signed either before or after the petition is filed. The court shall appoint the nominee as conservator unless the court finds that the appointment of the nominee is not in the best interests of the proposed conservatee.

Probate Code § 1811.

(a) Subject to Section 1813, the spouse, domestic partner, or an adult child, parent, brother, or sister of the proposed conservatee may nominate a conservator in the petition or at the hearing on the petition.

(b) Subject to Section 1813, the spouse, domestic partner, or a parent of the proposed conservatee may nominate a conservator in a writing signed either before or after the petition is filed and that nomination remains effective notwithstanding the subsequent legal incapacity or death of the spouse, domestic partner, or parent.

Probate Code § 1812.

(a) Subject to Sections 1810 and 1813, the selection of a conservator of the person or estate, or both, is solely in the discretion of the court and, in making the selection, the court is to be guided by what appears to be for the best interests of the proposed conservatee.

(b) Subject to Sections 1810 and 1813, of persons equally qualified in the opinion of the court to appointment as conservator of the person or estate or both, preference is to be given in the following order:

   (1) The spouse or domestic partner of the proposed conservatee or the person nominated by the spouse or domestic partner pursuant to Section 1811.
   (2) An adult child of the proposed conservatee or the person nominated by the child pursuant to Section 1811.
   (3) A parent of the proposed conservatee or the person nominated by the parent pursuant to Section 1811.
   (4) A brother or sister of the proposed conservatee or the person nominated by the brother or sister pursuant to Section 1811.
   (5) Any other person or entity eligible for appointment as a conservator under this code or, if there is no person or entity willing to act as a conservator, under the Welfare and Institutions Code.

(c) The preference for any nominee for appointment under paragraphs (2), (3), and (4) of subdivision (b) is subordinate to the preference for any other parent, child, brother, or sister in that class.

Probate Code § 1813.

(a) The spouse of a proposed conservatee may not petition for the appointment of a conservator for a spouse or be appointed as conservator of the person or estate of the proposed conservatee unless the petitioner alleges in the petition for appointment as conservator, and the court finds, that the spouse is not a party to any action or proceeding against the proposed conservatee for legal separation of the parties, dissolution of marriage, or adjudication of nullity of their marriage. However, if the court finds by clear and convincing evidence that the appointment of the spouse, who is a party to an action or proceeding against the proposed conservatee for legal separation of the parties, dissolution of marriage, or adjudication of nullity of their marriage, or has obtained a judgment in any of these proceedings, is in the best interests of the proposed conservatee, the court may appoint the spouse. Prior to making this appointment, the court shall appoint counsel to consult with and advise the conservatee, and to report to the court his or her findings concerning the suitability of appointing the spouse as conservator.

(b) The spouse of a conservatee shall disclose to the conservator, or if the spouse is the conservator, shall disclose to the court, the filing of any action or proceeding against the conservatee for legal separation of the parties, dissolution of marriage, or adjudication of nullity of the marriage, within 10 days of the filing of the action or proceeding by filing a notice with the court and serving the notice according to the notice procedures under this title. The court may, upon receipt of the notice, set the matter for hearing on an order to show cause why the appointment of the spouse as conservator, if the spouse is the conservator, should not be terminated and a new conservator appointed by the court.

Probate Code § 1813.1.

(a) (1) The domestic partner of a proposed conservatee may not petition for the appointment of a conservator for a domestic partner or be appointed as conservator of the person or estate of the proposed conservatee unless the petitioner alleges in the petition for appointment as conservator, and the court finds, that the domestic partner has not terminated and is not intending to terminate the domestic partnership as provided in Section 299 of the Family Code. However, if the court finds by clear and convincing evidence that the appointment of a domestic partner who has terminated or is intending to terminate the domestic partnership is in the best interests of the proposed conservatee, the court may appoint the domestic partner.

> (2) Prior to making this appointment, the court shall appoint counsel to consult with and advise the conservatee, and to report to the court his or her findings concerning the suitability of appointing the domestic partner as conservator.

(b) The domestic partner of a conservatee shall disclose to the conservator, or if the domestic partner is the conservator, shall notify the court, of the termination of a domestic partnership as provided in Section 299 of the Family Code within 10 days of its occurrence. The court may, upon receipt of the notice, set the matter for hearing on an order to show cause why the appointment of the domestic partner as conservator, if the domestic partner is the conservator, should not be terminated and a new conservator appointed by the court.

Probate Code § 1850.

1850.

(a) Except as provided in subdivision (b), each conservatorship initiated pursuant to this part shall be reviewed by the court as follows:

> (1) At the expiration of six months after the initial appointment of the conservator, the court investigator shall visit the conservatee, conduct an investigation in accordance with the provisions of subdivision (a) of Section 1851, and report to the court regarding the appropriateness of the conservatorship and whether the conservator is acting in the best interests of the conservatee regarding the conservatee's placement, quality of care, including physical and mental treatment, and finances. The court may, in response to the investigator's report, take appropriate action including, but not limited to:
>
> > (A) Ordering a review of the conservatorship pursuant to subdivision (b).
> > (B) Ordering the conservator to submit an accounting pursuant to subdivision (a) of Section 2620.

(2) One year after the appointment of the conservator and annually thereafter. However, at the review that occurs one year after the appointment of the conservator, and every subsequent review conducted pursuant to this paragraph, the court may set the next review in two years if the court determines that the conservator is acting in the best interest interests of the conservatee. In these cases, the court shall require the investigator to conduct an investigation pursuant to subdivision (a) of Section 1851 one year before the next review and file a status report in the conservatee's court file regarding whether the conservatorship still appears to be warranted and whether the conservator is acting in the best interests of the conservatee.

If the investigator determines pursuant to this investigation that the conservatorship still appears to be warranted and that the conservator is acting in the best interests of the conservatee regarding the conservatee's placement, quality of care, including physical and mental treatment, and finances, no hearing or court action in response to the investigator's report is required.

(b) The court may, on its own motion or upon request by any interested person, take appropriate action including, but not limited to, ordering a review of the conservatorship, including at a noticed hearing, and ordering the conservator to present an accounting of the assets of the estate pursuant to Section 2620.

(c) Notice of a hearing pursuant to subdivision (b) shall be provided to all persons listed in subdivision (b) of Section 1822.

(d) This chapter does not apply to either of the following:

(1) A conservatorship for an absentee as defined in Section 1403.
(2) A conservatorship of the estate for a nonresident of this state where the conservatee is not present in this state.

(e) The amendments made to this section by the act adding this subdivision shall become operative on July 1, 2007.

(f) A superior court shall not be required to perform any duties imposed pursuant to the amendments to this section enacted by Chapter 493 of the Statutes 2006 until the Legislature makes an appropriation identified for this purpose.

1850.5.

(a) Notwithstanding Section 1850, each limited conservatorship for a developmentally disabled adult, as defined in subdivision (d) of Section 1801, shall be reviewed by the court one year after the appointment of the conservator and biennially thereafter.

(b) The court may, on its own motion or upon request by any interested person, take appropriate action, including, but not limited to, ordering a review of the limited conservatorship, including at a noticed hearing, at any time.

(c) A superior court shall not be required to perform any duties imposed by this section until the Legislature makes an appropriation identified for this purpose.

1851.

(a) When court review is required pursuant to Section 1850, the court investigator shall, without prior notice to the conservator except as ordered by the court for necessity or to prevent harm to the conservatee, visit the conservatee. The court investigator shall inform the conservatee personally that the conservatee is under a conservatorship and shall give the name of the conservator to the conservatee. The court investigator shall determine whether the conservatee wishes to petition the court for termination of the conservatorship, whether the conservatee is still in need of the conservatorship, whether the present conservator is acting in the best interests of the conservatee, and whether the conservatee is capable of completing an affidavit of voter registration. In determining whether the conservator is acting in the best interests of the conservatee, the court investigator's evaluation shall include an examination of the conservatee's placement, the quality of care, including physical and mental treatment, and the conservatee's finances. To the extent practicable, the investigator shall review the accounting with a conservatee who has sufficient capacity. To the greatest extent possible, the court investigator shall interview individuals set forth in subdivision (a) of Section 1826, in order to determine if the conservator is acting in the best interests of the conservatee. If the court has made an order under Chapter 4 (commencing with Section 1870), the court investigator shall determine whether the present condition of the conservatee is such that the terms of the order should be modified or the order revoked.Upon request of the court investigator, the conservator shall make available to the court investigator during the investigation for inspection and copying all books and records, including receipts and any expenditures, of the conservatorship.

(b) (1) The findings of the court investigator, including the facts upon which the findings are based, shall be certified in writing to the court not less than 15 days prior to the date of review. A copy of the report shall be mailed to the conservator and to the attorneys of record for the conservator and conservatee at the same time it is certified to the court. A copy of the report, modified as set forth in paragraph (2), also shall be mailed to the conservatee's spouse or registered domestic partner, the conservatee' s relatives in the first degree, and if there are no such relatives, to the next closest relative, unless the court determines that the mailing will result in harm to the conservatee.

   (2) Confidential medical information and confidential information from the California Law Enforcement Telecommunications System shall be in a separate attachment to the report and shall not be provided in copies sent to the conservatee's spouse or registered domestic partner, the conservatee's relatives in the first degree, and if there are no such relatives, to the next closest relative.

(c) In the case of a limited conservatee, the court investigator shall make a recommendation regarding the continuation or termination of the limited conservatorship.

(d) The court investigator may personally visit the conservator and other persons as may be necessary to determine whether the present conservator is acting in the best interests of the conservatee.

(e) The report required by this section shall be confidential and shall be made available only to parties, persons described in subdivision (b), persons given notice of the petition who have requested the report or who have appeared in the proceeding, their attorneys, and the court. The court shall have discretion at any other time to release the report if it would serve the interests of the conservatee. The clerk of the court shall make provision for limiting disclosure of the report exclusively to persons entitled thereto under this section.

(f) The amendments made to this section by the act adding this subdivision shall become operative on July 1, 2007.

(g) A superior court shall not be required to perform any duties imposed pursuant to the amendments to this section enacted by Chapter 493 of the Statutes 2006 until the Legislature makes an appropriation identified for this purpose.

Probate Code § 1851.2. Each court shall coordinate investigations with the filing of accountings, so that investigators may review accountings before visiting conservatees, if feasible.

Probate Code § 1851.5. Each court shall assess each conservatee in the county for any investigation or review conducted by a court investigator with respect to that person. The court may order reimbursement to the court for the amount of the assessment, unless the court finds that all or any part of the assessment would impose a hardship on conservatee or the conservatee's estate. There shall be a rebuttable presumption that the assessment would impose a hardship if the conservatee is receiving Medi-Cal benefits.

Probate Code § 1852. If the conservatee wishes to petition the court for termination of the conservatorship or for removal of the existing conservator or for the making, modification, or revocation of a court order under Chapter 4 (commencing with Section 1870) or for restoration of the right to register to vote, or if, based on information contained in the court investigator's report or obtained from any other source, the court determines that a trial or hearing for termination of the conservatorship or removal of the existing conservator is in the best interests of the conservatee, the court shall notify the attorney of record for the conservatee, if any, or shall appoint the public defender or private counsel under Section 1471, to file the petition and represent the conservatee at the trial or hearing and, if such appointment is made, Section 1472 applies.

Probate Code § 1853.

(a) If the court investigator is unable to locate the conservatee, the court shall order the court investigator to serve notice upon the conservator of the person, or upon the conservator of the estate if there is no conservator of the person, in the manner provided in Section 415.10 or 415.30 of the Code of Civil Procedure or in such other manner as is ordered by the court, to make the conservatee available for the purposes of Section 1851 to the court investigator within 15 days of the receipt of such notice or to show cause why the conservatorship should not be terminated.

(b) If the conservatee is not made available within the time prescribed, unless good cause is shown for not doing so, the court shall make such a finding and shall enter judgment terminating the conservatorship and, in case of a conservatorship of the estate, shall order the conservator to file an account and to surrender the estate to the person legally entitled thereto. At the hearing, or thereafter on further notice and hearing, the conservator may be discharged and the bond given by the conservator may be exonerated upon the settlement and approval of the conservator's final account by the court.

(c) Termination of the conservatorship under this section does not preclude institution of new proceedings for the appointment of a conservator. Nothing in this section limits the power of a court to appoint a temporary conservator under Chapter 3 (commencing with Section 2250) of Part 4.

## Judicial Council Forms

Petition for Appointment (GC-310)

Confidential Supplemental Information (GC-312)

Confidential Conservator Screening Form (GC-314)

Notice of Hearing—Guardianship or Conservatorship (GC-020)

Proof of Service of Hearing (GC-020(P))

Citation (GC-320)

Order Appointing Investigator (GC-330)

Notice of Conservator's Rights (GC-341)

Capacity Declaration (GC-335)

Dementia Declaration (GC-335A) [attachment to GC-335]

Notice of Hearing—Probate (GC-020)

Order Appointing Probate Conservator(GC-340)

Duties of Conservator (GC-348)

Order Authorizing Conservator to Give Consent to Medical Treatment (GC-385)

Inventory and Appraisal (DE-160/GC-040)

Inventory and Appraisal Attachment (DE-161/GC041)

Order Prescribing Notice [if applicable] (DE-200/GC-022)

Order Dispensing with Notice (GC-021)

Letters of Conservatorship (GC-350)

## Conservatorship Process

Preparing a conservatorship can be very tricky. The first task is to print a copy of the Petition for Appointment of Probate Conservator (GC-310). This will provide the information that will be needed such as whether it is a conservatorship of the person and/or the estate, or if this is a limited conservatorship. If a successor conservator must be appointed, this form will also be used, the appropriate boxes will be checked, and information attached.

The second task, after reviewing the above code sections and the judicial council forms, is to check the Local Rules for any particular "local" forms that will need to be completed, and whether any other specific procedures must be followed.

The attorney will also need to decide whether this is to be a full, complete conservatorship of the person and/or the estate, or a limited conservatorship. The specific code sections will need to be reviewed to determine which ones apply to a limited conservatorship. The Petition should be reviewed, particularly, section 1(b)–(k) which will provide you with information regarding the powers, responsibilities, capacity and relevant Probate Code sections for a limited conservatorship.

# Limited Conservatorship

Probate Code § 1827.5(a)–(f) provides the basis for a hearing on a limited conservatorship, often referred to by the Courts and attorneys as an "LPS."

Probate Code § 1828.5

(a) At the hearing on the petition for appointment of a limited conservator for an allegedly developmentally disabled adult, the court shall do each of the following:

   (1) Inquire into the nature and extent of the general intellectual functioning of the individual alleged to be developmentally disabled.
   (2) Evaluate the extent of the impairment of his or her adaptive behavior.
   (3) Ascertain his or her capacity to care for himself or herself and his or her property.
   (4) Inquire into the qualifications, abilities, and capabilities of the person seeking appointment as limited conservator.
   (5) If a report by the regional center, in accordance with Section 1827.5, has not been filed in court because the proposed limited conservatee withheld his or her consent to assessment by the regional center, the court shall determine the reason for withholding such consent.

(b) If the court finds that the proposed limited conservatee possesses the capacity to care for himself or herself and to manage his or her property as a reasonably prudent person, the court shall dismiss the petition for appointment of a limited conservator.

(c) If the court finds that the proposed limited conservatee lacks the capacity to perform some, but not all, of the tasks necessary to provide properly for his or her own personal needs for physical health, food, clothing, or shelter, or to manage his or her own financial resources, the court shall appoint a limited conservator for the person or the estate or the person and the estate.

(d) If the court finds that the proposed limited conservatee lacks the capacity to perform all of the tasks necessary to provide properly for his or her own personal needs for physical health, food, clothing, or shelter, or to manage his or her own financial resources, the court shall appoint either a conservator or a limited conservator for the person or the estate, or the person and the estate.

(e) The court shall define the powers and duties of the limited conservator so as to permit the developmentally disabled adult to care for himself or herself or to manage his or her financial resources commensurate with his or her ability to do so.

(f) Prior to the appointment of a limited conservator for the person or estate or person and estate of a developmentally disabled adult, the court shall inform the proposed limited conservatee of the nature and purpose of the limited conservatorship proceeding, that the appointment of a limited conservator for his or her person or estate or person and estate will result in the transfer of certain rights set forth in the petition and the effect of such transfer, the identity of the person who has been nominated as his or her limited conservator, that he or she has a right to oppose such proceeding, and that he or she has a right to have the matter tried by jury. After communicating such information to the person and prior to the appointment of a limited conservator, the court shall consult the person to determine his or her opinion concerning the appointment.

The following are the code sections that relate to the powers that may be conveyed upon the conservator and the Court's findings in that respect.

Probate Code § 1830(b) provides the powers and responsibilities of the conservator as they should appear in the Order. It is extremely important to understand what powers should be conveyed in the Order before completing the Petition. They must mirror each other.

Probate Code § 1830(b): In the case of a limited conservator for a developmentally disabled adult, any order the court may make shall include the findings of the court specified in Section 1828.5. The order shall specify the powers granted to and duties imposed upon the limited conservator, which powers and duties may not exceed the powers and duties applicable to a conservator under this code. The order shall also specify the following:

(1) The properties of the limited conservatee to which the limited conservator is entitled to possession and management, giving a description of the properties that will be sufficient to identify them.

(2) The debts, rentals, wages, or other claims due to the limited conservatee which the limited conservator is entitled to collect, or file suit with respect to, if necessary, and thereafter to possess and manage.

(3) The contractual or other obligations which the limited conservator may incur on behalf of the limited conservatee.

(4) The claims against the limited conservatee which the limited conservator may pay, compromise, or defend, if necessary.

(5) Any other powers, limitations, or duties with respect to the care of the limited conservatee or the management of the property specified in this subdivision by the limited conservator which the court shall specifically and expressly grant.

(c) An information notice of the rights of conservatees shall be attached to the order. The conservator shall mail the order and the attached information notice to the conservatee and the conservatee's relatives, as set forth in subdivision (b) of Section 1821, within 30 days of the issuance of the order. By January 1, 2008, the Judicial Council shall develop the notice required by this subdivision.

Probate Code §§ 2351–2352 provide the basis and information on the various types of powers that may be requested:

Probate Code 2351.

(a) Subject to subdivision (b), the guardian or conservator, but not a limited conservator, has the care, custody, and control of, and has charge of the education of, the ward or conservatee.

(b) Where the court determines that it is appropriate in the circumstances of the particular conservatee, the court, in its discretion, may limit the powers and duties that the conservator would otherwise have under subdivision (a) by an order stating either of the following:

(1) The specific powers that the conservator does not have with respect to the conservatee's person and reserving the powers so specified to the conservatee.

(2) The specific powers and duties the conservator has with respect to the conservatee's person and reserving to the conservatee all other rights with respect to

the conservatee's person that the conservator otherwise would have under subdivision (a).

(c) An order under this section

(1) may be included in the order appointing a conservator of the person or
(2) may be made, modified, or revoked upon a petition subsequently filed, notice of the hearing on the petition having been given for the period and in the manner provided in Chapter 3 (commencing with Section 1460) of Part 1.

(d) The guardian or conservator, in exercising his or her powers, may not hire or refer any business to an entity in which he or she has a financial interest except upon authorization of the court. Prior to authorization from the court, the guardian or conservator shall disclose to the court in writing his or her financial interest in the entity. For the purposes of this subdivision, "financial interest" shall mean

(1) an ownership interest in a sole proprietorship, a partnership, or a closely held corporation, or
(2) an ownership interest of greater than 1 percent of the outstanding shares in a publicly traded corporation, or
(3) being an officer or a director of a corporation. This subdivision shall apply only to conservators and guardians required to register with the Statewide Registry under Chapter 13 (commencing with Section 2850).

Probate Code 2351.5.

(a) Subject to subdivision (b):

(1) The limited conservator has the care, custody, and control of the limited conservatee.
(2) The limited conservator shall secure for the limited conservatee those habilitation or treatment, training, education, medical and psychological services, and social and vocational opportunity as appropriate and as will assist the limited conservatee in the development of maximum self-reliance and independence.

(b) A limited conservator does not have any of the following powers or controls over the limited conservatee unless those powers or controls are specifically requested in the petition for appointment of a limited conservator and granted by the court in its order appointing the limited conservator:

(1) To fix the residence or specific dwelling of the limited conservatee.
(2) Access to the confidential records and papers of the limited conservatee.
(3) To consent or withhold consent to the marriage of, or the entrance into a registered domestic partnership by, the limited conservatee.
(4) The right of the limited conservatee to contract.
(5) The power of the limited conservatee to give or withhold medical consent.
(6) The limited conservatee's right to control his or her own social and sexual contacts and relationships.
(7) Decisions concerning the education of the limited conservatee.

(c) Any limited conservator, the limited conservatee, or any relative or friend of the limited conservatee may apply by petition to the superior court of the county in which the proceedings are pending to have the limited conservatorship modified by the elimination or addition of any of the powers which must be specifically granted to the limited conservator pursuant to subdivision (b). The petition shall state the facts alleged to establish that the limited conservatorship should be modified. The granting or elimination of those powers is discretionary with the court. Notice of the hearing on the petition shall be given for the period and in the manner provided in Chapter 3 (commencing with Section 1460) of Part

(d) The limited conservator or any relative or friend of the limited conservatee may appear and oppose the petition. The court shall hear and determine the matter according to the laws and procedures relating to the trial of civil actions, including trial by jury if demanded. If any of the powers which must be specifically granted to the limited conservator pursuant to subdivision (b) are granted or eliminated, new letters of limited conservatorship shall be issued reflecting the change in the limited conservator's powers.

Probate Code § 2352.

(a) The guardian may establish the residence of the ward at any place within this state without the permission of the court. The guardian shall select the least restrictive appropriate residence that is available and necessary to meet the needs of the ward, and that is in the best interests of the ward.

(b) The conservator may establish the residence of the conservatee at any place within this state without the permission of the court. The conservator shall select the least restrictive appropriate residence, as described in Section 2352.5, that is available and necessary to meet the needs of the conservatee, and that is in the best interests of the conservatee.

(c) If permission of the court is first obtained, a guardian or conservator may establish the residence of a ward or conservatee at a place not within this state. Notice of the hearing on the petition to establish the residence of the ward or conservatee out of state, together with a copy of the petition, shall be given in the manner required by subdivision (a) of Section 1460 to all persons entitled to notice under subdivision (b) of Section 1511 or subdivision (b) of Section 1822.

(d) An order under subdivision (c) shall require the guardian or conservator either to return the ward or conservatee to this state, or to cause a guardianship or conservatorship proceeding or its equivalent to be commenced in the place of the new residence, when the ward or conservatee has resided in the place of new residence for a period of four months or a longer or shorter period specified in the order.

(e) (1) The guardian or conservator shall file a notice of change of residence with the court within 30 days of the date of the change. The guardian or conservator shall include in the notice of change of residence a declaration stating that the ward's or conservatee's change of residence is consistent with the standard described in subdivision (b).

(2) The guardian or conservator shall mail a copy of the notice to all persons entitled to notice under subdivision (b) of Section 1511 or subdivision (b) of Section 1822 and shall file proof of service of the notice with the court. The court may, for good cause, waive the mailing requirement pursuant to this paragraph in order to prevent harm to the conservatee or ward.

(3) If the guardian or conservator proposes to remove the ward or conservatee from his or her personal residence, except as provided by subdivision (c), the guardian or conservator shall mail a notice of his or her intention to change the residence of the ward or conservatee to all persons entitled to notice under subdivision (b) of Section 1511 and subdivision (b) of Section 1822. In the ab-

sence of an emergency, that notice shall be mailed at least 15 days before the proposed removal of the ward or conservatee from his or her personal residence. If the notice is served less than 15 days prior to the proposed removal of the ward or conservatee, the guardian or conservatee shall set forth the basis for the emergency in the notice. The guardian or conservator shall file proof of service of that notice with the court.

(f) This section does not apply where the court has made an order under Section 2351 pursuant to which the conservatee retains the right to establish his or her own residence.

(g) As used in this section, "guardian" or "conservator" includes a proposed guardian or proposed conservator and "ward" or "conservatee" includes a proposed ward or proposed conservatee.

(h) This section does not apply to a person with developmental disabilities for whom the Director of the Department of Developmental Services or a regional center, established pursuant to Chapter 5 (commencing with Section 4620) of Division 4.5 of the Welfare and Institutions Code, acts as the conservator.

The following is an example of where an attorney and the client (proposed conservator) agree that a limited conservatorship, rather than a full conservatorship of the person and estate, should be filed with the court:

Mother requests conservatorship over her adult son. Son is unable to live on his own due to mental incapacity (previous drug use). Son has lived with mother since prior to his 18th birthday. He receives social security. Mother is payee for social security account. All money received from social security is used for the care of the son and is only enough to provide for the food, shelter and clothing. The son also receives Medi-Care benefits. He does not have any assets. Son can dress himself and heat leftovers in a microwave. He is able to read short, simple instructions. He has the comprehension level of a fourth grader. He does not drive and relies upon his mother and siblings (who live nearby) for all of his basic needs.

The process for preparing the limited conservatorship will be the same as preparing any other type of conservatorship. It is simply a matter of determining prior to beginning the process which type of conservatorship is needed and being requested by the Petitioner and best suited to meet the needs of the conservator and conservatee.

## Preparing the Petition for Appointment of Probate Conservator

As with any other judicial process it is wise to have a complete set of the forms to determine exactly what information is going to be needed from the client and others in order to properly prepare the documents and have them filed with the court. Missing information and/or documentation may cause delay. Additionally, the attorney will need to determine exactly what types of powers are to be granted to the conservator. In most cases, the Judicial Council forms provide the relevant code sections within the forms in the event the statute needs to be reviewed.

For example, review the confidential forms that are required of the conservator to insure that you have all of the personal information that is required. The attorney will also need to determine whether this is a conservatorship of the person and/or the estate. He or she will also need to decide if it is a "limited" conservatorship, as well as whether the conservatee is suffering from dementia or any other medical incapacity which will need to be documented by a doctor.

Note also that the conservator **must** purchase and **read** the *Judicial Council Handbook for Conservators*. The conservator must sign under penalty of perjury that they "possess" the book and have read it.

A person who possesses a Durable Power of Attorney appointing him/her as conservator will need to provide the Court with a copy of that document along with the Petition. The Power of Attorney will usually specify the type of conservatorship authorized and also identify the powers that are to be given to the conservator.

The Petition for Conservatorship will need to be served on the Public Defender in the County. It is the Public Defender's duty to protect all citizens of the County. This includes any potential conservatee and conservators. The Public Defender will confirm that the conservator does not have a criminal record and has the ability to perform the duties of the conservator. The Public Defender will also confirm that the conservatee's civil rights are not being violated by the conservatorship. The Public Defender must perform background checks and will also visit the conservatee to determine whether he or she understands the implications of the conservatorship. In the event the conservatee is mentally incapacitated and unable to submit to the conservatorship, the Public Defender will need to confirm that the conservatee is in fact incapacitated.

A conservatee, who is mentally incapacitated, must have that fact established by two physicians. In the event the conservatee is suffering from dementia, the Dementia Declaration (Form GC-355) must be attached to the Capacity Declaration. Each physician must sign a separate form verifying, under penalty of perjury, that the proposed conservatee is unable to make certain decisions on their own. The doctors' declarations are filed with the Court and also served on the Public Defender. A proof of service will need to be filed with the Court indicating that the Public Defender was served a copy of the Capacity Declarations and any attachments.

The issue of requirement of a bond as well as attorney and conservatorship compensation should be included in the initial Petition and Order and any subsequent annual filings. See Probate Code § 2300 for bond requirements and Probate Code §§ 2640–2646 for information regarding compensation.

A conservatorship must be renewed annually. The doctor's declarations must be submitted each year with the renewal. The doctors' declarations are often the most difficult portion of preparing the conservatorship. It can, at times, be difficult to schedule doctors' appointments, especially for a conservatee. In the event that your office has a client for whom you prepare an annual renewal, it is prudent to calendar the date of the renewal far enough in advance to remind the conservator to schedule a doctor's appointment for the conservatee. The form can then be sent to the conservator and taken with him or her to the doctor's appointment, so that the doctor can complete and sign the form prior to the deadline.

In the event the conservatorship has been established for both the person and the estate, or just the estate of the conservatee, an accounting will also need to be prepared annually. The Court has the discretion to order bi-annual, rather than annual, accountings. The conservator will have to provide a balance sheet of the conservatee's assets on hand, any income, and expenses paid during the previous year.

The accounting must be submitted to the Court prior to the scheduled hearing date. It is wise to obtain all of the information from the conservator well in advance, so that it can be prepared in proper format for submission to the Court. It is the conservator's responsibility to keep track of this information. It is best if the conservator (client) has kept the income and expense information in a spreadsheet format that can be attached to the pleading, which will be submitted to the Court for approval. In fact, it is wise to have the conservator set up such an accounting as soon as the conservatorship has been approved.

> For example, I have seen a situation where the conservator did not create a spreadsheet or any other similar accounting system. The conservator simply brought in all of their receipts and the check register when the law firm informed the conservator that the accounting was due. The paralegal was required to prepare the accounting using the receipts and a check register. While the attorney may ask the paralegal to prepare the accounting as a courtesy to the client, it is the client's (Conservator) responsibility to keep track of all the income and expenses of the conservatee. There is no additional compensation for the paralegal's time involved in having to do the conservator's work.

The initial Petition will be submitted to the Court and a hearing date will be obtained. All other required Judicial Council forms should be submitted along with the Petition. As soon as the hearing date is set, the documents must be served on all interested parties, including the Public Defender. The Proof of Service is then filed with the Court.

The tentative rulings should be checked approximately one week before the scheduled hearing date, or pursuant to the Local Rules, to determine if the file is in order. In the event this is an LPS, the Court may have specific Local Rules about obtaining the file notes. If there are any deficiencies, those need to be cleared with the probate attorney so that the matter can be recommended for approval. Even if the matter is recommended for approval, the attorney and the Petitioner will need to make an appearance at the hearing. Having the information from the tentative rulings will allow time to cure any deficiencies and/or for the attorney to be prepared to answer the Judge's questions and submit the documents at the hearing.

The Order and Letters should be prepared so that the attorney can take them with him or her to the hearing. The client should sign the Letters either prior to or at the hearing, and a check should be prepared to obtain a certified copy or copies. The attorney may also want a self-addressed, return envelope prepared so that he or she can leave the documents with the Clerk, who will then return them in the mail. The attorney will not need to wait for them in that case. Once the Order and the Letters have been returned from the Court, the client should be given the **original** Letters and a copy of the Order. A copy of the Letters should be retained in the client file. The conservator is now able to perform all of the duties that have been enumerated in the Order and Letters on behalf of the conservatee.

A renewal of a Petition for Conservatorship should indicate the chronological year in the case title on the Judicial Council form. For instance, it would say "First Annual" or "Second Annual" and so on. The conservator and/or the law firm should have received a renewal notice indicating the date by which the renewal must be submitted to the Court. The notice will, in most cases, indicate those documents that must be submitted and/or any duties with which the conservator must comply. Other Courts will have provided this information in the Order. Most commonly, the requirements will be the inventory and/or an accounting and the "Doctors Declarations."

*Note that if the Court Clerk does not send a renewal notice it is the responsibility of the Conservator (read: the Conservator's attorney) to calendar the renewal and prepare the documents (Petition, accounting, Notices, Letters, Order, etc.) prior to the renewal date.*

The same procedures are followed as previously indicated.

## Other Considerations

You will have noted upon reading the Petition for Appointment of Probate Conservator that there are several categories for individuals who may wish to be appointed as a conservator. (See Section 3(a)–(d) on the Petition.)

Specifically, the Court will need to know if the proposed conservatee is a resident of the State of California and if he/she are not, the reason for requesting the conservatorship in California.

Second, the Court needs to establish whether the proposed conservator is a creditor or debtor of the conservatee. In other words, does he/she have any financial interest in the conservatee's estate and property? In most cases, the Court will not appoint anyone having a financial interest in the Conservatee's property unless there is no other person who can serve. Even in that case, the Court will more likely appoint a private professional conservator, even the Public Defender, or Guardian's Office, if they are equipped to handle such matters.

Third, the proposed conservator must state the relationship to the conservatee. Box 3(c)(1) indicates nominee, who would be the person appointed by a Power of Attorney or Will. That document must be attached as Attachment 3c. Also, note that effective 2005, Registered Domestic Partners can be appointed to serve in the capacity of a conservator the same as a spouse. A person who is an entity (bank, trust company, non-profit charitable corporation, registered private conservator, etc.) must document the relationship and comply with the Probate Code sections listed under each category.

In the event, the conservatee dies, the conservator will have to file a final inventory and accounting for the Court in the Order Terminating or Closing to close the matter. Local Rules should be reviewed to determine the period under which this must occur.

## Key Terms

- Guardianship of the Person
- Guardianship of the Estate
- Guardian Ad Litem
- Conservatorship
- Conservator
- Conservatee
- Limited Conservatorship
- Public Defender
- Private Conservator
- Blocked Account

# Chapter Twelve

# Other Issues Affecting Probate and Estate Planning

This chapter contains information and probate codes sections that are not typical estate planning and probate issues that will influence the probate and estate planning paralegal on a daily basis. These sections are included to provide some additional information that may occasionally affect the manner in which wills, trusts, and other estate planning documents are prepared or administered.

Finally, the area of Registered Domestic Partners is included as it relates to estate planning and probate in general.

## Effects of Homicide or Elder Abuse

Probate Code §§ 250–259 set forth the considerations for the right to inherit property where there has been abuse or a homicide of a parent or other party with whom the party has a financial relationship or a fiduciary responsibility.

Probate Code § 250.

(a) A person who feloniously and intentionally kills the decedent is not entitled to any of the following:

(1) Any property, interest, or benefit under a will of the decedent, or a trust created by or for the benefit of the decedent or in which the decedent has an interest, including any general or special power of appointment conferred by the will or trust on the killer and any nomination of the killer as executor, trustee, guardian, or conservator or custodian made by the will or trust.

(2) Any property of the decedent by intestate succession.

(3) Any of the decedent's quasi-community property the killer would otherwise acquire under Section 101 or 102 upon the death of the decedent.

(4) Any property of the decedent under Part 5 (commencing with Section 5700) of Division 5.

(5) Any property of the decedent under Part 3 (commencing with Section 6500) of Division 6.

(b) In the cases covered by subdivision (a):

(1) The property interest or benefit referred to in paragraph (1) of subdivision (a) passes as if the killer had predeceased the decedent and Section 21110 does not apply.

(2) Any property interest or benefit referred to in paragraph (1) of subdivision (a) which passes under a power of appointment and by reason of the death of the decedent passes as if the killer had predeceased the decedent, and Section 673 not apply.

(3) Any nomination in a will or trust of the killer as executor, trustee, guardian, conservator, or custodian which becomes effective as a result of the death of the decedent shall be interpreted as if the killer had predeceased the decedent.

Probate Code §251. A joint tenant who feloniously and intentionally kills another joint tenant thereby effects a severance of the interest of the decedent so that the share of the decedent passes as the decedent's property and the killer has no rights by survivorship. This section applies to joint tenancies in real and personal property, joint and multiple-party accounts in financial institutions, and any other form of co-ownership with survivorship incidents.

Probate Code §252. A named beneficiary of a bond, life insurance policy, or other contractual arrangement who feloniously and intentionally kills the principal obligee or the person upon whose life the policy is issued is not entitled to any benefit under the bond, policy, or other contractual arrangement, and it becomes payable as though the killer had predeceased the decedent.

Probate Code §253. In any case not described in Section 250, 251, or 252 in which one person feloniously and intentionally kills another, any acquisition of property, interest, or benefit by the killer as a result of the killing of the decedent shall be treated in accordance with the principles of this part.

Probate Code §254.

(a) A final judgment of conviction of felonious and intentional killing is conclusive for purposes of this part.

(b) In the absence of a final judgment of conviction of felonious and intentional killing, the court may determine by a preponderance of evidence whether the killing was felonious and intentional for purposes of this part. The burden of proof is on the party seeking to establish that the killing was felonious and intentional for the purposes of this part.

Probate Code §255. This part does not affect the rights of any person who, before rights under this part have been adjudicated, purchases from the killer for value and without notice property which the killer would have acquired except for this part, but the killer is liable for the amount of the proceeds or the value of the property.

Probate Code §256. An insurance company, financial institution, or other obligor making payment according to the terms of its policy or obligation is not liable by reason of this part, unless prior to payment it has received at its home office or principal address written notice of a claim under this part.

Probate Code §257. This part does not apply where the decedent was killed before January 1, 1985; and the law applicable prior to January 1, 1985, continues to apply where the decedent was killed before January 1, 1985.

Probate Code §258. A person who feloniously and intentionally kills the decedent is not entitled to bring an action for wrongful death of the decedent or to benefit from the action brought by the decedent's personal representative. The persons who may bring an action for wrongful death of the decedent and to benefit from the action are determined as if the killer had predeceased the decedent.

Probate Code § 259.

(a) Any person shall be deemed to have predeceased a decedent to the extent provided in subdivision (c) where all of the following apply:

(1) It has been proven by clear and convincing evidence that the person is liable for physical abuse, neglect, or fiduciary abuse of the decedent, who was an elder or dependent adult.

(2) The person is found to have acted in bad faith.

(3) The person has been found to have been reckless, oppressive, fraudulent, or malicious in the commission of any of these acts upon the decedent.

(4) The decedent, at the time those acts occurred and thereafter until the time of his or her death, has been found to have been substantially unable to manage his or her financial resources or to resist fraud or undue influence.

(b) Any person shall be deemed to have predeceased a decedent to the extent provided in subdivision (c) if that person has been convicted of a violation of Section 236 of the Penal Code or any offense described in Section 368 of the Penal Code.

(c) Any person found liable under subdivision (a) or convicted under subdivision (b) shall not (1) receive any property, damages, or costs that are awarded to the decedent's estate in an action described in subdivision (a) or (b), whether that person's entitlement is under a will, a trust, or the laws of intestacy; or (2) serve as a fiduciary as defined in Section 39, if the instrument nominating or appointing that person was executed during the period when the decedent was substantially unable to manage his or her financial resources or resist fraud or undue influence. This section shall not apply to a decedent who, at any time following the act or acts described in paragraph (1) of subdivision (a), or the act or acts described in subdivision (b), was substantially able to manage his or her financial resources and to resist fraud or undue influence within the meaning of subdivision (b) of Section 1801 of the Probate Code and subdivision (b) of Section 39 of the Civil Code.

(d) For purposes of this section, the following definitions shall apply:

(1) Physical abuse as defined in Section 15610.63 of the Welfare and Institutions Code.

(2) Neglect as defined in Section 15610.57 of the Welfare and Institutions Code.

(3) False imprisonment as defined in Section 368 of the Penal Code.

(4) Fiduciary abuse as defined in Section 15610.30 of the Welfare and Institutions Code.

(e) Nothing in this section shall be construed to prohibit the severance and transfer of an action or proceeding to a separate civil action pursuant to Section 801.

# Health Care Surrogacy (PC § 4711)

Probate Code §§ 4711–4716 provide instructions for the appointment of a "Health Care Surrogate." In the event the person does not wish to execute an Advance Health Care Directive ("Living Will") this method may be used. Note, however, that most health care practitioners and hospitals rely on the formal Advance Health Care Directive. These sections also define capacity and health care decisions. They also include instructions and a standard of care for the health care provider in ascertaining and relying on the surrogate's instructions and decisions and are, therefore, a good frame of reference for understanding the Advance Health Care Directive.

Probate Code §4711.

(a) A patient may designate an adult as a surrogate to make health care decisions by personally informing the supervising health care provider. The designation of a surrogate shall be promptly recorded in the patient's health care record.
(b) Unless the patient specifies a shorter period, a surrogate designation under subdivision (a) is effective only during the course of treatment or illness or during the stay in the health care institution when the surrogate designation is made, or for 60 days, whichever period is shorter.
(c) The expiration of a surrogate designation under subdivision (b) does not affect any role the person designated under subdivision (a) may have in making health care decisions for the patient under any other law or standards of practice.
(d) If the patient has designated an agent under a power of attorney for health care, the surrogate designated under subdivision (a) has priority over the agent for the period provided in subdivision (b), but the designation of a surrogate does not revoke the designation of an agent unless the patient communicates the intention to revoke in compliance with subdivision (a) of Section 4695.

Probate Code §4714. A surrogate, including a person acting as a surrogate, shall make a health care decision in accordance with the patient's individual health care instructions, if any, and other wishes to the extent known to the surrogate. Otherwise, the surrogate shall make the decision in accordance with the surrogate's determination of the patient's best interest. In determining the patient's best interest, the surrogate shall consider the patient's personal values to the extent known to the surrogate.

Probate Code §4715. A patient having capacity at any time may disqualify another person, including a member of the patient's family, from acting as the patient's surrogate by a signed writing or by personally informing the supervising health care provider of the disqualification.

Probate Code §4716.

(a) If a patient lacks the capacity to make a health care decision, the patient's domestic partner shall have the same authority as a spouse has to make a health care decision for his or her incapacitated spouse. This section may not be construed to expand or restrict the ability of a spouse to make a health care decision for an incapacitated spouse.
(b) For the purposes of this section, the following definitions shall apply:
  (1) "Capacity" has the same meaning as defined in Section 4609.
  (2) "Health care" has the same meaning as defined in Section 4615.
  (3) "Health care decision" has the same meaning as defined in Section 4617.
  (4) "Domestic partner" has the same meaning as that term is used in Section 297 of the Family Code.
(a) Notwithstanding any other provision of law, within 24 hours of the arrival in the emergency department of a general acute care hospital of a patient who is unconscious or otherwise incapable of communication, the hospital shall make rea-

sonable efforts to contact the patient's agent, surrogate, or a family member or other person the hospital reasonably believes has the authority to make health care decisions on behalf of the patient. A hospital shall be deemed to have made reasonable efforts, and to have discharged its duty under this section, if it does all of the following:

(1) Examines the personal effects, if any, accompanying the patient and any medical records regarding the patient in its possession, and reviews any verbal or written report made by emergency medical technicians or the police, to identify the name of any agent, surrogate, or a family member or other person the hospital reasonably believes has the authority to make health care decisions on behalf of the patient.

(2) Contacts or attempts to contact any agent, surrogate, or a family member or other person the hospital reasonably believes has the authority to make health care decisions on behalf of the patient, as identified in paragraph (1).

(3) Contacts the Secretary of State directly or indirectly, including by voice mail or facsimile, to inquire whether the patient has registered an advance health care directive with the Advance Health Care Directive Registry, if the hospital finds evidence of the patient's Advance Health Care Directive Registry identification card either from the patient or from the patient's family or authorized agent.

(b) The hospital shall document in the patient's medical record all efforts made to contact any agent, surrogate, or a family member or other person the hospital reasonably believes has the authority to make health care decisions on behalf of the patient.

(c) Application of this section shall be suspended during any period in which the hospital implements its disaster and mass casualty program, or its fire and internal disaster program.

Probate Code §4717[1]. (a) Notwithstanding any other provision of law, within 24 hours of the arrival in the emergency department of a general acute care hospital of a patient who is unconscious or otherwise incapable of communication, the hospital shall make reasonable efforts to contact the patient's agent, surrogate, or a family member or other person the hospital reasonably believes has the authority to make health care decisions on behalf of the patient. A hospital shall be deemed to have made reasonable efforts, and to have discharged its duty under this section, if it does all of the following:

(1) Examines the personal effects, if any, accompanying the patient and any medical records regarding the patient in its possession, and reviews any verbal or written report made by emergency medical technicians or the police, to identify the name of any agent, surrogate, or a family member or other person the hospital reasonably believes has the authority to make health care decisions on behalf of the patient.

(2) Contacts or attempts to contact any agent, surrogate, or a family member or other person the hospital reasonably believes has the authority to make health care decisions on behalf of the patient, as identified in paragraph (1).

(3) Contacts the Secretary of State directly or indirectly, including by voice mail or facsimile, to inquire whether the patient has registered an advance health care directive with the Advance Health Care Directive Registry, if the hospital finds evi-

dence of the patient's Advance Health Care Directive Registry identification card either from the patient or from the patient's family or authorized agent.

(b) The hospital shall document in the patient's medical record all efforts made to contact any agent, surrogate, or a family member or other person the hospital reasonably believes has the authority to make health care decisions on behalf of the patient.

## Public Administrator (PC§§ 7600–7666)

There are instances where a public administrator will need to be appointed to probate a decedent's estate, particularly if the decedent was intestate. In most cases, this will be where the decedent does not have any known living relatives or if the relatives are not U.S. citizens and reside outside of the country. Sadly, there are also occasions where no family member is willing to take on this responsibility. Probate Code §7600 et seq. provides instructions for a hospital or other health care facility to notify the public administrator if they believe there are no living relatives. It will be the job of the public administrator to determine if, in fact, the decedent has any relatives.

Probate Code §7600. If a public officer or employee knows of property of a decedent that is subject to loss, injury, waste, or misappropriation and that ought to be in the possession or control of the public administrator, the officer or employee shall inform the public administrator.

Probate Code §7600.5. If a person dies in a hospital, convalescent hospital, or board and care facility without known next of kin, the person in charge of the hospital or facility shall give immediate notice of that fact to the public administrator of the county in which the hospital or facility is located. If the notice required by this section is not given, the hospital or facility is liable for (1) any cost of interment incurred by the estate or the county as a result of the failure and (2) any loss to the estate or beneficiaries caused by loss, injury, waste, or misappropriation of property of the decedent as a result of the failure.

Probate Code §7600.6. A funeral director in control of the decedent's remains pursuant to subdivision (c) of Section 7100 of the Health and Safety Code shall notify the public administrator if none of the persons described in paragraphs (2) to (6), inclusive, of subdivision (a) of Section 7100 of the Health and Safety Code exist, can be found after reasonable inquiry, or can be contacted by reasonable means.

Probate Code §7601.

(a) If no personal representative has been appointed, the public administrator of a county shall take prompt possession or control of property of a decedent in the county that is deemed by the public administrator to be subject to loss, injury, waste, or misappropriation, or that the court orders into the possession or control of the public administrator after notice to the public administrator as provided in Section 1220.

(b) If property described in subdivision (a) is beyond the ability of the public administrator to take possession or control, the public administrator is not liable for failing to take possession or control of the property.

Probate Code §7602.

(a) A public administrator who is authorized to take possession or control of property of a decedent under this article shall make a prompt search for other property, a will, and instructions for disposition of the decedent's remains.
(b) If a will is found, the public administrator or custodian of the will shall deliver the will as provided in Section 8200.
(c) If instructions for disposition of the decedent's remains are found, the public administrator shall promptly deliver the instructions to the person upon whom the right to control disposition of the decedent's remains devolves as provided in Section 7100 of the Health and Safety Code.
(d) If other property is located, the public administrator shall take possession or control of any property that, in the sole discretion of the public administrator, is deemed to be subject to loss, injury, waste, or misappropriation and that is located anywhere in this state or that is subject to the laws of this state. The public administrator does not have any liability for loss, injury, waste, or misappropriation of property of which he or she is unable to take possession or control.

Probate Code § 7603.

(a) A public administrator who is authorized to take possession or control of property of a decedent pursuant to this article may issue a written certification of that fact. The written certification is effective for 30 days after the date of issuance.
(b) The public administrator may record a copy of the written certification in any county in which is located real property of which the public administrator is authorized to take possession or control under this article.
(c) A financial institution, government or private agency, retirement fund administrator, insurance company, licensed securities dealer, or other person shall, without the necessity of inquiring into the truth of the written certification, without requiring a death certificate, without charge, and without court order or letters being issued:
  (1) Provide the public administrator complete information concerning property held in the sole name of the decedent, including the names and addresses of any beneficiaries.
  (2) Grant the public administrator access to a safe-deposit box rented in the sole name of the decedent for the purpose of inspection and removal of any will or instructions for disposition of the decedent's remains. Costs and expenses incurred in drilling or forcing a safe-deposit box shall be borne by the estate of the decedent.
  (3) Surrender to the public administrator any property of the decedent that, in the sole discretion of the public administrator, is deemed to be subject to loss, injury, waste, or misappropriation.
(d) Receipt of the written certification provided by this section: (1) Constitutes sufficient acquittance for providing information or granting access to the safe-deposit box, for removal of the decedent's will and instructions for disposition of the decedent's remains, and for surrendering property of the decedent. (2) Fully discharges the financial institution, government or private agency, retirement fund administrator, insurance company, licensed securities dealer, or other person from any liability for any act or omission of the public administrator with respect to the property or the safe-deposit box.

Probate Code § 7604. If the public administrator takes possession or control of property of a decedent under this article, but another person is subsequently appointed personal representative or subsequently takes control or possession, the public administrator is entitled to reasonable costs incurred for the preservation of the estate, together with reasonable compensation for services. The costs and compensation are a proper expense of administration.

Probate Code § 7620. The public administrator of the county in which the estate of a decedent may be administered shall promptly:

(a) Petition for appointment as personal representative of the estate if no person having higher priority has petitioned for appointment and the total value of the property in the decedent's estate exceeds one hundred thousand dollars ($100,000).

(b) Petition for appointment as personal representative of any other estate the public administrator determines is proper.

(c) Accept appointment as personal representative of an estate when so ordered by the court, whether or not on petition of the public administrator, after notice to the public administrator as provided in Section 7621.

(d) Proceed with summary disposition of the estate as authorized by Article 4 (commencing with Section 7660), if the total value of the property in the decedent's estate does not exceed the amount prescribed in Section 13100 and a person having higher priority has not assumed responsibility for administration of the estate.

Probate Code § 7621.

(a) Except as otherwise provided in this section, appointment of the public administrator as personal representative shall be made, and letters issued, in the same manner and pursuant to the same procedure as for appointment of and issuance of letters to personal representatives generally.

(b) Appointment of the public administrator may be made on the court's own motion, after notice to the public administrator as provided in Section 1220.

(c) Letters may be issued to "the public administrator" of the county without naming the public administrator.

(d) The public administrator's oath and official bond are in lieu of the personal representative's oath and bond. Every estate administered under this chapter shall be charged an annual bond fee in the amount of twenty-five dollars ($25) plus one-fourth of one percent of the amount of an estate greater than ten thousand dollars ($10,000). The amount charged is an expense of administration and that amount shall be deposited in the county treasury. If a successor personal representative is appointed, the amount of the bond fee shall be prorated over the period of months during which the public administrator acted as personal representative. Upon final distribution by the public administrator, any amount of bond charges in excess of one year shall be a prorated charge to the estate.

Probate Code § 7622. Except as otherwise provided in this chapter:

(a) The public administrator shall administer the estate in the same manner as a personal representative generally, and the provisions of this code concerning the administration of the decedent's estate apply to administration by the public administrator.

(b) The public administrator is entitled to receive the same compensation as is granted by this division to a personal representative generally. The attorney for the public administrator is entitled to receive the same compensation as is granted by this division to an attorney for a personal representative generally. However, the compensation of the public administrator and the public administrator's attorney may not be less than the compensation in effect at the time of appointment of the public administrator or the minimum amount provided in subdivision (b) of Section 7666, whichever is greater.

Probate Code § 7623.

(a) As used in this section, "additional compensation" means the difference between the reasonable compensation of the public administrator in administering the estate and the compensation awarded the public administrator under Chapter 1 (commencing with Section 10800) of Part 7.

(b) The public administrator may be awarded additional compensation if any of the following conditions are satisfied: (1) A person having priority for appointment as personal representative has been given notice under Section 8110 of the public administrator's petition for appointment, and the person has not petitioned for appointment in preference to the public administrator. (2) The public administrator has been appointed after the resignation or removal of a personal representative.

Probate Code § 7624.

(a) If after final distribution of an estate any money remains in the possession of the public administrator that should be paid over to the county treasurer pursuant to Chapter 5 (commencing with Section 11850) of Part 10, the court shall order payment to be made within 60 days.

(b) Upon failure of the public administrator to comply with an order made pursuant to subdivision (a), the district attorney of the county shall promptly institute proceedings against the public administrator and the sureties on the official bond for the amount ordered to be paid, plus costs.

Probate Code §§ 7640–7666 provide details on the actual probate administration of the estate that a public administrator must follow. It also enumerates the responsibilities, requirements, and powers under which the administrator may act. These sections should be reviewed by the paralegal in the event the firm becomes involved in a probate where a public administrator has been appointed.

# Priority for Appointment of Administrator (PC§§ 8460–8469)

As indicated in Chapter Three a Personal Representative (Administrator) will need to be appointed by the Court to probate a decedent's estate. In the event the decedent died intestate, or all Executors named in the decedent's Will have predeceased the decedent, or if for any reason he or she is unable to act, the Probate Code establishes the priority for making that appointment.

Probate Code § 8460.

(a) If the decedent dies intestate, the court shall appoint an administrator as personal representative.

(b) The court may appoint one or more persons as administrator.

Probate Code § 8461. Subject to the provisions of this article, a person in the following relation to the decedent is entitled to appointment as administrator in the following order of priority:

(a) Surviving spouse or domestic partner as defined in Section 37.
(b) Children.
(c) Grandchildren.
(d) Other issue.
(e) Parents.
(f) Brothers and sisters.
(g) Issue of brothers and sisters.
(h) Grandparents.
(i) Issue of grandparents.
(j) Children of a predeceased spouse or domestic partner.
(k) Other issue of a predeceased spouse or domestic partner.
(l) Other next of kin.
(m) Parents of a predeceased spouse or domestic partner.
(n) Issue of parents of a predeceased spouse or domestic partner.
(o) Conservator or guardian of the estate acting in that capacity at the time of death who has filed a first account and is not acting as conservator or guardian for any other person.
(p) Public administrator.
(q) Creditors.
(r) Any other person.

Probate Code § 8462. The surviving spouse or domestic partner of the decedent, a relative of the decedent, or a relative of a predeceased spouse or domestic partner of the decedent, has priority under Section 8461 only if one of the following conditions is satisfied:

(a) The surviving spouse, domestic partner, or relative is entitled to succeed to all or part of the estate.
(b) The surviving spouse, domestic partner, or relative either takes under the will of, or is entitled to succeed to all or part of the estate of, another deceased person who is entitled to succeed to all or part of the estate of the decedent.

Probate Code § 8463. If the surviving spouse is a party to an action for separate maintenance, annulment, or dissolution of the marriage of the decedent and the surviving spouse, and was living apart from the decedent on the date of the decedent's death, the surviving spouse has priority next after brothers and sisters and not the priority prescribed in Section 8461.

Probate Code § 8464. If a person otherwise entitled to appointment as administrator is a person under the age of majority or a person for whom a guardian or conservator of the estate has been appointed, the court in its discretion may appoint the guardian or conservator or another person entitled to appointment.

Probate Code § 8465.

(a) The court may appoint as administrator a person nominated by a person otherwise entitled to appointment or by the guardian or conservator of the estate of a person otherwise entitled to appointment. The nomination shall be made in writing and filed with the court.

(b) If a person making a nomination for appointment of an administrator is the surviving spouse or domestic partner, child, grandchild, other issue, parent, brother or sister, or grandparent of the decedent, the nominee has priority next after those in the class of the person making the nomination.

(c) If a person making a nomination for appointment of an administrator is other than a person described in subdivision (b), the court in its discretion may appoint either the nominee or a person of a class lower in priority to that of the person making the nomination, but other persons of the class of the person making the nomination have priority over the nominee. (d) This section shall become operative on January 1, 2016[2].

Probate Code § 8467. If several persons have equal priority for appointment as administrator, the court may appoint one or more of them, or if such persons are unable to agree, the court may appoint the public administrator or a disinterested person in the same or the next lower class of priority as the persons who are unable to agree.

Probate Code § 8468. If persons having priority fail to claim appointment as administrator, the court may appoint any person who claims appointment.

Probate Code § 8469.

(a) For good cause, the court may allow the priority given by Section 8461 to a conservator or guardian of the estate of the decedent serving in that capacity at the time of death that has not filed a first account, or that is acting as guardian or conservator for another person, or both.

(b) If the petition for appointment as administrator requests the court to allow the priority permitted by subdivision (a), the petitioner shall, in addition to the notice otherwise required by statute, serve notice of the hearing by mail or personal delivery on the public administrator.

# Federal "Uniform" Statutes

The following sections are those which relate to the administration of Wills and Trusts and the federal or "Uniform" Codes that have been established. California has adopted many of these sections, especially those that are needed to comply with federal rules regarding taxes.

## Uniform Testamentary Additions to Trust Act (PC§§ 6300–6303)

Probate Code § 6300. A devise, the validity of which is determinable by the law of this state, may be made by a will to the trustee of a trust established or to be established by the testator or by the testator and some other person or by some other person (including a funded or unfunded life insurance trust, although the settlor has reserved any or all rights of ownership of the insurance contracts) if the trust is identified in the testator's will and its terms are set forth in a written instrument (other than a will) executed before or concurrently with the execution of the testator's will or in the valid last will of a person who has predeceased the testator (regardless of the existence, size, or character of the trust property). The devise is not invalid because the trust is amendable or revocable, or both, or because the trust was amended after the execution of the will or after the death of the testator. Unless the testator's will provides otherwise, the property so devised (1) is not deemed to be held under a testamentary trust of the testator but becomes a part of the trust to which it is given and (2) shall be administered and disposed of in accordance with the provisions of the instrument or will setting forth the terms of the trust, including any amendments thereto made before or after the death of the testator (regardless of whether made before or after the execution of the testator's will). Unless otherwise provided in the will, a revocation or termination of the trust before the death of the testator causes the devise to lapse.

## Uniform International Wills Act (PC §§ 6380–6390)

Probate Code § 6380. In this chapter:

(a) "International will" means a will executed in conformity with Sections 6381 to 6384, inclusive.

(b) "Authorized person" and "person authorized to act in connection with international wills" means a person who by Section 6388, or by the laws of the United States including members of the diplomatic and consular service of the United States designated by Foreign Service Regulations, is empowered to supervise the execution of international wills.

Probate Code § 6381.

(a) A will is valid as regards form, irrespective particularly of the place where it is made, of the location of the assets and of the nationality, domicile, or residence of the testator, if it is made in the form of an international will complying with the requirements of this chapter.

(b) The invalidity of the will as an international will does not affect its formal validity as a will of another kind.

(c) This chapter does not apply to the form of testamentary dispositions made by two or more persons in one instrument.

Probate Code § 6382.

(a) The will shall be made in writing. It need not be written by the testator himself or herself. It may be written in any language, by hand or by any other means.

(b) The testator shall declare in the presence of two witnesses and of a person authorized to act in connection with international wills that the document is the testator's will and that the testator knows the contents thereof. The testator need not inform the witnesses, or the authorized person, of the contents of the will.

(c) In the presence of the witnesses, and of the authorized person, the testator shall sign the will or, if the testator has previously signed it, shall acknowledge his or her signature.

(d) If the testator is unable to sign, the absence of the testator's signature does not affect the validity of the international will if the testator indicates the reason for his or her inability to sign and the authorized person makes note thereof on the will. In that case, it is permissible for any other person present, including the authorized person or one of the witnesses, at the direction of the testator, to sign the testator's name for the testator if the authorized person makes note of this also on the will, but it is not required that any person sign the testator's name for the testator.

(e) The witnesses and the authorized person shall there and then attest the will by signing in the presence of the testator.

Probate Code § 6383.

(a) The signatures shall be placed at the end of the will. If the will consists of several sheets, each sheet shall be signed by the testator or, if the testator is unable to sign, by the person signing on his or her behalf or, if there is no such person, by the authorized person. In addition, each sheet shall be numbered.

(b) The date of the will shall be the date of its signature by the authorized person. That date shall be noted at the end of the will by the authorized person.

(c) The authorized person shall ask the testator whether the testator wishes to make a declaration concerning the safekeeping of the will. If so and at the express request of the testator, the place where the testator intends to have the will kept shall be mentioned in the certificate provided for in Section 6384.

(d) A will executed in compliance with Section 6382 is not invalid merely because it does not comply with this section.

Probate Code § 6384. The authorized person shall attach to the will a certificate to be signed by the authorized person establishing that the requirements of this chapter for valid execution of an international will have been fulfilled. The authorized person shall keep a copy of the certificate and deliver another to the testator. The certificate shall be substantially in the following form: CERTIFICATE (Convention of October 26, 1973)

1. I, _____, (name, address, and capacity) a person authorized to act in connection with international wills,
2. certify that on _____ at _____ (date) (place)
3. _____ (testator) (name, address, date and place of birth) in my presence and that of the witnesses
4. (a) -_____ (name, address, date and place of birth)

(b) -_____ (name, address, date and place of birth) has declared that the attached document is his will and that he knows the contents thereof.
5. I furthermore certify that:
6. (a) in my presence and in that of the witnesses

   (1) the testator has signed the will or has acknowledged his signature previously affixed.

   (2) following a declaration of the testator stating that he was unable to sign his will for the following reason _____, I have mentioned this declaration on the will, and the signature has been affixed by _____ (name and address)
7. (b) the witnesses and I have signed the will;
8. (c) each page of the will has been signed by _____ and numbered;
9. (d) I have satisfied myself as to the identity of the testator and of the witnesses as designated above;
10. (e) the witnesses met the conditions requisite to act as such according to the law under which I am acting;
11. (f) the testator has requested me to include the following statement concerning the safekeeping of his will: _____
12. PLACE OF EXECUTION

13. DATE

14. SIGNATURE and, if necessary, SEAL _____ to be completed if appropriate.

Probate Code § 6385. In the absence of evidence to the contrary, the certificate of the authorized person is conclusive of the formal validity of the instrument as a will under this chapter. The absence or irregularity of a certificate does not affect the formal validity of a will under this chapter.

Probate Code § 6386. The international will is subject to the ordinary rules of revocation of wills.

Probate Code § 6387. Sections 6380 to 6386, inclusive, derive from Annex to Convention of October 26, 1973, Providing a Uniform Law on the Form of an International Will. In interpreting and applying this chapter, regard shall be had to its international origin and to the need for uniformity in its interpretation.

Probate Code § 6388. Individuals who have been admitted to practice law before the courts of this state and who are in good standing as active law practitioners of this state are authorized persons in relation to international wills.

Probate Code § 6389. The Secretary of State shall establish a registry system by which authorized persons may register in a central information center information regarding the execution of international wills, keeping that information in strictest confidence until the death of the maker and then making it available to any person desiring information about any will who presents a death certificate or other satisfactory evidence of the testator's death to the center. Information that may be received, preserved in confidence until death, and reported as indicated is limited to the name, social security or other individual identifying number established by law, if any, address, date and place of birth of the testator, and the intended place of deposit or safekeeping of the instrument pending the death of the maker. The Secretary of State, at the request of the authorized person, may cause the information it receives about execution of any international will to be transmitted to the registry system of another jurisdiction as identified by the testator, if that other system adheres to rules protecting the confidentiality of the information similar to those established in this state.

Probate Code § 6390. After December 31, 1984, a reference in a written instrument, including a will, to the former law (repealed by Chapter 892 of the Statutes of 1984) shall be deemed to be a reference to the corresponding provision of this chapter.

## Uniform Principal and Income Act (PC§§ 16320–16347)

Probate Code § 16321. The definitions in this article govern the construction of this chapter.

Probate Code § 16322. "Accounting period" means a calendar year unless another 12-month period is selected by a fiduciary. The term includes a portion of a calendar year or other 12-month period that begins when an income interest begins or ends when an income interest ends.

Probate Code § 16323. "Fiduciary" means a personal representative or a trustee.

Probate Code § 16324. "Income" means money or property that a fiduciary receives as current return from a principal asset. The term includes a portion of receipts from a sale, exchange, or liquidation of a principal asset, to the extent provided in Article 5.1 (commencing with Section 16350), 5.2 (commencing with Section 16355), or 5.3 (commencing with Section 16360).

Probate Code § 16325. "Income beneficiary" means a person to whom net income of a trust is or may be payable.

Probate Code § 16326. "Income interest" means the right of an income beneficiary to receive all or part of net income, whether the trust requires it to be distributed or authorizes it to be distributed in the trustee's discretion.

Probate Code § 16327. "Mandatory income interest" means the right of an income beneficiary to receive net income that the trust requires the fiduciary to distribute.

Probate Code § 16328. "Net income" means the total receipts allocated to income during an accounting period minus the disbursements made from income during the accounting period, plus or minus transfers under this chapter to or from income during the accounting period. During any period in which the trust is being administered as a unitrust, either pursuant to the powers conferred by Sections 16336.4 to 16336.6, inclusive, or pursuant to the terms of the governing instrument, "net income" means the unitrust amount, if the unitrust amount is no less than 3 percent and no more than 5 percent of the fair market value of the trust assets, whether determined annually or averaged on a multiple year basis.

## Uniform Prudent Management of Institutional Funds Act (PC §§ 18500–18509)

Probate Code § 18501. This part may be cited as the Uniform Prudent Management of Institutional Funds Act.

Probate Code § 18502. As used in this part, the following terms shall have the following meanings:

(a) "Charitable purpose" means the relief of poverty, the advancement of education or religion, the promotion of health, the promotion of a governmental purpose, or any other purpose the
achievement of which is beneficial to the community.
(b) "Endowment fund" means an institutional fund or part thereof that, under the terms of a gift instrument, is not wholly expendable by the institution on a current basis. The term does not include assets that an institution designates as an endowment fund for its
own use.
(c) "Gift instrument" means a record or records, including an institutional solicitation, under which property is granted to, transferred to, or held by an institution as an institutional fund.
(d) "Institution" means any of the following:
(1) A person, other than an individual, organized and operated exclusively for charitable purposes.
(2) A government or governmental subdivision, agency, or instrumentality, to the extent that it holds funds exclusively for a charitable purpose.
(3) A trust that had both charitable and noncharitable interests, after all noncharitable interests have terminated.

(e) "Institutional fund" means a fund held by an institution exclusively for charitable purposes. The term does not include any of the following:

(1) Program-related assets.

(2) A fund held for an institution by a trustee that is not an institution.

(3) A fund in which a beneficiary that is not an institution has an interest, other than an interest that could arise upon violation or failure of the purposes of the fund.

(f) "Person" means an individual, corporation, business trust, estate, trust, partnership, limited liability company, association, joint venture, public corporation, government or governmental

subdivision, agency, or instrumentality, or any other legal or commercial entity.

(g) "Program-related asset" means an asset held by an institution primarily to accomplish a charitable purpose of the institution and not primarily for investment.

(h) "Record" means information that is inscribed on a tangible medium or that is stored in an electronic or other medium and is retrievable in perceivable form.

Probate Code § 18503. (a) Subject to the intent of a donor expressed in a gift instrument, an institution, in managing and investing an institutional fund, shall consider the charitable purposes of the institution and the purposes of the institutional fund.

(b) In addition to complying with the duty of loyalty imposed by law other than this part, each person responsible for managing and investing an institutional fund shall manage and invest the fund in good faith and with the care an ordinarily prudent person in a like position would exercise under similar circumstances.

(c) In managing and investing an institutional fund, an institution is subject to both of the following:

(1) It may incur only costs that are appropriate and reasonable in relation to the assets, the purposes of the institution, and the skills available to the institution.

(2) It shall make a reasonable effort to verify facts relevant to the management and investment of the fund.

(d) An institution may pool two or more institutional funds for purposes of management and investment.

(e) Except as otherwise provided by a gift instrument, the following rules apply:

(1) In managing and investing an institutional fund, all of the following factors, if relevant, must be considered:

(A) General economic conditions.

(B) The possible effect of inflation or deflation.

(C) The expected tax consequences, if any, of investment decisions or strategies.

(D) The role that each investment or course of action plays within the overall investment portfolio of the fund.

(E) The expected total return from income and the appreciation of investments.

(F) Other resources of the institution.

(G) The needs of the institution and the fund to make distributions and to preserve capital.

(H) An asset's special relationship or special value, if any, to the charitable purposes of the institution.

(2) Management and investment decisions about an individual asset must be made not in isolation but rather in the context of the institutional fund's portfolio of investments as a whole and as a part of an overall investment strategy

having risk and return objectives reasonably suited to the fund and to the institution.

(3) Except as otherwise provided by law other than this part, an institution may invest in any kind of property or type of investment consistent with this section.

(4) An institution shall diversify the investments of an institutional fund unless the institution reasonably determines that, because of special circumstances, the purposes of the fund are
better served without diversification.

(5) Within a reasonable time after receiving property, an institution shall make and carry out decisions concerning the retention or disposition of the property or to rebalance a portfolio, in order to bring the institutional fund into compliance with the purposes, terms, and distribution requirements of the institution as necessary to meet other circumstances of the institution and the requirements of this part.

(6) A person that has special skills or expertise, or is selected in reliance upon the person's representation that the person has special skills or expertise, has a duty to use those skills or that
expertise in managing and investing institutional funds.

(f) Nothing in this section alters the duties and liabilities of a director of a nonprofit public benefit corporation under Section 5240 of the Corporations Code.

Probate Code § 18504. (a) Subject to the intent of a donor expressed in the gift instrument, an institution may appropriate for expenditure or accumulate so much of an endowment fund as the institution determines is prudent for the uses, benefits, purposes, and duration for which the endowment fund is established. Unless stated otherwise in the gift instrument, the assets in an endowment fund are donor-restricted assets until appropriated for expenditure by the institution. In making a determination to appropriate or accumulate, the institution shall act in good faith, with the care that an ordinarily prudent person in a like position would exercise under similar circumstances, and shall consider, if relevant, all of the following factors:

(1) The duration and preservation of the endowment fund.
(2) The purposes of the institution and the endowment fund.
(3) General economic conditions.
(4) The possible effect of inflation or deflation.
(5) The expected total return from income and the appreciation of investments.
(6) Other resources of the institution.
(7) The investment policy of the institution.

(b) To limit the authority to appropriate for expenditure or accumulate under subdivision (a), a gift instrument must specifically state the limitation.

(c) Terms in a gift instrument designating a gift as an endowment, or a direction or authorization in the gift instrument to use only "income," "interest," "dividends," or "rents, issues, or profits," or "to preserve the principal intact," or words of similar import have both of the following effects:

(1) To create an endowment fund of permanent duration unless other language in the gift instrument limits the duration or purpose of the fund.

(2) To not otherwise limit the authority to appropriate for expenditure or accumulate under subdivision (a).

(d) The appropriation for expenditure in any year of an amount greater than 7 percent of the fair market value of an endowment fund, calculated on the basis of market values determined at least quarterly and averaged over a period of not less than three years immediately preceding the year in which the appropriation for expenditure is made, creates a rebuttable presumption of imprudence.

For an endowment fund in existence for fewer than three years, the fair market value of the endowment fund shall be calculated for the period the endowment fund has been in existence.

This subdivision does not do any of the following:

(1) Apply to an appropriation for expenditure permitted under law other than this part or by the gift instrument.

(2) Apply to a private or public postsecondary educational institution, or to a campus foundation established by and operated under the auspices of such an educational institution.

(3) Create a presumption of prudence for an appropriation for expenditure of an amount less than or equal to 7 percent of the fair market value of the endowment fund.

Probate Code § 18505. (a) Subject to any specific limitation set forth in a gift instrument or in law other than this part, an institution may delegate to an external agent the management and investment of an institutional fund to the extent that an institution could prudently delegate under the circumstances. An institution shall act in good faith, with the care that an ordinarily prudent person in a like position would exercise under similar circumstances, in all of the following:

(1) Selecting an agent.

(2) Establishing the scope and terms of the delegation, consistent with the purposes of the institution and the institutional fund.

(3) Periodically reviewing the agent's actions in order to monitor the agent's performance and compliance with the scope and terms of the delegation.

(b) In performing a delegated function, an agent owes a duty to the institution to exercise reasonable care to comply with the scope and terms of the delegation.

(c) An institution that complies with subdivision (a) is not liable for the decisions or actions of an agent to which the function was delegated except to the extent a trustee would be liable for those actions or decisions under Sections 16052 and 16401.

(d) By accepting delegation of a management or investment function from an institution that is subject to the laws of this state, an agent submits to the jurisdiction of the courts of this state in all proceedings arising from or related to the delegation or the performance of the delegated function.

(e) An institution may delegate management and investment functions to its committees, officers, or employees as authorized by law of this state other than this part.

Probate Code § 18506. (a) If the donor consents in a record, an institution may release or modify, in whole or in part, a restriction contained in a gift instrument on the management, investment, or purpose of an institutional fund. A release or modification may not allow a fund to be used for a purpose other than a charitable purpose of the institution.

(b) The court, upon application of an institution, may modify a restriction contained in a gift instrument regarding the management or investment of an institutional fund if the restriction has become impracticable or wasteful, if it impairs the management or investment of the fund, or if, because of circumstances not anticipated by the donor, a modification of a restriction will further the purposes of the fund. The institution shall notify the Attorney General of the application, and the Attorney General must be given an opportunity to be heard. To the extent practicable, any modification must be made in accordance with the donor's probable intention.

(c) If a particular charitable purpose or a restriction contained in a gift instrument on the use of an institutional fund becomes unlawful, impracticable, impossible to achieve, or wasteful, the

court, upon application of an institution, may modify the purpose of the fund or the restriction on the use of the fund in a manner consistent with the charitable purposes expressed in the gift instrument. The institution shall notify the Attorney General of the application, and the Attorney General must be given an opportunity to be heard.

(d) If an institution determines that a restriction contained in a gift instrument on the management, investment, or purpose of an institutional fund is unlawful, impracticable, impossible to achieve, or wasteful, the institution, 60 days after notification to the Attorney General and to the donor at the donor's last known address in the records of the institution, may release or modify the restriction, in whole or part, if all of the following apply:

(1) The institutional fund subject to the restriction has a total value of less than one hundred thousand dollars ($100,000).

(2) More than 20 years have elapsed since the fund was established.

(3) The institution uses the property in a manner consistent with the charitable purposes expressed in the gift instrument. An institution that releases or modifies a restriction under this subdivision may, if appropriate circumstances arise thereafter, use the property in accordance with the restriction notwithstanding its release or modification, and that use is deemed to satisfy the consistency requirement of this paragraph.

Probate Code § 18507. Compliance with this part is determined in light of the facts and circumstances existing at the time a decision is made or action is taken, and not by hindsight.

Probate Code § 18508. This part applies to institutional funds existing on or established after January 1, 2009. As applied to institutional funds existing on January 1, 2009, this part governs only decisions made or actions taken on or after that date.

Probate Code § 18509. This part modifies, limits, and supersedes the Electronic Signatures in Global and National Commerce Act (15 U.S.C. Sec. 7001 et seq.), but does not modify, limit, or supersede Section 101 of that act (15 U.S.C. Sec. 7001(a)), or authorize electronic delivery of any of the notices described in Section 103 of that act (15 U.S.C. Sec. 7003(b)).

Probate Code § 18510. In applying and construing this uniform act, consideration must be given to the need to promote uniformity of the law with respect to its subject matter among states that enact it.

# Effects of a Registered Domestic Partnership

Effective January 1, 2005 and as amended October 2005, the Probate Code provides language that includes Registered Domestic Partners in much the same capacity, powers, and responsibilities previously given only to a spouse. Both parties must sign the Declaration of Domestic Partnership (which is available on the California Secretary of State website) before a notary public and the document must be filed with the California Secretary of State. As previously indicated, the definition of Domestic Partnership and its relation to the area of probate and trust law can be found at Probate Code § 37. Family Code § 297 also provides information on California Domestic Partnerships.

## Termination of Domestic Partnership/Revocation of Bequests

Once the Domestic Partnership is terminated, the powers, rights and responsibilities are no longer valid. Any person who previously had registered as a Domestic Partner named his/her partner as a Executor, Trustee, Agent, surrogate, or in any other capacity needs to change any and all documents to avoid confusion. Specific probate code reference regarding the termination of conservatorships and Wills can be found at Probate Code §§ 1813.1 and 6122.1, respectively.

## Hospital and Health Care Facility Visitation Rights (H&S Code § 1261)

Health and Safety Code § 1261.
 (a) A health facility shall allow a patient's domestic partner, the children of the patient's domestic partner, and the domestic partner of the patient's parent or child to visit, unless one of the following is met:
  (1) No visitors are allowed.
  (2) The facility reasonably determines that the presence of a particular visitor would endanger the health or safety of a patient, member of the health facility staff, or other visitor to the health facility, or would significantly disrupt the operations of a facility.
  (3) The patient has indicated to health facility staff that the patient does not want this person to visit.
 (b) This section may not be construed to prohibit a health facility from otherwise establishing reasonable restrictions upon visitation, including restrictions upon the hours of visitation and number of visitors.
 (c) For purposes of this section, "domestic partner" has the same meaning as that term is used in Section 297 of the Family Code.

# Taxes and Definitions

This section contains some of the California Probate Codes that relate to federal tax codes that are relevant to simple estate planning and administration. This is only a small sampling and should not be construed as the complete tax-related codes and/or advice for following same. Related codes should be reviewed by an attorney and/or a certified public accountant to be verified for accuracy and as being the current tax laws and regulations.

Probate Code § 20100. Except where the context otherwise requires, the following definitions shall govern the construction of this chapter:

(a) "Estate tax" means a tax imposed by any federal or California estate tax law, now existing or hereafter enacted, and includes interest and penalties on any deficiency.

(b) "Person interested in the estate" means any person, including a personal representative, entitled to receive, or who has received, from a decedent while alive or by reason of the death of the decedent any property or interest therein.

(c) "Personal representative" includes a guardian, conservator, trustee, or other person charged with the responsibility of paying the estate tax.

(d) "Property" means property included in the gross estate for federal estate tax purposes.

(e) "Value" means fair market value as determined for federal estate tax purposes.

Probate Code § 20101.

(a) This chapter does not apply to persons interested in the estate of a decedent who died before January 1, 1987.

(b) Notwithstanding the repeal of former Article 4a (commencing with Section 970) of Chapter 15 of Division 3 of the Probate Code by Chapter 783 of the Statutes of 1986, the provisions of that former article remain applicable where the decedent died before January 1, 1987. No inference as to the applicable law in effect before January 1, 1987, shall be drawn from the enactment of this chapter

Probate Code § 20110.

(a) Except as provided in subdivision (b), any estate tax shall be equitably prorated among the persons interested in the estate in the manner prescribed in this article.

(b) This section does not apply: (1) To the extent the decedent in a written inter vivos or testamentary instrument disposing of property specifically directs that the property be applied to the satisfaction of an estate tax or that an estate tax be prorated to the property in the manner provided in the instrument. As used in this paragraph, an "instrument disposing of property" includes an instrument that creates an interest in property or an amendment to an instrument that disposes of property or creates an interest in property. (2) Where federal law directs otherwise. If federal law directs the manner of proration of the federal estate tax, the California estate tax shall be prorated in the same manner.

Probate Code § 20111. The proration required by this article shall be made in the proportion that the value of the property received by each person interested in the estate bears to the total value of all property received by all persons interested in the estate, subject to the provisions of this article.

Probate Code § 20112.

(a) In making a proration of the federal estate tax, allowances shall be made for credits allowed for state or foreign death taxes in determining the federal tax payable and for exemptions and deductions allowed for the purpose of determining the taxable estate.

(b) In making a proration of the California estate tax, allowances shall be made for

(1) credits (other than the credit for state death taxes paid) allowed by the federal estate tax law and attributable to property located in this state, and

(2) exemptions and deductions allowed by the federal estate tax law for the purpose of determining the taxable estate attributable to property located in this state.

(c) In making a proration of an estate tax, interest on extension of taxes and interest and penalties on any deficiency shall be charged to equitably reflect the benefits and burdens of the extension or deficiency and of any tax deductions associated with the interest and penalties.

Probate Code § 20113. If a trust is created, or other provision made whereby a person is given an interest in the income of, an estate for years or for life in, or other temporary interest in, any property, the estate tax on both the temporary interest and on the remainder thereafter shall be charged against and paid out of the corpus of the property without apportionment between remainders and temporary estates.

Probate Code § 20114.

(a) As used in this section, "qualified real property" means qualified real property as defined in Section 2032A of the Internal Revenue Code (26 U.S.C. Sec. 2032A).

(b) If an election is made pursuant to Section 2032A of the Internal Revenue Code (26 U.S.C. Sec. 2032A), the proration shall be based upon the amount of federal estate tax that would be payable but for the election. The amount of the reduction in federal estate tax resulting from an election pursuant to Section 2032A of the Internal Revenue Code (26 U.S.C. Sec. 2032A) shall reduce the tax that is otherwise attributable to the qualified real property that is the subject of the election. If the tax that is otherwise attributable to the qualified real property is reduced to zero pursuant to this subdivision, any excess amount of reduction shall reduce the tax otherwise payable with respect to the other property, this amount to be equitably prorated in accordance with Section 20111.

(c) If additional federal estate tax is imposed under subsection (c) of Section 2032A of the Internal Revenue Code (26 U.S.C. Sec. 2032A) by reason of early disposition or cessation of qualified use, the additional tax shall be a charge against the portion of the qualified real property to which the additional tax is attributable, and shall be equitably prorated among the persons interested in that portion of the qualified real property in proportion to their interests.

Probate Code § 20114.5.

(a) As used in this section: (1) A reference to Section 4980A of the Internal Revenue Code means Section 4980A of the federal Internal Revenue Code of 1986 as amended (26 U.S.C. Sec. 4980A) and also means former Section 4981A of the federal Internal Revenue Code of 1986. (2) "Excess retirement accumulation" has the meaning given it in paragraph (3) of subsection (d) of Section 4980A.

(b) If the federal estate tax is increased under subsection (d) of Section 4980A of the Internal Revenue Code, the amount of the increase shall be a charge against the persons who receive the excess retirement accumulation that gives rise to the increase, and shall be equitably prorated among all persons who receive interests in qualified employer plans and individual retirement plans to which the excess retirement accumulation is attributable.

Probate Code § 20115. Where the payment of any portion of the federal estate tax is extended under the provisions of the federal estate tax law, the amount of extended tax shall be a charge against the persons who receive the specific property that gives rise to the extension.

Probate Code § 20116.

(a) If all property does not come into the possession of the personal representative, the personal representative is entitled, and has the duty, to recover from the persons interested in the estate the proportionate amount of the estate tax with which the persons are chargeable under this chapter.

(b) If the personal representative cannot collect from any person interested in the estate the amount of an estate tax apportioned to the person, the amount not recoverable shall be equitably prorated among the other persons interested in the estate who are subject to proration.

Probate Code § 20117.

(a) If a person is charged with or required to pay an estate tax greater than the amount prorated to that person because another person does not pay the amount of estate tax prorated to the other person, the person charged with or required to pay the greater amount has a right of reimbursement against the other person.

(b) The right of reimbursement may be enforced through the personal representative in the discretion of the personal representative, or may be enforced directly by the person charged with or required to pay the greater amount, and for the purpose of direct enforcement the person is subrogated to the position of the personal representative.

(c) The personal representative or person who has a right of reimbursement may commence a proceeding to have a court determine the right of reimbursement. The provisions of Article 3 (commencing with Section 20120) shall govern the proceeding, with changes necessary to make the provisions appropriate for application to the proceeding, and the court order determining the right of reimbursement is an enforceable judgment.

Probate Code § 20200. Except where the context otherwise requires, the following definitions shall govern the construction of this chapter:

(a) "Generation-skipping transfer tax" means a tax imposed by any federal or California generation-skipping transfer tax law, now existing or hereafter enacted, and includes interest and penalties on any deficiency.

(b) "Property" means property on which a generation-skipping transfer tax is imposed.

(c) "Transferee" means any person who receives, who is deemed to receive, or who is the beneficiary of, any property.

(d) "Trustee" means any person who is a trustee within the meaning of the federal generation-skipping transfer tax law, or who is otherwise required to pay a generation-skipping transfer tax.

(e) "Value" means fair market value as determined for generation-skipping transfer tax purposes.

Probate Code § 20201 (a) This chapter does not apply to transferees of property of a decedent who died before January 1, 1987. (b) No inference as to the applicable law in effect before January 1, 1987, shall be drawn from the enactment of this chapter.[4]

Probate Code § 20210.

(a) Except as provided in subdivision (b), any generation-skipping transfer tax shall be equitably prorated among the transferees in the manner prescribed in this article.

(b) This section does not apply:

(1) To the extent the transferor in a written instrument transferring property specifically directs that the property be applied to the satisfaction of a generation-skipping transfer tax or that a generation-skipping transfer tax be prorated to the property in the manner provided in the instrument.

(2) Where federal law directs otherwise. If federal law directs the manner of proration of the federal generation-skipping transfer tax, the California generation-skipping transfer tax shall be prorated in the same manner.

Probate Code § 20211. The proration required by this article shall be made in the proportion that the value of the property received by each transferee bears to the total value of all property received by all transferees, subject to the provisions of this article.

Probate Code § 20212. In making a proration required by this article:

(a) Allowances shall be made for credits, exemptions, and deductions allowed for the purpose of determining the tax payable.

(b) Interest and penalties on any deficiency shall be charged to equitably reflect the benefits and burdens of the deficiency and of any tax deductions associated with the interest and penalties.

Probate Code § 20213. If a trust is created or other provision made whereby a transferee is given an interest in income, or an estate for years or for life, or another temporary interest in property, the tax on both the temporary interest and other interests in the property shall be charged against, and paid out of, the corpus of the property without apportionment between the temporary and other interests.

Probate Code § 20214.

(a) If all property does not come into the possession of the trustee, the trustee is entitled, and has the duty, to recover from the transferees, the proportionate amount of the tax with which the transferees are chargeable under this chapter.

(b) If the trustee cannot collect from any transferee the amount of tax apportioned to the transferee, the amount not recoverable shall be equitably prorated among the other transferees who are subject to proration.

Probate Code § 20215.

(a) If a person is charged with, or required to pay, a generation-skipping transfer tax greater than the amount prorated to that person because another person does not pay the amount of generation-skipping transfer tax prorated to the other person, the person charged with or required to pay the greater amount has a right of reimbursement against the other person.

(b) The right of reimbursement may be enforced through the trustee in the discretion of the trustee, or may be enforced directly by the person charged with, or required to pay, the greater amount and, for the purpose of direct enforcement, the person is subrogated to the position of the trustee.

(c) The trustee or person who has a right of reimbursement may commence a proceeding to have a court determine the right of reimbursement. The provisions of Article 3 (commencing with Section 20220) shall govern the proceeding, with changes necessary to make the provisions appropriate for application to the proceeding, and the court order determining the right of reimbursement is an enforceable judgment.

Probate Code § 21500. As used in this part, "Internal Revenue Code" means the Internal Revenue Code of 1986, as amended from time to time. A reference to a provision of the Internal Revenue Code includes any subsequent provision of law enacted in its place.

Probate Code § 21501.

(a) This part applies to a distribution made on or after January 1, 1988, whether the transferor died before, on, or after that date.

(b) A distribution made on or after January 1, 1983, and before January 1, 1988, is governed by the applicable law in effect before January 1, 1988.

Probate Code § 21502.

(a) This part does not apply to an instrument the terms of which expressly or by necessary implication make this part inapplicable.

(b) By an appropriate statement made in an instrument, the transferor may incorporate by reference any or all of the provisions of this part. The effect of incorporating a provision of this part in an instrument is to make the incorporated provision a part of the instrument as though the language of the incorporated provision were set forth verbatim in the instrument. Unless an instrument incorporating a provision of this part provides otherwise, the instrument automatically incorporates the provision's amendments.

Probate Code § 21503.

(a) If an instrument includes a formula intended to eliminate the federal estate tax, the formula shall be applied to eliminate or to reduce to the maximum extent possible the federal estate tax.

(b) If an instrument includes a formula that refers to a maximum fraction or amount that will not result in a federal estate tax, the formula shall be construed to refer to the maximum fraction or amount that will not result in or increase the federal estate tax.

# Marital Deduction

Probate Code § 21520. As used in this chapter:

(a) "Marital deduction" means the federal estate tax deduction allowed for transfers under Section 2056 of the Internal Revenue Code or the federal gift tax deduction allowed for transfers under Section 2523 of the Internal Revenue Code.

(b) "Marital deduction gift" means a transfer of property that is intended to qualify for the marital deduction.

Probate Code § 21521. Sections 21524 and 21526 do not apply to a trust that qualifies for the marital deduction under Section 20.2056(e)–2(b) of the Code of Federal Regulations (commonly referred to as the "estate trust").

Probate Code § 21522. If an instrument contains a marital deduction gift:

(a) The provisions of the instrument, including any power, duty, or discretionary authority given to a fiduciary, shall be construed to comply with the marital deduction provisions of the Internal Revenue Code.

(b) The fiduciary shall not take any action or have any power that impairs the deduction as applied to the marital deduction gift.

(c) The marital deduction gift may be satisfied only with property that qualifies for the marital deduction.

Probate Code § 21523.

(a) The Economic Recovery Tax Act of 1981 was enacted August 13, 1981. This section applies to an instrument executed before September 12, 1981 (before 30 days after enactment of the Economic Recovery Tax Act of 1981).

(b) If an instrument described in subdivision (a) indicates the transferor's intention to make a gift that will provide the maximum allowable marital deduction, the instrument passes to the recipient an amount equal to the maximum amount of the marital deduction that would have been allowed as of the date of the gift under federal law as it existed before enactment of the Economic Recovery Tax Act of 1981, with adjustments for the following, if applicable: (1) The provisions of Section 2056(c)(1)(B) and (C) of the Internal Revenue Code in effect immediately before enactment of the Economic Recovery Tax Act of 1981. (2) To reduce the amount passing under the gift by the final federal estate tax values of any other property that passes under or outside of the instrument and qualifies for the marital deduction. This subdivision does not apply to qualified terminable interest property under Section 2056(b)(7) of the Internal Revenue Code.

Probate Code § 21524. If a marital deduction gift is made in trust, in addition to the other provisions of this chapter, each of the following provisions also applies to the marital deduction trust:

(a) The transferor's spouse is the only beneficiary of income or principal of the marital deduction property as long as the spouse is alive. Nothing in this subdivision precludes exercise by the transferor's spouse of a power of appointment included in a trust that qualifies as a general power of appointment marital deduction trust.

(b) Subject to subdivision (d), the transferor's spouse is entitled to all of the income of the marital deduction property not less frequently than annually, as long as the spouse is alive.

(c) The transferor's spouse has the right to require that the trustee of the trust make unproductive marital deduction property productive or to convert it into productive property within a reasonable time.

(d) Notwithstanding Section 16347, in the case of qualified terminable interest property under Section 2056(b)(7) or Section 2523 (f) of the Internal Revenue Code, on termination of the interest of the transferor's spouse in the trust all of the remaining accrued or undistributed income shall pass to the estate of the transferor's spouse, unless the instrument provides a different disposition that qualifies for the marital deduction.

Probate Code § 21525.

(a) If an instrument that makes a marital deduction gift includes a condition that the transferor's spouse survive the transferor by a period that exceeds or may exceed six months, other than a condition described in subdivision (b), the condition shall be limited to six months as applied to the marital deduction gift.

(b) If an instrument that makes a marital deduction gift includes a condition that the transferor's spouse survive a common disaster that results in the death of the transferor, the condition shall be limited to the time of the final audit of the federal estate tax return for the transferor's estate, if any, as applied to the marital deduction gift.

(c) The amendment of subdivision (a) made by Chapter 113 of the Statutes of 1988 is declaratory of, and not a change in, either existing law or former Section 1036 (repealed by Chapter 923 of the Statutes of 1987).

Probate Code § 21526. A fiduciary is not liable for a good faith decision to make any election, or not to make any election, referred to in Section 2056(b)(7) or Section 2523(f) of the Internal Revenue Code.

## Charitable Gifts

Probate Code § 21540. If an instrument indicates the transferor's intention to comply with the Internal Revenue Code requirements for a charitable remainder unitrust or a charitable remainder annuity trust as each is defined in Section 664 of the Internal Revenue Code, the provisions of the instrument, including any power, duty, or discretionary authority given to a fiduciary, shall be construed to comply with the charitable deduction provisions of Section 2055 or Section 2522 of the Internal Revenue Code and the charitable remainder trust provisions of Section 664 of the Internal Revenue Code in order to conform to that intent. In no event shall the fiduciary take an action or have a power that impairs the charitable deduction. The provisions of the instrument may be augmented in any manner consistent with Section 2055(e) or Section 2522(c) of the Internal Revenue Code on a petition provided for in Section 17200. 21541. If an instrument indicates the transferor's intention to comply with the requirements for a charitable lead trust as described in Section 170(f)(2)(B) and Section 2055(e)(2) or Section 2522(c)(2) of the Internal Revenue Code, the provisions of the instrument, including any power, duty, or discretionary authority given to a fiduciary, shall be construed to comply with the provisions of that section in order to conform to that intent. In no event shall the fiduciary take any action or have any power that impairs the charitable deduction. The provisions of the instrument may be augmented in any manner consistent with that intent upon a petition provided for in Section 17200.

These sections provide detail regarding the payment and/or pro rata payment of taxes, including those due to the Internal Revenue Service.

## California Inheritance Tax

As previously indicated, California does not currently have inheritance tax. There are some estates, however, that are not exempt under the California Tax Code. In the event that a decedent died prior to the repeal of this tax and the estate is still pending, the personal representative will have to file an IT-22 with the State of California as that is state would be liable for inheritance tax. Additionally, if a surviving spouse did not pay California Estate Tax, the tax could be levied and inheritance tax would therefore be due. Estate or inheritance might also been levied by the State of California on real property.

The attorney will need to verify whether the estate is exempt and confirm the current status of any California Inheritance Tax statutes.

## Key Terms

- Health Care Surrogate
- Public Administrator
- Uniform Testamentary Additions to Trust Act
- Uniform International Wills Act
- Uniform Principal and Income Act
- Uniform Management of Institutional Funds Act
- Domestic Partnership Act
- Hospital and Health Care Facility Visitation Rights

# The California Probate Paralegal

# Appendices

# Table of Contents

| | | |
|---|---|---|
| Appendix 1A | Table of Consanguinity | 289 |
| Appendix 1B | Distribution Charts | 290 |
| Appendix 2A | Intake Form | 292 |
| Appendix 3A | Sample Will | 295 |
| Appendix 3B | Shores Will (Signed) | 301 |
| Appendix 4A | Client Fact Sheet (Completed) | 307 |
| Appendix 4B | Verification | 310 |
| Appendix 4C | Proof of Subscribing Witness (DE-131) | 311 |
| Appendix 4D | Waiver of Bond | 312 |
| Appendix 5A | Probate Accounting Spreadsheets | 313 |
| Appendix 5B | Petition for Final Distribution | 317 |
| Appendix 5C | Waiver of Notice | 324 |
| Appendix 5D | Receipt | 325 |
| Appendix 5E | Order for Final Distribution | 326 |
| Appendix 5F | Ex Parte Petition for Discharge | 329 |
| Appendix 6A | Affidavit—Death of Spouse | 330 |
| Appendix 6B | Death of Owner (form) | 331 |
| Appendix 6C | Preliminary Change of Ownership Form | 333 |
| Appendix 6D | Declaration for Collection of Compensation Owed to Spouse | 335 |
| Appendix 6E | Affidavit—Death of Joint Tenant | 336 |
| Appendix 6F | Declaration under Probate Code §13100, et seq | 337 |
| Appendix 6G | Spousal Property Petition Attachments | 339 |
| Appendix 7A | Federal Estate Tax Exemption Chart | 343 |
| Appendix 7B | Annual Exclusion Chart | 344 |
| Appendix 7C | Disclaimer Requirements | 345 |
| Appendix 8A | Assignment to Trust | 346 |
| Appendix 8B | Trust Transfer Deed | 349 |
| Appendix 9A | Durable Power of Attorney—Powers | 351 |
| Appendix 9B | Durable Power of Attorney—Care & Control of Person | 359 |
| Appendix 9C | Durable Power of Attorney—Incidental Provisions | 361 |
| Appendix 9D | Durable Power of Attorney—Health Care Powers | 366 |
| Appendix 10A | Trustee Accounting (Spreadsheet) | 370 |
| Appendix 10B | Petition for Instructions | 372 |

# Appendix 1A
## Table of Consanguinity
*(Degrees of Blood Relationship)*

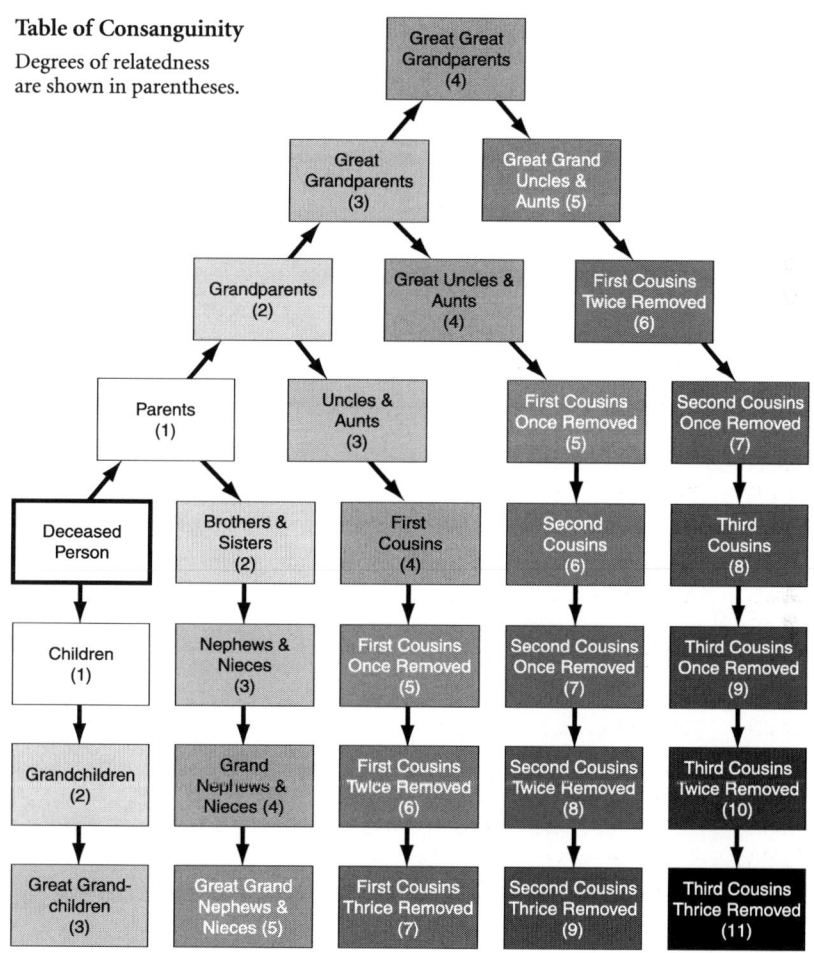

# Appendix 1B_1
## Distribution Charts

Per Stirpes- Right of Representation Distribution (predeceased child)
Probate Code §246-Child #1 receives one-half of parent's estate; Child #2 is deceased. His/her share is distributed equally between two living children; Grandchild #1 and Grandchild #2 each receive one-quarter of the grandparent's estate.

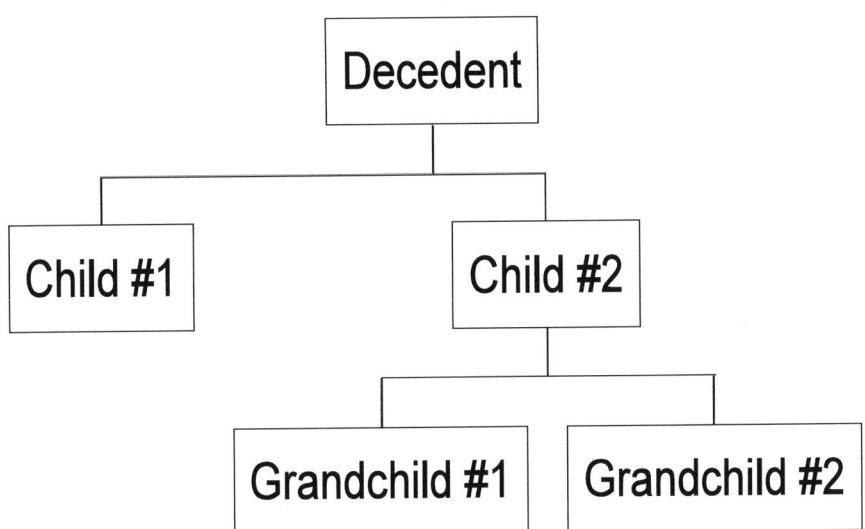

# Appendix 1B_2
## Distribution Charts *continued*

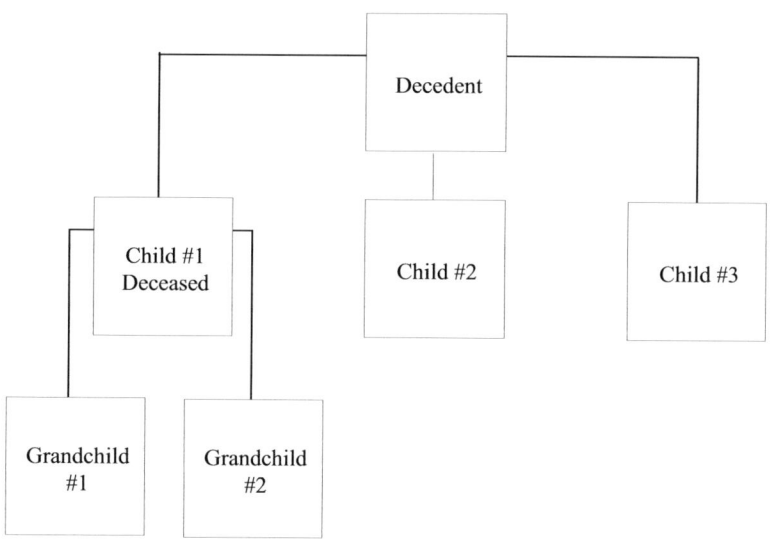

Probate Code §240 (Right of Representation)

Child #2 receives one-third; Child #3 receives one-third; Child #1 is deceased, his/her one-third is divided equally between two children = Grandchild#1 receives one-sixth and Grandchild #2 receives one-sixth.

# Appendix 2A
## Probate Intake Form

**PROBATE INTAKE FORM**

Date of Meeting: _____ Date Received: _____

Client: _____ Client's Spouse _____

Address: _____

Home Phone: _____ Work Phone: _____ Cell Phone: _____

Relationship to Decedent: _____

Name of Decedent: _____ Date of Birth: _____

Date of Death: _____ Social Security No: _____ Death Certificates? _____

Last Address of Decedent: _____

Location of Death: _____

Did the Decedent have a Will? _____ Date of the Will: _____

Was there a Codicil? _____ Location of Original Will? _____

Executor Named in Will? _____

Name of Decedent's Spouse: _____

Address of Decedent's Spouse: _____

If Decedent's Spouse is Predeceased on what date? _____

Did the Decedent own Real Property: _____ If Yes, list address(es) below; How is Title Held?

_____

_____

_____

Insurance Policies: _____

_____

Has Social Security Been Notified? _____

Appendix 2A

# Appendix 2A
## Probate Intake Form *continued*

Retirement Benefits: _____

Name; Address; Telephone No; Birth dates; Social Security No. of All Living Children

_____

_____

_____

_____

_____

Name; Birth dates; Social Security No. of All Deceased Children

_____

_____

_____

Name; Address; Telephone No; Birth dates; Grandchildren (Children of predeceased Child)

_____

_____

_____

_____

_____

Did Decedent Leave Make Any Specific Bequests?

_____

_____

Did Decedent Receive Any Medi-Cal Benefits? _____

Appendix 2A

# Appendix 2A
## Probate Intake Form *continued*

Did Decedent Have Last Illness Expenses? _____

OTHER ASSETS:

Automobiles/Boats/RVs: _____

_____

_____

_____

Cash: _____

Bank/Savings Accounts: _____

_____

_____

Stocks/Bonds/Mutual Funds: _____

_____

_____

Business/Other Assets: _____

_____

_____

Other Property of Value Such as Artwork, Jewelry, Collectibles:

_____

_____

_____

_____

# Appendix 3A
## Sample Will

**LAST WILL
OF**

_____

# appendix 3A
## Sample Will *continued*

### LAST WILL AND TESTAMENT
### OF
_____

**Introductory Clause**. I, _____, a resident of and domiciled in the County of _____, State of California, do hereby make, publish and declare this to be my Last Will and Testament, hereby revoking all Wills and Codicils at any time heretofore made by me.

I am married to _____, and all references to my husband/wife shall specifically mean him/her.

I have two living children: _____, born _____, ____ and _____, born _____, ____.

I have no deceased children.

### ARTICLE I

**Direction to Pay Debts**. I direct that all my legally enforceable debts, secured and unsecured, be paid as soon as practicable after my death. If at the time of my death any of the real property herein devised is subject to any mortgage, I direct that the devisee taking such mortgaged property shall take it subject to such mortgage and that the devisee shall not be entitled to have the obligation secured thereby paid out of my general estate.

### ARTICLE II

**No Contractual Agreement**. My husband/wife and I are executing reciprocal Wills. The Will are not the result of any contract or agreement between us. Either of us may revoke this Will at our sole discretion.

### ARTICLE III

**Outright Gift of Residuary**. I give, devise and bequeath all the rest, residue and remainder of my property of every kind and description (including lapsed legacies and devises) wherever situate and whether acquired before or after the execution of this Will, outright and free of trust to my husband/wife. If my husband/wife predeceases me I give my property to my children, in equal shares. In the event that either of my children predecease me, then that child's share shall be distributed to their issue by right of representation. If either of my children do not have any issue, that child's share shall lapse and become part of the residue of my estate.

Last Will and Testament of _____

# Appendix 3A
## Sample Will *continued*

### ARTICLE IV

**Naming the Executor, Executor Succession, Executor's Fees and Other Matters** . The provisions for naming the Executor, Executor succession, Executor's fees and other matters are set forth below:

(1)**Naming an Individual Executor** . I hereby nominate, constitute and appoint as Executor of this my Last Will and Testament _____ my husband/wife, and direct that he/she shall serve without bond.

(2)**Naming Individual Successor or Substitute Executor** . If my individual Executor should fail to qualify as Executor hereunder, or for any reason should cease to act in such capacity, the successor or substitute Executor who shall also serve without bond shall be the next person willing to serve from the list below in the order named:

        _____ [name of alternate executor]
        _____ [name of alternate executor]

### ARTICLE V

**Powers for Executor** . The Executor shall have full authority to administer my estate under the Independent Administration of Estates Act. By way of illustration and not of limitation and in addition to any inherent, implied or statutory powers granted to Executors generally, my Executor is specifically authorized and empowered with respect to any property, real or personal, at any time held under any provision of this my Will: to allot, allocate between principal and income, assign, borrow, buy, care for, collect, compromise claims, contract with respect to, continue any business of mine, convey, convert, deal with, dispose of, enter into, exchange, hold, improve, incorporate any business of mine, invest, lease, manage, mortgage, grant and exercise options with respect to, take possession of, pledge, receive, release, repair, sell, sue for, to make distributions or divisions in cash or in kind or partly in each without regard to the income tax basis of such asset, and in general, to exercise all the powers in the management of my Estate which any individual could exercise in the management of similar property owned in his or her own right, upon such terms and conditions as to my Executor may seem best, and to execute and deliver any and all instruments and to do all acts which my Executor may deem proper or necessary to carry out the purposes of this my Will, without being limited in any way by the specific grants of power made, and without the necessity of a court order.

**Definition of Executor** . Whenever the word "Executor" or any modifying or substituted pronoun therefor is used in this my Will, such words and respective pronouns shall include both the singular and the plural, the masculine, feminine and neuter gender thereof, and shall apply equally to the Executor named herein and to any successor or substitute Executor acting hereunder, and such successor or substitute Executor shall possess all the rights, powers and duties, authority and responsibility conferred upon the Executor originally named herein.

### ARTICLE VI

**Provision for Executor to Act as Trustee for Beneficiary Under Age Twenty-One**. If any share or property hereunder becomes distributable to a beneficiary who has not attained the age of Twenty-one (21) years or if any real property shall be devised to a person who has not attained the age of Twenty-one (21) years at the date of my death, then such share or property shall immediately vest in the beneficiary, but notwithstanding the provisions herein, my Executor acting as Trustee shall retain possession of the share or property in trust for the beneficiary until the beneficiary attains the age of Twenty-one (21), using so much of the net income and principal of the share or property as my Executor deems necessary to provide for the medical care, education, support and maintenance in reasonable comfort of the beneficiary, taking into consideration to the extent my Executor deems advisable any other income or resources of the beneficiary or his or her parents known to my Executor. Any income not so paid or applied shall be accumulated and added to principal. The beneficiary's share or property shall be paid over, distributed and conveyed to the beneficiary upon attaining age Twenty-one (21), or if he or she shall sooner die, to his or her executors or administrators. Whenever my Executor determines it appropriate to pay any money for the benefit of a beneficiary for whom a trust is created hereunder, then the amounts shall be paid out by my Executor in such of the following ways as my Executor deems best: (1) directly to the beneficiary; (2) to the legally appointed guardian of the beneficiary; (3) to some relative or friend for the care, support and education of the beneficiary; (4) by my Executor using such amounts directly for the beneficiary's care, support and education; (5) to a custodian for the beneficiary under the Uniform Gifts or Transfers to Minors Act. My Executor as trustee shall have with respect to each share or property so retained all the powers and discretions conferred upon it as Executor.

### ARTICLE VII

**Discretion Granted to Executor in Reference to Tax Matters** My Executor as the fiduciary of my estate shall have the discretion, but shall not be required when allocating receipts of my estate between income and principal, to make adjustments in the rights of any beneficiaries, or among the principal and income accounts to compensate for the consequences of any tax decision or election, or of any investment or administrative decision, that my Executor believes has had the effect, directly or indirectly, of preferring one beneficiary or group of beneficiaries over others; provided, however, my Executor shall not exercise its discretion in a manner which would cause the loss or reduction of the marital deduction as may be herein provided. In determining the state or federal estate and income tax liabilities of my estate, my Executor shall have discretion to select the valuation date and to determine whether any or all of the allowable administration expenses in my estate shall be used as state or federal estate tax deductions or as state or federal income tax deductions.

## Appendix 3A
### Sample Will *continued*

#### ARTICLE VIII

**Guardianship**. [Optional/as necessary] If a guardian should need to be appointment for any my children, I direct that _____ (my husband/wife) shall serve as guardian, without bond. If _____ is unable to serve as guardian, then I direct that _____ be appointed to serve as guardian, without bond.

#### ARTICLE IX

**Definition of Children** . For purposes of this Will, "children" means the lawful blood descendants in the first degree of the parent designated; and "issue" and "descendants" mean the lawful blood descendants in any degree of the ancestor designated; provided, however, that if a person has been adopted, that person shall be considered a child of such adopting parent and such adopted child and his or her issue shall be considered as issue of the adopting parent or parents and of anyone who is by blood or adoption an ancestor of the adopting parent or either of the adopting parents. The terms "child," "children," "issue," "descendant" and "descendants" or those terms preceded by the terms "living" or "then living" shall include the lawful blood descendant in the first degree of the parent designated even though such descendant is born after the death of such parent.

The term "per stirpes" as used herein has the identical meaning as the term "taking by representation" as defined in the California Probate Code.

#### ARTICLE X

**Definition of Words Relating to the Internal Revenue Code** . As used herein, the words "gross estate," "adjusted gross estate," "taxable estate," "unified credit" ("unified credit" shall also mean "applicable credit amount"), "applicable exclusion amount," "state death tax credit," "maximum marital deduction," "marital deduction," "pass,"  and any other word or words which from the context in which it or they are used refer to the Internal Revenue Code shall have the same meaning as such words have for the purposes of applying the Internal Revenue Code to my estate. Reference to sections of the Internal Revenue Code and to the Internal Revenue Code shall refer to the Internal Revenue Code amended to the date of my death.

#### ARTICLE XI

**Simultaneous Death Provision Presuming Beneficiary Predeceases Testator** . If any beneficiary and I should die under such circumstances as would make it doubtful whether the beneficiary or I died first, then it shall be conclusively presumed for the purposes of this Will that the beneficiary predeceased me.

**Testimonium, Attestation and Self-Proving Affidavit** . I, _____, the Testator, sign my name to this instrument this ____ day of _____, 20__, and being first duly sworn, do hereby declare to the undersigned authority that I sign and execute this instrument as my last will

# Appendix 3A
## Sample Will *continued*

and that I sign it willingly (or willingly direct another to sign for me), that I execute it as my free and voluntary act for the purposes therein expressed, and that I am eighteen years of age or older, of sound mind, and under no constraint or undue influence.

_____ [name of testator]

The foregoing will, consisting of five (5) pages, including the page signed by the testator, was on that date, by _____, subscribed to and declared to be his/her last will in our presence, we at his/her request and in his/her presence, and in the presence of each other, sign the will as witnesses to the will; we further declare that at the time of signing this will, _____ appeared to be of sound mind and memory, and not acting under duress, menace, fraud or undue influence.

We declare under penalty of perjury that the foregoing is true and correct.

_____          _____
Witness Name (print)                              (Witness Signature)

_____
Address

_____
City                State

_____          _____
Witness Name (print)                              (Witness Signature)

_____
Address

_____
City                State

Last Will and Testament of _____

# Appendix 3B
## Shores Will (Signed)

**LAST WILL
OF
CORAL LEIGH SHORES**

# Appendix 3B
## Shores Will (Signed) *continued*

### LAST WILL AND TESTAMENT
### OF
### CORAL LEIGH SHORES

**Introductory Clause**. I, **Coral Leigh Shores**, also known as Coral Redd Shores, a resident of and domiciled in the County of Sacramento, State of California, do hereby make, publish and declare this to be my Last Will and Testament, hereby revoking all Wills and Codicils at any time heretofore made by me.

I am not currently married. I was married to Eddy Cliff Shores, who died on March 10, 2010.

I have two living children: **Eddy Wade Shores**, born September 1, 1975, and **Shelley P. Line (Shores)** born May 30, 1978.

I have no deceased children.

#### ARTICLE I

**Direction to Pay Debts**. I direct that all my legally enforceable debts, secured and unsecured, be paid as soon as practicable after my death. If at the time of my death any of the real property herein devised is subject to any mortgage, I direct that the devisee taking such mortgaged property shall take it subject to such mortgage and that the devisee shall not be entitled to have the obligation secured thereby paid out of my general estate.

#### ARTICLE III

**Outright Gift of Residuary** I give, devise and bequeath all the rest, residue and remainder of my property of every kind and description (including lapsed legacies and devises) wherever situate and whether acquired before or after the execution of this Will, outright and free of trust in equal shares to my children. In the event that either of my children predecease me, then that child's share shall be distributed to their issue by right of representation. If either of my children do not have any issue, that child's share shall lapse and become part of the residue of my estate.

In the event I leave a Memorandum with this Will, any items of property on that list should be distributed to the individual named therein. The distribution of the property on the Memorandum is not mandatory, however, I request that my Executor distribute the property as directed to the best of his or her ability.

# Appendix 3B
## Shores Will (Signed) *continued*

### ARTICLE IV

**Naming the Executor, Executor Succession, Executor's Fees and Other Matters**. The provisions for naming the Executor, Executor succession, Executor's fees and other matters are set forth below:

(1) **Naming an Individual Executor**. I hereby nominate, constitute and appoint as Executor of this my Last Will and Testament **Eddy Wade Shores,** my son, and direct that he shall serve without bond.

(2) **Naming Individual Successor or Substitute Executor**. If my individual Executor should fail to qualify as Executor hereunder, or for any reason should cease to act in such capacity, the successor or substitute Executor who shall also serve without bond shall be the next person willing to serve from the list below in the order named:

      **Shelley P. Line**, my daughter
      **Elmer J. Mudd**, my brother

### ARTICLE V

**Powers for Executor**. The Executor shall have full authority to administer my estate under the Independent Administration of Estates Act. By way of illustration and not of limitation and in addition to any inherent, implied or statutory powers granted to Executors generally, my Executor is specifically authorized and empowered with respect to any property, real or personal, at any time held under any provision of this my Will: to allot, allocate between principal and income, assign, borrow, buy, care for, collect, compromise claims, contract with respect to, continue any business of mine, convey, convert, deal with, dispose of, enter into, exchange, hold, improve, incorporate any business of mine, invest, lease, manage, mortgage, grant and exercise options with respect to, take possession of, pledge, receive, release, repair, sell, sue for, to make distributions or divisions in cash or in kind or partly in each without regard to the income tax basis of such asset, and in general, to exercise all the powers in the management of my Estate which any individual could exercise in the management of similar property owned in his or her own right, upon such terms and conditions as to my Executor may seem best, and to execute and deliver any and all instruments and to do all acts which my Executor may deem proper or necessary to carry out the purposes of this my Will, without being limited in any way by the specific grants of power made, and without the necessity of a court order.

**Definition of Executor**. Whenever the word "Executor" or any modifying or substituted pronoun therefor is used in this my Will, such words and respective pronouns shall include both the singular and the plural, the masculine, feminine and neuter gender thereof, and shall apply equally to the Executor named herein and to any successor or substitute Executor acting hereunder, and such successor or substitute Executor shall possess all the rights, powers and duties, authority and responsibility conferred upon the Executor originally named herein.

# Appendix 3B
## Shores Will (Signed) *continued*

### ARTICLE VI

**Provision for Executor to Act as Trustee for Beneficiary Under Age Twenty-One**. If any share or property hereunder becomes distributable to a beneficiary who has not attained the age of Twenty-one (21) years or if any real property shall be devised to a person who has not attained the age of Twenty-one (21) years at the date of my death, then such share or property shall immediately vest in the beneficiary, but notwithstanding the provisions herein, my Executor acting as Trustee shall retain possession of the share or property in trust for the beneficiary until the beneficiary attains the age of Twenty-one (21), using so much of the net income and principal of the share or property as my Executor deems necessary to provide for the medical care, education, support and maintenance in reasonable comfort of the beneficiary, taking into consideration to the extent my Executor deems advisable any other income or resources of the beneficiary or his or her parents known to my Executor. Any income not so paid or applied shall be accumulated and added to principal. The beneficiary's share or property shall be paid over, distributed and conveyed to the beneficiary upon attaining age Twenty-one (21), or if he or she shall sooner die, to his or her executors or administrators. Whenever my Executor determines it appropriate to pay any money for the benefit of a beneficiary for whom a trust is created hereunder, then the amounts shall be paid out by my Executor in such of the following ways as my Executor deems best: (1) directly to the beneficiary; (2) to the legally appointed guardian of the beneficiary; (3) to some relative or friend for the care, support and education of the beneficiary; (4) by my Executor using such amounts directly for the beneficiary's care, support and education; (5) to a custodian for the beneficiary under the Uniform Gifts or Transfers to Minors Act. My Executor as trustee shall have with respect to each share or property so retained all the powers and discretions conferred upon it as Executor.

### ARTICLE VII

**Discretion Granted to Executor in Reference to Tax Matters**. My Executor as the fiduciary of my estate shall have the discretion, but shall not be required when allocating receipts of my estate between income and principal, to make adjustments in the rights of any beneficiaries, or among the principal and income accounts to compensate for the consequences of any tax decision or election, or of any investment or administrative decision, that my Executor believes has had the effect, directly or indirectly, of preferring one beneficiary or group of beneficiaries over others; provided, however, my Executor shall not exercise its discretion in a manner which would cause the loss or reduction of the marital deduction as may be herein provided. In determining the state or federal estate and income tax liabilities of my estate, my Executor shall have discretion to select the valuation date and to determine whether any or all of the allowable administration expenses in my estate shall be used as state or federal estate tax deductions or as state or federal income tax deductions.

## ARTICLE VIII

**Definition of Children**. For purposes of this Will, "children" means the lawful blood descendants in the first degree of the parent designated; and "issue" and "descendants" mean the lawful blood descendants in any degree of the ancestor designated; provided, however, that if a person has been adopted, that person shall be considered a child of such adopting parent and such adopted child and his or her issue shall be considered as issue of the adopting parent or parents and of anyone who is by blood or adoption an ancestor of the adopting parent or either of the adopting parents. The terms "child," "children," "issue," "descendant" and "descendants" or those terms preceded by the terms "living" or "then living" shall include the lawful blood descendant in the first degree of the parent designated even though such descendant is born after the death of such parent.

The term "per stirpes" as used herein has the identical meaning as the term "taking by representation" as defined in the California Probate Code.

## ARTICLE IX

**Definition of Words Relating to the Internal Revenue Code**. As used herein, the words "gross estate," "adjusted gross estate," "taxable estate," "unified credit" ("unified credit" shall also mean "applicable credit amount"), "applicable exclusion amount," "state death tax credit," "maximum marital deduction," "marital deduction," "pass," and any other word or words which from the context in which it or they are used refer to the Internal Revenue Code shall have the same meaning as such words have for the purposes of applying the Internal Revenue Code to my estate. Reference to sections of the Internal Revenue Code and to the Internal Revenue Code shall refer to the Internal Revenue Code amended to the date of my death.

## ARTICLE X

**Simultaneous Death Provision Presuming Beneficiary Predeceases Testator**. If any beneficiary and I should die under such circumstances as would make it doubtful whether the beneficiary or I died first, then it shall be conclusively presumed for the purposes of this Will that the beneficiary predeceased me.

**Testimonium, Attestation and Self-Proving Affidavit**. I, *Coral Leigh Shores*, the Testator, sign my name to this instrument this 2nd day of August, 2012, and being first duly sworn, do hereby declare to the undersigned authority that I sign and execute this instrument as my last will and that I sign it willingly (or willingly direct another to sign for me), that I execute it as my free and voluntary act for the purposes therein expressed, and that I am eighteen years of age or older, of sound mind, and under no constraint or undue influence.

*Coral Leigh Shores*
_____
Coral Leigh Shores

# Appendix 3B
## Shores Will (Signed) *continued*

The foregoing will, consisting of five (5) pages, including the page signed by the testator, was on that date, by **Coral Leigh Shores**, subscribed to and declared to be her last will in our presence, we at her request and in her presence, and in the presence of each other, sign the will as witnesses to the will; we further declare that at the time of signing this will, **Coral Leigh Shores** appeared to be of sound mind and memory, and not acting under duress, menace, fraud or undue influence.

We declare under penalty of perjury that the foregoing is true and correct.

Alfred B. Neumann  *Alfred B. Neumann*
Witness Name (print)  (Witness Signature)

22220 Wonderful Place
Address

Elk Grove, CA   95624
City                State

Sally F. Neumann  *Sally F. Neumann*
Witness Name (print)  (Witness Signature)

22220 Wonderful Place
Address

Elk Grove, CA   95624
City                State

# Appendix 4A
## Client Fact Sheet (Completed)

**PROBATE INTAKE FORM**

Date of Meeting: 1/25/13    Date Received: 1/25/13

Client: EDDY WADE SHORES    Client's Spouse: N/A

Address: 22222 WONDERFUL PLACE    ELK GROVE, CA  95624

Home Phone: 916-XXX-XXXX    Work Phone: 916-XXX-XXXX    Cell Phone: 916-XXX-XXXX

Relationship to Decedent: SON, NAMED EXECUTOR

Name of Decedent: CORAL LEIGH SHORES aka CORAL REDD SHORES
DOB 10/4/58

Date of Death: 1/5/13 ; Social Security No: XXX-XX-XXXX   Death Certificates? YES

Last Address of Decedent: 22222 WONDERFUL PLACE, ELK GROVE, CA

Location of Death: KAISER HOSPITAL, SOUTH SACRAMENTO, CA

Did the Decedent have a Will? YES    Date of the Will: 8/2/12

Was there a Codicil? NO    Location of Original Will? SON HAS

Executor Named in Will? EDDY WADE SHORES

Name of Decedent's Spouse: ROCKY CLIFF SHORES

Address of Decedent's Spouse: N/A

If Decedent's Spouse is Predeceased on what date? 3/10/10

Did the Decedent own Real Property: YES    If Yes, list address(es) below; How is Title Held?

22222 WONDERFUL PLACE, ELK GROVE, CA    SOLE OWNER
SEE DEED PROVIDED; AFFIDAVIT DEATH OF JOINT TENANT
RECORDED AFTER HUSBANDS DEATH

Insurance Policies: YES TERM LIFE W/ XYZ INSURANCE CO.
BENEFICIARIES: 50% EDDY W SHORES / 50% SHELLE P. LINE

# Appendix 4A
## Client Fact Sheet (Completed) *continued*

Has Social Security Been Notified? __YES__

Retirement Benefits: __YES; CAL PERS__

Name; Address; Telephone No; Birth dates; Social Security No. of All Living Children

EDDY WADE SHORES   22222 WONDERFUL PL. ELK GROVE, CA
916-XXX-XXXX   9/1/75   XXX-XX-XXXX
SHELLEY PEBBLES (SHORE) LINE
7777 LITTLETON WY, STOCKTON, CA 95722
209-XXX-XXXX   5/30/78   XXX-XX-XXXX

Name; Address; Telephone No; Birth dates; Social Security No. of All Deceased Children

NONE

Name; Address; Telephone No; Birth dates; Grandchildren (Children of predeceased Child)

~~Bo~~ N/A

Did Decedent Leave Make Any Specific Bequests?

EDDY TO RECEIVE FATHER'S (ROCKY SHORES) JEWELRY
SHELLEY TO RECEIVE (DECEDENT) MOTHERS JEWELRY

# Appendix 4A
## Client Fact Sheet (Completed) *continued*

Did Decedent Receive Any Medi-Cal Benefits? **No**

Did Decedent Have Last Illness Expenses? **UNKNOWN**

OTHER ASSETS:

Automobiles/Boats/RVs: **2010 Buick Century**
**1994 Toyota PU**

Cash: **$64**

Bank/Savings Accounts: **GOLDEN ONE CREDIT UNION - BAL - $1158**
**MUTUAL FUND - BAL - $20,235**

Stocks/Bonds/Mutual Funds: **NONE**

Business/Other Assets: **PERS SAVINGS PLUS ACCT - BENEFICIARY: CHILDREN**
**IRA ACCOUNT - BENERICIARY: CHILDREN**

Other Property of Value Such as Artwork, Jewelry, Collectibles:
**THOMAS KINCAID PAINTING**
**ROY ROGERS MEMORABILIA**

# Appendix 4B
## Verification

**VERIFICATION**

I, _____, declare that I am the [Executor/Petitioner] in the above entitled action; I have read the foregoing _____ [name of document] and know the contents thereof; the same is true of my own knowledge, except as to those matters which are therein stated upon my information and belief, and as to those matter I believe to be true.

I declare under penalty of perjury that the foregoing is true and correct and that this verification was executed on _____, 200_, at _____, California.

_____

_____, Petitioner

# Appendix 4C
## Proof of Subscribing Witness (DE-131)

**DE-131**

ATTORNEY OR PARTY WITHOUT ATTORNEY *(Name, state bar number, and address)*:
NANCY NOE-NONSENSE, SBN ********
Law Offices of Nancy Noe-Nonsense
11111 Courthouse Plaza
Sacramento, CA 95826

TELEPHONE AND FAX NOS.: ***-***-****

FOR COURT USE ONLY

ATTORNEY FOR *(Name)*: EDDY WADE SHORES, Petitioner

**SUPERIOR COURT OF CALIFORNIA, COUNTY OF** SACRAMENTO
STREET ADDRESS: 3341 Power Inn Road
MAILING ADDRESS: 3341 Power Inn Road
CITY AND ZIP CODE: Sacramento, CA 95826
BRANCH NAME: Probate Division

ESTATE OF *(Name)*:
CORAL LEIGH SHORES aka CORAL REDD SHORES
DECEDENT

**PROOF OF SUBSCRIBING WITNESS**

CASE NUMBER:

---

1. I am one of the attesting witnesses to the instrument of which Attachment 1 is a photographic copy. I have examined Attachment 1 and my signature is on it.
   a. [✓] The name of the decedent was signed in the presence of the attesting witnesses present at the same time by
      (1) [✓] the decedent personally.
      (2) [ ] another person in the decedent's presence and by the decedent's direction.
   b. [✓] The decedent acknowledged in the presence of the attesting witnesses present at the same time that the decedent's name was signed by
      (1) [✓] the decedent personally.
      (2) [ ] another person in the decedent's presence and by the decedent's direction.
   c. [✓] The decedent acknowledged in the presence of the attesting witnesses present at the same time that the instrument signed was decedent's
      (1) [✓] will.
      (2) [ ] codicil.

2. When I signed the instrument, I understood that it was decedent's [✓] will [ ] codicil.

3. I have no knowledge of any facts indicating that the instrument, or any part of it, was procured by duress, menace, fraud, or undue influence.

I declare under penalty of perjury under the laws of the State of California that the foregoing is true and correct.

Date: xx/xx/2007

Alfred B. Neumann
(TYPE OR PRINT NAME)

▶ _____
(SIGNATURE OF WITNESS)

22220 Wonderful Place, Elk Grove, CA
(ADDRESS)

---

## ATTORNEY'S CERTIFICATION
*(Check local court rules for requirements for certifying copies of wills and codicils)*

I am an active member of The State Bar of California. I declare under penalty of perjury under the laws of the State of California that Attachment 1 is a photographic copy of every page of the [✓] will [ ] codicil presented for probate.

Date: xx/xx/2007

Nancy Noe-Nonsense
(TYPE OR PRINT NAME)

▶ _____
(SIGNATURE OF ATTORNEY)

---

Form Approved by the
Judicial Council of California
DE-131 [Rev. January 1, 1998]

**PROOF OF SUBSCRIBING WITNESS**
(Probate)

Probate Code, § 8220
American LegalNet, Inc.
www.USCourtForms.com

# Appendix 4D
# Waiver of Bond

_____
_____
_____
_____

Telephone: _____
Facsimile: _____

Attorneys for _____, Petitioner

IN THE SUPERIOR COURT OF THE STATE OF CALIFORNIA

IN AND FOR THE COUNTY OF _____

IN RE THE ESTATE OF

_____

CASE NO.

**WAIVER OF _____**
**[BOND/ACCOUNTING, PETITION**
**FOR FINAL DISTRIBUTION]**

_____/

I, _____, am the [son/daughter] and beneficiary entitled to distribution in the estate of _____. I have reviewed the [petition, accounting] prepared by Petitioner and the attorney of record in this matter. I hereby agree that [bond, accounting, petition for final distribution] may be waived.

Dated: _____          _____
                                 Name/Relationship

# Appendix 5A
## Probate Accounting Spreadsheets

| INVENTORY | DATE OF DEATH VALUE | |
|---|---|---|
| REAL PROPERTY | $200,000 | (Decedent's One-Half) |
| 2010 Buick Century | 2,500 | (Decedent's One-Half) |
| Personal Property | 5,000 | |
| IRA | 20,000 | |
| Bank Account | 500 | (Decedent's One-Half) |
| **Total** | **$228,000** | |

| ESTATE EXPENSES | AMOUNT | DATE PAID |
|---|---|---|
| Burial Expenses | 20,000 | |
| Publication Fee | 200 | |
| Probate Referee | 125 | |
| Filing Fee | 250 | |
| Misc Administrative | 50 | |
| Credit Card | 2,000 | |
| **Total** | **22,625** | |

# Appendix 5A
## Probate Accounting Spreadsheets *continued*

**PROBATE ACCOUNTING - CORAL LEIGH SHORES**   (Widow w/2 children)

| INVENTORY | DATE OF DEATH VALUE | | |
|---|---|---|---|
| REAL PROPERTY | $450,000 | $200,000 debt | $250,000 net |
| 2010 Buick Century | 5,000 | | |
| 1994 Toyota Pick Up | 1,000 | | |
| Personal Property | 5,000 | | |
| Bank Account | 1,158 | | |
| CD Account | 20,223 | | |
| **Total** | **$482,381** | | |

| ESTATE EXPENSES | AMOUNT | DATE PAID |
|---|---|---|
| Burial Expenses | 20,000 | |
| Publication Fee | 250 | |
| Probate Referee | 150 | |
| Filing Fee | 350 | |
| Misc Administrative | 50 | |
| Credit Card | 2,000 | |
| Utilities | 300 | |
| **Total** | **23,100** | |

# Appendix 5A
## Probate Accounting Spreadsheets *continued*

**PROBATE ACCOUNTING - CORAL LEIGH SHORES**   (Married - Distribution to Husband)

| INVENTORY | DATE OF DEATH VALUE | |
|---|---|---|
| REAL PROPERTY | $225,000 | (Decedent's One-Half) |
| 2010 Buick Century | 2,500 | (Decedent's One-Half) |
| Personal Property | 5,000 | (Distributed or sold) |
| CD | 10,000 | (Decedent's One-Half) |
| Bank Account | 500 | (Decedent's One-Half) |
| **Total Inventory/Assets** | **$243,000** | |

**ESTATE EXPENSES**

| | | |
|---|---|---|
| Burial Expenses | 20,000 | |
| Publication Fee | 200 | |
| Probate Referee | 125 | |
| Filing Fee | 250 | |
| Misc Administrative | 50 | |
| Credit Card | 2,000 | |
| Attorney Fees | 7,530 | |
| Executor Fees | 0 | (Waived) |
| **Total Expenses** | **30,155** | |

| | |
|---|---|
| Net Estate to be Transferred to Spouse  (FMV) | 243,000 |
| Less Debts | -30,155 |
| **Total Net Estate** (In Cash and Kind) | **212,845** |

# Appendix 5A
## Probate Accounting Spreadsheets *continued*

**PROBATE ACCOUNTING - SANDY SHORES**   (Widowed - Distribution to 2 Children)

| INVENTORY | DATE OF DEATH VALUE | | |
|---|---:|---|---|
| REAL PROPERTY | $200,000 | Sold | (Net - $450,000 - 200,000 debt) |
| 2010 Buick Century | 5,000 | Sold | |
| 1994 Toyota Pick up | 1,000 | Distributed/Sold | |
| Personal Property | 5,000 | Distributed/Sold | |
| Bank Account | 1,000 | Liquidated | |
| CD Account | 20,233 | Liquidated | |
| Thomas Kincaid Painting | 1,000 | Distributed/Sold | |
| Roy Rogers Collection | 500 | Distributed/Sold | |
| Interest - checking account | 85 | | |
| **Total Inventory/Assets** | **$233,818** | | |

**ESTATE EXPENSES**

| | | |
|---|---:|---|
| Burial Expenses | 20,000 | |
| Publication Fee | 200 | |
| Probate Referee | 125 | |
| Filing Fee | 250 | |
| Misc Administrative | 50 | |
| Credit Card | 2,000 | |
| Attorney Fees | 12,173 | (Excludes Extraordinary Fees for Sale of House) |
| Executor Fees | 0 | (Waived) |
| **Total Expenses** | **34,798** | |
| Net Estate to Distributed to Children   (FMV) | 233,818 | |
| Less Debts | -34,798 | |
| **Total Net Estate** | **199,020** | |
| One-half to each child | 99,510.00 | |

# Appendix 5B
## Petition for Final Distribution

_____
_____
_____
_____

Telephone: _____
Facsimile: _____

Attorneys for _____, Petitioner

IN THE SUPERIOR COURT OF THE STATE OF CALIFORNIA

IN AND FOR THE COUNTY OF _____

IN RE THE ESTATE OF

_____

_____ /

CASE NO.

**PETITION FOR FINAL DISTRIBUTION ON WAIVER OF ACCOUNT AND FOR ALLOWANCE OF COMPENSATION EXECUTOR, ATTORNEY FEES AND EXTRAORDINARY SERVICES**

Petitioner, _____, renders to the court for settlement her Report of Administration of the above-entitled estate from _____, ____ to _____, 200_, and a Financial Statement, and petitioner for an order for final distribution and for an award of Executor fees and costs, Attorney fees and compensation for extraordinary services rendered by Petitioner's attorney, _____, as follows:

### A. ACCOUNT NOT REQUIRED

No account is required because as shown by the records and file herein, each of the person entitled to distribution from the estate has executed and filed herein a written waiver of account or acknowledgment that the person's interest has been satisfied.

# Appendix 5B
## Petition for Final Distribution *continued*

**B. REPORT OF ADMINISTRATION**

1. Decedent died on _____, 200_ and at the date of death was a resident of _____ County. Decedent had a will, which was lodged with the court herein on _____, 200_.

The will appointed _____, as executor.

2. The Letters of Administration were issued on _____, 200_.

3. Petitioner has performed all of the duties required of him/her as Executor.

<u>Statement of Liabilities</u>

4. Notice to creditors was published in the manner prescribed by law, and more than four months has elapsed since the date of letters were issued to petitioner. In addition, the notice prescribed by law was duly mailed to all known and reasonably ascertainable creditors of the estate prescribed in Probate Code Section 9050 and 9051, and more than 30 days has elapsed since the date notice was so given.

5. The claims against the estate are listed in Schedule E, below, and shall be paid as set forth herein.

6. All claims against the estate paid prior to the notice prescribed by law were debts justly due, paid in good faith, the amount paid did not exceed the amount due, and were paid out of decedent's bank account.

7. No personal property taxes are due or payable by the estate.

8. Neither the decedent, nor decedent's spouse received MediCal benefits.

9. All California and federal income taxes due and payable by the estate have been paid. There are no nonresident devisees of the estate.

10. Neither the executor nor the attorney for the estate has any financial relationship with any creditor or other person who provided services to the decedent and his/her estate.

11. The estate is of insufficient value to require the filing of a federal estate tax return and therefore, no federal estate tax return has been or will be filed for the estate.

# Appendix 5B
## Petition for Final Distribution *continued*

<u>Cash Investments and Inventory and Appraisal</u>

  11. On or about _____, 200\_, an Inventory and Appraisement was filed showing the value of the estate to be $_____. The inventory lists all of the assets of the decedent's estate that have come into the Petitioner's possession under her control. On or about _____, 200\_, concurrently with the Inventory and Appraisement, a Property Tax Certification was filed with the _____ Superior Court. Further, a complete, true and correct account of all receipts of the estate received by Petitioner, as well as sum expended by Petitioner on behalf of the estate, from the period _____ to _____, inclusive, as set forth below.

  On or about _____, 200\_, Petitioner opened an interest bearing checking account at Bank of _____, _____, _____ California, from the proceeds of the sale of the family home.

  12. An offer was made on the real property on or about _____, 200\_ in the amount of $_____, resulting in a gain/loss in the value of the estate of $_____. A Notice of Proposed Action for Sale was filed and served on _____, 2000. There were no objections filed.

  A draft in the amount of $_____ was issued to the Estate of _____ on _____, 200\_ and was deposited in the estate account on _____, 200\_. A copy of the escrow closing is attached herein showing the net proceeds of the sale dispersed.

  13. No heirs have received any preliminary distributions of the estate

  14. Petitioner requests reimbursement for expenses related to the administration of the estate in the amount of: $_____, as set forth below. Said amount shall be paid prior to the final distribution of the estate.

  15. The estate is now ready to be closed and distributed to the heirs of the estate, as set forth in the decedent's will, as referenced below:

Estate of _____; Petition for Final Distribution

# Appendix 5B
## Petition for Final Distribution *continued*

**C. ESTATE DISTRIBUTIONS**

    GROSS VALUE OF THE ESTATE (Inventory & Appraisement)      $_____

    Estate Expenses (funeral, estate administration, taxes, debts)      $_____

        Debts of the Decedent -    $_____
        Funeral Expenses -    $_____
        Federal Income Taxes -    $_____
        Administration Expenses - $_____

    Closing Costs on sale of real property      $_____

    Gain/Loss on Sale of Property      $_____

        Sale of property      $_____
        Interest on checking account      $_____
    Subtotal:      $_____

    **TOTAL PROPERTY REMAINING ON HAND**      $_____
    (Net value of estate)

**D. PROPERTY TO BE DISBURSED**

    Creditors Claims

        _____ (Utility Co.)      _____
        _____ (Yard Maintenance)      _____
        _____ (Cable Co.)      _____
        _____ (Credit Card)      _____
        _____ (Burial expenses)      _____

    Total Creditors Claims      $_____

    Administrative Expenses

        _____ (filing fee)      _____
        _____ (publication fee)      _____
        _____ (bond)      _____
        _____ (probate referee)      _____

    Total Administrative Expenses      $_____

    Compensation (as set forth in E, below)

        _____, Attorney      $_____
        _____, Attorney - Extraordinary Fees      $_____

        _____, Executor      $_____

    Total Compensation      $_____

Estate of _____; Petition for Final Distribution

# Appendix 5B
## Petition for Final Distribution *continued*

    **TOTAL DISBURSEMENTS TO BE MADE** .......................... $_____
    (Total of Creditors claims, administrative expenses and compensation)

E.    COMPENSATION OF EXECUTOR AND ATTORNEY

The total statutory compensation due to Petitioner and her attorney, calculated on the basis of $_____, is as follows:

| Amount of Estate | Compensation |
|---|---|
| $_____ at 4% | _____ |
| $_____ at 3% | _____ |
| $_____ at 2% | _____ |
| Total | $_____ |

Petitioner is entitled to a total statutory compensation of $_____. Petitioner has waived/has not waived his/her statutory fees. Petitioner's attorney is entitled to the statutory fee of $_____.

Petitioner's attorney, _____, has for the benefit of the estate, performed extraordinary services as set forth in Exhibit "B" which is attached and made a part hereof, for which he is entitled to reasonable compensation in addition to his statutory compensation. A reasonable compensation for these services is $_____.

F. **DISTRIBUTION OF NET ESTATE TO BENEFICIARIES**

The total remaining property to be distributed to the decedent's beneficiaries, pursuant to the terms of the will, is the sum of $_____. Said $_____ shall be distributed as follows:

    Child #1     _____

    Child #2     _____

    Child #3     _____

WHEREFORE, Petitioner prays for an order that:

1. The administration of this estate be closed.

2. Petitioner's first and final account as set forth herein be settled, allowed and approved.

3. The compensation of Petitioner, _____, for all services as executor [is/is not] waived.

4. The compensation of Petitioner's attorney, _____, for all services rendered in the Estate of _____; Petition for Final Distribution     Page 5

# Appendix 5B
## Petition for Final Distribution *continued*

estate proceedings be fixed and allowed.

    5. Petitioner's attorney, _____, be allowed the additional sum of $_____ as reasonable compensation for extraordinary services rendered for the benefit of the estate.

    6. The remaining estate property, in the amount of $_____, shall be distributed as set forth in [the decedent's will/Probate Code Section 246], as follows:

| Beneficiary | Distributive Share |
|---|---|
| _____ | $_____ [1/3 amount] |
| _____ | $_____ [1/3 amount] |
| _____ | $_____ [1/3 amount] |

    7. Any property acquired after the date of execution of this Petition shall be distributed as follows:

| Beneficiary | Distributive Share |
|---|---|
| _____ | 1/3 |
| _____ | 1/3 |
| _____ | 1/3 |

Dated: _____     _____
                                                _____, Attorney

# Appendix 5B
## Petition for Final Distribution *continued*

**VERIFICATION**

I, _____, declare that I am the Executor/Petitioner in the above entitled action; I have read the foregoing Petition for Final Distribution on Waiver of Account and for Allowance of Compensation of Executor, Attorney Fees and Extraordinary Services and know the contents thereof; the same is true of my own knowledge, except as to those matters which are therein stated upon my information and belief, and as to those matter I believe to be true.

I declare under penalty of perjury that the foregoing is true and correct and that this verification was executed on _____, 200_, at _____, California.

_____, Petitioner

# Appendix 5C
## Waiver of Notice

```
_____
_____
_____
```
Telephone: _____
Facsimile: _____

Attorneys for _____, Petitioner

IN THE SUPERIOR COURT OF THE STATE OF CALIFORNIA

IN AND FOR THE COUNTY OF _____

| | |
|---|---|
| IN RE THE ESTATE OF | CASE NO. |
| _____ | **WAIVER OF _____ [BOND/ACCOUNTING, PETITION FOR FINAL DISTRIBUTION]** |
| _____ / | |

I, _____, am the [son/daughter] and beneficiary entitled to distribution in the estate of _____. I have reviewed the [petition, accounting] prepared by Petitioner and the attorney of record in this matter. I hereby agree that [bond, accounting, petition for final distribution] may be waived.

Dated: _____          _____
                                                Name/Relationship

# Appendix 5D
## Receipt

_____
_____
_____

Telephone: _____
Facsimile: _____

Attorneys for _____, Petitioner

IN THE SUPERIOR COURT OF THE STATE OF CALIFORNIA

IN AND FOR THE COUNTY OF _____

IN RE THE ESTATE OF           CASE NO.

_____         **RECEIPT** _____

_____/

    I, _____, am the [son/daughter] and beneficiary entitled to distribution in the estate of _____.

I hereby acknowledge receipt of my distributive share. I make no further claims on the estate.

Dated: _____          _____

                                                                          Name/Relationship

# Appendix 5E
## Order for Final Distribution

```
_____
_____
_____
_____
```

Telephone: _____
Facsimile: _____

Attorneys for _____, Petitioner

IN THE SUPERIOR COURT OF THE STATE OF CALIFORNIA

IN AND FOR THE COUNTY OF _____

IN RE THE ESTATE OF

_____

_____ /

CASE NO.

**ORDER FOR FINAL DISTRIBUTION, WAIVER OF ACCOUNT AND FOR ALLOWANCE OF COMPENSATION EXECUTOR, ATTORNEY FEES AND EXTRAORDINARY SERVICES**

This matter came on regularly for hearing on _____, 200_. Petitioner, and his/her attorney of record appeared before the Honorable _____.

**FINDINGS & ORDERS**:

The Court makes the following Findings and Orders for Final Distribution:

1. No account is required as each of the person entitled to distribution from the estate has executed and filed herein a written waiver of account or acknowledgment that the person's interest has been satisfied.

2. Petitioner has performed all of the duties required of him/her as Executor.

3. All claims against the estate paid prior to the notice prescribed by law were debts justly due, paid in good faith, the amount paid did not exceed the amount due, and were paid out of decedent's bank account.

4. No personal property taxes are due or payable by the estate.

5. Neither the decedent, nor decedent's spouse received MediCal benefits.

# Appendix 5E
## Order for Final Distribution *continued*

6. All California and federal income taxes due and payable by the estate have been paid. There are no nonresident devisees of the estate.

7. Neither the executor nor the attorney for the estate has any financial relationship with any creditor or other person who provided services to the decedent and his/her estate.

8.. The estate is of insufficient value to require the filing of a federal estate tax return and therefore, no federal estate tax return has been or will be filed for the estate.

**PROPERTY TO BE DISBURSED**

9. The following sums are authorized and shall be paid as set forth in the Petition:

Administrative Expenses to be reimbursed to the Petitioner:

| | |
|---|---|
| _____ (filing fee) | $ _____ |
| _____ (publication fee) | $ _____ |
| _____ (bond) | $ _____ |
| _____ (probate referee) | $ _____ |
| Total Administrative Expenses due to Petitioner | $ _____ |

10. The following Compensation shall be paid from the estate:

| | |
|---|---|
| _____, Attorney | $ _____ |
| _____, Attorney - Extraordinary Fees | $ _____ |
| _____, Executor | $ _____ |
| Total Compensation | $ _____ |

**TOTAL DISBURSEMENTS TO BE MADE** ............................. $ _____
(Total of Creditors claims, administrative expenses and compensation)

**TOTAL REMAINING (NET) ESTATE TO BE DISTRIBUTED**     $ _____
(Amount remaining in the estate account after dispersal listed above)

/ / / / / /

/ / / / / /

/ / / / / /

# Appendix 5E
## Order for Final Distribution *continued*

**DISTRIBUTION OF NET ESTATE TO BENEFICIARIES**

11. The remaining estate property, in the amount of $_____, shall be distributed as se in [the decedent's will/Probate Code Section 246], as follows:

| Beneficiary | Distributive Share |
|---|---|
| _____ | $_____ [1/3 amount] |
| _____ | $_____ [1/3 amount] |
| _____ | $_____ [1/3 amount] |

12. Any property acquired after the date of execution of this Petition shall be distribu follows:

| Beneficiary | Distributive Share |
|---|---|
| _____ | 1/3 |
| _____ | 1/3 |
| _____ | 1/3 |

Dated: _____            _____
                             Judge of the Superior Court

EX PARTE PETITION FOR DISCHARGE

# Appendix 5F
# Ex Parte Petition for Discharge

**DE-295/GC-395**

| ATTORNEY OR PARTY WITHOUT ATTORNEY *(Name, State Bar number, and address):* | FOR COURT USE ONLY |
|---|---|
| TELEPHONE NO.:  FAX NO. *(Optional):* | |
| E-MAIL ADDRESS *(Optional):* | |
| ATTORNEY FOR *(Name):* | |

**SUPERIOR COURT OF CALIFORNIA, COUNTY OF**
STREET ADDRESS:
MAILING ADDRESS:
CITY AND ZIP CODE:
BRANCH NAME:

☐ ESTATE ☐ CONSERVATORSHIP ☐ GUARDIANSHIP OF
*(Name):*
☐ DECEDENT ☐ CONSERVATEE ☐ MINOR

**EX PARTE PETITION FOR FINAL DISCHARGE AND ORDER**

CASE NUMBER:

1. Petitioner is the ☐ personal representative ☐ conservator ☐ guardian of the estate of the above-named decedent, conservatee, or minor. Petitioner has distributed or transferred all property of the estate as required by the final order ☐ and all preliminary orders for distribution or liquidation filed in this proceeding on *(specify date each order was filed):*

2. All required acts of distribution or liquidation have been performed as follows *(check all that apply):*
   a. ☐ All personal property, including money, stocks, bonds, and other securities, has been delivered or transferred to the distributees or transferees as ordered by the court. The receipts of all distributees or transferees are now on file or are filed with this petition. Conformed copies of all receipts previously filed are attached on Attachment 2.
   b. ☐ No personal property is on hand for distribution or transfer.
   c. ☐ Real property was distributed or transferred. The order for distribution or transfer of the real property; the personal representative's, conservator's, or guardian's deed; or both, were recorded as follows *(specify documents recorded, dates and locations of recording, and document numbers or other appropriate recording information):*

   d. ☐ No real property is on hand for distribution or transfer.
   e. ☐ No receipts are required because Petitioner is the sole distributee.
   f. ☐ The minor named above attained the age of majority on *(date):*
3. Petitioner requests discharge as personal representative, conservator, or guardian of the estate.

I declare under penalty of perjury under the laws of the State of California that the foregoing is true and correct.

Date:

_____        ▶    _____
(TYPE OR PRINT NAME OF PETITIONER)                          (SIGNATURE OF PETITIONER)

**ORDER FOR FINAL DISCHARGE**

**THE COURT FINDS** that the facts stated in the foregoing *Ex Parte Petition for Final Discharge* are true.
**THE COURT ORDERS** that *(name):*
is discharged as ☐ personal representative ☐ conservator ☐ guardian of the estate of the above-named decedent, conservatee, or minor, and sureties are discharged and released from liability for all acts subsequent hereto.

Date: _____
                                              _____
                                                         JUDICIAL OFFICER
                                              ☐ SIGNATURE FOLLOWS LAST ATTACHMENT.

Page 1 of 1

Form Adopted for Mandatory Use
Judicial Council of California
DE-295/GC-395
[New January 1, 2006]

**EX PARTE PETITION FOR FINAL DISCHARGE AND ORDER**
**(Probate—Decedents' Estates and Conservatorships and Guardianships)**

Probate Code, §§ 2100, 2627, 2631, 11753, 12250;
www.courtinfo.ca.gov

# Appendix 6A
## Affidavit—Death of Spouse

**RECORDING REQUESTED BY**

**WHEN RECORDED MAIL TO:**

---

**AFFIDAVIT - DEATH OF SPOUSE**

**STATE OF CALIFORNIA**

**COUNTY OF** _____

_____, of legal age, being duly sworn, deposes and says:

That _____, the decedent mentioned in the attached certified copy of Certificate of Death, is the same person as _____ named as one of the parties in that certain _____ dated _____ and executed by _____ to _____ as [husband and wife, community property] recorded as Instrument No. _____ on _____ Book _____ Page \_\_\_\_\_, of official records of _____ County, California, covering the following described property situated in the _____, County of _____, State of California:

[legal description]


Assessor's Parcel No:

I declare under penalty of perjury that the foregoing statement is true and correct.

_____
_____, Surviving Spouse
Dated: _____

SUBSCRIBED AND SWORN TO before me this _____ day of _____, 200\_

_____ [seal]

# Appendix 6B
## Death of Property Owner Assessor

BOE-502-D (P1) REV. 06 (12-12)

**CHANGE IN OWNERSHIP STATEMENT**
**DEATH OF REAL PROPERTY OWNER**

This notice is a request for a completed Change in Ownership Statement. Failure to file this statement will result in the assessment of a penalty.

NAME AND MAILING ADDRESS
*(Make necessary corrections to the printed name and mailing address)*

SACRAMENTO COUNTY ASSESSOR
Property Transfer Section
3701 Power Inn Road, Suite 3000
Sacramento, CA 95826-4329
(916) 875-0750

Section 480(b) of the Revenue and Taxation Code requires that the personal representative file this statement with the Assessor in each county where the decedent owned property at the time of death. **File a separate statement for each parcel of real property owned by the decedent.**

NAME OF DECEDENT | DATE OF DEATH

☐ YES  ☐ NO   Did the decedent have an interest in real property in this county? If **YES**, answer all questions. If **NO**, sign and complete the certification on page 2.

STREET ADDRESS OF REAL PROPERTY | CITY | ZIP CODE | ASSESSOR'S PARCEL NUMBER (APN)

**DESCRIPTIVE INFORMATION** ☑ *(IF APN UNKNOWN)*   **DISPOSITION OF REAL PROPERTY** ☑

☐ Copy of deed by which decedent acquired title is attached.
☐ Copy of decedent's most recent tax bill is attached.
☐ Deed or tax bill is not available; legal description is attached.

☐ Succession without a will
☐ Probate Code 13650 distribution
☐ Affidavit of death of joint tenant

☐ Decree of distribution pursuant to will
☐ Action of trustee pursuant to terms of a trust

**TRANSFER INFORMATION** ☑ Check all that apply and list details below.

☐ Decedent's spouse            ☐ Decedent's registered domestic partner

☐ Decedent's child(ren) or parent(s). If qualified for exclusion from assessment, a *Claim for Reassessment Exclusion for Transfer Between Parent and Child* must be filed (see instructions).

☐ Decedent's grandchild(ren). If qualified for exclusion from assessment, a *Claim for Reassessment Exclusion for Transfer from Grandparent to Grandchild* must be filed (see instructions).

☐ Cotenant to cotenant. If qualified for exclusion from assessment, an *Affidavit of Cotenant Residency* must be filed (see instructions).

☐ Other beneficiaries.

☐ A trust.

NAME OF TRUSTEE | ADDRESS OF TRUSTEE

List names and percentage of ownership of all beneficiaries:

| NAME OF BENEFICIARY | RELATIONSHIP TO DECEDENT | PERCENT OF OWNERSHIP RECEIVED |
|---|---|---|
|  |  |  |
|  |  |  |
|  |  |  |
|  |  |  |
|  |  |  |
|  |  |  |
|  |  |  |

☐ This property has been or will be sold prior to distribution. (Attach the conveyance document and/or court order).

NOTE: Sale of the property does not relieve the need to file a *Claim for Reassessment Exclusion for Transfer Between Parent and Child* if appropriate.

**THIS DOCUMENT IS NOT SUBJECT TO PUBLIC INSPECTION**

# Appendix 6B

## Death of Property Owner Assessor *continued*

BOE-502-D (P2) REV. 06 (12-12)

☐ YES  ☐ NO   Will the decree of distribution include distribution of an ownership interest in any legal entity that owns real property in this county? If **YES**, will the distribution result in any person or legal entity obtaining control of more than 50% of the ownership of that legal entity? ☐ YES  ☐ NO   If **YES**, complete the following section.

| NAME AND ADDRESS OF LEGAL ENTITY | NAME OF PERSON OR ENTITY GAINING SUCH CONTROL |
|---|---|
|   |   |

☐ YES  ☐ NO   Was the decedent the lessor or lessee in a lease that had an original term of 35 years or more, including renewal options? If **YES**, provide the names and addresses of all other parties to the lease.

| NAME | MAILING ADDRESS | CITY | STATE | ZIP CODE |
|---|---|---|---|---|
|   |   |   |   |   |
|   |   |   |   |   |
|   |   |   |   |   |
|   |   |   |   |   |

**MAILING ADDRESS FOR FUTURE PROPERTY TAX STATEMENTS**

| ADDRESS | CITY | STATE | ZIP CODE |
|---|---|---|---|
|   |   |   |   |

**CERTIFICATION**

I certify (or declare) under penalty of perjury under the laws of the State of California that the information contained herein is true, correct and complete to the best of my knowledge and belief.

| SIGNATURE OF PERSONAL REPRESENTATIVE ▶ | PRINTED NAME OF PERSONAL REPRESENTATIVE |
|---|---|
| TITLE | DATE |
| E-MAIL ADDRESS | DAYTIME TELEPHONE ( ) |

## INSTRUCTIONS

**IMPORTANT** — Failure to file a Change in Ownership Statement within the time prescribed by law may result in a penalty of either $100 or 10% of the taxes applicable to the new base year value of the real property or manufactured home, whichever is greater, but not to exceed five thousand dollars ($5,000) if the property is eligible for the homeowners' exemption or twenty thousand dollars ($20,000) if the property is not eligible for the homeowners' exemption if that failure to file was not willful. This penalty will be added to the assessment roll and shall be collected like any other delinquent property taxes and subjected to the same penalties for nonpayment.

Section 480 of the Revenue and Taxation Code states, in part:

(a) Whenever there occurs any change in ownership of real property or of a manufactured home that is subject to local property taxation and is assessed by the county assessor, the transferee shall file a signed change in ownership statement in the county where the real property or manufactured home is located, as provided for in subdivision (c). In the case of a change in ownership where the transferee is not locally assessed, no change in ownership statement is required.

(b) The personal representative shall file a change in ownership statement with the county recorder or assessor in each county in which the decedent owned real property at the time of death that is subject to probate proceedings. The statement shall be filed prior to or at the time the inventory and appraisal is filed with the court clerk. In all other cases in which an interest in real property is transferred by reason of death, including a transfer through the medium of a trust, the change in ownership statement or statements shall be filed by the trustee (if the property was held in trust) or the transferee with the county recorder or assessor in each county in which the decedent owned an interest in real property within 150 days after the date of death.

The above requested information is required by law. Please reference the following:

- Passage of Decedent's Property: Beneficial interest passes to the decedent's heirs effectively on the decedent's date of death. However, a document must be recorded to vest title in the heirs. An attorney should be consulted to discuss the specific facts of your situation.

- Change in Ownership: California Code of Regulations, Title 18, Rule 462.260(c), states in part that "[i]nheritance (by will or intestate succession)" shall be "the date of death of decedent."

- Inventory and Appraisal: Probate Code, Section 8800, states in part, "Concurrent with the filing of the inventory and appraisal pursuant to this section, the personal representative shall also file a certification that the requirements of Section 480 of the Revenue and Taxation Code either:
  (1) Are not applicable because the decedent owned no real property in California at the time of death
  (2) Have been satisfied by the filing of a change in ownership statement with the county recorder or assessor of each county in California in which the decedent owned property at the time of death."

- Parent/Child and Grandparent/Grandchild Exclusions: A claim must be filed within three years after the date of death/transfer, but prior to the date of transfer to a third party; or within six months after the date of mailing of a Notice of Assessed Value Change, issued as a result of the transfer of property for which the claim is filed. An application may be obtained by calling XXX-XXX-XXXX.

- Cotenant to cotenant. An affidavit must be filed with the county assessor. An affidavit may be obtained by calling XXX-XXX-XXXX.

This statement will remain confidential as required by Revenue and Taxation Code Section 481, which states in part: "These statements are not public documents and are not open to inspection, except as provided by Section 408."

# Appendix 6C
## Preliminary Change of Ownership Form

COUNTY OF SACRAMENTO, OFFICE OF THE ASSESSOR
KENNETH D. STIEGER, ASSESSOR
KATHLEEN KELLEHER, ASSISTANT ASSESSOR
PROPERTY TRANSFER DIVISION
3701 Power Inn Rd., Suite 3000, Sacramento, CA, 95826-4329
www.saccounty.net/assessor

FOR ASSISTANCE
PHONE: (916)875-0750 9 a.m. – 4 p.m.

**ASSESSOR'S USE ONLY**
Sal. Pr._____
Rel. Cd._____
Sal. Ty._____
C.E._____
Cond._____

**PRELIMINARY CHANGE OF OWNERSHIP REPORT**

[To be completed by transferee (buyer) prior to transfer of subject property in accordance with Section 480.3 of the Revenue and Taxation Code.] A Preliminary Change of Ownership Report must be filed with each conveyance in the County Recorder's Office for the county where the property is located; this particular form may be used in all 58 counties of California.

**THIS REPORT IS NOT A PUBLIC DOCUMENT**

Seller/Transferor_____
Buyer/Transferee_____
Assessor's Parcel Number (s)_____
Property Address or Location_____

Mail Tax Information to:
Name_____
Address_____
Phone_____

**NOTICE:** A lien for property taxes applies to your property on January 1 of each year for the taxes owing in the following fiscal year, July 1 through June 30. One-half of these taxes is due November 1, and one-half is due February 1. The first installment becomes delinquent on December 10, and the second installment becomes delinquent on April 10. One tax bill is mailed before November 1 to the owner of record. **IF THIS TRANSFER OCCURS AFTER JANUARY 1 AND ON OR BEFORE DECEMBER 31, YOU MAY BE RESPONSIBLE FOR THE SECOND INSTALLMENT OF TAXES DUE FEBRUARY 1.**

The property which you acquired may be subject to a supplemental assessment in an amount to be determined by the Sacramento County Assessor. For further information on your supplemental roll obligation, please call the Sacramento County Assessor at 875-0700.

### PART I: TRANSFER INFORMATION (please answer all questions)

YES NO
☐ ☐ A. Is this transfer solely between husband and wife (Addition of a spouse, death of a spouse, divorce settlement, etc.)?
☐ ☐ B. Is this transaction only a correction of the name(s) of the person(s) holding title to the property (For example, a name change upon marriage?) Please explain_____
☐ ☐ C. Is this document recorded to create, terminate, or reconvey a lender's interest in the property?
☐ ☐ D. Is this transaction recorded only as a requirement for financing purposes or to create, terminate, or reconvey a security interest (e.g. cosigner)? Please explain_____
☐ ☐ E. Is this document recorded to substitute a trustee of a trust, mortgage, or other similar document?
☐ ☐ F. Did this transfer result in the creation or a joint tenancy in which the seller (transferor) remains as one of the joint tenants?
☐ ☐ G. Does this transfer return property to the person who created the joint tenancy (original transferor)?
☐ ☐ H. Is this transfer of property:
☐ ☐   1. to a revocable trust that may be revoked by the transferor?of the ☐ Grantor, or ☐ Grantor's spouse?
☐ ☐   2. to a trust that may be revoked by the Creator/Grantor who is also a joint tenant, and which names the other joint tenant(s) as beneficiaries when the Creator/Grantor dies?
☐ ☐   3. to an irrevocable trust for the benefit of the ☐ Creator/Grantor and/or ☐ Grantor's spouse?
☐ ☐   4. to an irrevocable trust from which the property reverts to the Creator/Grantor within 12 years?
☐ ☐ I. If this property is subject to a lease, is the remaining lease term 35 years or more including written options?
☐ ☐ *J. IS THIS TRANSFER BETWEEN ☐ PARENT(S) AND CHILD(REN) OR ☐ FROM GRANDPARENT(S) TO GRANDCHILD(REN)?
☐ ☐ *K. Is this transaction to replace a principal residence by a person 55 years of age or older? Within the same County? ☐ Yes ☐ No
☐ ☐ *L. Is this transaction to replace a principal residence by a person who is severely disabled as defined by Revenue and Taxation Code Section 69.5? Within the same County? ☐ Yes ☐ No
☐ ☐ M. Did this transfer result from the death of a domestic partner currently registered with the California Secretary of State?

*If you checked yes to J, K, or L, you may qualify for a property tax reassessment exclusion, which may result in lower taxes on your property. **IF YOU DO NOT FILE A CLAIM, YOUR PROPERTY WILL BE REASSESSED.**

Please provide any other information that would help the Assessor to understand the nature of the transfer.
If the conveying document constitutes an exclusion from a change in ownership as defined in section 62 of the Revenue and Taxation Code for any reason other than those listed above, set forth the specific exclusions claimed:_____

*Please answer all questions in each section. If a question does not apply, indicate with "N/A." Sign and date at bottom of second page.*

### PART II: OTHER TRANSFER INFORMATION

A. Date of transfer if other than recording date_____
B. Type of transfer. Please check appropriate box.
☐ Purchase ☐ Foreclosure ☐ Gift ☐ Trade or Exchange ☐ Merger, Stock, or Partnership Acquisition
☐ Contract of Sale -- Date of Contract_____
☐ Inheritance --Date of Death_____ ☐ Other: Please explain:_____
☐ Creation of Lease ☐ Assignment of Lease ☐ Termination of Lease ☐ Sale/Leaseback
☐ Date Lease Began_____
☐ Original term in years (Including written options)_____
☐ Remaining term in years (including written options)_____
Monthly Payment_____ Remaining Term_____
C. Was only a partial interest in the property transferred? ☐ Yes ☐ No
If **yes**, indicate the percentage transferred_____%.

BOE-502-A (Front) Rev. 6 (8-04)

# Appendix 6C
## Preliminary Change of Ownership Form *continued*

*Please answer, to the best of your knowledge, all applicable questions, then sign and date. If a question does not apply, indicate with "N/A".*

**PART III: PURCHASE PRICE AND TERMS OF SALE**

A. CASH DOWN PAYMENT OR value of trade or exchange (excluding closing costs)    Amount $_____

B. FIRST DEED OF TRUST @____% Interest for_____years. Pymts./Mo=$_____(Prin & Int only)    Amount $_____
- ☐ FHA (__Discount Points)    ☐ Fixed Rate    ☐ New Loan
- ☐ Conventional    ☐ Variable Rate    ☐ Assumed Existing Loan Balance
- ☐ VA (__Discount Points)    ☐ All inclusive D.T. ($_____Wrapped)    ☐ Bank or Savings & Loan
- ☐ Cal-Vet    ☐ Loan Carried by Seller    ☐ Finance Company
- Balloon Payment ☐ Yes ☐ No    Due Date_____    Amount $_____

C. SECOND DEED OF TRUST @__% interest for_____years. Pymts./Mo=$_____(Prin & Int only)    Amount $_____
- ☐ Bank or Savings & Loan    ☐ Fixed Rate    ☐ New Loan
- ☐ Loan Carried by Seller    ☐ Variable Rate    ☐ Assumed Existing Loan Balance
- Balloon Payment ☐ Yes ☐ No    Due Date_____    Amount $_____

D. OTHER FINANCING: Is other financing involved not covered in (b) or (c) above? ☐ Yes ☐ No    Amount $_____
- Type_____ @_____% interest for____years. Pymts./Mo=$_____(Prin & Int only)
- ☐ Bank or Savings & Loan    ☐ Fixed Rate    ☐ New Loan
- ☐ Loan Carried by Seller    ☐ Variable Rate    ☐ Assumed Existing Loan Balance
- Balloon Payment ☐ Yes ☐ No    Due Date_____    Amount $_____

E. Was an Improvement Bond assumed by the Buyer? ☐ Yes ☐ No    Outstanding Balance: Amount $_____

F. TOTAL PURCHASE PRICE (or acquisition price, if traded or exchanged, include real estate commission if paid.)    **TOTAL ITEMS A THROUGH E** $_____

G. PROPERTY PURCHASED ☐ Through a Broker ☐ Direct from Seller ☐ From a family member ☐ Other (please explain)_____
If purchased through a broker, provide broker's name and phone number:_____
Please explain any special terms, seller concessions, or financing and any other information that would help the Assessor understand the purchase price and terms of sale._____

**PART IV: PROPERTY INFORMATION**

A. TYPE OF PROPERTY TRANSFERRED:
- ☐ Single-Family Residence    ☐ Agricultural    ☐ Timeshare
- ☐ Multiple-family residence (no. of units:_____)    ☐ Co-op/Own-your own    ☐ Manufactured Home
- ☐ Commercial/Industrial    ☐ Condominium    ☐ Unimproved lot
- ☐ Other (Description): _____

B. IS THIS PROPERTY INTENDED AS YOUR PRINCIPAL RESIDENCE? ☐ YES ☐ NO
If **yes**, enter date of occupancy ____/____, 20____ or intended occupancy ____/____, 20____
   (month) (day) (year)    (month) (day) (year)

C. IS PERSONAL PROPERTY INCLUDED IN PURCHASE PRICE (i.e. furniture, farm equipment, machinery, etc.)
(other than a manufactured home subject to local property tax)? ☐ Yes ☐ No
If **yes**, enter the value of the personal property included in the purchase price $_____ (Attach itemized list of personal property.)

D. IS A MANUFACTURED HOME INCLUDED IN PURCHASE PRICE? ☐ Yes ☐ No
If **yes**, how much of the purchase price is allocated to the manufactured home? $_____
Is the manufactured home subject to local property tax? ☐ Yes ☐ No    What is the decal number?_____

E. DOES THE PROPERTY PRODUCE INCOME? ☐ Yes ☐ No    If yes, is the income from:
☐ Lease/Rent ☐ Contract ☐ Mineral Rights ☐ Other *(please explain)*:_____

F. WHAT WAS THE CONDITION OF THE PROPERTY AT THE TIME OF SALE?
☐ Good ☐ Average ☐ Fair ☐ Poor
Please explain the physical condition of the property and provide any other information (such as restrictions. etc.) that would assist the Assessor in determining the value of the property._____

**CERTIFICATION**

| OWNERSHIP TYPE (✓) | | |
|---|---|---|
| Proprietorship ☐ | *I certify that the foregoing is true, correct and complete to the best of my knowledge and belief.* | |
| Partnership ☐ | ***This declaration is binding on each and every co-owner and/or partner.*** | |
| Corporation ☐ | | |
| Other ☐ | | |

| NAME OF NEW OWNER / CORPORATE OFFICER | TITLE |
|---|---|
| | |

| SIGNATURE OF NEW OWNER / CORPORATE OFFICER | DATE |
|---|---|
| ✍ | |

| NAME OF ENTITY *(typed or printed)* | FEDERAL EMPLOYER ID NUMBER |
|---|---|
| | |

| ADDRESS *(typed or printed)* | E-Mail address *(optional)* | DATE |
|---|---|---|
| | | |

**(Note: The Assessor may contact you for further information.)**
If a document evidencing a change of ownership is presented to the recorder for recordation without the concurrent filing of a preliminary change of ownership report, the recorder may charge an additional recording fee of twenty dollars ($20).

BOE-502-A (BACK) Rev. 6 (8-04)

# Appendix 6D
## Declaration for Collection of Compensation Owed to Spouse

**DECLARATION FOR COLLECTION OF COMPENSATION OWED TO DECEASED SPOUSE PURSUANT TO PROBATE CODE §§13600-13606**

I, _____, declare:

1. The name of the decedent is _____, who died in the City of _____, County of _____, State of California, on _____, 20___.

2. The declarant (or affiant) is the surviving spouse of the decedent;

or  2. The declarant (or affiant) is the guardian or conservator of the estate of the surviving spouse of the decedent.

3. The surviving spouse of the decedent is entitled to the earnings of the decedent under the decedent's will or by intestate succession and no one else has a superior right to the decedent's estate.

4. No proceeding is now being or has been conducted in California for administration of the decedent's estate.

5. Sections 13600 to 12606, inclusive, of the California Probate Code require that the earnings of the decedent, including compensation for unused vacation, not in excess of $15,000 net, be paid promptly to the declarant or affiant.

6. Neither the surviving spouse, nor anyone acting on behalf of the surviving spouse, has a pending request to collect compensation owned by another employer for personal services of the decedent under sections 13600 to 13606, inclusive, of the California Probate Code except the sum of $_____, which was collected from _____.

7. Neither the surviving spouse, nor anyone acting on behalf of the surviving spouse, has colleted compensation owned by another employer for personal services of the decedent under sections 13600 to 13606, inclusive, of the California Probate Code except the sum of $_____, which was collected from _____.

8. The declarant (or affiant) requests that he/she be paid the salary or other compensation owed by you for personal services of the decedent, including compensation for unused vacation, not to exceed $15,000 net (less the amount of $_____ that was previously collected.)

9. The declarant (or affiant) declares (or affirms) under penalty of perjury under the laws of the State of California that the foregoing is true and correct.

Executed at _____, California, this _____ day of _____, 20___.

_____
Declarant

# Appendix 6E
## Affidavit—Death of Joint Tenant

**RECORDING REQUESTED BY**

**WHEN RECORDED MAIL TO:**

---

### AFFIDAVIT - DEATH OF JOINT TENANT

**STATE OF CALIFORNIA**

**COUNTY OF** _____

_____, of legal age, being duly sworn, deposes and says:

That _____, the decedent mentioned in the attached certified copy of Certificate of Death, is the same person as _____ named as one of the parties in that certain _____ dated _____ and executed by _____ to _____ as joint tenants, recorded as Instrument No. _____ on _____ Book _____ Page \_\_\_\_\_, of official records of _____ County, California, covering the following described property situated in the _____ , County of _____ State of California:

[legal description]

Assessor's Parcel No:

I declare under penalty of perjury that the foregoing statement is true and correct.

_____
_____, Joint Tenant

Dated: _____

SUBSCRIBED AND SWORN TO before me this _____ day of _____, 200\_

_____    [seal]

# Appendix 6F
## Declaration under Probate Code §13100, et seq

**Affidavit Regarding Personal Property  
Under California Probate Code §§13100-13106**

The undersigned state(s) as follows:

1. _____ died on _____, 20___, in the County of _____, State of California.

2. At least forty (40) days have elapsed since the death of the decedent, as shown on the attached certified copy of the decedent's death certificate.

3. No proceeding is now being or has been conducted in California for administration of the decedent's estate.

4. The gross value of the decedent's real and personal property in California, excluding the property described in Section 13050 of the California Probate Code, does not exceed $150,000.

5. An inventory and appraisal of the real property is attached; or There is no real property in the estate.

6. The following property is to be paid, transferred or delivered to the undersigned under the provisions as set forth in California Probate Code Section 13100.
[insert description]


7. The successor(s) of the decedent, as defined in Probate Code Section 13006, is/are:

_____

8. The undersigned is/are successor(s) the decedent to the decedent's interest in the described property; or is/are authorized under California Probate Code Section 130151 to act on behalf of the successor(s) of the decedent with respect to the decedent's interest in the described property.

9. No other person has a right to the interest of the decedent in the described property.

# Appendix 6F
## Declaration under Probate Code §13100, et seq *continued*

10. The undersigned request(s) that the described property be paid, delivered or transferred to the undersigned.

I/we declare under penalty of perjury under the laws of the State of California that the foregoing is true and correct.

Dated: _____, 20_____

_____
_____
_____

[attach notarial acknowledgment for each signature]

[attach certified death certificate]

# Appendix 6G
## Spousal Property Petition Attachments

### **Attachment 7 a**

Estate of _____ (decedent)

Spousal Property Petition

Legal description of the deceased spouse's property passing to the surviving spouse:

Community Property

Undivided one-half (½) interest in the following community property:

1. Real property known as _____, Street, City, California, title of which is in the name of Jon Doe and Jane Doe, husband and wife, more fully described as:

    Lot 25, Block 87, The Plat of My Home Estates, Anytown, California, in the Parcel Map recorded on June 12, 1905, Book 10 of Maps, Page 4, records of City of Anytown, _____ County, California.

# Appendix 6G
## Spousal Property Petition Attachments *continued*

**Attachment 7 b**

Estate of Jane Doe (decedent)

Spousal Property Petition

Legal description of the deceased spouse's property confirmed to the surviving spouse:

Community Property

Undivided one-half (½) interest in the following community property:

1. Real property known as _____, Street, City, California, title of which is in the name of Jon Doe and Jane Doe, husband and wife, more fully described as:

    Lot 25, Block 87, The Plat of My Home Estates, Anytown, California, in the Parcel Map recorded on June 12, 1905, Book 10 of Maps, Page 4, records of City of Anytown, _____ County, California.

# Appendix 6G
## Spousal Property Petition Attachments *continued*

**Attachment 5a**

Estate of _____ (decedent)

Spousal Property Order

Legal description of the deceased spouse's property passing to the surviving spouse:

Community Property

Undivided one-half (½) interest in the following community property:

1. Real property known as _____, Street, City, California, title of which is in the name of Jon Doe and Jane Doe, husband and wife, more fully described as:

    Lot 25, Block 87, The Plat of My Home Estates, Anytown, California, in the Parcel Map recorded on June 12, 1905, Book 10 of Maps, Page 4, records of City of Anytown, _____ County, California.

# Appendix 6G
## Spousal Property Petition Attachments *continued*

**Attachment 5 b**

Estate of Jane Doe (decedent)

Spousal Property Order

Legal description of the deceased spouse's property confirmed to the surviving spouse:

Community Property

Undivided one-half (½) interest in the following community property:

1. Real property known as _____, Street, City, California, title of which is in the name of Jon Doe and Jane Doe, husband and wife, more fully described as:

    Lot 25, Block 87, The Plat of My Home Estates, Anytown, California, in the Parcel Map recorded on June 12, 1905, Book 10 of Maps, Page 4, records of City of Anytown, _____ County, California.

# Appendix 7A
## Federal Estate Tax Exemption Chart

Annual Federal Estate Tax Exemption Chart

| Date of Decedent's Death | Applicable Exemption Amount |
|---|---|
| 2000<br>2001 | $675,000 |
| 2002<br>2003 | 1,000,000 |
| 2004<br>2005 | $1,500,000 |
| 2006<br>2007<br>2008 | $2,000,000 |
| 2009 | $3,500,000 |
| 2010 | no federal estate tax |
| 2011 | 5,000,000 |
| 2012 | 5,120,000 |
| 2013 | 5,250,000 |
| 2014 | 5,000,000 + inflation |

# Appendix 7B
## Annual Exclusion Chart

**Annual Exclusion Chart**

| Year of Decedent's Death | Applicable Exclusion Amount |
|---|---|
| 2005<br>2006<br>2007 | $11,000 |
| 2008<br>2009<br>2010 | $12,000 |
| 2011<br>2012<br>2013 | $13,000 |
| 2014 | $14,000 |

# Appendix 7C
## Disclaimer Requirements

### Disclaimer Requirements

1) The disclaiming beneficiary must sign an agreement stating they have disclaimed the property.

2) The Disclaimer must be filed within nine (9) months of the date of death.

3) The Disclaimer must be presented to the Trustee so that the Trustee can make the appropriate transfers to the new beneficiary.

4) A Disclaimer is irrevocable.

5) A partial Disclaimer is allowed.

6) If an heir has received and accepted the property they can no longer disclaim the property.

7) The Disclaimer must be unconditional.

# Appendix 8A
## Assignment to Trust

RECORDING REQUESTED BY:

AND WHEN RECORDED MAIL TO:

---

[Space above for Recorder's Use]

## **GENERAL TRANSFER**

      THIS AGREEMENT is entered into at _____, California, by _____ and _____ of _____, _____ County, California, as the Settlors and _____ and _____, as the Trustees of the _____ Trust executed earlier this day (the "Trust").

### **RECITALS**

    A. The Settlors wish to transfer certain assets to the Trust and change certain beneficiary designations from themselves to the Trust.

    B. The Trustees are willing to accept the transfer and designations.

    C. These transfers and designations are made without consideration, and shall be subject to all the terms and provisions of the Trust. The Settlors have the right to revoke or amend the Trust, in whole or in part, at any time and from time to time.

### **TRANSFERS**

    1. The Settlors hereby grant, transfer, assign and convey to the Trustees all of the Settlors' interest in all real property, of whatever nature and wherever situated. Further, the Settlors hereby transfer and convert all real property held as joint tenants between them to community property which real property shall be designated as the Grantor's community property pursuant to terms of the Trust Agreement.

# Appendix 8A
## Assignment to Trust *continued*

   2. The Settlors hereby transfer and assign to the Trustees all of the Settlors' interests in all tangible and intangible personal property of whatever nature and wherever situated. This includes, but is not limited to, personal articles, jewelry, stocks, bonds, mutual funds, partnership interests, leases, promissory notes, savings accounts, checking accounts and motor vehicles.

   3. Notwithstanding the foregoing, no interest of either or both Settlors shall be transferred to the Trust if the interest would thereby become subject to any of the following:

      A. Any right, duty or option to purchases, repurchase, liquidate or terminate all or any portion of such interest, of any person or entity not a party to this Agreement.

      B. The right of any depository, creditor or other person or entity not a party to this Agreement to impose penalties, interest, or charges in excess of $50.00 per asset.

   4. This Agreement shall become effective as to all assets not transferred because of the preceding Paragraph 3, upon waiver or release by the third party of the rights which precluded the transfer.

   5. However, none of the Settlors' right, title or interest in life insurance policies owned by a Grantor shall be transferred to the Trustees of the Trust unless the Settlors assign a right, title, or interest in such policy or policies to the Trust in an instrument separate from this General Transfer. Similarly, the Trustees shall not be deemed a beneficiary of any such life insurance policy unless the beneficiary designation for such policy specifically names the Trustees of the Trust as a beneficiary.

   6. Further, none of the Settlors' right, title or interest in any qualified pension, profit-sharing and stock bonus plan as defined in Section 401 of the Internal Revenue Code of 1986, as amended from time to time, and any Individual Retirement Account as defined in Section 408 of such Code, shall be transferred to the Trustees of the Trust unless the Settlors assign a right, title or interest in such plans or accounts to the Trust in an instrument separate from this General Transfer. Similarly, the Trustees shall not be deemed to be a beneficiary or any such plans unless the beneficiary designation for such plans or accounts specifically names the Trustees of the Trust as a beneficiary.

   7. This Agreement shall be effective when assigned as to all assets and benefits of the Settlors unless a Grantor specifically excludes an asset from the

# Appendix 8A
## Assignment to Trust *continued*

Trust in writing. It shall also be effective prospectively to all other assets and benefits hereafter acquired by the Settlors, except as follows:

 A. This Agreement shall be ineffective as to any future acquisition of either Grantor if the Grantor, at the time of such acquisition, so provides and gives written notice thereof to the Trustees.

 B. If either Grantor gives written notice to the Trustees of the termination of this General Transfer or the Trust Agreement, this General Transfer shall not be effective to transfer that Grantor's assets to the Trust after the Trustees' receipt of such notice. Complete revocation of a Grantor's interest in the Trust shall also constitute notice of termination of this General Transfer.

 IN MUTUAL RECOGNITION of the terms and conditions hereof, the parties have executed this Agreement.

DATED: _____, 200_

_____
_____, individually and as Settlor and Trustee of _____ Trust

_____
_____, individually and as Settlor and Trustee of _____ Trust

STATE OF CALIFORNIA

COUNTY OF _____

On _____, 200_, before me, _____, personally appeared, _____ **and** _____, personally known to me or proved to me on the basis of satisfactory evidence to be the person(s) whose name(s) is/are subscribed to the within instrument and acknowledged to me that he/she/they executed the same in his/her/their authorized capacity(ies), and that by his/her/their signature(s) on the instrument the person(s), or the entity upon behalf of which the person(s) acted, executed the instrument.

WITNESS my hand and official seal.

_____

# Appendix 8B
## Trust Transfer Deed

**RECORDING REQUESTED BY
AND RETURN TO:**

**MAIL TAX STATEMENTS TO:**

---

## TRUST TRANSFER DEED

The undersigned Grantor(s) declare(s) under penalty of perjury that the following is true and correct:

DOCUMENTARY TRANSFER TAX: $___-0-___      Pursuant to R&T Code §62, transfer is exempt
                                          Grantors is/are transferring to a Revocable Trust

( ) computed on full value of property conveyed, or
( ) computed on full value less of value of liens and
    encumbrances remaining at time of sale.
( ) Unincorporated area: City of _____, and

FOR VALUABLE CONSIDERATION, receipt of which is hereby acknowledged,

hereby grants to _____, trustee of the _____ Revocable Trust, dated _____

the following described real property in the county of Sacramento, State of California:

Assessor's Parcel Number:

DATED:_____      _____
                                 [Trustee]

MAIL TAX STATEMENTS AS DIRECTED ABOVE

Appendix 8B

# Appendix 8B
## Trust Transfer Deed *continued*

STATE OF CALIFORNIA    )
                                         )
COUNTY OF _____    )

    On _____ before me, _____, personally appeared, _____ personally known to me (or proved to me on the basis of satisfactory evidence) to be the person(s) whose name(s) is/are subscribed to the within instrument and acknowledged to me that he/she/they executed the same in his/her/their authorized capacity(ies), and that by his/her/their signature(s) on the instrument the person(s), or the entity(ies) upon behalf of which the person(s) acted, executed the instrument.

(seal)                  WITNESS my hand and official seal.

_____

# Appendix 9A
## Durable Power of Attorney—Powers

### MANAGEMENT OF PROPERTY

**Introduction**. My Agent is authorized in my Agent's sole and absolute discretion from time to time and at any time, with respect to any and all of my property and interests in property, real, personal, intangible and mixed, as follows:

**Power to Sell**. To sell, transfer, assign, convey and hypothecate any and every kind of property that I may own now or in the future, real, personal, intangible and/or mixed, including without being limited to contingent and expectant interests, marital rights and any rights of survivorship incident to joint tenancy or tenancy by the entirety, on such terms and conditions and security as my Agent shall deem appropriate and to grant options with respect to sales thereof; to make such disposition of the proceeds of such sale or sales, including expending such proceeds for my benefit, as my Agent shall deem appropriate.

**Power to Buy**. To buy every kind of property, real, personal, intangible and/or mixed, on such terms and conditions as my Agent shall deem appropriate; to obtain options with respect to such purchases; to arrange for appropriate disposition, use, safekeeping and/or insuring of any such property; to buy United States Government bonds redeemable at par in payment of the federal estate tax imposed at my death; to borrow money for the purposes described herein and to secure such borrowings in such manner as my Agent shall deem appropriate; to use any credit card held in my name to make such purchases and to sign such charge slips as may be necessary to use such credit cards; to repay from any funds belonging to me any money borrowed and to pay for any purchases made or cash advanced using credit cards issued to me.

**Power to Invest**. To invest and reinvest all or any part of my property in any property or interests, including undivided interests, in property, real, personal, intangible and/or mixed, wherever located, including without being limited to securities of all kinds, stocks of corporations regardless of class, interests in limited partnerships, real estate or any interest in real estate whether or not productive at the time of investment, commodities contracts of all kinds, interests in trusts, investment trusts, whether of the open and/or closed fund types, and participation in common, collective or pooled trust funds or annuity contracts without being limited by any statute or rule of law concerning investments by fiduciaries; to sell, including short sales, and terminate any investments whether made by me or my Agent; to establish, utilize and terminate savings and money market accounts with financial institutions of all kinds; to establish, utilize and terminate accounts with securities brokers and in such accounts, to make short sales and to buy on margin and, for such purposes, my Agent may pledge any securities so held or purchased with such brokers as security for loans and advances made to the account; to

# Appendix 9A
## Durable Power of Attorney—Powers *continued*

establish, utilize and terminate agency accounts with corporate fiduciaries; to employ, compensate and terminate the services of financial and investment advisors and consultants.

**Power to Manage Real Property.** With respect to real property, including but not limited to any real property I may hereafter acquire or receive and my personal residence, my Agent is authorized to lease, sublease, release; to eject and remove tenants or other persons from, and recover possession of by all lawful means; to accept real property as a gift or as security for a loan; to collect, sue for, receive and receipt for rents and profits and to conserve, invest or utilize any and all of such rents, profits and receipts for the purposes described in this paragraph; to do any act of management and conservation, to pay, compromise, or to contest tax assessments and to apply for refunds in connection therewith; to employ laborers; to subdivide, develop, dedicate to public use without consideration, and/or dedicate easements over; to maintain, protect, repair, preserve, insure, build on, demolish, alter or improve all or any part thereof; to obtain or vacate plats and adjust boundaries; to adjust differences in valuation on exchange or partition by giving or receiving consideration; to release or partially release real property from a lien; to sell and to buy real property; to mortgage and/or convey by deed of trust or otherwise encumber any real property now or hereafter owned by me, whether acquired by me or for me by my Agent.

**Power to Manage Personal Property.** With respect to personal property; to lease, sublease, and release; to recover possession of by all lawful means; to collect, sue for, receive and receipt for rents and profits therefrom; to maintain, protect, repair, preserve, insure, alter or improve all or any part thereof; to sell and to buy the same or other personal property; to mortgage or grant deeds of trust, pledge and/or grant other security interests in any personal property or intangibles now or hereafter owned by me, whether acquired by me or for me by my Agent.

**Power to Operate Businesses.** To continue the operation of any business (including a ranch or farm) belonging to me or in which I have a substantial interest, for such time and in such manner as my Agent shall deem appropriate, including but not limited to hiring and discharging my employees, paying my employees' salaries and providing for employee benefits, employing legal, accounting, financial and other consultants; continuing, modifying, terminating, renegotiating and extending any contractual arrangements with any person, firm, association or corporation whatsoever made by me or on my behalf; executing business tax returns and other government forms required to be filed by my business, paying all business related expenses, transacting all kinds of business for me in my name and on my behalf, contributing additional capital to the business, changing the name and/or the form of the business, incorporating the business, entering into such partnership agreement with other persons as my Agent shall

# Appendix 9A
## Durable Power of Attorney—Powers *continued*

deem appropriate, joining in any plan of reorganization, consolidation or merger of such business, selling, liquidating or closing out such business at such time and on such terms as my Agent shall deem appropriate and representing me in establishing the value of any business under "Buy-out" or "Buy-Sell" agreements to which I may be a party; to create, continue or terminate retirement plans with respect to such business and to make contributions which may be required by such plans; to borrow and pledge business assets; to exercise any right, power, privilege or option I may have or may claim under any contract of partnership whether as a general, special or limited partner; to modify or terminate my interest on such terms and conditions as my Agent may deem appropriate; to enforce the terms of any such partnership agreement for my protection, whether by action, proceeding or otherwise as my Agent shall deem appropriate; to defend, submit to arbitration, settle or compromise any action or other legal proceeding to which I am a party because of my membership in such partnership.

**Power to Exercise Rights in Securities.** To exercise all rights with respect to corporate securities which I now own or may hereafter acquire, including the right to sell, grant security interests in and to buy the same or different securities; to establish, utilize and terminate brokerage accounts, including margin accounts; to make such payments as my Agent deems necessary, appropriate, incidental or convenient to the owning and holding of such securities; to receive, retain, expend for my benefit, invest and reinvest or make such disposition of as my Agent shall deem appropriate all additional securities, cash or property, including the proceeds from the sales of my securities, to which I may be or become entitled by reason of my ownership of any securities; to vote at all meetings of security holders, regular or special; to lend money to any corporation in which I hold any shares and to guarantee or endorse loans made to such corporation by third parties.

**Power to Demand and Receive.** To demand, arbitrate, settle, sue for, collect, receive, deposit, expend for my benefit, reinvest or make such other appropriate disposition of as my Agent deems appropriate, all cash, rights to the payment of cash, property, real, personal, intangible and/or mixed, debts, dues rights, accounts, legacies, bequests, devises, dividends, annuities, rights and/or benefits to which I am now or may in the future become entitled, regardless of the identity of the individual or public or private entity involved, including but not limited to benefits payable to or for my benefit by any governmental agency or body, such as Supplemental Social Security (SSI), Medicaid, Medicare, and Social Security Disability Insurance (SSDI) and for the purposes of receiving Social Security benefits, my Agent is herewith appointed my "Representative Payee"; to utilize all lawful means and methods to recover such assets and/or rights, qualify me for such benefits and claim such benefits on my behalf, and to compromise claims and grant discharges in regard to the matters described herein; to utilize all lawful means and methods to recover such assets and/or rights, qualify me for such

# Appendix 9A
## Durable Power of Attorney—Powers *continued*

benefits and claim such benefits on my behalf. The authority herein granted shall include but not be limited to converting my assets into assets that do not disqualify me from receiving such benefits or divesting me of such assets. In any divestment actions or asset conversions, I direct that my Agent, to the extent reasonably possible, avoid disrupting the dispositive provisions of any estate plan of mine known to my Agent whether or not such estate plan is embodied in a will, a trust, non-probate property, or otherwise. If it is necessary to disrupt such plan, then my Agent is directed to use my Agent's best efforts to restore such plan as and when the opportunity to do so is available to my Agent. If a transfer of cash by my Agent is made to a pecuniary legatee under my will, my Agent shall ensure that such transfer is deemed a satisfaction of such legacy, pro tanto.

**Power to Exercise Elective Share Rights.** To elect to take against any will and conveyances of any person, if appropriate; to retain any property which I have the right to elect to retain; to file petitions pertaining to the election, including petitions to extend the time for electing and petitions for orders, decrees and judgments; and to take all other actions that my Agent deems appropriate in order to effectuate the election; provided, however, that if any such actions by my Agent require the approval of any court, my Agent is authorized to seek such approval.

**Power with Respect to Employment Benefits.** To create and contribute to an employee benefit plan, including a plan for a self-employed individual, for my benefit; to elect retirement on my behalf; to select any payment option under any IRA or employee benefit plan in which I am a participant, including plans for self-employed individuals, or to change options I have selected; to make voluntary contributions to such plans; to make "roll-overs" of plan benefits into other retirement plans; to apply for and receive payments and benefits; to waive rights given to nonemployee spouses under state or federal law; to borrow money and purchase assets therefrom and sell assets thereto, if authorized by any such plans; to make revocable and irrevocable beneficiary designations and to change revocable beneficiary designations; to consent and/or waive consent in connection with the designation of beneficiaries and the selection of joint and survivor annuities under any employee benefit plan.

**Power with Respect to Bank Accounts.** To establish accounts of all kinds, including checking and savings, for me with financial institutions of any kinds, including but not limited to banks and thrift institutions; to modify, terminate, make deposits to and write checks on or make withdrawals from and grant security interests in all accounts in my name or with respect to which I am an authorized signatory, except accounts held by me in a fiduciary capacity, whether or not any such account was established by me or for me by my Agent, to negotiate, endorse or transfer any checks or other instruments with respect to any such accounts; to contract for any services rendered by any bank or financial institution,

# Appendix 9A
## Durable Power of Attorney—Powers *continued*

and to execute, on my behalf as principal, agency or power of attorney forms furnished by any bank with respect to accounts with such bank, appointing as my Agent or any other person or persons.

**Power with Respect to Safe-Deposit Boxes.** To contract with any institution for the maintenance of a safe-deposit box in my name; to have access to all safe-deposit boxes in my name or with respect to which I am an authorized signatory, whether or not the contract for such safe-deposit box was executed by me, either alone or jointly with others, or by my Agent in my name; to add to and remove from the contents of any such safe deposit box and to terminate any and all contracts for such boxes.

**Power with Respect to Legal and Other Actions.** To institute, supervise, prosecute, defend, intervene in, abandon, compromise, arbitrate, settle, dismiss, and appeal from any and all legal, equitable, judicial or administrative hearings, actions, suits, proceedings, attachments, arrests or distresses, involving me in any way, including but not limited to claims by or against me arising out of property damages or personal injuries suffered by or caused by me or under such circumstances that the loss resulting therefrom will or may be imposed on me and otherwise engage in litigation involving me, my property or any interest of mine, including any property or interest or person for which or whom I have or may have any responsibility.

**Power to Borrow Money (Including Insurance Policy Loans).** To borrow money from any lender for my account on such terms and conditions as my Agent shall deem appropriate and to secure such borrowing by the granting of security interests in any property or interests in property which I may now or hereafter own; to borrow money on any life insurance policies owned by me on my life for any purpose and to grant a security interest in such policy to secure any such loans, including the assignment and delivery of any such policies as security; and no insurance company shall be under any obligation whatsoever to determine the need for such loan or the application of the proceeds by my Agent.

**Power to Create, Fund, Amend and Terminate Trusts Solely for the Benefit of the Principal.** To execute a revocable trust agreement with such trustee or trustees as my Agent shall select, and such trust shall provide that all income and principal shall be paid to me, to some person for my benefit or applied for my benefit in such amounts as I or my Agent shall request or as the trustee or trustees shall determine, and that on my death any remaining income and principal shall be paid to my personal representative, and that the trust may be revoked or amended by me or my Agent at any time and from time to time; provided, however, that any amendment by my Agent must be such that by law or under the provisions

# Appendix 9A
## Durable Power of Attorney—Powers *continued*

of this instrument such amendment could have been included in the original trust agreement; to deliver and convey any or all of my assets to the trustee or trustees thereof; to add any or all of my assets to such a trust already in existence at the time of the creation of this instrument or created by me at any time thereafter; and for the purpose of funding any trust, to enter and remove any of my assets from any safe-deposit box of mine, whether the box is registered in my name alone or jointly with one or more persons and my Agent may be sole trustee of the trust or one of several trustees.

**Power to Fund Trusts Created by the Principal**. To transfer from time to time and at any time to the trustee or trustees of any revocable trust agreement created by me before or after the execution of this instrument, as to which trust I am, during my lifetime, a primary income and principal beneficiary, any and all of my cash, property or interests in property, including any rights to receive income from any source; and for this purpose to enter and remove from any safe-deposit box of mine, whether the box is registered in my name alone or jointly with one or more other persons, any of my assets and to execute such instruments, documents and papers to effect the transfers described herein as may be necessary, appropriate, incidental or convenient; to make such transfers absolutely in fee simple or for my lifetime only with the remainder or reversion of the property so transferred, remaining in me so that such property will be disposed of at my death by my will or by the intestacy laws of the state in which I shall die a resident.

**Power to Withdraw Funds from Trusts**. To withdraw and/or receive the income or corpus of any trust over which I may have a right of receipt or withdrawal; to request and receive the income or corpus of any trust with respect to which the trustee thereof has the discretionary power to make distributions to or on my behalf, and to execute and deliver to such trustee or trustees a receipt and release or similar document for the income or corpus so received; to exercise in whole or in part, release or let lapse any power of appointment held by me, whether general or special, or any power of amendment or revocation under any trust including any trust with respect to which I may exercise any such power only with the consent of another person, even if my Agent is such other person, whether or not such power of appointment was created by me, subject, however, to any restrictions on such exercise imposed on my Agent and set forth in other provisions of this instrument.

**Power to Renounce and Resign from Fiduciary Positions**. To renounce any fiduciary position to which I have been or may be appointed or elected, including but not limited to personal representative, trustee, guardian, attorney-in-fact, and officer or director of a corporation; and any governmental or political office or position to which I have been or may be elected or appointed; to resign any such positions in which capacity I am presently serving; to file an

# Appendix 9A
## Durable Power of Attorney—Powers *continued*

accounting with a court of competent jurisdiction or settle on a receipt and release or such other informal method as my Agent shall deem appropriate.

**Power to Disclaim, Renounce, Release, or Abandon Property Interests**. To renounce and disclaim any property or interest in property or powers to which for any reason and by any means I may become entitled, whether by gift, testate or intestate succession; to release or abandon any property or interest in property or powers which I may now or hereafter own, including any interests in or rights over trusts, including the right to alter, amend, revoke or terminate, and to exercise any right to claim an elective share in any estate or under any will. In exercising such discretion, my Agent shall consider any reduction in estate or inheritance taxes that may be due on my death, and the effect of such renunciation or disclaimer on persons interested in my estate and persons who would receive the renounced or disclaimed property; provided, however, that my Agent shall make no disclaimer that is expressly prohibited by other provisions of this instrument.

**Power with Respect to Insurance**. To purchase, maintain, surrender, collect, or cancel (a) life insurance or annuities of any kind on my life or the life of any one in whom I have an insurable interest, (b) liability insurance protecting me and my estate against third party claims, (c) hospital insurance, medical insurance, Medicare supplement insurance, custodial care insurance, and disability income insurance for me or any of my dependents, and (d) casualty insurance insuring assets of mine against loss or damage due to fire, theft or other commonly insured risk; to pay all insurance premiums, to select any options under such policies; to increase coverage under any such policy, to borrow against any such policy, to pursue all insurance claims on my behalf, to adjust insurance losses, and the foregoing powers shall apply to private and public plans, including but not limited to Medicare, Medicaid, SSI and Worker's Compensation; to decrease coverage under or cancel any of the policies described herein; to receive and make such disposition of the cash value on termination of any such policy as my Agent shall deem appropriate.

**Power with Respect to Taxes**. To represent me in all tax matters; to prepare, sign, and file federal, state, and/or local income, gift and other tax returns of all kinds, including, where appropriate, joint returns, FICA returns, payroll tax returns, claims for refunds, requests for extensions of time to file returns and/or pay taxes, extensions and waivers of applicable periods of limitation, protests and petitions to administrative agencies or courts, including the tax court, regarding tax matters, and any and all other tax related documents, including but not limited to consents and agreements under Section 2032A of the Internal Revenue Code or any successor section thereto and consents to split gifts, closing agreements and any power of attorney form required by the Internal Revenue Service and/or any state and/or local taxing authority with respect to any tax year; to pay taxes due, collect

# Appendix 9A
## Durable Power of Attorney—Powers *continued*

and make such disposition of refunds as my Agent shall deem appropriate, post bonds, receive confidential information and contest deficiencies determined by the Internal Revenue Service and/or any state and/or local taxing authority; to exercise any elections I may have under federal, state or local tax law; to allocate any generation-skipping tax exemption to which I am entitled, and generally to represent me or obtain professional representation for me in all tax matters and proceedings of all kinds and for all periods before all officers of the Internal Revenue Service and state and local authorities and in any and all courts; to engage, compensate and discharge attorneys, accountants and other tax and financial advisers and consultants to represent and/or assist me in connection with any and all tax matters involving or in any way related to me or any property in which I have or may have an interest or responsibility; and on my behalf to execute IRS Form 2848 and appoint my Agent or any suitable person selected by my Agent as my representative before the Internal Revenue Service.

**Power to Provide Support to Others**. To support and/or continue to support any person whom I have undertaken to support or to whom I may owe an obligation of support, in the same manner and in accordance with the same standard of living as I may have provided in the past, adjusted if necessary by circumstances and inflation, including but not limited to the payment of real property taxes, payments on loans secured by my residence, maintenance of my residence, food, clothing and shelter, health care, dental and psychiatric care, normal vacations and travel expenses and education, including education at vocational and trade schools, training in music, stage, arts and sports, special training provided at institutions for the mentally or physically handicapped, undergraduate and graduate study in any field at public or private universities, colleges or other institutions of higher learning, and in providing for such education to pay for tuition, books and incidental charges made by the educational institutions, travel costs to and from such institutions, room and board, and a reasonable amount of spending money.

**Power to Make Loans**. To lend money and property at such interest rate, if any, and on such terms and conditions, and with such security, if any, as my Agent may deem appropriate; to renew, extend, and modify any such loans or loans that I may have previously made; to guarantee the obligations of any such person; to consent to the renewal, extension and modification of such obligations; provided, however, that my Agent shall not lend my money or property to my Agent, but this provision shall not be interpreted to require that any loan made by me personally, and not on my behalf by any agent, to my Agent, must be repaid earlier than (i) its scheduled maturity date or (ii) in case of a demand note, that demand for payment be made unreasonably.

# Appendix 9B
## Durable Power of Attorney — Care & Control of Person

### CARE AND CONTROL OF THE PERSON

**Introduction.** My Agent is authorized in my Agent's sole and absolute discretion from time to time and at any time, with respect to the control and management of my person, as follows:

**Power to Provide for Principal's Support.** To do all acts necessary for maintaining my customary standard of living, to provide a place of residence by purchase, lease or other arrangement, or by payment of the operating costs of my existing place of residence, including interest, amortization payments, repairs and taxes, to provide normal domestic help for the operation of my household, to provide clothing, transportation, medicine, food and incidentals, and if necessary to make all necessary arrangements, contractual or otherwise, for me at any hospital, hospice, nursing home, convalescent home or similar establishment, or in my own residence should I desire it, and to assure that all of my essential needs are provided for at such a facility or in my own residence, as the case may be. If in the judgment of my Agent I will never be able to return to my place of residence from a hospital, hospice, nursing home, convalescent home or similar establishment, to lease, sublease or assign my interest as lessee in any lease or protect or sell or otherwise dispose of my place of residence, investing the proceeds of any such sale as my Agent deems appropriate, for such price and on such terms, conditions and security, if any, as my Agent shall deem appropriate; and to store and safeguard or sell for such price and on such terms, conditions and security, if any, as my Agent shall deem appropriate or otherwise dispose of any items of tangible personal property remaining in my place of residence which my Agent believes I will never need again, and pay all costs thereof. As an alternative to such storage and safeguarding, to transfer custody and possession, but not title, for such storage and safekeeping of any such tangible personal property of mine to the person, if any, named in my will or any trust as the recipient of such property entitled to receive such property on my death.

**Power to Provide for Recreation and Travel.** To provide opportunities for me to engage in recreational and sports activities, including travel, as my health permits.

**Power to Provide for Spiritual or Religious Needs.** To provide for the presence and involvement of religious clergy or spiritual leaders in my care, provide them access to me at all times, maintain my memberships in religious or spiritual organizations or arrange for membership in such groups, and enhance my opportunities to derive comfort and spiritual satisfaction from such activities, including religious books, tapes and other materials.

**Power to Provide for Companionship.** To provide for such

# Appendix 9B
## Durable Power of Attorney—Care & Control of Person *continued*

companionship for me as will meet my needs and preferences at a time when I am disabled or otherwise unable to arrange for such companionship myself.

**Power to Make Advance Funeral Arrangements.** To make advance arrangements for the disposition of my remains and such other related arrangements as my Agent shall deem appropriate.

**Power to Make Donation of Anatomical Gifts.** My agent may make arrangements for the donation of anatomical gifts as is deemed appropriate.

**Power to Change Domicile.** To establish a new residency or domicile for me, from time to time and at any time, within or without the state, and within or without the United States, for such purposes as my Agent shall deem appropriate, including but not limited to any purpose for which this instrument was created.

# Appendix 9C
## Durable Power of Attorney — Incidental Provisions

### INCIDENTAL POWERS

**Introduction.** In connection with the exercise of the powers and discretions herein described, my Agent is fully authorized and empowered to perform any acts and things and to execute and deliver any documents, instruments, affidavits, certificates, and papers necessary or appropriate, to such exercise or exercises, including without limitation the following:

**Resort to Courts.** To seek on my behalf and at my expense:

(a) a declaratory judgment from any court of competent jurisdiction interpreting the validity of this instrument and any of the acts authorized by this instrument, but such declaratory judgment shall not be necessary in order for my Agent to perform any act authorized by this instrument.

(b) a mandatory injunction requiring compliance with my Agent's instructions by any person, organization, corporation, or other entity obligated to comply with instructions given by me.

(c) actual and punitive damages and the recoverable costs, fees and expenses of such litigation, against any person, organization, corporation or other entity obligated to comply with instructions given by me who negligently or willfully fails or refuses to follow such instructions.

**Hire and Fire - All Personnel.** To employ, compensate and discharge such domestic, health care and professional personnel including lawyers, accountants, doctors, nurses, brokers, financial consultants, advisors, consultants, companions, servants and employees as my Agent deems appropriate.

**Sign Documents and Incur Costs in Implementing the Agent's Instructions.** To sign, execute, endorse, seal, acknowledge, deliver and file or record instruments and documents, including but not limited to contracts, agreements and conveyances of real and personal property, instruments granting and perfecting security instruments and obligations, orders for the payment of money, receipts, releases, waivers, elections, vouchers, consents, satisfactions and certificates. In addition, any Agent of mine who has the authority to incur costs on my behalf may render the bills for such costs to any Agent of mine who has been granted the authority to pay such costs or to any trustee of any revocable living trust of mine, or guardian, committee or conservator who has authority to pay such costs I request that costs be paid promptly. Any recipient thereof (i.e. my Agent with authority to pay or my trustee) shall promptly such costs.

**Payment of Medical Expenses.** My Agent is directed to pay, or cause to be paid, all bills incurred and presented by any agent representing me under a Durable Power of Attorney for Health Care.

**Borrow, Spend, Liquidate, Secure**. To expend my funds and to liquidate my property or to borrow money to produce such funds and to secure any such borrowings with security interests in any property, real, personal, or intangible that I may now or hereafter own.

**Power to Do Miscellaneous Acts**. To open, read, respond to and redirect my mail; to represent me before the U.S. Postal Service in all matters relating to mail service; to establish, cancel, continue or initiate my membership in organizations and associations of all kinds, to take and give or deny custody of all of my important documents, including but not limited to my will, codicils, trust agreements, deeds, leases, life insurance policies, contracts and securities and, bearing in mind the confidential nature of such documents, to disclose or refuse to disclose such documents; to obtain and release or deny information or records of all kinds relating to me, to any interest of mine or to any person for whom I am responsible; to house or provide for housing, support and maintenance of any animals or other living creatures that I may own and to contract for and pay the expenses of their proper veterinary care and treatment; and if the care and maintenance of such animals or other living creatures shall become unreasonably expensive or burdensome in my Agent's opinion, to irrevocably transfer such animals to some person or persons willing to care for and maintain them.

## THIRD PARTY RELIANCE

**Introduction**. For the purpose of inducing all persons, organizations, corporations and entities including but not limited to any physician, hospital, nursing home, health care provider, bank, broker, custodian, insurer, lender, transfer agent, taxing authority, governmental agency, or other party (all of whom will be referred to in this Article as a "Person") to act in accordance with the instructions of my Agent as authorized in this instrument, I hereby represent, warrant and agree that:

**Third Party Liability for Revocation and Amendments**. If this instrument is revoked or amended for any reason, I, my estate, and my executor or administrator will hold any person, organization, corporation or entity, hereinafter referred to in the aggregate as "Person", harmless from any loss suffered, or liability incurred by such Person in acting in accordance with the instructions of my Agent acting under this instrument prior to the receipt by such Person of actual written notice of any such revocation or amendment.

# Appendix 9C
## Durable Power of Attorney—Incidental Provisions *continued*

**Agent Has Power to Act Alone.** The powers conferred on my Agent by this instrument may be exercised by my Agent alone and my Agent's signature or act under the authority granted in this instrument may be accepted by persons as fully authorized by me and with the same force and effect as if I were personally present, competent, and acting on my own behalf. Consequently, all acts lawfully done by my Agent hereunder are done with my consent and shall have the same validity and effect as if I were personally present and personally exercised the powers myself, and shall inure to the benefit of and bind me and my estate and my executor or administrator.

**When Less Than the Required Number of Agents May Act.** If this instrument appoints more than one person to act concurrently as my Agent, and under the terms of this instrument such persons may act only by the consent of all or by the consent of a specified number of such Agents, then:

(a) on the death of one or more of such Agents, or

(b) on the legal and/or mental incapacity of one or more of such Agents (in the opinion and judgment of my remaining Agents, supported by the written opinion of a physician licensed to practice in any state of the United States), or

(c) if the consent of the required number of Agents cannot readily be obtained within the time reasonably available for emergency action or other action necessary to implement the purposes of this instrument,

actions taken with the consent of less than all or less than the specified number of the surviving Agents, as the case may be, shall be valid and enforceable acts under this instrument. Any party dealing with any person named as Agent, including any person named as an Alternate Agent hereunder, may rely conclusively on an affidavit or certificate under penalty of perjury of such Agent that if the consent of any other person or persons named as Agent herein is required in order for affiant or declarant to act, that:

(i) affiant or declarant has been given the requisite number of such consents and such consents continue to be effective, or

(ii) because of the death, legal or mental incapacity of one or more such other Agents, affiant or declarant either may act alone or has the consent of those Agents as are not deceased or legally or mentally incapacitated, or

(iii) the consent of other Agents is not required if such consent cannot be

# Appendix 9C
## Durable Power of Attorney—Incidental Provisions *continued*

readily obtained within the time reasonably available for emergency action or other action necessary to implement the purposes of this instrument.

**No Liability to Third Parties for Reliance on Agent.** No Person who relies in good faith on the authority of my Agent under this instrument shall incur any liability to me, my estate or my executor or administrator. In addition, no Person who acts in reliance on any representations my Agent may make as to (a) the fact that my Agent's powers are then in effect, (b) the scope of my Agent's authority granted under this instrument, (c) my competency at the time this instrument is executed, (d) the fact that this instrument has not been revoked or amended, or (e) the fact that my Agent continues to serve as my Agent shall incur any liability to me, my estate or my executor or administrator for permitting my Agent to exercise any such authority, nor shall any Person who deals with my Agent be responsible to determine or insure the proper application of funds or property by my Agent. Any party dealing with any Person named as Agent (including any Person named as an Alternate Agent hereunder) may rely on as conclusively correct an affidavit or certificate of such Agent that (i) my Agent's powers are then in effect, (ii) the action my Agent desires to take is within the scope of my Agent's authority granted under this instrument, (iii) I was competent at the time this instrument was executed, (iv) this instrument has not been revoked, and/or (v) my Agent continues to serve as my Agent.

**Alternate Agent May Give Affidavit or Certificate That He or She Currently Serves.** Any party dealing with any person named as Alternate Agent hereunder may rely on as conclusively correct an affidavit or certificate under penalties of perjury of such Alternate Agent that those persons named as prior Agents are no longer serving.

**Affidavits or Certificates Given by Agent Bind Principal.** No Person who relies on any affidavit or certificate under penalties of perjury that this instrument specifically authorizes my Agent to execute and deliver to such person shall incur any liability to me, my estate or my executor or administrator for permitting my Agent to exercise any such authority, nor shall any Person who deals with my Agent be responsible to determine or insure the proper application of funds or property by my Agent.

**Authorization to Release Information to Agent.** All Persons from whom my Agent may request information regarding me, my personal or financial affairs or any information which I am entitled to receive are hereby authorized to provide such information to my Agent without limitation and are released from any legal liability whatsoever to me, my estate or my executor or administrator for complying with my Agent's requests.

# Appendix 9C
## Durable Power of Attorney—Incidental Provisions *continued*

**Authorization to Release Medical Information.** I hereby authorize all physicians and psychiatrists who have treated me, and all other providers of health care, including hospitals, to release to my Agent all information or photocopies of any records which my Agent may request. If I am incapacitated at the time my Agent shall request such information, all Persons are authorized to treat any such request for information by my Agent as the request of my legal representative and to honor such requests on that basis. I hereby waive all privileges which may be applicable to such information and records and to any communication pertaining to me and made in the course of any confidential relationship recognized by law. My Agent may also disclose such information to such Persons as my Agent shall deem appropriate.

# Appendix 9D
## Durable Power of Attorney — Health Care Powers

**HEALTH CARE**

**Introduction.** My Agent is authorized in my Agent's discretion from time to time and at any time to exercise the authority described below relating to matters involving my health care. In exercising the authority granted to my Agent herein, I first direct my Agent to try to discuss with me the specifics of any proposed decision regarding my health care and treatment if I am able to communicate in any manner, however rudimentary. If I am unable to consent, or refuse to consent, to health care, and my Agent cannot determine the choice I would want made under the circumstances, my Agent shall give, withhold, modify, or withdraw such consent for me based on any health care choices that I may previously have expressed on the subject while competent, whether under this instrument or otherwise. If my Agent cannot determine the treatment choice I would want made under the circumstances, then my Agent shall make such choice for me based on what my Agent believes to be in my best interests. Accordingly, my Agent is authorized as follows:

**Power of Access and Disclosure of Medical Records and Other Personal Information.** To request, receive and review any information, verbal or written, regarding my personal affairs or my physical or mental health, including medical and hospital records, and to execute any releases or other documents that may be required to obtain such information, and to disclose or deny such information to such persons, organizations, firms or corporations as my Agent shall deem appropriate.

**Power to Employ and Discharge Health Care Personnel.** To employ and discharge health care personnel including physicians, psychiatrists, dentists, nurses, and therapists as my Agent shall deem necessary for my physical, mental and emotional well-being, and to pay them, or cause them to be paid, reasonable compensation.

**Power to Give, Withhold, or Withdraw Consent to Health Care Treatment.** To give, withhold, withdraw or modify consent to any health care procedures, tests or treatments, including surgery; to arrange for my hospitalization, convalescent care, hospice or home care; to summon paramedics or other emergency medical personnel and seek emergency treatment for me, as my Agent shall deem appropriate; to give, withhold, withdraw or modify consent to such procedures, tests and treatments, as well as hospitalization, convalescent care, hospice or home care which I or my Agent may have previously allowed or consented to or which may have been implied due to emergency conditions. My Agent's decisions should be guided by taking into account (1) the provisions of this instrument, (2) any reliable evidence of preferences that I may have expressed on the subject whether before or after the execution of this document, (3) what my

# Appendix 9D
## Durable Power of Attorney—Health Care Powers *continued*

Agent believes I would want done in the circumstances if I were able to express myself, and (4) any information given to my Agent by the physicians treating me as to my health care diagnosis and prognosis and the intrusiveness, pain, risks, and side effects of the treatment.

**Power to Give or Withhold Consent to Psychiatric Treatment.** To arrange, on the execution of a certificate by two independent psychiatrists who have examined me and in whose opinions I am in immediate need of hospitalization because of mental disorder, alcoholism or drug abuse, for my voluntary admission to an appropriate hospital or institution for treatment of the diagnosed problem or disorder; to arrange for private psychiatric and psychological treatment for me; and to revoke, modify, withdraw or change consent to such hospitalization, institutionalization or private treatment which I or my Agent may have previously given. The consent of my Agent to my hospitalization for psychiatric help, alcoholism or drug abuse shall have the same legal effect, subject to applicable local law, as a voluntary admission made by me.

**Power to Maintain Me in My Residence.** To take whatever steps are necessary or advisable to enable me to remain in my personal residence as long as it is reasonable under the circumstances. I realize that my health may deteriorate so that it becomes necessary to have round-the-clock nursing care if I am to remain in my personal residence, and I direct my Agent to obtain such care, including any equipment that might assist in such care, as is reasonable under the circumstances. Specifically, I do not want to be hospitalized or put in a convalescent or similar home as long as it is reasonable to maintain me in my personal residence.

**Power to Exercise My Health Care Right of Privacy.** To exercise all state and federal rights that I may have, including but not limited to my right of privacy to make decisions regarding my health care even though the exercise of those rights might hasten my death or be contrary to conventional health care advice.

**Power to Authorize Relief from Pain.** To consent to and arrange for the administration of pain-relieving drugs of any kind, or other surgical or health care procedures calculated to relieve my pain, including unconventional pain-relief therapies which my Agent believes may be helpful to me, even though such drugs or procedures may lead to permanent physical damage, addiction or even hasten the moment of, but not intentionally cause, my death.

**Power to Grant Releases.** To grant, in conjunction with any instructions given under this Article, releases to hospital staff, physicians, nurses and other health care providers who act in reliance on instructions given by my Agent or who render written opinions to my Agent in connection with any matter described in this

# Appendix 9D
## Durable Power of Attorney—Health Care Powers *continued*

Article from all liability for damages suffered or to be suffered by me; to sign documents titled or purporting to be a "Refusal to Permit Treatment" and "Leaving Hospital Against Medical Advice" as well as any necessary waivers of or releases from liability required by any hospital or physician to implement my wishes regarding medical treatment or nontreatment.

### REFUSAL OF HEALTH CARE TREATMENT

**Introduction and Recitals**. I wish to live and enjoy life as long as possible. However, I do not wish to receive health care treatment that will only postpone the moment of my death from an incurable and terminal condition or prolong an irreversible coma. Therefore, my Agent is authorized to:

1) direct that health care which will only postpone the moment of my death or prolong my irreversible coma, whether or not such treatment is directed toward my terminal condition, be withheld or, if previously begun, to direct that such treatment be withdrawn whether or not such treatment is related to my terminal condition or irreversible coma; and

2) request, require or consent to the writing of a "No-Code" or "Do Not Resuscitate" order by any of my attending physician; and

3) sign on my behalf any documents necessary to carry out the authorizations described in this instrument, including waivers or releases of liability required by any health care provider; and

4) order whatever is appropriate to keep me as comfortable and free of pain as is reasonably possible, including the administration of pain relieving drugs of any kind or other surgical or medical procedures calculated to relieve my pain, including unconventional pain-relief therapies which my Agent believes may be helpful, even though such drugs or procedures may lead to permanent physical damage, addiction or hasten the moment of, but not intentionally cause, my death.

I desire that my wishes be carried out through the authority given to my Agent by this instrument despite any contrary feelings, beliefs or opinions of members of my family, relatives, friends, conservator or guardian.

In exercising the authority given to my Agent herein, my Agent shall first follow the instructions of this document and any other subsequent instructions, oral or written, that I may give my Agent while I am competent. Notwithstanding such instruction, if my Agent cannot determine the treatment choice I would want made under the circumstances, then my Agent should make such choice for me based on

# Appendix 9D
## Durable Power of Attorney—Health Care Powers *continued*

what my Agent believes to be in my best interest.

If no Agent designated in this instrument is available or able or willing to serve as my Agent or to exercise the powers granted in this Article, then I request that this instrument be given the same force and effect as any other written expression of intent under applicable law.

It is my intention that this instrument, both as a self-executing document and a delegation of power to my Agent, shall be deemed an exercise of all rights and interests that I may have under the United States Constitution, the constitution of the state of my domicile, state and federal laws, rules, regulations and decisions, judicial and administrative, to refuse health care treatment, including but not limited to artificial nutrition and artificial hydration.

I authorize my Agent to establish a new residency or domicile for me, from time to time and at any time, within or without the state, and within or without the United States, for the purpose of exercising effectively the powers granted to my Agent in this Article.

In addition, if I have been in an irreversible coma, as defined above, for sixty (60) days or more, or if because of my terminal condition as defined above it is no longer possible to nourish me without severe discomfort, and the two physicians described above also conclude that the nourishment will not improve my physical condition and I will not experience pain as a result of the withdrawal of nutrition and hydration, then my Agent may require that procedures used to provide me with nutrition and hydration, including, by way of example only, all forms of intravenous and parenteral feeding, all forms of tube feeding and misting, be withheld or, if previously instituted, to require that they be withdrawn.

In addition, my Agent is authorized to receive and retain custody of any instrument signed by me that is effective under law to require the withdrawal or withholding of life sustaining treatment or procedures, including but not limited to an "Advance Health Care Directive" and if the circumstances described above authorizing my Agent to require that life sustaining treatment be withheld or withdrawn have occurred, then as an alternative or supplemental act, I authorize my Agent to deliver to my physicians, health care providers and other appropriate recipients, this instrument and any other writings and an Advance Health Care Directives signed by me that express my desire under the circumstances to require the withholding or withdrawal of futile, health care treatment, and to instruct such physicians, health care providers and other appropriate recipients to act immediately in accordance with my desires.

# Appendix 10A
## Trustee Accounting (Spreadsheet)

**PROBATE ACCOUNTING - CORAL LEIGH SHORES**   (Married - Distribution to Husband)

**INVENTORY**                     **DATE OF DEATH VALUE**

| | | |
|---|---|---|
| REAL PROPERTY | $400,000 | (Decedent's One-Half) |
| 2010 Buick Centruy | 2,500 | (Decedent's One-Half) |
| 1994 Toyota Pickup | 500 | (Decedent's One-Half) |
| Personal Property | 25,000 | (Distributed or sold) |
| IRA | 20,000 | |
| Bank Account | 500 | (Decedent's One-Half) |

**Total Inventory/Assets**         $448,500

**ESTATE EXPENSES**

| | |
|---|---|
| Burial Expenses | 20,000 |
| Credit Card | 2,000 |

**Total Expenses**                 **22,000**

Net Estate to be Transferred to Spouse
Less Debts

428,500
-22,000

**Total to Spouse**                **406,500**

# Appendix 10A
## Trustee Accounting (Spreadsheet) *continued*

**ESTATE ACCOUNTING - CORAL LEIGH SHORES)**     (Widowed - Distribution to 2 Children)

| INVENTORY | DATE OF DEATH VALUE | |
|---|---:|---|
| REAL PROPERTY | $800,000 | Sold |
| 2010 Buick Century | 5,000 | Sold |
| 1994 Toyota Pickup | 1,000 | Sold |
| Personal Property | 5,000 | Distributed/Sold |
| IRA | 20,000 | Liquidated |
| Bank Account | 1,000 | Liquidated |
| CD Account | 20,233 | Liquidated |
| Gain on Sale of House | 10,328 | |
| Interest - checking account | 85 | |
| **Total Inventory/Assets** | **$862,646** | |

**ESTATE EXPENSES**

| | | |
|---|---:|---|
| Burial Expenses | 20,000 | |
| Credit Card | 2,000 | |
| **Total Expenses** | **22,000** | |
| Net Estate to Distributed to Children | | |
| Less Debts | | |
| **Total Net Estate** | **840,646** | |
| One-half to each child (FMV) | **425,823** | |

# Appendix 10B
## Petition for Instructions

_____
_____
_____
_____

Telephone: _____
Facsimile: _____

Attorney for Petitioner
_____

SUPERIOR COURT OF CALIFORNIA

COUNTY OF _____

In Re: 

_____
REVOCABLE TRUST DATED


_____ /

CASE NO:

PETITION FOR INSTRUCTIONS

[Probate Code §§17200, 9883]
Hearing Date: _____
Time: _____
Dept: _____

**FORMATION AND TERMS OF THE TRUST**

_____, Successor Trustee, petitions and alleges as follows:

1. _____ created a revocable living trust on _____, entitled "The _____ Trust."

Said Trust allocated the real property located at _____, _____ [city/town] _____ County, California, Assessor's Parcel _____ Number: _____ and as referenced in the Schedule of Trust Assets. A copy of the Trust is attached hereto as Exhibit A.

The Trust also stated that the all property listed in Schedule of Trust Assets and all other real or personal property in the Settlor's name henceforth such assets shall and will belong to The Trust of _____.

On _____, _____ executed a Grant Deed transferring said property into said trust and the Grant Deed was recorded in Book _____ on page _____ [or as Instrument No. _____] in the records of _____ County. A

# Appendix 10B
## Petition for Instructions *continued*

copy of that Deed is attached hereto as Exhibit B.

  On _____. _____ refinanced his/her home. As part of that refinance he/she was required to take the property out of the Trust and grant it back to him/herself as a single man/woman. That deed which was recorded in Book No. _____ at Page \_\_\_\_ and is attached hereto as Exhibit C. After the loan was completed _____ neglected to transfer the property back into the Trust.

  2. On _____. 20\_\_, _____ died in _____ County, California. A certified copy of the death certificate is attached hereto as Exhibit D.

  3. Petitioner is informed and believes that it was an oversight that the real estate located at _____, _____, California was not transferred back into her revocable trust after the refinance took place in 20\_\_.

  Petitioner believes that it was the intention of the Trustor to dispose of this property as set forth in the terms of The _____Trust. Moreover, the probate of decedents' pour-over will would accomplish the same objective sought through this petition, namely to transfer title from the decedents' name(s) to that of petitioner as Successor Trustee of the Trust.

  4. The original will of _____ has been lodged with the Court and a copy is attached hereto as Exhibit E.

  5. In <u>Estate of Heggstad</u>, 16 Cal.App.4th 943 (1993) the settlor of a revocable living trust similarly failed to execute and record a deed to transfer title to real property to the settlor's trust. However, the declaration of trust had a schedule of assets attached with a declaration that he held the property as trustee of the trust. The court held that the declaration of trust alone was sufficient to transfer title to the property to the trust.

  6. As part of the Trust the deceased also executed a General Transfer/Assignment on _____, _____. Said Assignment states:

  "The undersigned, as settlor of "The _____ Trust ", declare that all of the following assets and property, whether individually, particularly, or generally as hereafter described, whether presently owned or hereafter acquired by settlor, are hereby forever conveyed, transferred, assigned and deed over to the trustee of "The _____

# Appendix 10B
## Petition for Instructions *continued*

Trust" to form a part of the trust estate, to be held by the said trustee for the use and purpose and upon the terms and conditions of said trust:

> All of my tangible and intangible personal property including without limitation all household furniture and furnishings, bank accounts, certificates of deposit, mutual and money market funds of all kind, securities, agency and custody accounts, notes, **real estate wherever located** (including mortgages, land contract interest, leaseholds, and mineral interests), jewelry, antiques, and any and all other assets wherever located."

A copy of the General Assignment is attached hereto as Exhibit F.

7. The following are the names and addresses of the trust beneficiaries:

   A. _____, _____;

   B. _____, _____;

   C. _____, _____.

### REQUEST FOR INSTRUCTIONS

8. Upon the death of the Settlor, the Trust dated _____ provides for distribution as follows:

   A. [Insert language regarding appointment of trustee and executor.]

   B. [Insert language regarding distribution of estate.]

   C. The trustor/executor is given power to set up any trust needed to administer my wishes and will have all authority as far as the investment decision within that trust."

9. The trust instrument identifies the assets referenced herein as trust property. Without an order from the court as requested in this petition, a formal probate proceeding will be required to transfer title from the decedent's name to the decedent's estate and then to the trust. The purpose of this petition is to achieve the identical result but without the expense and delay of a probate proceeding.

WHEREFORE, Petitioner request that the Court issue the following orders:

1. The real property located at _____, _____, California described

# Appendix 10B
## Petition for Instructions *continued*

as "_____ [insert legal description or attach]

    2. The court appoints Petitioner _____ to act as Successor Trustee of The _____ Trust and to perform all duties necessary to complete the transfer of assets to the beneficiaries as set forth in The _____ Trust. The following real property shall be considered to be part of the Trust Estate passing under The _____ Trust.

[Insert legal description or reference to description on attachment]

    3. For such other orders and directions as may be proper.

Dated: _____       _____
                                                    Nancy Noe-Nonsense, Attorney for Petitioner

### VERIFICATION

I, _____, declare that:

I am the Petitioner, in the above entitled matter; I have read the foregoing Petition for Instructions, and know the contents thereof; the same is true of my own knowledge, except as to those matters which are therein stated upon my information or belief, and as to those matters, I believe to be true.

I declare under penalty of perjury that the foregoing is true and correct and that this Verification was executed on_____, at _____, California.

                            _____, Petitioner and Successor Trustee

# Glossary

**Abatement**
The process of determining the distribution of bequests as directed by the decedent in his or her will when there are not assets sufficient to satisfy the bequests.

**Abstract of Title**
A summary of the history of real property. The trail of succession of ownership.

**Acknowledgment**
Notarized statement which identifies the person executing the document and which confirms the authenticity of his or her signature on the document.

**Ad Litem**
Person appointed to act, during the pendency of a matter, as guardian for a minor child. Person may also bring action on behalf of the child.

**Adjusted basis**
The basis of property used when computing gains for income tax purposes. The cost minus depreciation plus capital improvements.

**Administration of Estate**
The mismanagement of a decedent's estate. An administrator is appointed to collect all assets and debts of the decedent so that administrative expenses and taxes are paid and the remaining assets are distributed to the heirs or beneficiaries.

**Administrator**
The person appointed by the court to manage the estate of decedent when there is **no** will.

**Advance Directive**
May also be referred to as a "living will." Document that expresses a person's wishes about his or her medical care in the event they are unable to communicate their desires or have a terminal illness.

**Adverse Party**
A party having a substantial beneficial interest in a trust who would be adversely affected by the exercise or non-exercise of the power he or she has with respect to the trust.

**Alternate Valuation Date**
The administrator may choose an alternative date to the date of death for the valuation of the decedent's estate for federal estate tax purposes.

**Ancillary Administration**
Probate proceeding required in another jurisdiction when the decedent owned assets in another state.

**Annual Exclusion**
    The amount of money that a person can "gift" each year which is free from federal gift tax. Requires the filing of a gift tax return. Currently the allowable gift is $11,000 per person. A married couple may gift $22,000 per person and there is no limit to the number of persons who may receive a gift.

**Annuity**
    Similar to an insurance policy. A contract between the owner of the annuity provider and the purchaser (annuitant) The annuitant funds the account and interest accrues. The annuitant is then able to receive a yearly payment of a fixed amount for a specific period of time or for a specific amount until all of the value has been paid to the owner.

**Appraisal**
    Valuation or determination of worth.

**Appreciation**
    Increase in value.

**Asset**
    Anything that has value which is owned by a individual, company or organization. Assets include real property, tangible and intangible property, including businesses, goodwill, promissory notes and accounts receivable.

**Attorney-in-Fact**
    An agent. Person who acts for another under a power of attorney.

**Bad Faith**
    Deceitful or devious intent, which is motivated by self-interest, concealed purpose or ill will.

**Basis**
    The basis of real property is the original purchase price; adjusted purchase price of property.

**Beneficiary**
    A person who inherits or who is entitled to inherit under a will or trust or who is entitled to the proceeds of an insurance policy when the insured dies.

**Bequest**
    Testamentary gift of personal property; Property left to a named individual by the decedent in his or her will.

**Blockage Discount**
    If the sale of an entire piece of property at the same time would decrease the value of the property, a discount in valuation may be allowed.

**Blocked Account**
    A secure account that holds fund, usually proceeds from sales, or other estate assets until distribution is to be made. Can also be a custodian account for a minor.

**Bond**
    A deposit of money that ensures that the personal representative will perform his or her duties.

**Book Value**
    The value of an asset as reflected by the books of the company holding the asset.

**Burden of Proof**
    The duty to establish the truth of the matter; duty to prove a fact being disputed.

**Bypass Trust**
    A trust which intends to save a "second tax" when the second spouse dies by "bypassing" his or her estate. May also be called a credit shelter trust or B Trust.

## Capital Gains Tax
Income tax upon financial gain resulting from the sale or exchange of capital assets.

## Carry-over Basis
A basis for computing the taxes on property after it is sold.

## Charitable Deduction
A tax deduction allowed on federal income taxes for contributions or gifts made to tax-exempt charitable organizations, which have been approved by the IRS.

## Charitable Lead Trust
Trust which provides charity with benefits for a specified period of time, after which the benefits are paid to the settlor and/or his or her family.

## Charitable Remainder Annuity Trust
A trust that allows the donor to receive a fixed percentage of the value of the trust, which is determined annually. The trust is usually for a limited period of time after which the remainder of the trust is distributed to charity.

## Charitable Remainder Trust
A trust that benefits the settlor and/or his or her family for a specified period of time, after which the remainder is distributed to charity.

## Charitable Trust
Also called a public trust. Trust created for charitable benefit.

## Chattel
An item of personal property, not real property.

## Class Gift
A group of beneficiaries who are designated to receive a gift from the decedent by general reference rather than by their specific names, for example: "my children."

## Closely Held Business
A corporation wherein a few persons own all of the stock and which is not traded on the public stock exchange. Also called a Closely Held Corporation.

## Codicil
An amendment or addition to an existing will.

## Collateral Relative
Person related to the decedent who are not his or her "issue." Siblings, aunts, uncles, cousins, nieces and nephews are collateral relatives. Descendants of the decedent's parents are "first-line" collateral relatives; descendants of the decedent's grandparents are "second-line" collateral relatives. See Table of Consanguinity.

## Community Property
Property acquired by either spouse during the marriage, except by gift, bequest or inheritance.

## Conflict of Interest
The existence of varying interests between the parties involved in a fiduciary relationship.

## Conservator
A person granted authority by the Court to oversee the person and/or property of an incompetent person.

## Conservatorship
A proceeding requesting the Court approve a conservator.

## Contest
A contest of a will by an interested party who claims that the decedent's Will is not valid.

**Corporation**
　　A legal business entity wherein the shareholders may contract, operate, sue and control the business operation, its assets and debts.

**Corpus**
　　Latin meaning "the body"; The capital of a trust or an estate, the principal and not the interest or income.

**Creditor's Claim**
　　Creditors are required to file a "claim" in an estate requesting that they be paid from the assets of the estate within the course of the probate process.

**Crummey Trust**
　　Type of trust named as set forth in *Crummy v Commissioner*, (1978) 397 F2d. 82, 9th Circuit. Considered an Irrevocable Trust. Contributions made to the trust qualify for annual exclusions.

**Curtesy Rights**
　　The interest in a deceased wife's real estate that passes upon her death to her husband for his lifetime if they have had children who are able to inherit the property.

**Death Certificate**
　　The official proof of death which issued by the county clerk in the county where the decedent died.

**Decedent**
　　Legal term for a person who has died.

**Declaration of Trust**
　　The creation of a trust by a settlor. The settlor declares him or herself to be the trustee, gives him/herself fiduciary powers and responsibilities and transfers the property to the trust which will convey the property to the trust's beneficiaries.

**Deed**
　　Written document granting or transferring title of property to another individual.

**Deemed Transferor**
　　A person who transfers the property.

**Depreciation**
　　The value of the deterioration of property with the passage of time or through wear; allowance made for the decrease in property with income-producing value. The original purchase price is divided by the estimated useful life of the property.

**Descendant**
　　Person related to the decedent and descending in a lineal manner; children or grandchildren. Also referred to as issue.

**Devise**
　　A gift of property through a Will. Prior to 1985, California used only in reference to real property gifts.

**Devisee**
　　Person who receives a gift of property (real or personal).

**Direct Skip**
　　Transfer that skips a generation; used to calculate taxes imposed in the transfer.

**Directive to Physicians**
　　Also called the Advance Directive or Living Will.

**Disclaimer**
　　The right to refuse the acceptance of property.

**Discretionary Trust**
　　A trust that gives the Trustee broad discretion in carrying out the purposes and distribution of the trust.

**Distributable Net Income**
A beneficiary's actual taxes owed.
**Domicile**
A person's permanent residence or the place to which they intend to return.
**Done**
Person receiving property.
**Donor**
Person giving or transferring property.
**Dower Rights**
The interest in a widow's deceased husband's real property that is allowed for her lifetime.
**Durable Power of Attorney**
Power of attorney that continues even if the principal is incapacitated.
**Duress**
Threat of physical harm.
**Dynasty Trust**
Trust created for the benefit of the settlor's descendants that has unlimited duration.
**Earned Income**
As defined by law, the income from personal services rather than real estate.
**Encumbrance**
Claim or charge against property; debt.
**Equity of Redemption**
The right of a mortgagor, who is in default, to pay the debt on the mortgage in full, thus avoiding foreclosure.
**Equivalent Exemption**
The amount of property, including lifetime transfers, exempt from tax at death. Equals the unified tax credit.
**Escheat**
The right of the state to take title to property after the death of a decedent with no has not executed a will and who has no heirs.
**Escrow**
Written instrument, money or property that is held by a third party until a contractual obligation has been met or an event has occurred. Upon the completion of the obligation, the property is transferred or delivered to the grantee.
**Estate Planning**
The protection of family assets through legal means.
**Estate Tax**
Tax imposed by the federal government on estates.
**Ex Parte Proceeding**
Proceeding where only one party appears. Usually a hearing that requires shortened notice and which will require a formal notice of a future hearing.
**Exculpatory Clause**
Trust provision that reduces the standard of care customarily required of the trustee.
**Executor**
The person designated by a testator in his or her will. Directions for the disposition of property according to the will.
**Exoneration**
Beneficiary or devisee receives the property without encumbrances.

**Extraordinary Fees**
　The executor and/or attorney fees allowed by Probate Code for services that are not within the normal scope of the estate administration.

**Fair Market Value**
　Value of property defined as the amount a willing buyer would pay the seller if neither had to buy or sell.

**Family Allowance**
　The sum allowed by the Court for the maintenance and support of the decedent's family (wife and/or children).

**Family Pot Trust**
　A Trust created after the death of the surviving spouse that keeps all assets together "in one pot" rather than dividing it in separate shares.

**Fee Simple**
　The absolute ownership right in real property.

**Fiduciary**
　A person entrusted to handle money or property for another person. An executor, trustee, agent or guardian is considered a fiduciary.

**Fiscal Year**
　An accounting period. A different period may be chosen for an estate rather than a calendar year.

**Five-by-Five**
　The power of a Trustee to remove up to $5,000 or 5% of the trust principal, whichever is greater.

**Forfeiture Clause**
　No-contest clause.

**Form 706**
　Federal Estate Tax Return.

**Form 709**
　Federal Gift Tax Return.

**Franchise Tax Board**
　State agency designated to collect California income tax.

**Freehold**
　An estate for life.

**Funded Trust**
　Property that has been transferred to and is held by a "living" trust.

**Future Interest**
　An estate or interest in land or personal property that is to come into existence in the future. May be real estate or personal property, including money.

**Garnishment**
　Procedure by a creditor to obtain satisfaction of a debt from money owed or property in the possession of the debtor or a third person or the creditor.

**General Power of Appointment**
　Power under IRC § 2014(b) which allows a future interest in property. Is considered to be favorable to the decedent, his or her estate and/or creditors.

**General Power of Attorney**
　Power of attorney with broad powers that authorize the agent to take any action the principal would take.

**Generation-Skipping Transfer Tax**
　Estate tax imposed when decedent's interest in a trust passes to persons who are at least one generation younger than the donor.

**Gift**

Transfer of property from one person to another without consideration or compensation.

**Gift Tax**

Tax imposed on transfers of the donor's estate property during his or her lifetime. Estate tax is imposed upon death.

**Good Faith**

The honest and reasonable belief that one's conduct is performed without improper motive or negligent disregard.

**Goodwill**

The result of a good reputation of a business that is acquired which is not a tangible asset.

**Grantor**

One who grants something. The person who creates a trust or the person who transfers property from one person or entity to another.

**Gross Estate**

All property in which the decedent had an interest at death.

**Guardian**

The person appointed by the Court to represent and protect the interests of a minor child.

**Guardian Ad Litem**

The person appointed by the Court to represent and protect the interests of a minor child or incompetent person during the pendency of a civil matter.

**Guardianship**

Procedure for the appointment of a guardian for a minor child.

**Heirs**

Person(s) entitled to inherit the property (real or personal) of the decedent who dies without a will; person(s) receiving property by descent.

**Holographic Will**

Will written entirely by the testator in his or her own handwriting.

**Homestead Property**

Real property that is free and clear of claims of creditors as long as the owner occupies the property as his or her primary residence.

**Income**

Earnings or other profits made by the property after it has been conveyed to a trust.

**Income Beneficiary**

Person who is entitled to trust income.

**Independent Administration of Estates Act**

The probate code provision that provides the executor with the ability to administer the estate more informally and with minimal court supervision.

**Inheritance Tax**

The tax imposed by state law on property inherited from decedent. Tax was abolished in California.

**Insolvent**

Debts exceed assets; without funds.

**Installment Sale**

Proceeds of a sale are paid in installments to reduce the taxable gain over a period of time.

**Inter Vivos Trust**
Living Trust; A trust that is effective during the lifetime of the creator of the trust.
**Interest in Property**
The right, claim share or title to property.
**Intestate**
Estate of a person who dies without leaving a valid Will.
**Intestate Succession**
The manner in which property passes when the descendant died without a valid will.
**Inventory**
Schedule of assets and debts of the decedent; includes real and person property, money, vehicles and contains the date of death value of the property.
**IRA**
Individual Retirement Account. Individuals who are not eligible for an employment retirement plan may deposit money (as allowed by the IRS) in an account for their retirement.
**Irrevocable Trust**
Trust created by the Settler wherein he or she gives up control of the trust property. A trustee who is not the Settler administers the trust.
**Issue**
The persons who descend in a direct line from an ancestor: child, grandchild, great-grandchild and all lineal descendants.
**Joint Account**
Account that is payable upon the request of one or more of the account holders.
**Joint Tenancy**
Manner in which title is held in real or personal property wherein they share equal rights to the property. There is a right of survivorship to the surviving tenant.
**Keogh Account**
Type of retirement account available to self-employed persons or partners of an incorporated business (as allowed by the IRS).
**Kinship**
Being related by blood; kin.
**Lapsed Gift**
Gift intended for a beneficiary who predeceases the testator or donor.
**Leasehold**
Right under a lease to hold property for a specific term.
**Legacy**
Usually refers to cash left as a bequest in a Will.
**Legatee**
The person who is the beneficiary of either real or personal property in a Will.
**Letters of Administration**
Document issued by the Court appointing a personal representative of a decedent who died intestate.
**Letters Testamentary**
Document issued by the Court that appoints the executor or personal representative when the decedent had a valid Will.
**Lien**
Claim or encumbrance against real or personal property.
**Life Estate**
Ownership interest provided in property for the lifetime of a designated person, usually the owner of the estate.

## Life Tenant
Person who receives the benefits use of as well as the rent and income from property during their lifetime receives a life estate.

## Limited Partnership
Type of partnership wherein there are one or more general partners who manage the business or partnership and assume liability; while limited partners have limited responsibility and liability.

## Lineal Descendant
Person in direct line: child, grandchild, great-grandchild.

## Liquid Assets
Assets that can easily be converted to cash.

## Living Trust
Trust created by the settlor(s) that takes effect will he, she, they are alive; Inter Vivos Trust.

## Marital Deduction Trust
Trust created for a surviving spouse that will reduce federal income tax. The deceased spouse's estate is entitled to an unlimited marital deduction.

## Minor
Person under the age of eighteen.

## Mutual Wills
Reciprocal wills

## Natural Heirs
Heirs of the body.

## Negligence
Failure to act or do what a reasonable person would do under the circumstance.

## No-Contest Clause
Provision contained in the Will that disinherits any person who contests the validity of the Will; Forfeiture clause.

## Nonlinear Descendant
Beneficiary who is not related to the decedent but is assigned to a generation based on his or her birthrate.

## Nonprobate Property
Property owned by the decedent, but that is distributed by other means rather than the decedent's Will; life insurance, annuities, retirement accounts, property held in joint tenancy or that has a right of survivorship.

## Non-Resident Alien
A person who is not a resident nor a citizen of the United States.

## Notice of Creditors
Notice to all creditors of the decedent of his or her death and that they must file their claim, if any, with the court.

## Notice of Proposed Action
Formal notice that informs the persons required to receive notice that an action is pending.

## Nuncupative Will
An oral will made by the testator on his or her death bed, which is later transcribed by a person who was present.

## Ordinary Fees
Fees allowed by Probate Code to be paid to the attorney and personal representative for customary and usual services in the administration of the state.

**Partition**
Court proceeding that separates the interests of co-owners.

**Partnership**
A business or organization wherein two or more persons carry out the business for profit. All partners are equally liable and responsible for the business and liabilities, and receive equal share of the profits.

**Patent**
The right to use, manufacturer or sell an invention which is issued by the Federal Government.

**Pendente Lite**
Pending litigation.

**Pension**
Retirement benefit through an employer created by employer contributions and employee contributions during the period the employee is employed. Governed by Federal Rules and the IRS.

**Per Capita**
Latin meaning "by the head." Method for distributing the and intestate estate. The decedent's estate where all persons are equally related. Each heir will receive an equal share of the decedent's estate.

**Per Stirpes**
Descendants take the decedent's estate by right of representation; distribution by "the root."

**Personal Property**
All property that is not real estate; tangible and intangible property.

**Personal Representative**
The executor or administrator of the decedent's estate. General name given whether or not there was a Will.

**Petition for Instructions**
A summary procedure used to request that the court order tangible property, which was not transferred to a trust, be treated as a trust asset.

**P.O.D. Payee**
Pay on Death Account. The payee is the recipient of funds from the owner's account upon the death of the decedent. The owner has total control of the account during their lifetime.

**Posthumous**
That which is done after one's death.

**Post-Marital Agreement**
Also called a post-nuptial agreement. An agreement executed by spouse after their marriage that sets forth the individual rights to property or transmutes property from separate to community.

**Pour-Over Will**
A will created at the same time as a trust to "catch" or "pour over" any assets that were not transferred to the trust.

**Power of Appointment**
The ability to appoint a new owner of the property or act for another, including an interest in the subject of the action.

**Power of Attorney**
Formal document which authorizes one person to act as an "agent" for another (the principal).

**Prayer**
Portion of the petition, motion, or other pleading which requests equitable relief sought.

**Precatory Language**
Language that is nonbinding that requests or recommends that a person do a certain act; "I wish."

**Predeceased**
Person who dies before another.

**Preliminary Distribution**
A partial distribution of the estate which is made prior to the final distribution or when the estate would normally be closed.

**Pre-Marital Agreement**
Also called a pre-nuptial agreement. An agreement executed by spouses prior to their marriage that sets forth their separate property rights.

**Present Interest**
Interest that is vested rather than a future interest.

**Pretermitted**
A child or other issue who is unintentionally omitted from the Will.

**Primogeniture**
Rule of descent used in the Middle Ages, wherein the oldest male inherited the real property of decedent and excluded all other children.

**Principal**
The body (corpus) of a trust; or the person who creates a power of attorney.

**Pro Rata**
"In proportion to"; A person's share, interest.

**Probate**
The judicial proceeding whereby a Will is proven to be valid to the court.

**Property**
A person's *right* to use, possess, enjoy and dispose of any thing.

**Proprietorship**
Business that is owned by one person.

**Prudent Person Standard**
Trustee is held to a degree of care that would be required of an "ordinary and prudent person" if they were dealing with their own property.

**Publishing the Will**
Statement made by the testator that the document is her or her Will.

**Qualified Disclaimer**
Property being disclaimed must satisfy the conditions of Internal Revenue Code §2518.

**Qualified Domestic Trust**
Trust created to preserve the marital deduction property that passes to a non-citizen spouse. Referred to as a Q-DOT trust.

**Qualified Terminable Interest Property**
The interest in property that ends with the death of the person who holds the interest. Ownership interest is not absolute.

**Qualified Terminable Interest Property Trust**
A (Q-TIP) trust that allows the surviving spouse with a life estate in order to qualify for the marital deduction. The surviving spouse will receive income and principal, if needed. May also provide an eventual gift to charity.

**Quasi-Community Property**
  Property belonging to residents of a community property state, California, which is acquired or located in another state.

**Real Property**
  Land, including all things attached or located on the property directly or indirectly; real estate.

**Reciprocal Wills**
  Wills that contain parallel dispositive provisions. Usually prepared by husband and wife or domestic partners; also called mutual wills.

**Redemption**
  Recovery of property pledged for payment or upon the performance of a condition.

**Remainder**
  An estate in land that takes effect immediately after the expiration of a prior estate. Created at the same time and by the same instrument.

**Res**
  The principal property in a trust.

**Residence**
  Place where a person currently lives; it may not be their permanent domicile.

**Residuary Clause**
  A clause in a will or trust that provides for the distribution of any property that remains in the estate after the distribution of specific bequests.

**Residuary Devisee**
  The beneficiary who will receive the remainder of the estate after distribution of specific bequests and all debts and expenses of the decedent are paid.

**Reversion**
  Future interest in real estate that is in favor of the grantor or his heirs after the termination of a prior estate. The property is returned to the grantor or his heirs once the grant is over.

**Reversionary Interest**
  Future interest or the right to enjoy future interest in a reversion.

**Revocable Trust**
  Trust created by the settlor (grantor) which he or she is able to revoke.

**Right of Representation**
  Inheritance received by right of representation is one that distributes the decedent's estate to the heirs by whatever share their predeceased parent would have taken if he or she had survived. May be used with terms such as per capita or per stirpes.

**Right of Survivorship**
  A joint tenant automatically receives the other joint tenant's share upon death.

**Rule Against Perpetuities**
  Rule determining how long an interest in property may remain invested. California allows twenty-one years.

**Salvage Value**
  Estimated value that would be obtained at the end of the asset's "useful" life. Used in tax law. May also be referred to as "garage sale" value.

**Savings Statute**
  Statute that allows an invalid Will to stand even though it does not meet the state law requirements for a valid will.

**Self-Proving Will**
Will that includes an attestation or affidavit by the testator and the witnesses as to the valid execution of the Will.

**Separate Property**
Property that is acquired by married person before the marriage, during marriage by gift, bequest or inheritance, or after the date of their separation. The property must be continued to be held separately during the marriage to be identified as such.

**Settlor**
Person who creates a trust, sets for the duties and responsibilities of the trustee, and who transfers the property into the trust. May also be called the Trustee, Grantor or Donor.

**Simple Trust**
Straightforward transfer of property from one person to another.

**Situs**
Location (jurisdiction) of real property.

**Skip Person**
Person who is at least two generations removed (younger) than the transferor.

**Special Administrator**
Administrator who is appointed by the Court to administer some portion of the estate, or who is appointed as an interim administrator until the Letters Testamentary have been filed and the administrator officially appointed.

**Special Power of Appointment**
Power of appointment wherein the donor specifies who may be appointees. The donor may not appoint creditor or the donee's estate.

**Spendthrift Clause**
Clause which prevents creditors from making claims on a trust beneficiary's interest and which also prevents bankruptcy.

**Spousal Attribution Rule**
If the grantor's spouse is living with the grantor at the time the trust was created the grantor may continue to hold the power or interest in the trust property.

**Springing Power of Attorney**
Power of Attorney created to become effective upon the person's disability and/or incapacity.

**Sprinkling Power**
Trustee's power of distribution is limited to an ascertainable standard as set forth in the trust; conditions are placed on the distribution of income to the beneficiaries.

**Statute of Limitations**
State statute that prescribes the maximum period of time during which an action (civil or criminal) can be brought after the occurrence of the injury or event.

**Statutory Fees**
Fees allowed by statute to be paid to the personal representative and the attorney.

**Stepped-Up Basis**
Value of property that is inherited is "stepped up" to its fair market value as of the date of death rather than at the date of purchase.

**Straight Life Annuity**
Yearly payment of a fixed sum of money until the death of the annuitant.

**Strict Privity Test**
A closes relationship between two parties who have some legal right.

**Subscribing Witness**
    Person who sees the testator sign his or her Will and thereafter acknowledges that he or she witnessed the signing and affixes his or her name to the Will. The person attests to the validity of the document.

**Summary Probate**
    Used in small estates where an abbreviated (summary) procedure will be more timely and beneficial to the estate.

**Surety Company**
    Company who engages in a business that promises to pay the debt or satisfy an obligation of another.

**Survival Period**
    Statute that specifies the minimum period by which a beneficiary must outlive the testator in order for them (or their estate) to receive the gift.

**Survivorship**
    Right to receive property by operation of law when the property is held in joint tenancy.

**Taxable Apportionment**
    Death taxes may be apportioned to individual gifts rather than charged against the estate or residuary gift.

**Taxable Distribution**
    Distribution from a trust to a skip person, other than a taxable termination or a direct skip.

**Taxable Termination**
    Termination to an interest in trust property that occurs upon death, lapse of time, release of power to a nonskip person. After such termination, a transfer may not be made to a skip person upon such termination.

**Tenancy by the Entirety**
    Form of joint tenancy between spouses.

**Tenant in Common**
    Type of tenancy wherein the persons owning the property own equal, undivided portions in real estate. If one of the owners of the property dies, that person's share is distributed to their heirs and not the remaining tenants, unless a Will or other document h as directed that their share should be transferred to the remaining living tenants.

**Term Life Insurance**
    Life insurance purchased which is paid if the insured dies during the designated term.

**Terminable Interest**
    Interest in property that ends upon the death of the person who holds the interest or upon the occurrence of some event.

**Testamentary Capacity**
    Capacity to make a valid will; mentally competent.

**Testamentary Trust**
    A trust created by a will.

**Testate**
    Person who dies leaving a valid will.

**Testate Succession**
    The manner in which property passes under a valid will.

**Testator**
    Person who makes a valid will.

**Totten Trust**
Trust created by a person, using his or her own money and depositing it into a bank account, naming him or herself as trustee for another person.

**Tracing**
Tracking the transfer of property from one person to another.

**Transferor**
Person who places money or property in the hands of another.

**Trust**
Fiduciary relationship between a trustee and the beneficiary. The trustee holds the trust property for the benefit of the beneficiary.

**Trust Equivalent**
An arrangement that has substantially the same effect as a trust and which may include life estates, remainder estates, insurance and annuity accounts.

**Trustee**
Person who holds legal title to trust property; manages the trust property and has a fiduciary duty to the settlor.

**Trustor**
Person who creates a trust, the grantor.

**Unclaimed Property**
Property that has been abandoned may be distributed to the state through escheat.

**Uncontrolled Discretion**
Trustee is not held to a standard of reasonable discretion but to good faith.

**Unfunded Trust**
Trust that was created but property was not put in it.

**Unified Estate & Gift Tax**
IRS rules which became effective January 1, 1977 wherein estate and gift tax schedules were created to determine tax rate on lifetime gifts and estates.

**Uniform Gifts to Minors Act**
Law that allows gifts of money to be transferred to a custodian rather than directly to the minor child.

**Uniform Probate Code**
Federal Act that was also adopted by several states, which seeks to simplify the probate process.

**Unitary Transfer Taxes**
Gift taxes transferred to a Clifford trust will be valued over a ten-year period.

**Universal Life Insurance**
Whole life insurance that receives a competitive rate of return.

**Unlimited Marital Deduction**
Tax law that allows non-terminable interest gifts, in any amount, to the donor's spouse, that is generally deductible from gift and estate taxes.

**Void**
Null; without legal effect.

**Voidable**
The ability to determine that something was defective or invalid.

**Whole Life Insurance**
Life insurance policy wherein the proceeds are paid whenever the insured dies.

**Will**
Instrument by which the testator disposes of his or her property upon their death.

**Window Minor's Trust**
> Trust created for minors that distributes the property upon the minor reaching the age of twenty-one. The trust gives the trustee the discretion to extend the trust beyond that time.

**Younger Generation Beneficiary**
> Person of a younger generation than the person who created the trust.

# Index

Abatement, 377
Abstract, 194-195, 205, 377
Abstract of Title, 367
Acknowledgment, 54, 107, 114, 156, 317, 326, 338, 377
Accounts, 4, 25, 52, 60, 61, 102-104, 111, 113, 120-122, 143, 144, 150, 152, 153, 155, 156, 221, 232, 260, 294, 298, 304, 347, 351-355, 374, 378, 385, 391
Accounting, 13, 109, 115, 116, 120, 220, 222, 223, 226, 234, 235, 257, 272, 273, 288, 312-316, 324, 352, 357, 370, 371, 382
Actuary, 231
Ad Litem, 239, 241-242, 255, 258, 377
Adjusted basis, 148, 184, 227, 377
Administration of Estate, 13, 27, 51, 59, 68, 73, 75, 81, 85, 92, 96, 101, 102, 108-110, 112, 122, 128, 129, 139, 143-158, 235, 266, 267, 278, 297, 298, 303, 304, 317, 319-321, 335, 337, 382
Administrator, 28, 49, 60, 65, 69-71, 73, 74, 79, 80, 90, 91, 103, 107, 114, 115, 144, 156, 264-269, 286, 362-364, 377, 386, 389
"Advance Directive" Advance Health Care Directive, 261-264, 369
Adverse Party, 18-19, 377
Affidavit, 3, 68, 107, 143-145, 147, 150-152, 154-156, 158, 167, 288, 299, 305, 330, 336, 337, 363, 364
Affidavit of Death of Joint Tenant, 68, 147, 288, 336
Affidavit of Death of Spouse, 144, 145, 147, 288, 330

Affidavit of Death of Trustee, 225
Affidavit of Domicile, 156, 158
Agent, 6, 37, 56, 60, 112-114, 154-156, 209, 216, 262-264, 276, 278, 351-369, 378, 382, 383, 387
Allocation, 185, 231
Allocation Agreement, 230-231
Alternate Valuation Date, 148, 377
Amendment, 21, 168, 174, 279, 285, 355, 356, 362, 379
Ancillary Administration, 377
Ancillary Probate, 27, 68, 377
Annual Exclusion, 228, 288, 344
Annuity, 3, 24, 68, 104, 285, 351, 378, 391
Appraisal, 85, 96, 101-106, 113-115, 118, 122, 125-127, 134-137, 149, 319, 332, 337, 378
Appraiser, 9, 104, 231
Appreciation, 232, 274, 275, 378
Asset, 3, 4, 5, 12, 20-23, 60, 72, 104, 109, 111, 113, 143, 150, 231, 233, 272-274, 297, 303, 347, 354, 378, 383, 386, 389
Assignment of Property, 196, 205, 346, 373
Attestation, 33-34, 44, 56, 299, 305, 389
Attorney fees, 68, 69, 72, 109-111, 116-119, 121, 122, 145, 153, 231, 315-317, 320, 321, 323, 326, 327, 382, 386, 390
Attorney in Fact, 207
Bad Faith, 261, 378
Bank, 20-21, 25, 30-31, 36, 42, 50, 60, 70, 104, 113-115, 121, 143, 144, 150, 153, 155, 156, 172, 179, 193, 195, 196, 201, 208, 221, 222, 224, 225, 231, 232, 258, 354
Basis, 148, 184, 227, 367, 377-379

Beneficiary, 3, 7-8, 11, 17, 18, 20, 22, 25, 27, 28, 30, 31, 41, 55, 61, 68, 69, 102, 110, 111, 116, 141, 143, 147-151, 167, 171-173, 175-177, 179, 180, 182, 184, 191, 192, 199, 203, 211, 219-225, 228, 232, 233-235, 260, 273, 274, 281, 284, 298-299, 304-305, 354, 378

Beneficiary designation, 177, 192, 211, 346-347, 354

Bequest, 115, 146, 220, 378, 379, 384, 389

*Biakanja v Irving* (1958) 49 Cal.2d 647, 320 P2d 16, 10

Blocked account, 241-242, 258, 378

Blockage discount, 378

Bond(s), 5, 15, 21, 49-51, 55, 57, 71, 72, 73, 74, 75, 78-80, 90, 91, 103-105 113-115, 120, 122, 144, 152, 153, 155-157, 196, 202, 232, 243, 260, 266, 267, 288, 294, 297, 299, 303, 312, 320, 324, 327, 329, 347, 351, 358, 378

Book value, 378

Burden of Proof, 64, 260, 378

Bypass Trust, 190, 230, 378

Capital Gains Tax, 379

Carry-over basis, 379

Certification, 109, 116, 155, 196, 265, 319, 332

Certified Abstract, 194 -195, 205, 379

Chain of title, 201, 205

Charitable deduction, 226, 228, 229, 285, 379

Charitable Lead Trust, 285, 379

Charitable Remainder Trust, 230, 285, 379

Charitable Trust, 230, 273, 285, 379

Chattel, 379

Children, 6, 7, 12, 15, 17, 19-21, 25, 26, 27, 30, 32-38, 45-50, 52-56, 59-62, 65, 68, 71, 75, 76, 81, 92, 109, 111, 118, 119, 121, 143-146, 149, 187, 189, 221, 222, 224-226, 234, 268, 278, 289-291, 293, 296, 299, 302, 305, 314, 316, 371, 379, 380, 382, 387

Class gift, 379

Clifford Trust, 194, 391

Closely Held Corporation, 379

Codicil, 35, 44, 60, 73, 80, 81, 91, 92, 292, 379

Collateral Relative 28, 379

Community Property, 22, 61, 64, 143-147, 149, 151-153, 157, 196, 228, 330, 339-342, 346, 379, 386, 388,

Confidentiality, 9, 28, 165, 167, 272

Conflict check, 5, 36, 42, 67

Conflict of interest, 5, 10, 144, 218, 379

Conservator" Conservatee" Conservatorship, 5,12, 29, 172, 173, 210, 213, 239, 241, 244, 241-249, 250, 379

Contest, 54, 57, 352, 358, 379

Corporate fiduciary, 50, 51, 57, 80, 91

Corporation, 114, 144, 253, 274, 275, 352, 353, 356, 361, 362, 379, 380

Corpus, 191, 280, 282, 356, 380, 380

Credit Shelter Trust, 230, 238, 380

Creditor's claim, 101, 106-110, 113, 128, 129, 145

Crummey letter, 176, 193

Crummey Trust, 174-175, 228, 380

*Crummey v. Commissioner* (1978) 397 F.2d 82 (9th Circuit), 175

Custodial account, 54, 56, 122, 172, 173-174

Custodian, 20, 21, 52, 53, 57, 121, 259, 260, 265, 298, 304, 362, 378, 391

Custodianship, 53

Death Certificate, 103, 144, 145, 147, 152, 153, 155, 224, 265, 272, 330, 336-338, 373

Decedent, 11-16, 18-19, 23, 25, 26, 47-49, 51, 52, 54, 56, 59-71, 73-76, 78-86, 90-96, 100-116, 118, 120, 121, 128, 129, 143-157, 171, 217, 219, 221, 222, 231-233, 259-261, 264-269, 279, 281, 285, 289, 291-294, 313, 315, 318-322, 326-332, 335-337, 339-344, 370, 374, 377-388

Declaration for Collection of Compensation, 146, 288, 334, 335

Declaration of Spouse, 146, 278, 288, 335

Declaration of Trust, 145, 373, 380

Declaration Under Probate Code Section 13100, 143, 158, 226, 337,

Deed(s), 13, 14, 20, 23, 25, 36, 42, 50, 104, 147, 152, 154, 167, 172, 178, 192, 195, 196, 197, 199, 200-203, 205, 218, 224, 231, 236, 237, 240, 288

Deemed transferor, 380

Dementia Declaration 248, 250, 256

Department of Health Services, 110, 111, 113

Department of Motor Vehicles, 146, 152, 154, 155
Depreciation, 377, 380
Descendant, 28, 299, 305, 380, 384
Devise, Devisee, 64, 102, 118, 296-298, 253, 380
Directive to Physicians, 207, 211, 213-215, 228, 369
Direct skip, 390
Disburse, 115-116, 120, 151, 157, 235, 241, 273
Disclaimer, 174, 191, 226, 230, 288, 345, 357, 380
Disclaimer Trust, 191, 226, 230, 288, 345, 380
Discretionary Trust, 356
Disinherit, 20, 27, 54
Disinheritance, 27, 39, 54, 57
Distributable net income, 381
Distribution, 11, 15-17, 27, 47-50, 52, 53, 55, 56, 60, 61, 64-66, 71, 101-103, 109-118, 120-122, 168, 184, 186, 188, 190, 220, 222, 266, 267, 275, 283, 288, 290, 291, 302, 312, 315-329, 331, 332, 370, 371, 374, 377, 378, 381
Documentary Transfer Tax, 145, 147, 153, 349
Domestic partnership, 20, 21-22, 24, 143, 151, 246, 253, 278, 286
Domestic Partnership Act, 286
Domicile, 16, 22-24, 30, 45, 67, 156, 158, 270
Donee, 26, 52, 170, 389
Donor, 52, 228, 274-277, 379, 381
Dower Rights, 381
Durable Power of Attorney, 28, 207, 209-210, 212, 214, 216, 218, 256, 288, 351-369, 381
Durable Power of Attorney for Health Care, 207, 211, 212-213, 214, 288, 362, 366-368
Durable Power of Attorney for Property Management, 173, 176-177, 207, 221, 212-213
Duties and Responsibilities, 10, 50, 51, 73, 74, 78, 87-89, 98-100, 275, 381
Duress, 300, 306, 381
Dynasty Trust, 175, 381
Earned Income, 121, 381

Encumbrance, 381, 385
Equity of redemption, 381
Equivalent exemption, 381
Escheat, 27, 28, 63, 65, 381, 391
Escrow, 109, 111-115, 120, 319, 381
Estate planning, 3, 6, 13, 29, 59, 176, 219, 227, 229, 259, 278, 381
Estate tax, 5, 8, 15, 20, 55, 69, 111, 114, 144, 148, 219, 227-229, 231, 232, 278-285, 288, 297-299, 303-305, 318, 319, 327, 343, 351, 377, 378, 382, 383, 385, 391
Executor, 6, 7, 10, 14, 17-19, 20, 21, 28, 46, 49-55, 57, 60, 61, 66-70, 72, 74-76, 79, 80, 90, 91, 107, 109-111, 113, 115, 117-120, 122, 148, 166, 178, 218, 259, 260, 278, 292, 297, 298, 302-304, 310, 315-318, 320, 321, 323, 326, 327, 362-364, 374, 381, 385, 386
Executor fees, 50, 55, 109, 111, 117-120, 122, 166, 297, 303, 315-317, 320, 323, 326, 327, 381
Exclusion of Reassessment, 147, 148, 331, 381
Exculpatory clause, 381
Ex Parte proceeding, 381
Exoneration, 382
Extraordinary Fees, 13, 111, 116, 117, 119, 122, 316, 317, 320, 323, 326, 327
Fair Market Value, 64, 71, 72, 75, 80, 91, 114, 148, 150, 273, 276, 279, 281, 382, 390
Family allowance, 110, 382
Family Pot Trust, 382
Federal tax, 5, 8, 15, 20, 55, 69, 114, 148, 226-229, 278-284, 288, 377-379, 382, 385
Federal Estate Tax Return, 114, 227, 232, 284, 318, 327, 382
Fee Simple, 119, 356
Fiduciary, 10, 27, 49, 54, 69, 107, 113, 220, 224, 259, 382
Fiduciary Tax Return, 114
Final Distribution, 52, 71, 102, 103, 110, 112-118, 120-122, 266, 267, 288, 312, 317-324, 326-329
Financial Institutions, 77, 119, 144, 153, 201, 221, 260, 351, 354
Fiscal year, 30, 382
Five-by-Five, 174, 194, 382

Forfeiture Clause, 382, 385
Form 706, 225, 238, 382
Form 709, 382
Franchise Tax Board, 382
Freehold, 382
Funded trust, 59, 224, 269, 382
Future interest, 170, 228, 382, 387, 388
Garnishment, 382
General Power of Appointment, 259, 284, 356, 382
General Power of Attorney 284, 382
Generation-Skipping Transfer Tax (GST), 175, 185-186,193, 217, 227, 231-232, 281-281, 358, 383
Gift, 16, 52, 53, 64, 146, 227-229, 231, 273-277, 283, 284, 296, 302, 352, 357, 378-380, 382-384, 388-391
Gift Tax, 170, 186, 193, 227-229, 230, 231, 283, 284, 357, 378, 382, 383, 391
Good Faith, 28, 64, 107, 108, 274-276, 182, 274-275, 285, 318, 326, 364, 383, 391
Goodwill, 67, 378, 383
Grantee, 383
Grantor, 169, 193, 346-349, 383, 388, 389, 391
Gross estate, 55, 71, 72, 75, 80, 91, 118, 150, 279, 299, 305, 320, 337, 383
Guardian/Guardianship, 4, 5, 12, 17, 19-21, 28, 28, 31, 32, 34, 35, 37-39, 52-54, 56, 57, 172, 174, 176, 178, 208, 210-211, 239-244 250 253-258, 259-260, 268, 298-299, 383
Guardian Ad Litem, 239, 241-242, 258, 377, 383
Guardian of the Estate, 17, 39, 242, 268, 269, 279, 329, 335
Guardian of the Person, 53, 242, 268, 279, 377, 383
Health care surrogate, 261-264, 286
Heirs, 7, 15, 16, 18, 25, 26, 27, 28, 33, 45, 48, 50, 54-56, 60, 61, 64, 65, 68, 71-73, 75, 77, 78, 80, 85, 91, 96, 110, 111, 115-117, 119-121, 143, 144, 146, 150, 157, 166, 170, 172, 188, 189, 190, 224, 319, 377, 381, 383, 385, 388, 390
Holographic Will, 17, 28, 29, 32, 34, 44, 74
Homestead property, 150, 383
Housing and Urban Development, 155
Income, 24, 38, 69, 75, 80, 91, 120, 121, 146, 148, 156, 170, 235, 272-275, 280, 282, 284, 286, 297, 298, 303, 304, 318, 320, 327, 355-357, 377, 379-383, 385, 388, 389
Income Beneficiary, 69, 148, 273, 284, 298, 304, 356, 383
Independent Administration of Estates Act, 43, 51,75, 79, 81, 85, 90, 92, 96, 297, 303
Inheritance tax, 148,228, 285
*In re Allen's Estate* (1941) 42 Cal.App.2d, 346, 110
*In re Conduct of Morin* (1994) 319 Or. 547, 878 P.2d 393, 11,
*In re Cornitius' Estate* (1957) 154 Cal.App.2d 422, 110
*In re Estate of Devine* (1994) 263 ILL APP.3d 799, 635 N.E. 2d 581, 11
*In re Jameson's Estate* (1949) 93 CalApp.2d 35, 110
*In Re Ockerlander's Estate* (1961) 195 Cal.App.2d 185, 110
Insolvent, 384
Issue, 18, 28, 45, 48-50, 61-66, 69, 71, 75, 79, 81, 90, 92, 144, 145, 152, 156, 265, 268, 269, 296, 299, 302, 305, 374, 379, 380, 384, 387
Installment sale, 384
Insurance Trust, 175, 176, 196, 224, 240, 269, 347, 362, 378, 391
Inter Vivos Trust, 165, 384
Interest in Property, 25, 55, 81, 92, 147-149, 152, 228, 230, 259, 260, 279, 280, 282, 284, 331, 332, 337, 339-342, 346, 355, 357, 358, 381-383, 385, 387-390
Intestate, 16, 18, 26, 27, 49, 59, 61, 62, 64-66, 69, 70, 75, 76, 80, 91, 101, 106, 112, 115, 143, 146, 147, 152, 259, 264, 267, 335, 357, 384, 386
Intestate Succession, 16, 61, 64-66, 69, 146, 147, 259, 335, 357
Inventory, 70, 85, 96, 101-106, 113-116, 118, 122, 125-127, 134-137, 149, 313-316, 319, 320, 337, 370, 371, 384
Inventory and Appraisal, 85, 96, 101-106, 113, 115, 122, 125-127, 134-137, 149, 319, 337
Individual Retirement Account (IRA), 16, 34, 143,150, 167, 178, 203, 347, 384

Interspousal Transfer Deed, 196, 197, 200
Irrevocable Trust, 169, 380
Issue, 18, 28, 45, 48-50, 61-66, 69, 71, 75, 79, 81, 90, 92, 144, 145, 152, 156, 265, 268, 269, 296, 299, 302, 305, 374, 379, 380, 384, 387
Joint account, 25, 150
Joint tenancy, 25, 60, 61, 68, 104, 143, 144, 146, 147, 150-152, 154, 157, 236, 351, 385, 390
Keogh account, 203, 384
Kinship, 62, 63, 384
Lapsed gift, 296, 302, 384
Laws of perpetuity, 52
Leasehold, 384
Legacy, 354, 384
Legatee, 354, 384
Letters, 50, 73, 75, 77-80, 85, 90, 91, 96, 101, 102, 105, 106, 110, 112, 113, 115, 122, 124, 128, 133, 149, 257, 265, 266, 318, 389
Letters of Administration, 79, 90, 102, 122, 149, 318
Letters of Instruction, 195
Letters Testamentary, 77, 79, 90, 101, 112, 385, 389
Lien, 110, 113, 149, 352, 385
Life estate, 146, 147, 149, 230, 280, 282, 357, 382, 385, 388
Life tenant, 149, 385
Limited Partnership, 105, 226, 274, 347, 353, 385
Lineal Descendant, 380, 384, 385
Liquid assets, 109, 385
Living Will, 48, 81, 92, 221, 261, 264, 377, 380, 385
Living Trust, 48, 174, 221, 361, 372, 373, 382, 384, 389
*Lucas v Hamm* (1961) 56 Cal2d. 583, 15 Cal.Rptr. 821, 364 P.2d 685, 10
Lodging the will, 70, 78
Marital Deduction Trust, 171, 175, 229, 230, 283, 284, 387, 388
Medallion Signature Guarantee, 114, 153, 156-158, 203, 205
Medi-Cal, 4, 12, 14, 110, 113, 115, 116, 222, 249, 293
Medicare, 4, 222, 353, 357
Memorandum of personal property, 189, 195, 221, 224, 225, 302

Minor, 25, 46, 52-54, 57, 75, 121, 149, 174, 228, 329, 377, 378, 383, 385, 391, 392
Mobile Homes, 155, 203
Motor Vehicles, 146, 152-155, 202, 347
Mutual Funds, 103, 113, 115, 152, 153, 156, 172, 203, 224, 294, 347, 374
Mutual Wills, 385, 388
Natural heirs, 11, 385
National Association for Paralegal Associations, Inc. (NFPA), 5, 10, 11, 13
Negligence, 10, 11, 66, 183, 385
Net estate, 50, 51, 110, 118-120, 149, 150, 222, 315, 316, 319-321, 327, 328, 370, 371
No-Contest clause, 54, 57, 382, 385
Nonlinear descendant, 385
Nonprobate property, 3, 17, 26, 28, 56, 68, 365
Non-resident alien, 27, 385
Notary public, 25, 38, 40, 42, 75, 114, 145, 147, 153, 203, 205, 208, 215, 278
Notice of Hearing, 51, 60, 73-76, 78, 82-84, 93-95, 102, 112, 120, 153, 157, 161, 162, 269, 381
Notice of Creditors; Notice to Creditors, 85, 106-108, 113, 122, 128, 129, 140, 141, 318, 385, 386
Notice of Petition to Administer Estate, 73, 75, 76, 78, 84-86, 96, 97, 122, 138, 139
Notice of Proposed Action, 51, 102, 112, 122, 319
Nuncupative Will, 386
Ombudsmen, 215
Omission of heirs, 54
Order for Distribution, 116, 121, 288, 317, 326-329
Order for Probate, 77, 101, 102, 104, 122, 123, 132, 145, 149, 153, 281, 288, 329
Order on Petition for Instructions,167, 177, 217, 226, 235-237, 238, 288, 372-375, 386
Ordinary Fees, 386
Parent-Child Exclusion, 154
Partition, 352, 386
Partnership, 22, 105, 151, 152, 226, 274, 278, 286, 347, 352, 353, 385, 386
Patent, 386
Pay On Death Account (POD), 3, 25, 31, 44, 232, 386
Pay On Death Payee, 386

Pendente Lite, 386
Pension, 60, 232, 347, 386
Per Capita, 48, 49, 56, 388
Personal property, 47, 53, 56, 63, 64, 75, 80, 81, 91, 92, 102-104, 111-113, 115, 116, 118, 120, 122, 144, 145, 148-152, 157, 221, 224, 231, 260, 264, 266, 272, 279, 281, 297, 303, 313-316, 318, 326, 329, 331, 332, 337, 347, 351-353, 355, 359, 361, 362, 370-372, 374, 378-385, 390
Personal Representative, 49, 59-61, 69-71, 74-76, 78, 80, 81, 85, 87, 88, 91, 92, 96, 98-100, 102-119, 121, 122, 128, 144, 148, 261, 264, 266, 267, 272, 279, 281, 329, 331, 355, 356, 378, 384-386, 390
Per Stirpes, 19, 48, 49, 56, 290, 299, 305, 388
Petition for Probate, 56, 59-61, 68, 70, 71, 73-75, 78-82, 85, 90-93, 96, 101, 112, 113, 116, 117, 128, 143-145, 149-153, 255, 288, 329, 372
Petition for Instructions, 149, 235, 236, 288, 372-375
Petition to Determine Succession, 143, 148, 149
Post-Marital Agreement, 23, 386
Posthumous, 386
Posthumously conceived child, 26
Pour-Over Will, 34, 57, 59, 165, 176-177, 373, 386
Power of Appointment, 55, 259, 260, 284, 356, 374, 389
Power of Attorney, 25, 55, 90, 96, 262, 288, 351-369, 378, 381, 383, 387, 389
Prayer, 387
Precatory Language, 187, 194, 387
Predeceased, 46, 54, 62-64, 71, 81, 92, 144, 260, 261, 267-269, 292, 293, 299, 305, 387, 388
Preliminary Change of Ownership (PCOR), 154, 201, 205, 225, 237, 288, 233-234,
Preliminary Distribution, 102, 103, 110, 116-117, 121, 122, 168, 319, 329, 387
Pre-Marital Agreement, 47, 146, 387
Present Interest, 170
Pretermitted, 387
Primogeniture, 387
Principal, 207, 209, 213, 216, 260, 272, 273, 275, 284, 286, 297, 298, 303, 304, 355, 356, 359, 364, 380-383, 387, 388
Probate, 1, 3, 4, 11-13, 15, 16, 18, 19, 25, 27, 30, 41, 45-52, 54-56, 59-61, 65-82, 85, 86, 90-93, 96, 100-124, 128, 132, 133, 143-155, 158, 166, 177, 204, 217, 219, 222, 226, 244, 250, 255, 259-285, 287, 288, 290-294, 299, 305, 313-316, 318, 320, 322, 327-329, 331, 335, 337, 338, 370, 372-374, 377, 380, 382, 383, 386, 387, 388
Probate Examiner, 76-78, 153
Probate Referee, 5, 14, 101-105, 109, 111, 113-115, 120, 145, 149, 313-316, 320, 327
Process Service, 74
Proof of Subscribing Witness, 32, 34, 35, 41, 44, 56, 74, 76, 77, 288, 311, 390
Property, 4, 13, 15, 20, 22, 23, 25, 26, 35, 45-49, 51-56, 60-69, 71-73, 75, 76, 78, 80, 81, 91, 92, 102-106, 109, 111-116, 118-122, 143-160, 163, 177, 179, 189, 192, 196, 199, 213, 219-221, 224-237, 240, 259-261, 264-266, 269, 270, 272, 273, 275, 277, 279-285, 288, 292, 294, 296-298, 302-304, 313-316, 318-322, 326-332, 336-342, 345-347, 349, 351-359, 361, 362, 364, 370-375, 377-390
Proprietorship, 387
Pro rata, 109, 110, 285
Prudent Person Standard, 251, 274, 276, 388
Public Administrator, 264-269, 286
Public Defender, 249, 256-258
Publication, 74-76, 79, 90, 109, 145, 313-316, 320, 327
Publishing, 388
Qualified Domestic Trust, 387
Qualified Terminable Interest Property Trust (Q-TIP), 190, 193, 229, 230, 238, 334, 388
Quasi-Community Property, 23, 24, 61, 64, 144, 145, 259, 388
*Quigley v Nash* (1934) 1 Cal.2d 502, 110
Real Property, 61, 62, 68, 69, 72, 75, 80, 81, 91, 92, 104, 109, 111-113, 115, 116, 118, 119, 143, 144, 147-154, 199, 231, 233, 234, 237, 260, 265, 280, 285, 292, 296-298, 302-304, 313-316, 319, 320, 329,

331, 332, 337, 339-342, 346, 349, 351-353, 358, 361, 362, 370-375, 377-388
Reciprocal Wills, 47, 56, 296, 385, 388
Recreational Vehicle, 113, 114, 155
Redemption, 388
Remainder, 146, 193, 226, 230, 280, 285, 296, 302, 356, 379, 388, 391
Request for Special Notice, 85, 96, 102, 122
Res, 388
Residence, 69, 79, 86, 90, 120, 129, 230, 255, 270, 352, 358, 359, 367, 381, 383, 388
Residuary clause, 388
Residuary devisee, 388
Retirement, 12, 15, 25, 60, 61, 68, 104, 143, 144, 150, 177, 178, 188, 196, 203, 225, 232, 265, 280, 293, 347, 353, 354, 384-386
Reversion, 356, 388
Revocable Trust, 3, 13, 23, 31, 73, 171-175, 179, 193, 196, 204, 205, 270, 349, 355, 356, 361, 372, 373, 388
Revocation of Trust, 185, 197, 204, 205, 249, 270, 348, 356
Right of representation, 11, 19, 48, 49, 56, 189, 270, 290, 291, 296, 302, 386, 388
Right of survivorship, 24, 26, 64, 145, 147, 151, 157, 158, 202, 225, 384, 385, 388
Rule Against Perpetuities, 52, 55, 57, 389
Sale of Property, 51, 78, 111-113, 115, 154, 155, 319, 320, 331, 349, 378, 379
Salvage Value, 389
Savings Statute, 389
Securities and Exchange Commission, 114, 152, 155, 156
Self-proving attestation, 56,
Self-proving will, 30, 34, 35, 56, 57, 76, 80, 91, 299, 305
Service of Process, 74
Separate property, 61, 64, 143, 145-147, 158, 331, 382, 386, 387
Separate Share Trust, 191, 193
Settlor, 7, 165, 166, 168-169, 170-176, 179, 180-185, 187, 193, 204, 217, 223, 234, 236, 269, 348, 372-374, 379-381, 385, 388, 389, 389
Simple Trust, 48, 52, 54, 217, 233, 234, 389
Simultaneous death, 55, 57, 299, 305
Situs, 389

Skip person, 390
Soldiers and Seaman, 30
Special Administrator, 69, 79, 80, 90, 91
Special Needs Trust, 191
Special Power of Appointment, 259, 356
Spendthrift clause, 168, 192-194, 389
Spousal attribution rule, 389
Spousal Property Petition, 26, 144, 151-153, 157, 159, 160, 288, 339-342
Spousal Property Order, 152, 153, 157, 163, 341, 342
Springing Power of Attorney, 210-213, 216, 389
Sprinkling power, 389
Statement of residency, 72
State tax, 144
Statute of Limitations, 108, 389
Statutory fees, 68, 109, 110, 117, 145, 321, 390
Statutory Will, 19-22, 28, 33-34
Stepped-up basis, 227, 390
Stocks, 103-105, 113-115, 144, 148, 152, 155, 156, 172, 202, 231, 232, 294, 329, 347, 351
Straight Life Annuity, 390
Strict Privity Test, 390
Subchapter S, 155, 203
Subscribing Witness, 56, 74, 76, 77, 288, 311
Summary Probate, 45, 144, 145, 271, 390
Surety company, 49, 75, 390
Survivor benefit, 13
Survival period, 390
Survivorship, 25, 64, 145, 147, 151, 157, 158, 260, 351, 384, 385, 390
Table of Consanguinity, 18, 76, 289, 379
Taxable apportionment, 390
Taxable distribution, 390
Taxable termination, 390
Taxes, 4, 8, 20, 47, 55, 69, 109-111, 114, 115, 119, 120, 144, 146-148, 153, 167, 172, 173, 177, 186, 204, 226-229, 233, 269, 278-280, 285, 318, 320, 326, 327, 357-359, 377, 379-381, 390, 391
Tax Identification Number, 15, 170, 156, 195, 221, 231, 232
Tenancy by the entirety, 351
Tenants in common, 25, 26, 28, 146, 147, 152, 158, 174, 180, 181, 200

Term life insurance, 390
Terminable interest, 149, 230, 284
Testamentary capacity, 57
Testamentary Trust, 54, 57, 269, 270, 286, 378
Testate, 16, 28, 61, 66, 68, 70, 76, 101, 106, 357, 391
Testate Succession, 16, 357
Testator, 28, 38, 45-56, 60, 61, 68-70, 269-272, 299, 300, 305, 306, 381, 383, 384, 386, 387, 389-392
Totten Trust, 31, 44, 56, 391
Tracing, 391
Transferor, 48, 49, 282-285, 389, 391
Transmutation, 3, 23, 24, 47, 146, 176, 195-197, 201, 205
Trust, 5, 25, 34, 47-49, 52-57, 59, 81, 83, 84, 92, 94, 95, 102, 114, 121, 151, 166-171, 174-177, 179, 185, 187, 190-192, 195-198, 204, 205, 217, 220-224, 226-231, 233-236, 239, 240, 259-261, 269, 270, 273, 274, 278, 280, 282-286, 288, 296, 298, 302, 304, 331, 332, 346-352, 354-356, 359, 361, 362, 372-375, 377-392
Trust Amendment, 204, 356
Trust Equivalent, 391
Trustee, 6, 7, 10, 19, 22, 28, 52, 54, 81, 92, 114, 121, 169, 174, 180-185, 193, 195, 217-224, 231, 233-236, 259, 260, 269, 272-274, 276, 278, 279, 281, 282, 284, 288, 298, 304, 331, 345, 348, 349, 355, 356, 361, 370-375, 380-382, 384, 387, 389, 391, 392
Trustor, 169, 180, 193, 373, 374, 391
Trust Transfer Deed, 192, 196-197, 200, 201, 204, 205, 288, 348-350, 373

Unauthorized Practice of Law (UPL), 8, 11, 208
Unclaimed property, 391
Uncontrolled discretion, 391
Unfunded Trust, 269, 391
Unified Estate & Gift Tax, 391
Uniform Gifts to Minors Act (UTMA), 31, 52-53, 56, 121, 172, 220,
Uniform Probate Code, 16, 27, 45, 391
Uniform Statutory Form Power of Attorney Act, 208
Unitary Transfer Taxes, 391
Universal Life Insurance, 391
Vehicle Registration, 13, 25
Venue, 12
Verification, 53, 72, 106, 112, 120, 122, 288, 310, 323, 375
Void, 25, 31, 118, 203, 208, 392
Voidable, 392
Waiver, 60, 74, 75, 78, 80, 91, 104, 116, 117, 288, 312, 317, 323, 324, 326, 347
Waiver of accounting, 288, 312, 324
Waiver of bond, 74, 75, 78, 288, 311, 312, 324
Waiver of notice, 288, 324
Whole life insurance, 391
Will, 5, 14-16, 18, 22, 25, 26, 28, 32-35, 39, 41, 45-57, 59-61, 65-81, 85, 90-92, 96, 101-122, 128, 143-157, 213, 217-231, 234-236, 240, 259-261, 264, 265, 267-272, 277, 283-285, 288, 292, 295-306, 318, 319, 321, 322, 327, 328, 331, 332, 335, 354-357, 359, 360, 362, 368, 369, 372-374, 377-381, 383-392
Window Minor's Trust, 392
Younger generation beneficiary, 392